Finance and Capital Markets Series

The Finance and Capital Markets series is designed to bring you high-quality, cutting-edge information on the latest issues and developments in the financial world. These authoritative yet accessible books, written by experts in their field, provide clear, practical guidance not only for industry professionals, but also serve as a framework of current analysis for scholars and form a comprehensive reference resource for libraries.

Ross K. McGill

Cross-Border Investment Withholding Tax

A Practical Guide for Investors and Intermediaries

Second Edition

palgrave
macmillan

Ross K. McGill
TConsult Ltd.
Yateley, UK

Finance and Capital Markets Series
ISBN 978-3-031-32784-1 ISBN 978-3-031-32785-8 (eBook)
https://doi.org/10.1007/978-3-031-32785-8

This Palgrave Macmillan imprint is published by the registered company Springer Nature Switzerland AG
The registered company address is: Gewerbestrasse 11, 6330 Cham, Switzerland

For Kirsty

Foreword

This second edition of Ross K. McGill's ground-breaking book on withholding tax is even more important than the first. The first edition is, even now, still used by many as the prime source of introductory and explanatory reference material for this sector of the financial services industry.

However, in the years since that first edition, much has changed, and the pace of that change is accelerating rapidly. Withholding tax has been notable as one of the last bastions of paper-based, manual processing in financial institutions, constrained by inadequate legislation and archaic regulation.

The US, OECD and the EU, representing together a large majority of the world's economic activity, have focused in the last ten years on the need to improve and streamline cross-border taxation while at the same time strengthening mechanisms to detect and deter tax evasion and tax fraud.

The purpose of investing is to increase wealth and income. That wealth and income is created by only two mechanisms—(i) the inherent increase in value of the assets themselves, through trading (buying low and selling high) or (ii) through receiving benefits (passive income) as a reward for holding onto the investment. Both of these draw the attention of governments for tax revenues whether that be capital gains tax, taxes on gross proceeds or taxation of dividends and interest. While direct taxation rates had been relatively low until mid-2022, indirect taxation rates, particularly on cross-border passive income, have remained stubbornly high at an average statutory rate of 25–35%. In the absence of double tax treaties, that generally reduce these rates to a more equitable 15% or even 0%, cross-border withholding tax would be a significant drag on global investment and growth.

Even so, billions have been lost in fraud cases, only a small proportion of which is being recovered through litigation. These are dwarfed however by the billions more lost each year simply because investors have a low awareness of the issue and because financial institutions and tax administrations are still mired in costly, slow, manual, paper-based processes that often leave the cost of applying the correct rate of tax substantially higher than the value of the tax itself.

Governments and tax administrations have however changed their approach markedly, responding to many industry body research reports, all of which point in one direction—change the legislative landscape, change the regulatory landscape, simplify and harmonise the procedures, remove the paper and allow new technologies to change the tax processing paradigm.

So, the importance of this second edition of Mr. McGill's book cannot be over-stated. While he explains the basics, as he did in the first edition, he has added substantial new content relating to the new withholding tax paradigm that is emerging. This is a must-read for investors that want to optimise their returns on their investments and for those in financial institutions responsible for planning strategy, technology and operational implementation.

Johannesburg, South Africa

Daniel Ginsburg
Founder and CEO, WTAX
a division of VAT IT Group

Preface to the Second Edition

As global growth slows and the gap between the rich and poor grows, taxation naturally becomes a target of fierce controversy. The terms tax evasion and tax avoidance have become highly emotive and politicised. Its easy therefore to consider anything connected with tax "*optimisation*" as potentially suspect.

This book is concerned with *correct* taxation through the proper and effective application of established and globally agreed mechanisms whose purpose is to avoid double taxation.

This book is about a very narrow, yet incredibly valuable and important aspect of taxation—investment withholding tax. Corporations and governments raise money by the creation of financial instruments, most commonly equities (e.g. stocks and shares) or fixed income instruments (e.g. bonds and gilts). In order to raise money effectively these financial instruments are made available on a global basis through stock exchanges and sold through chains of financial intermediaries such as banks and brokers. One of the benefits for investors of owning these financial instruments is that they pay the investor what is called "passive income" such as a dividend on an equity or an interest payment or coupon on a bond.

Problems occur when the issuer of the financial instrument is resident for tax purposes in one jurisdiction and makes a payment (also known as a distribution) to an investor that is resident in a different tax jurisdiction. Both countries often claim a right to tax these payments and the rate of taxation in each jurisdiction is often different. This is called double taxation and is recognised as being harmful to the free movement of capital. So, over time, pairs of countries have entered bilateral double tax treaties ("DTTs") that provide for such income to be taxed only once and at a mutually agreed (treaty) rate.

However, the practicality of achieving this objective is neither simple nor easy. While double tax treaties establish the basis for an entitlement to a lower rate of taxation on cross-border investment income, they do not specify how this is to happen. That is left to the respective tax administrations who establish complex sets of rules, processes, forms and deadlines that are required to demonstrate an investor's entitlement to a lower tax rate. Those evidentiary rules can, and often are different depending on the nature of the investor.

There are three main ways that these double tax treaties are implemented in practice. They are (i) relief at source, (ii) quick refund and (iii) standard refund. Relief at source and quick refunds are managed by financial institutions as part of the payment process on financial instruments. Standard refunds, also called post pay date claims or long form claims, are claims made by investors or their agents directly to tax administrations. The legal frameworks in each jurisdiction determine which one or more of these mechanisms are available.

This means that, although the concepts of withholding tax are individually simple to understand, the reality of how it all works in practice is very much more complex. Unlike other sectors of finance, the withholding tax industry has historically operated in a paper-based environment. One of the reasons for writing this second edition of my book is to update readers on the changes that have happened in the last few years.

The main driver for change in this industry has been the consequence of this complexity. There is a substantial amount of tax each year that is over-withheld and that never gets returned to its rightful owners. In the European Commission Tax Barriers Business Advisory Group report of 2013,[1] reference is made to European Commission research indicating that the current cost of all this complexity on financial institutions is estimated to €1.09 billion annually while the amount of tax that is never recovered is estimated at €5.57 billion annually. Extrapolating this up from an EU level to a global level and taking into account statutes of limitations that allow for retrospective claims to be made over a period of years, and accounting for inflationary effects since the report's publication, it is easy to estimate that the cost to industry of these complex, paper-based processes would be over €8 billion annually and the amount of tax over withheld and never recovered would be over €50 billion.

---

[1] https://ec.europa.eu/info/sites/default/files/tbag-report-24052013_en.pdf.

Only with a greater understanding by all those in the investment chain between the issuer of these financial instruments and the investor, can effective strategies be devised to improve performance.

This book, the second edition of the third that I have written on this topic, is written for the full range of professional investors, their advisors and financial intermediaries, to bring such awareness to a higher level and to bring together the various threads of the issue into focus. Much has changed since my previous works were published:

1. The OECD and the EU have both settled on similar frameworks that favour tax relief at source over the more traditional standard refunds
2. Tax administrations and governments have progressively adapted their legal frameworks to allow for the evolution of digital technologies to replace paper
3. Tax administrations and governments are moving towards self-certifications of residency as opposed to residency certificates issued by tax administrations
4. Tax administrations have been subjected to major cases of treaty abuse and fraud leaving them more sensitive to the control procedures in place surrounding tax relief and reclaims.

These are merely the outward signs of more fundamental changes including changes in attitude and political will within major trading blocks. To that extent, this book has become more important than its predecessors as a practical repository for aggregated information. It's not enough longer for professionals in the industry to know the practical issues in a global context, although in this edition, all of these issues are enumerated, discussed and updated from the original works. They must also know of the strategic shifts taking place. These include changes in paradigms of processing, including the advent of Distributed ledger Technology ("DLT") processing as the precursor for full STP in withholding tax, which I still estimate still to be at least a decade away. Also of importance are the views of major groups on the commercial side such as G30 as well as on the political side such as Giovanini and FISCO. The work of the OECD is also valuable to understand. So, in this edition, you will find more extensive references to the work of these bodies and in some cases, reproduction of important tracts. Since I take some time to discuss the context and relevance of the work of these bodies, it is useful to be able to reference the significant parts of their work in one place. In the previous editions, I gave scale and scope to the effects of withholding tax, so its apposite to review the situation five years on. Global assets under management (AUM) in 2008 exceeded US$108 trillion. Of this 27.7% (US$30 trillion) were held cross-border. At a 5% yield, the tax imposed by foreign governments on the income from these assets was around US$300 billion. This figure is compounded to over US$1.56 trillion when statutes of limitation are included.

Since the global financial markets are founded on cross-border trade, it's clearly in the interests of each market to balance its need for tax revenue with the need to stimulate and maintain inward investment in the face of strong global competition. This has been brought into clearer focus by the upheaval in the financial markets in late 2008, the global COVID-19 pandemic in 2020–2021 followed in each case by general global slow-downs in 2009 and 2022. As companies struggle to survive, dividends will decrease in number and size. So tax revenues will decrease both from corporate taxation and the taxation of investment distributions. With linked economies, attracting inward investment will become more important providing a driver for more efficiencies in withholding tax processes while at the same time, increased regulation will make the job of financial services firms more complex and more costly. It used to be common for fund managers to be sanguine about a 2.5% performance improvement available from having an active tax reclamation policy in place since overall performances were typically already 20–30%. Now, that situation has changed. Funds are closing at an unprecedented pace, new market strategies are developing and regulation requires greater transparency between investor and fund manager and that 2.5% is now very material to performance. From whichever perspective you view it, withholding tax optimisation has never been more important for the investment world and I therefore believe that this book is important for everyone in the investment chain.

Yateley, UK

Ross K. McGill
Chairman

Acknowledgements

I would like to thank the following people who have provided me with invaluable support:

Kirsty Pitkin and Neil Moorhouse for proof reading.

Stuart Lipo & Rhodri Lougher for taking up much of my workload while I was writing this book.

Stefan Darmanin for creating all the diagrams.

Martin Foont, CEO of GlobeTax Inc. for allowing me to use information about ESP® and MIDAS®.

Alexander Lerch, CEO of RAQUEST GmbH for contributing his views on vendor dynamics.

About This Book

This book is about cross-border withholding tax on investment income. The subject matter may sound arcane, but it has, over the last few years, become the subject of intense debate as governments and business struggle to develop more efficient ways to ensure fair and correct taxation of cross-border passive income.

The first edition of this book, and on this subject matter was published by Euromoney in 2003. I have since changed publisher to Palgrave Macmillan. Under this new publisher, I wrote a new version on the subject, of which this is the second edition. So, depending on how you look at it, this is either the second edition published by Palgrave or the third edition of the book as a treatise on the subject.

Either way, the fact that this edition is being published at all stands testament to the changes that are occurring ever more rapidly, particularly in the US, the European Union and the member states of the OECD.

The basic premise on which this book is founded is that, if someone who is resident in one country, invests in a company that is resident in another country, when the company distributes a dividend, the company, or its financial agent, must withhold tax from that distribution and remit it to its local tax administration. When the investor receives the dividend, it will be reduced by the amount of foreign tax withheld, but the investor may also be liable to pay tax on that income to its local tax administration. This is essentially double taxation. Pairs of countries have entered into Double Tax Agreements ("DTAs") to prevent this double taxation. In the European

Union, the purpose of these agreements is to facilitate the free movement of capital.

So, this book is dedicated to describing the different methods, by means of which, this double taxation can be prevented. There are three major components: Tax relief at source ("RAS") in which the payor of the distribution withholds the correct amount of tax at the time the payment is made—to do which, they will need evidence of the investor's residence, eligibility and entitlement. The second is Quick Refund ("QR") in which the payor refunds the investor from the tax it has already withheld prior to paying its tax administration. The third is Standard Refund in which an investor or their agent claims the over-withheld tax back directly from the foreign tax administration.

With only three models, you would assume that this should be a short book. However, between the company issuing dividends and the investor receiving them, there are a plethora of different financial institutions each playing a different role. Equally, there are criminals out there who, on seeing such a complex tax system, choose to try to gain an unfair advantage. This book seeks to highlight some of the more recent high-profile legal cases which show that tax administrations are very aware of these types of activity and have sophisticated tools at their disposal to detect and prevent tax fraud.

Finally, again driven by concerns over tax evasion, global frameworks have arisen to detect and prevent investors from evading their tax obligations. These were led by the US in 2010, with its Foreign Account Tax Compliance Act ("FATCA") and extended by the OECD with the Automatic Exchange of Information ("AEoI") and Common Reporting Standard ("CRS") in 2013. While all this work was going on, technology was also not standing still. Most tax administrations now have online portals and most financial institutions now onboard clients digitally rather than with paper forms.

This book tries to bring all these threads together to explain what withholding tax is, why its complicated, how criminals try to subvert the frameworks and what technological advances have been made since the publication of the prior edition of this book. I also try to predict where this is all heading.

Contents

About the Author

Ross K. McGill is the co-founder and Chairman of TConsult Ltd., a specialist withholding tax regulatory consulting firm. He lives in northeast Hampshire in the United Kingdom. Since his entry into the financial services industry in 1996, he has held the roles of Managing Director of GlobeTax and Group Managing Director of the GOAL group of companies, both of which are focused on cross-border withholding tax reclamation. The former delivers services in a business process outsourcing model ("BPO"). The latter delivers products by licensing of software for use in-house by financial institutions. It can thus be said of Mr. McGill that he has a wide base of subject knowledge as well as a deep understanding of the different business models in use in the industry today.

Mr. McGill holds an Honours Degree in Materials Science and Certificate in Education from Bath University in England. Mr. McGill has contributed to several influential international bodies including as an expert witness to the European Union Fiscal Compliance Committee ("FISCO").[1] He subsequently contributed to and edited the final report of the Tax Barriers Business Advisory Group in 2013[2] which led to the EU Withholding Tax Code of Conduct.[3]

---

[1] https://ec.europa.eu/info/sites/default/files/fact-finding-study-19042006_en.pdf.

[2] https://ec.europa.eu/info/publications/report-tax-barriers-business-advisory-group-tbag_en.

[3] https://taxation-customs.ec.europa.eu/system/files/2017-12/code_of_conduct_on_witholding_tax.pdf.

Mr. McGill is passionate about regulatory reform, technology and standards. He sits on three subcommittees of the International Standards Organisation (ISO) Securities Evaluation Group (SEG), notably, corporate actions, fund administration and proxy voting. He also sits on the Advisory Board of RAQUEST GmbH a withholding tax software company based in Raubling, Germany.

Mr. McGill is the author of nine books, two of which, including this one, are now in their second editions, dealing with cross-border taxation and anti-tax evasion.

Abbreviations

ADR	American Depositary Receipt
AEoI	Automatic Exchange of Information
AML	Anti Money Laundering
ASCII	American Standard Code for Information Exchange
AUM	Assets Under Management
BIC	Bank Identifier Code
BOT	Short-Term Zero-Coupon Government Debt Securities
BP	Basis Points
BPO	Business Process Outsourcing
CAA	Competent Authority Agreement (bilateral) or Credit Advice Authorisation
CDC FFI	Certified Deemed Compliant FFI
CEDEAR	Certificados de Depósito Argentinos
CP	Compliance Program
CRS	Common Reporting Standard
CSD	Central Securities Depository
CSR	Corporate Social Responsibility
D-QI	Disclosing Qualified Intermediary (1446(a) and (f))
D-NQI	Disclosing Non-Qualified Intermediary
DAC6	European Union Council Directive 2011/16
DEP	Dividend Equivalent Payment
DR	Depositary Receipt
DTT	Double Tax Treaty
ECJ	European Court of Justice
EFTPS	Electronic Federal Tax Payment System

EIN	Employer Identification Number
ELI	Equity Linked instrument
ESG	Environmental Social Governance
EU	European Union
FATCA	IRC Chapter 4 Sections 1471–1474
FDAP	Income from US sources that is Fixed, Determinable, Annual or Periodic
FFI	Foreign (non-US) Financial Intermediary
FIRE	Filing Information Returns Electronically
GDR	Global Depositary Receipt
GIIN	Global Intermediary Identification Number
HNWI	High Net Worth Individual
HTTP	Hyper Text Transfer Protocol
ICSD	International Central Securities Depository
IGA	Inter-Governmental Agreement
IRC	US Internal Revenue Code
IRS	US Internal Revenue Service
ISD	Investor Self Declaration
ISO	International Standards Organisation
KYC	Know Your Customer
KYT	Know Your Transaction
LOB	Limitation Of Benefit
LPP	Legal Professional Privilege (DAC6)
MBT	Main Benefits Test (DAC6)
MCAA	Multi-Lateral Competent Authority Agreement
MeF	Modernized e-File
MoU	Memorandum of Understanding
ND-NQI	Non-Disclosing Non-Qualified Intermediary
NPC	Notional Principal Contract
NP-FFI	Non-Participating FFI
NQI	Non-Qualified Intermediary
NRA	Non-Resident Alien
NWQI	Non-Withholding Qualified Intermediary
OECD	Organisation for Economic Cooperation and Development
PDF	Portable Document Format
QDD	Qualified Derivatives Dealer
QI	Qualified Intermediary
QIEIN	QI Employer Identification Number
RDC-FFI	Registered Deemed Compliant FFI
REIT	Real Estate Investment Trust
RO	Responsible Officer
SEC	US Securities & Exchange Commission
SEG	(ISO) Securities Evaluation Group
SET	Substantial Equivalence Test

SICAF	Société d'Investissement a Capital Variable
SICAV	Société d'Investissement a Capital Fixe
SLA	Service Level Agreement
SWIFT	Society for Worldwide Interbank Financial Telecommunication
T-BAG	Tax Barriers Business Advisory Group
TCC	Transmitter Control Code
TRA	Transfer Risk Assessment
UBO	Ultimate Beneficial Owner
UHNWI	Ultra High Net Worth Individual
WQI	Withholding Qualified Intermediary
WRPS	Withholding Rate Pool Statement
WS	Withholding Statement

List of Exhibits

Part I

Essentials

1

Introduction

It is an accepted truism that there is nothing certain in this life other than death and taxes.[1] It is also a truism that, in the world of tax, the answer to every question starts with two words—"It depends".[2] With that in mind, we are about to embark on a story that will become more detailed as we proceed. For now, we need to understand the core concepts and principles.

We must start by setting the scene. This book is about what happens when someone resident in one jurisdiction, has bought financial assets that were issued by someone in another jurisdiction and those financial assets create a return on the investment. The tax administration of the country where the assets were created wants a slice of that cake (tax). The tax administration of the country where the investor has a permanent residence also wants a slice of that cake (tax on foreign passive income).

So, what are the essentials that every investor, adviser, financial institution, tax administration and financial instrument issuer needs to know about withholding tax? I am going to explain this as simply as I can. Then I'm going to explain each of those terms and concepts.

An **Issuer** is generally a legal entity or government that creates **financial instruments** and **lists** them on a **stock exchange**. Investors buy the financial instruments using a **broker** who, after the purchase, transfers them to a **custodian bank**, for safekeeping and to process any **corporate actions** such

[1] Benjamin Franklin circa 1789.

[2] Ross McGill 1996.

R. K. McGill, *Cross-Border Investment Withholding Tax*, Finance and Capital Markets Series,
https://doi.org/10.1007/978-3-031-32785-8_1

as dividends. **Withholding tax** must be applied whenever a **distribution** is processed as a **corporate action** by a **financial intermediary** on behalf of a **beneficial owner** who holds a **position** in the financial instrument on the **record date** with an expectation of receiving payment on the pay date. The payment may be taxed at a **treaty rate** under a **relief at source** or **quick refund procedure** or the beneficial owner, or their agent, may claim their entitlement from a tax authority using a **standard refund** procedure if, in all cases, the beneficial owner has provided at least a **certificate of residency,** evidence of their **entitlement** in, or the taxation of the financial instrument and the claim is within the tax administration's **statute of limitations.**

If you're new to this whole area, and many of my readers are either new investors or are newly employed in a financial institution and presented with this book as an introduction, then much of the preceding paragraph will be difficult to understand. So, we probably need to get a few terms and meanings straight. Please note, I am not giving dictionary definitions here. These are descriptions of important concepts that apply in the withholding tax space. These terms may have different meanings in different circumstances. They are not presented in alphabetical order, they are presented in the order that one would typically come across them in a typical sentence used in a withholding tax context. If you're familiar with these terms already, you can skip this part.

Issuer	Means generally a corporation or other legal entity type, e.g., a government, that can create a financial instrument and "issue" that instrument to an investor or make it available for purchase, for example at a stock exchange. Microsoft, Apple, Tesla and Amazon are all issuers of financial instruments as is the US Treasury when it issues bonds
Financial instruments	Can be many and varied as the industry seeks to package value in different ways to suit different needs. Examples include American Depositary Receipts (ADRs), Global Depositary Receipts (GDRs), Certificados de Depósito Argentinos (CEDEARs), Exchange Traded Funds (ETFs), Contracts for Difference (CFDs). The most common financial instruments that we'll talk about in this book are simply equities and fixed income. Equities just means owning shares in a private or listed company. Fixed Income just means owning a bond. All these instruments have withholding tax consequences that depend on their structure and who owns them
Broker	Is a type of financial institution that buys and sells financial instruments on behalf of its customers (beneficial owners)
Custodian Bank	Is a different type of financial institution that specialises in looking after assets after they have been purchased and, in particular, is responsible for processing corporate actions including the payment of dividends and coupon payments (distributions)

Withholding Tax	Is an amount that must be withheld from a distribution, the terms of which are usually defined in domestic legislation
Distribution	Is just a fancy way of saying a payment made from one person, usually a corporation, to a number of people e.g., shareholders. Distributions from equities are usually dividends and distributions from fixed income instruments are usually coupon payments or returns of capital. A distribution is in fact a sub-type of corporate action
Corporate Action	As the name implies a corporate action is an activity or process that takes place in relation to a corporate body. So, the processing of a dividend payment or a coupon payment are both corporate actions. There are many types of corporate action and many of those have no tax component. Registering shareholder votes at a general meeting, for example, is also a corporate action
Financial intermediaries	Generally speaking, the two most important people are the issuers and their investors. The issuer usually has strict legal liability associated with any tax that is withholdable on any of its distributions. However, most issuers want to focus on their day job—whatever their business is, so they outsource their obligations to financial intermediaries. This might be a business that specialises in processing payments—a paying agent. It might be a business that specialises in keeping records of share transfers—a transfer agent. It might be a business that specialises in recording the shareholder votes at a general meeting—a proxy voting agent. It might also be a business that specialises in withholding tax—a withholding agent. All these businesses will be regulated. There are three other types of financial institutions pertinent to this book. They are custodians, brokers and depositories. These firms do not generally work for issuers, they work for the market as infrastructures and for investors. Brokers provide services that allow investors to buy and sell securities. Once a security has been sold, it is passed to a custodian whose job is the safe keeping and processing of any corporate actions related to the security. A depository, and particularly a central securities depository (CSD) is the legal owner of record of the asset (but not the owner of the income, see below)

Beneficial owner	This is usually the person or entity that is the ultimate owner of the income derived from a financial instrument. It's an important nuance to understand that you don't always have to be the legal owner of a financial asset, to be the beneficial owner of the income derived from that asset. It is very often the case, but just not always, especially when we are talking about the way that financial assets are held by chains of financial intermediaries, as we will see later. So, usually, the term beneficial owner is modified by either income, as in beneficial owner of the income[3] or by asset, as in beneficial owner of the asset
Position	This just means the number of shares or the face value of the coupons that an investor owns at any time. If I buy 100 Tesla shares, my *position* in Tesla is 100 shares
Ex date	The ex-dividend date, or ex-date, is one of four stages that companies go through when they pay dividends to their shareholders. The ex-dividend date is important because it determines whether the buyer of a stock will be entitled to receive its upcoming dividend. To receive a dividend, the buyer must have purchased the shares before the ex-date
Record date	This is the date set by an issuer to decide who owns the security and is entitled to the distribution. The term used is that ownership is *crystallised* on the record date. This is a very complex area (and has been the subject of abuse scandals that will be described later)
Pay date	The pay date, as the name suggests, is the date on which the issuer will make the distribution. In line with the "it depends" rule, even here pay date may not be a constant. For example, an American Depositary Receipt is a derivative security linked to underlying ordinary securities. However, the pay date of an ADR may not be the same pay date as the pay date of the securities it represents
Statutory Rate	This term will be explained in context and in more detail later. Suffice it to say for the present, that the statutory rate is the legal rate of tax that must be applied in the absence of any other lower rate that can be claimed. In Switzerland, France and the USA, this rate is 30% at the time of writing
Treaty Rate	The treaty rate, as the name implies, is the rate that is set between parties to a double tax treaty. There are a range of treaty rates, including 5, 10 and 25%, but the most common by far is 15%

[3] For example, refer to the certification text on US Form W-8BEN: https://www.irs.gov/pub/irs-pdf/fw8ben.pdf "I certify that I am the individual that is the beneficial owner [...] of all the income [...] to which this form relates".

Residency Certificate	This is an important component of withholding tax because it is a common requirement for any of the processes described in the following three concepts. As the name implies, this is a certificate that establishes the tax residency of a beneficial owner. There are two types of residency certificates. A certificate of residency is issued by a competent authority, usually a tax administration. Sometimes it is required to be validated by another department of the same authority in what is called an Apostille process that attaches a special stamp to the original certificate. The second type of residency certificate is a self-certification. These are certifications made by beneficial owners themselves, usually under some legal rule such as penalty of perjury. Note that a residency certificate does not usually determine the basis of that residency e.g., citizenship versus permanent residence—it merely establishes the residency *for tax purposes*
Tax relief at source	As we will see later, tax relief at source means that an investor has met all the conditions to prove that they are entitled to a tax treaty rate (or an exemption). They must typically provide all the required evidence between the record date and the pay date so that the payment that is eventually made is taxed at the correct rate. Tax relief at source must be a legally allowable process in the issuer's jurisdiction
Quick Refund	Is a process that relies on the fact that the financial intermediary that has withheld the statutory rate of tax on the pay date, will not remit that tax to its tax administration for some time, typically thirty days. In that time, again, if the process is legally allowed in the issuer's jurisdiction, an investor can still claim their entitlement from the financial intermediary
Standard Refund	Sometimes also called a "long form reclaim" or a "tax reclaim", this means a claim made by an investor or their agent to a tax authority. In other words, the statutory rate of withholding tax was applied and the tax has already been remitted to the tax administration of the Issuer. It's important to understand the difference—a tax reclaim is not the same as tax relief at source. A tax reclaim involves reclaiming tax after it has been overwithheld. Tax relief at source involves being taxed at the correct rate in the first instance—so no reclaim is necessary (or possible)

- **Lack of service offering**. If the custodian does not provide a service, ALL the possible claims on all their client's holdings go into the "not claimed" pot.
- **Threshold**. Claim values below a certain threshold never get filed. The threshold varies per custodian.
- **Lack of scope of offering**—income type. Many custodians do not claim on particular types of income e.g., ADRs for perceived complexity reasons.
- **Lack of scope of offering**—beneficial owner type. Some beneficial owner types, typically tax transparent vehicles, are very expensive and complex to process.
- **Lack of scope of offering**—by market. Above all things, the cost of research is a critical factor, not least because it must be relative to the client and investment bases and be used only after independent verification from at least two sources. Key main markets are often the limitation of custodians.
- **Type of client base**. A custodian's client base has an important impact. If there are many "retail" investors compared to institutional, it may be that only the institutional investors are offered a service thus dis-intermediating part of the customer base, and their entitlements, for simple commercial reasons.
- **Lack of scope of offering**—structure. Some custodians will not do claims for clients with complex structures because the risk is too high, and the cost is too high.
- **Structure**. Some investment structures, e.g., complex trusts are deemed transparent. the claim at the fund level would be viable, but with thousands of investors, claims at the investor level are just not worth filing (cost too high), so never get done
- **Lack of scope of offering**—systems limitations. Some custodians cannot process certain types of claims because their systems are not structured to aggregate data in the right way
- **Claims filed incorrectly**—many tax authorities reject claims if the correct paperwork is not completed accurately. Sometimes, they even tell the claimant!
- **Location**—some investors, who would have an entitlement if they invested directly, choose to invest via a specific market structure e.g., Cayman corporate. They lose out on entitlements because of that choice as their entitlement is subsumed by the investment vehicle which has a different or no entitlement.

I could go on, but I'm sure you see the problem both of scaling the issue and even describing it concisely. Many of the players in the list above are unlikely to admit to any of the relevant "misses" let alone the scale and scope of their potential client entitlements. So, while the concept might be very simple to understand, clearly the message is often not getting received or applied somewhere along the line.

Investors have an unambiguous interest in the subject—where they have any knowledge of it at all. Financial intermediaries have a rather more subtle interest. That interest borders on the one hand at the level of fiduciary duty—the responsibility to act on your specialist knowledge in the best interests of your customers; and on the other hand, the self-interest driven by the fact that the more tax that is credited back into your client's accounts, the higher your custody fees will be.

Essentially withholding tax must be understood in terms of the principles and the context in which they apply. To try to apply knowledge of only one of these areas leads to failure.

In this first part of the book, we will look at Principles, Context and Primary factors. These three issues will set out what withholding tax is, how the issue is currently addressed by the various interested parties in the investment chain and some of the key factors that are affecting change in the industry, of which both investors and financial intermediaries should be cognisant.

Principles establish the broad issues to be addressed. For instance, the principle of withholding tax establishes that an investor can be entitled to a lower rate of tax than would otherwise perhaps be applied. However, having an entitlement doesn't do an investor very much good if they don't know about it, understand it or exercise that entitlement. The only way to exercise the entitlement is to understand the context in which the principle applies. The context, in this case for example, establishes that there are three broad operational processing regimes under which an entitlement might be obtained—relief at source, long form claims or combination. This is just one of many contextual issues that must be understood alone and in concert and both under the overarching principles that guide them.

The next chapter seeks to explain the principles and associated contexts in such a way that subsequent parts of the book are more easily understood and integrated.

2

Principles

This chapter establishes what cross-border withholding tax is and why it is important. Withholding tax, in the context of this book, will be the tax withheld on passive investment income when paid to a recipient that is resident in a jurisdiction that is different from that of the Issuer of the security on which the payment is based. In most cases, this will be dividends on equities or bond interest paid on fixed income instruments. The chapter will explain the international context (double tax treaties), the operating models (relief at source, quick refund, and standard refund) and then spend some time describing the types of financial instrument covered, the types of recipients (beneficial owner) and introduce the reader to the principles that make this area of taxation simultaneously extremely valuable and extremely complex and challenging.

There are a set of general principles that underpin withholding tax. They are:

Double taxation	The concept that in a multi-jurisdictional world, tax can be levied on the same income more than once and that this double taxation is undesirable and has a drag effect on international investment
Jurisdictional	The concept that each jurisdiction can adopt one or more of three legal frameworks to allow for the minimisation of double taxation
Transparency	The concept that certain types of investors can appear to be eligible for tax relief but should not benefit

R. K. McGill, *Cross-Border Investment Withholding Tax*, Finance and Capital Markets Series,
https://doi.org/10.1007/978-3-031-32785-8_2

Process and Procedure	The concept that, while governments establish the legal frameworks for double tax relief, tax administrations are tasked with implementing processes and procedure to give effect to those frameworks while protecting them against abuse
Automation	The concept that increasing automation, using inference standards, the principles of double taxation can more easily and affectively be delivered
Interests	The concept that there are many actors that are affected by these principles, and each has a different perspective, capability and motivation for implementing these principles

Double Tax Principle

The primary subject of this book is *cross-border* withholding tax. This means that we are talking about investment income e.g., dividends on stocks and interest on bonds. To be cross-border, the income from these investments must be beneficially owned by an investor resident in a different tax jurisdiction from the entity that created the financial instrument that generated the income. It is important to understand, as we shall see later, that beneficial ownership of a financial asset and beneficial ownership of the income derived from that asset are not the same thing.

When investment income is generated across borders, the tax authority in the country where the income was generated (country of issue) requires that, unless they have reason to know otherwise, the Issuer of such income must tax the income distributions to non-resident investors at a specified rate (The Statutory Rate).

Under normal circumstances, the recipient of such income would also be required, under their own domestic law, to declare the income for domestic income tax purposes in their country of residence. There are two effects that flow from this, an investor-specific effect and a jurisdictional effect.

Clearly, for the investor there is a potential for double taxation of a single item of income to occur. Equally, when we come to discuss tax evasion, the rules for cross-border taxation also provide the opportunity for double non-taxation in which neither jurisdiction receives any tax from the income. The lines that differentiate these situations and the temptations to cross those lines can be very compelling.

For the economy of the jurisdiction of issue, the consequential effect of double taxation, would be that inward investment to that market could be significantly damaged. Global investment strategies are often based on industry sectors e.g., health, technology and manufacturing. Many strategies also focus on price fluctuations—the difference between buying and selling prices to create gains. However, for many, the return on investment (ROI) through dividends and interest that occurs between buying a security and selling a security is also often important for certain kinds of investors notably pension funds. The tax effect of these investments can reduce the overall ROI quite substantially, leaving that sector less attractive than the same sector in a different jurisdiction.

Exhibit 2.1 demonstrates this. In this example, the statutory rate of tax in the market is 35%. In the absence of any other process, the tax deducted at source by the Issuer, or their agent, will be the statutory rate. So, the investor receives only 65% of what the Issuer intended them to receive when they distributed the dividend. However, if there are mechanisms that can reduce that effective tax rate, a matter that we will be discussing in detail later in the rest of this book, then the eventual payment could be between 85[1] and 100% depending on the tax status of the person or entity receiving the payment.

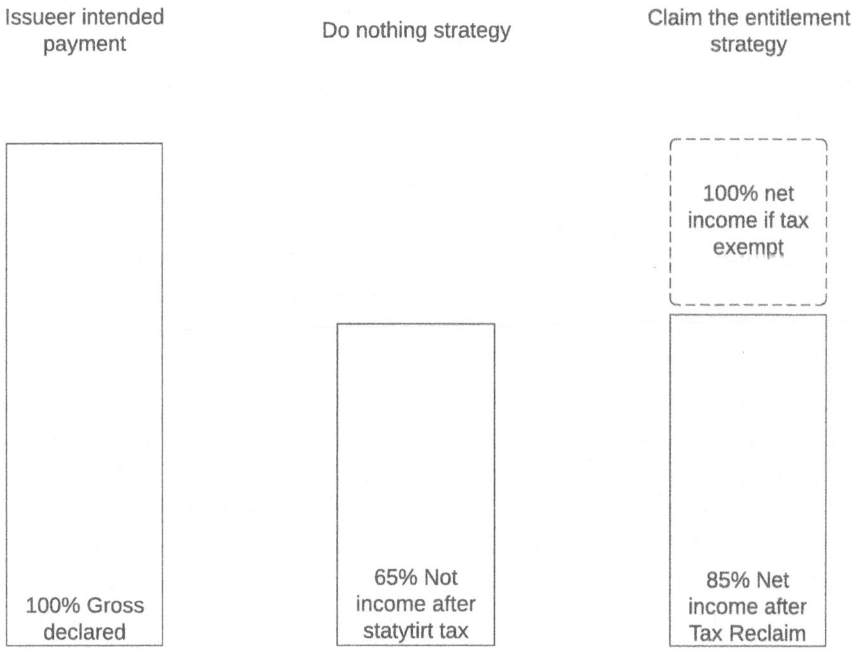

Exhibit 2.1 The withholding tax effect (*Source* Author's Own)

[1] Assumes that a 15% treaty rate of tax applies.

To avoid these effects, pairs of countries with common economic interests have, and continue to enter into bilateral Double Taxation Agreements or Treaties (DTAs or DTTs). By doing this they establish a Treaty Rate of withholding usually substantially lower than the statutory rate. These lower rates often come with strings attached. Because the DTAs are bilateral, the treaty rates can vary on a jurisdiction-by-jurisdiction basis, although, to be fair, most jurisdictions take a relatively flat rate approach with all their partner jurisdictions.

There are currently over 10,000 double tax treaties[2] in force worldwide which is an increase of over 2000 since 2018.

Many jurisdictions, although notably not the USA, also use a template framework provided by the Organisation for Economic Cooperation & Development (OECD), that is the Model Tax Convention on Income and Capital.[3] This establishes "Articles" that define how each jurisdiction will treat different types of income paid to different types of residents of the other jurisdiction. As we will see later, there can be cases where investors in one jurisdiction believe that they are being treated unfairly by the tax administration rules of another jurisdiction. This can lead to what are called Competent Authority discussions in which teams from each tax administration seek to iron out any inconsistencies or legal judgements, such as a European Court of Justice (ECJ) claims, to resolve such differences. Notwithstanding this, the effect of the DTAs and their Articles is to create the concept of entitlement. An entitlement is a property of an investor that is defined by their type (e.g., individual or entity), their tax residency, the type of income they are receiving and which jurisdiction they are receiving it from. When combined with the DTA rules and procedures, this means that the investor *should* be taxed on their cross-border income at a specified lower rate.

This means that the world of tax is not as static as one might at first suppose for such a process bound up in administration and intergovernmental negotiation. There are, on average 70 to 80 new treaties brought into force each year. These figures do not include around 200 changes to existing treaties each year. The combination of new treaties and changes to existing ones means that professional investors, wealth managers, portfolio managers and financial institutions must all keep a watching brief if they are to optimise returns on investment to the maximum extent possible (Exhibit 2.2).

---

[2] Source: International Bureau of Fiscal Documentation (IBFD).

[3] OECD (2019), *Model Tax Convention on Income and on Capital 2017 (Full Version)*, OECD Publishing, Paris, https://doi.org/10.1787/g2g972ee-en.

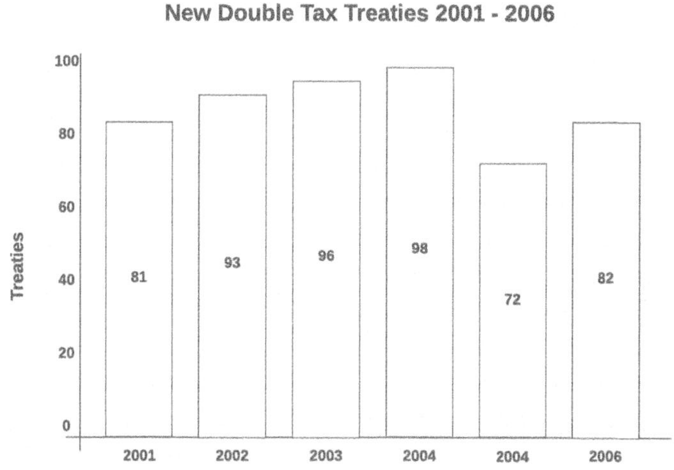

Exhibit 2.2 Double tax treaties 2001–2006 (*Source* Author)

However, it's one thing to *have* an entitlement and quite another to *gain the benefit* of that entitlement. Treaties commonly do not prescribe the detailed process by which entitlements can be realised. Instead, this is left to the tax administrations within each market to define. As we'll see later, the variety of processes and procedures causes a great deal of cost and risk for investors and intermediaries alike.

Even at this top level, we see the "it depends" effect at work. This statutory and treaty tax rate principle would be good if it weren't for the fact that there is not always one statutory rate in all markets of issue. For example, one eastern European country has a statutory rate of 20% applied to non-resident aliens EXCEPT if the company making the distribution is an oil company in which case the statutory rate is 25%.

When I was training to be a scientist in the 1970s, I learned about variables and constants and that the way we described the way things work in the world was through equations using those variables and constants. What I learned when I joined the financial services industry in 1996, and the withholding tax area, is that there are very few constants—it's almost all variables and that there really aren't many equations that hold true in all circumstances. Finance may be the world of Newton, where the rules are clear and always apply, but tax is the world of Heisenberg which is far more uncertain.

Jurisdictional Principle

So, as a given, we have a situation where an investment made cross-border is about to generate a distribution. This might be a cash dividend on a long equity position, or it might be a coupon payment on a bond. For the new reader, "long" in this context merely means that an investor owned the security across a specific date. In the case of equities (shares) that would usually be the "record date" and for fixed income instruments (bonds), that would usually be the "coupon date".

Technically, the treaty would provide the basis for an entitlement based on the residence and legal form of the investor, the nature of the income and the year in which the income is to be paid. Local law would provide for the statutory rate that would be applied and the treaty would establish the treaty rate that might apply, the difference being the entitlement. When it comes to obtaining the entitlement, there are different ways this can be done. All are based on two things—data and documentation. There are three broad categories of process:

- Relief at Source claim (RAS)
- Quick Refund
- Standard Refund Claim.

Relief at Source is a pre pay date process. If the beneficial owner can prove their entitlement prior to the pay date, according to the correct procedures, the correct "treaty" rate of tax will be deducted. Clearly, relief at source is a preferable taxation method because it ensures that investors receive correct distributions, properly taxed, in the fastest possible way. However, the time frame in which this documentation needs to be provided can be very tight. The result is that, although preferable, it's not always feasible.

Quick Refund is a process offered commercially by withholding agents mainly to other custodian banks and brokers. Essentially, the withholding agent will usually make payments to the tax authority on a regular basis, as opposed to every time a payment is distributed. So, in some cases, the withholding agent offers to make a book adjustment to the tax it has, if the beneficial owner or intermediary provides enough documentation to prove eligibility for a treaty rate. The tax is therefore remitted to the claimant by the withholding agent not the tax authority. This can occur all the way up to the date that the withholding agent remits tax to its local tax administration. As a result, quick refund processes are very fragmented in the nature of the rules, dates and types of documentation required. Once the quick refund window has passed, the withholding agent will pass the tax to the tax authority.

Standard refund claims are a post payment process. The beneficial owner is taxed at the Statutory Rate for that market and, within a certain given period (Statute of Limitations), if a retrospective claim is filed, the over-withheld tax is remitted back to the beneficial owner. In some cases, tax authorities also pay interest on amounts that take longer than expected to remit.

The problem, described as the jurisdictional principle, is that the availability of these processes varies. Some jurisdictions permit only relief at source mechanism. If the beneficial owner fails to apply for it, there is no quick refund or standard refund process available. At the other end of the spectrum are jurisdictions like Switzerland where there is no relief at source process (except on ADRs), only the standard refund process. In between, there are jurisdictions that allow both. So, if the beneficial owner does not make the deadline for relief at source, they still have an opportunity to file standard refund claims. These are called "Combination" jurisdictions.

These latter are important because they are likely to form the basis of any harmonisation that takes place in the market. The European Union and OECD have already settled that a combination approach would be the preferred common process for all jurisdictions. This nicely sidesteps the thorny and all but impossible alternative interpretation of harmonisation, that of the tax rates themselves. All the actors in the market agree that individual States should retain the rights to tax as they see fit both for the benefit of domestic taxpayers and also for non-resident aliens (inbound investors).

Transparency Principle

The entitlement we have spoken about so far has been created from the existence of the treaty and the wish of governments to encourage inward investment and avoid double taxation. However, in a complex financial world, there are different ways in which investors can group themselves to make investments cross-border.

Some of those mechanisms are viewed suspiciously by tax authorities and give rise to limitations on the benefits that some investors may be entitled to, merely because of the way that they invest. It also means that certain kinds of collective investment vehicle ("CIV") are seen as potential means for tax evasion or abuse of treaty (see below). These kinds of vehicles are often treated as fiscally transparent in order that tax administrations have a method to pierce through the CIV to the underlying investors.

This means, as shown in Exhibit 2.3, that a group of investors resident in a jurisdiction without a DTT with a target jurisdiction (a country of investment), could create a vehicle that is tax resident in a jurisdiction that does have a DTT with a target jurisdiction. In the absence of the transparency principle, the investors can access a favourable rate of tax on their investment that they could not have obtained if they had invested directly in the target market. There are innumerable variations on this theme and new constructs are being invented all the time, which means that financial institutions and tax administrations need to be continually researching these new vehicles to determine their tax transparency status.

Another aspect of transparency of principle that does not constitute treaty abuse but does affect tax processing, is that of *fiscal opacity*.

A pension fund, even though it may be comprised of thousands or even hundreds of thousands of individual investors, is typically looked at as the beneficial owner of income i.e., they are opaque for tax purposes. Partnerships on the other hand are typically fiscally transparent for tax purposes so any claim for an entitlement would be at the partner level and not the partnership level. In practice, some partnership structures can argue that a claim at the

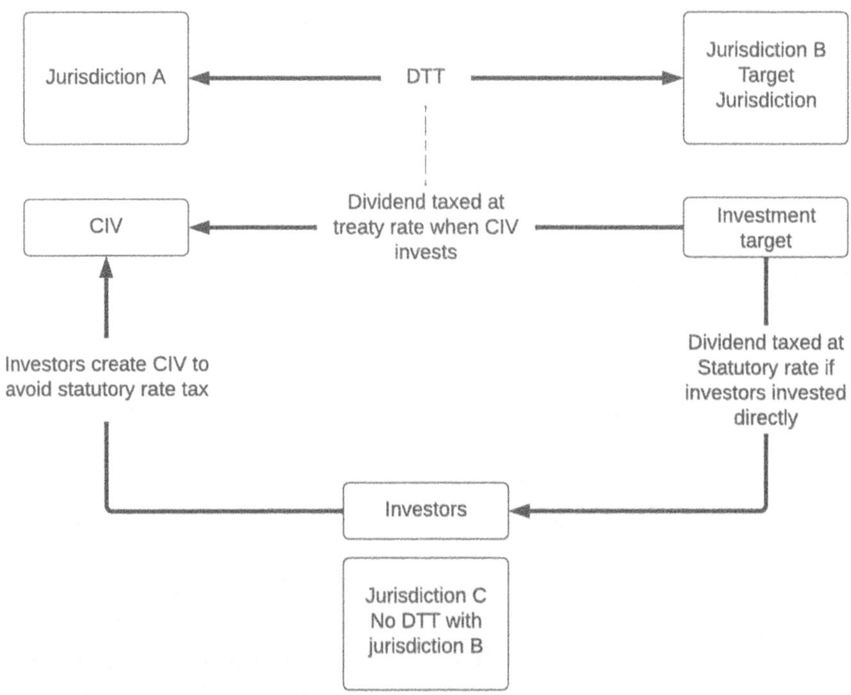

Exhibit 2.3 Treaty abuse (*Source* Author's own)

partnership level should be allowed, if they can demonstrate that the partners in the partnership are entitled to the same tax entitlement as the partnership would be claiming.

Good examples of these groupings include pension funds, hedge funds, SICAVs and SICAFs, unit trusts, etc. A pension fund for example would typically be exempt from withholding tax, so if investing directly, would be able to claim the whole of an entitlement to bring it up to 100% of a distributed dividend. However, if the pension fund is invested in the market by being an investor in a unit trust, as far as a foreign tax authority is concerned, the unit trust may well be the ultimate beneficial owner who can only access a treaty rate, say of 15%. In such a case, the pension fund loses out on tax that it cannot recover simply because of the way in which it invested in the market. The unit trust in that case was "fiscally opaque" i.e., the tax authority did not need to penetrate any deeper than the fund level, but equally the investors in the fund lost out. A US hedge fund that invests cross-border is typically viewed as a partnership. Tax authorities generally view partnerships as flow-through or fiscally transparent entities i.e., the fund is not the actual ultimate beneficial owner, the individual partners are. To that end, the transparency principle may seem to make the situation simpler as the entitlement will be at the partner level (based on the partner's residency and legal form as opposed to that of the fund).

However, when combined with the process and procedure principles we will discuss next, as far as tax is concerned, the hedge fund has an enormous administrative load placed upon it, if it wants to provide its investor partners with good value. The result is that many US hedge funds never attempt to recover the tax. Some tax authorities also require 100% transparency. So, if a hedge fund made a claim, all of its partners would need to be documented and disclosed to the foreign government even if some of them did not want to claim. Some hedge funds refuse to claim on this basis and so their entitlement is lost.

Even where these entitlements exist and the nature of the transparency principle makes it clear where the entitlement is within a collective investment vehicle, there is also an issue of disclosure. Many high net worth (HNWI) and ultra-high net worth individuals (UHNWI) are not always so happy about disclosing their income to a foreign government. This does not so much affect corporate entities like pension funds etc. who are regulated anyway. However, it's an important part of the transparency principle that to get tax back from a foreign government, to which you are entitled, you have to disclose yourself to that government or to an entity with which that government has contracted for that purpose.

Process and Procedure Principles

So, now we understand that there is a double taxation effect and in principle, that effect can be mitigated through the application of treaties to generate an entitlement. Access to those entitlements is mitigated in part by transparency issues. Now, depending on the market, an investor may be able to realise that entitlement in one of several ways.

The first myth to "bust" is the offset principle. Many beneficial owners are of the opinion that any tax they over-pay abroad can be taken as a tax credit against their domestic tax liability, effectively an offset process. In most cases this is not completely accurate. In most jurisdictions, the rules are that you can only take a credit on your domestic tax return for the "irrecoverable" portion of foreign tax overpaid. If there are recovery procedures, irrespective of how complex they may be, an investor would normally only be able to take a deduction for that portion of the foreign tax that could not be recovered.

With the offsetting myth put in context, the key ways in which these entitlements can be realised are through process and procedure. Unfortunately, the processes and procedures are different for each market of investment. However, they do share some common characteristics. They all require the claimant to provide evidence of their legal form and residency for tax purposes. However, the forms of evidence that are required by each market, of each claimant type—also vary.

Exhibit 2.4 shows what information is generally required from an investor to establish (i) whether they have an entitlement based on who they are, what they are and where they are tax residents, (ii) what the actual entitlement is and whether it is valid and (iii) whether the correct form(s) have been completed where the tax administration requires them. These components can then be fed into one of the three procedural processes I have already described.

Generally, once evidence of legal form and residency are established, for standard refund claims, all markets have a form on which the details of the income on which tax was over-deducted, must be provided. These forms are also the basis of the tax authority asking common questions of claimants to assure themselves that a false claim is not being filed e.g., the length of time that security was held by the claimant prior to the pay date, the reason for the claimant's ownership of the security, the answers to both of which, might indicate dividend washing or treaty shopping.

The forms vary by year sometimes and vary in many cases depending on the type of income received. So, for example, the form to recover tax on dividends in Austria is different from the form needed to claim tax back on

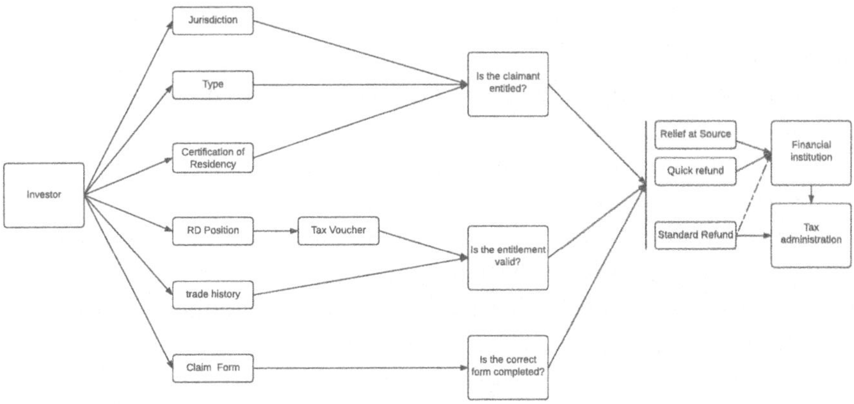

Exhibit 2.4 Key components of entitlement and procedure (*Source* Author's own)

interest. The questions asked on each of these forms is also different. Finally, in addition to evidence of the claimant's status and details of the claim, the claimant must also provide evidence that the income was in fact received by them and that it was over-taxed. In classical terms, this would be done with a tax voucher. For custodians, however, electronic records, including copies of SWIFT messages, are also sometimes accepted by tax authorities.

On the procedural front, life is not much easier, as we'll see in more detail later. For some markets the standard refund claim, once compiled, can be filed directly to the tax authority. In others however, e.g., France, the claim must be filed with an agent bank, which undertakes to review the claim's validity and process it through to the tax authority, for which of course they charge a fee. This is a jurisdictional procedure. There are also different procedures for some income types, irrespective of the market concerned. A good example is American Depositary Receipts (ADRs) which are generally "sponsored" by one of four ADR sponsoring banks—Citi, JPMorgan Chase, Bank of New York Mellon and Deutsche Bank. Claims on ADR positions cannot be filed to a tax authority or an agent bank because they are derivative products. The claim must be filed back to the depositary that sponsored the issue. More on that later.

Automation Principles

Automation, and its adjunct, standardisation, have been talked about in the withholding tax industry for decades. The problem has always been that the truly fragmented nature of what would appear to be a homogenous concept at the DTT level, has previously rendered attempts at standardisation and automation largely ineffectual. The scale of the manual processing problem has meant that although theoretical models were created, none have gained enough political traction and where there was enough traction, there was not enough industry participation because those expected to invest in these improvements could see no benefit for themselves.

I have come across this in many ways. For example, most tax processing functions in custodian banks have never had to undergo a cost–benefit analysis. The client is charged a flat fee measured as a number of basis points (BP) charged on the value of assets under management (AUM). The services that custodians deliver to investors, for that fee, are rarely split into components to determine what contribution each makes to profitability. In addition, of the three process and procedural principles (relief at source, quick refund and standard refund), most custodians do not explicitly charge for the first two. Standard refunds are usually the only transactions that are separately chargeable. So, if you don't know what components of tax processing are costing your firm, there's no real basis for comparing an automation or standardisation initiative and so there's very little incentive to participate.

However, as will be described later, the political landscape has changed markedly in the last few years, not least due to initiatives from the OECD and European Union which, added to the US QI model, start to provide a greater degree of certainty about the direction in which the industry is trending and the types of change that regulators ae prepared to accept and actively support. Over the same period, technology developments have increasingly been deployed in the securities space where previously they had been restricted to the payments environment. Securities processing, of which tax forms a part, is much more complex than payments processing. Two new breeds of financial firm have emerged—"fintechs" and "regtechs" who focus on the use of disruptive technologies in the financial space. Distributed Ledger Technology ("DLT"), the ultimate disruptor and disintermediator has also finally been used in a proof of concept within withholding tax.

So much for automation, but the problem that we have always had is that automation has tended to be driven by self-interest. The result is that many of these new technologies have created their own unique standards that don't play well with other solutions, very similar to the battle between JVC (VHS) and Sony (Betamax) in the video-standard wars of the last century. These unique standards were intended to destroy a competitor's offering by making it so popular that only their solution would be widely adopted. This model depends on rapid rates of adoption to be successful—something that the financial services industry and tax, are not well known for. A good example can be seen in the current adoption of self-certifications of tax residency in which the US uses a model—the W-8 (for QI and FATCA) while the OECD uses another for TRACE and CRS (the Investor Self Declaration or ISD). Both contain large amounts of data overlap and are still mainly output using paper. Both groups permit the development of digital alternatives, but their definitions of digital are not the same and they are taking no part, individually or collectively, in the development of a single standard. If we've learned anything, it should be that automation and standards go hand-in-hand. One cannot be effective without the other.

Principle of Interests

In this complex world of cross-border tax, to improve, we must first establish the answer to one question—in whose interest is it to change the paradigm? It's all very well to propose that these fragmented, manual systems could be harmonised, standardised and automated, and many have done so over the years, but it cannot happen without collaboration and common intent. Other than by disruption and disintermediation it's not clear that there is yet enough groundswell of support to change much. In this section, we can look at what some of the drivers are.

Issuers

Issuers are the listed corporate entities (and governments) whose financial instruments investors purchase. Many large corporations have institutional investments inbound from many different sources some of which are resident in other countries.

If an Issuer wants to attract investment, typically to fund or sustain growth, it's in its interests to make some efforts not to disadvantage its future shareholders. Yet until recently, in prospectuses, it was common to see legal wording about tax issues that put the entire responsibility for tax on investment income squarely on the investor's shoulders. "Not our problem" is essentially what the Issuers were saying to the market. This is rather odd because, in most legal frameworks, the ultimate responsibility for the taxation of distributions lies with the Issuer. We have become so used to innumerable financial intermediaries taking on some of the responsibilities of the Issuers, that we have perhaps forgotten this basic principle.

So, it is clearly in the best interests of investors and Issuers to have a taxation system that is efficient and fair. Fairness is established by the DTTs.

Efficiency is determined by the legal frameworks available (the jurisdictional principle) and the ease with which all parties can access and use the available methods (the procedural principles). While I recognise that tax may not always be the primary objective of investment, the fact is that it can, unaddressed, create up to a 250-basis point reduction in returns. So, an Issuer in a jurisdiction with a high statutory tax rate and an inefficient tax system may not be as attractive to an investor as a similar Issuer in the same sector in a different jurisdiction where the tax rates are more favourable and more easily accessed.

Issuers are also a key lobby group to their own domestic tax administrations. The argument is that an inefficient cross-border withholding tax system, such as one that does not allow for relief at source, harms an Issuer's ability to attract inward investment.

Intermediaries

Intermediaries clearly have a role to play and an interest. For most investors, the effort of finding out, understanding, researching and filing claims is too much. Intermediaries thus fall into three categories—those who advise investors, those who provide securities safe keeping services—custodians and those who provide clearing and settlement—the (international) central securities depositories (I)CSDs.

Much of the rest of this book will highlight issues of withholding tax primarily from a custodian's perspective because it is here that the main weight both of responsibility (contractual and fiduciary) and opportunity lies. Any intermediary who provides safe keeping services must assess the degree to which they offer withholding tax processing services. This will be a complex decision because the cost of providing a service is proportional to a number of factors including:

- the size of the custodian's client base
- the residencies of beneficial owners represented in the client base
- the types of beneficial owner or pooling of assets by investment vehicles represented in the client base
- the number and type of markets into which investments are made
- the expertise available to the custodian
- the availability of external expertise via an agent bank network or superior global custodian network

- competitive offerings by other custodians.

Of course, these factors must be considered with the cost associated with providing a service. This leads to limitations. Custodians essentially cut their cloth according to their perceived needs. However, custodians also derive, on the surface at least, financial benefit from the provision of these services. Most custodians make money by charging custody fees based on the value of the assets they manage. Ergo, if they recover extra tax, the value of assets goes up and the fees they receive increase. Unfortunately, while this is a simple concept to understand, most custodians provide their services on a pooled or bundled basis. In other words, it's often difficult, if not impossible to extract either the cost or the revenue associated with the provision of a service.

As the changes to this edition will attest, custodians, in fact, all intermediaries, are also now being required to apply a whole new level of effort in the withholding tax space. It's no longer enough simply to be able to process tax relief, quick refunds, and standard refund claims services. There have been enough cases of fraud, abuse of treaty and tax evasion in the last few years, that most tax administrations have now regulated the aspect of governance in the form of control and oversight. This usually takes the form of annual reporting to tax administrations so that they can hold financial institutions directly accountable for the tax they withhold. However, some administrations have gone further and have required financial institutions to appoint responsible officers and conduct regular independent reviews and certifications of compliance. This substantially increases costs for custodians while not really being capable of being re-charged out to clients except where special conditions apply and costs are allocable at a client level.

As these cost burdens increase, it is inevitable that, at least, the AUM charging rate will increase over time and/or that specialist areas such as tax are excluded from the AUM rate and charged separately based on the value they deliver to the client. At the same time, intermediaries are looking for ways to reduce the cost burden overall. This is where some automation is useful, particularly in the documentation of investors which is still predominantly paper-based even though several administrations have regulated to allow digital or electronic alternatives.

Advisors

Advisors have a key role to play. In this category, I also include trustees and administrators. The latter two have not only a financial interest but also a fiduciary interest. As we will see later, this fiduciary interest creates the potential for a longer term risk. For the banking community, this is critical. In 2008, the market crash was, in the most part, the result of banks engaging in activity, the risk of which was not properly understood or communicated. When the reality was understood, the global financial crisis of the century (so far) began. One of the questions that went unasked at the time, surprisingly, was—if we didn't anticipate the way in which banks were acting with respect to debt risk, what else do we not know about their activities and what else do they themselves not know about the systemic risks they may inadvertently be creating?

Advisors are also important as influencers and they have a vested interest to make sure that they understand the principles and mechanisms of withholding tax so that they can advise their clients properly.

Vendors

Vendors come in many forms. In general, we define a vendor as a firm that is not an intermediary (in the payment chain), issuer, advisor or investor but is a firm that provides a service, based on their expertise, that is useful to one of the foregoing.

Unusually, in withholding tax circles, most vendors are relatively small firms with very specific and niche knowledge. Their growth is usually within their geographic locale and within a very specific type of client. As their growth continues, they will generally present a more global image.

Therefore, understanding the complexities of withholding tax as well as the benefits that can be gained by that understanding is critical for vendors because it will make their solutions more relevant today and more future-proofed against tomorrow.

Many of the interested parties have different views of what they should be doing, what they can be doing and what they will do on behalf of their clients. For administrators of funds, for instance, this may include advising fund managers and trustees of the withholding tax issue at one end and supporting any claims made at the other. In many cases, fiscally transparent funds-making claims cannot succeed without providing a list of underlying beneficial owner investors. This is so that the receiving tax authority can be assured that the claim being made at the fund level would essentially be the same as that made by the investors were they have invested directly i.e., they would in effect be subject to the same entitlement. To that extent, non-custodial intermediaries have more need for information tools than processing tools.

For custodians, the issue is different. They are more likely to be filing the claims and therefore have need of both informational tools and processing tools or access to them.

The net result is that there is a small but important support industry focusing on providing information and processing tools to a variety of other interested parties. Generally speaking, any fees incurred in the provision of those tools is usually either paid for by the investor directly out of optimised tax or indirectly through custody fees.

Investors

And finally, we get to the most important interested party—the investor. For most private, retail, level investors with a few hundred shares, it's unlikely that there will ever be a realistic way for them to gain access to their entitlements. On the one hand, they lack the knowledge, skill, and experience (and time) to do the job and equally, the amount of time spent on such activity would not equal the likely return. It falls to the institutional investors to have the most interest because once assets are pooled in any way, the value of tax recoverable does make the recovery financially viable.

On the other hand, once assets are pooled, it makes the claim process more complex because one of the key concerns of tax authorities is that the pooling is done for the purpose of avoiding tax as opposed to optimising it. Thus, many claims are straightforward when filed for a simple direct beneficial owner but become subject to more scrutiny when filed at a pooled level. Much of the unrecovered tax extant today exists because it has been deducted from the income to a pooled asset vehicle and the underlying beneficial owners have no way to either claim their portion directly or force their asset vehicle manager to do so.

With so many interested parties, many of whom have a financial interest in increasing the return of tax refunds to investors, it does therefore seem counter-intuitive that so little is achieved.

Tax Administrations

Last, but certainly not least, on the list of interested parties are tax administrations. These have the job of translating the DTTs into a framework that meets their domestic law. One of the common myths about tax administrations and the way that they implement DTTs is that they believe that if they make claim processing difficult, there will be a large proportion of entitled

Materiality

There's a saying that when times are good, no one pays much attention to withholding tax and investors don't always care about their entitlements. When times are bad *everyone* pays attention to withholding tax. The reason is easy to understand, although more difficult to empathise with if you're an investor. In the period 2019–2020 fund performances were in the range 13.25% (equity markets)—31.5% (S&P 500).[1] In that context, explaining to someone that they could add another 1.5% to that performance by engaging in a difficult, long winded, complex process where that return might be a year or more down the line—generally meets with a negative response. However, when fund values are more volatile, as was the case in early 2022, suddenly that 1.5–2.5% can make a significant difference and, as a proportion of fund performance, becomes material. There's also a case to consider in the larger context when we look at the overall trends in investment and the absolute amounts involved.

While this area is relatively poorly researched from an investor perspective, as we've seen, there are published articles that indicate that as much as $200Bn of tax could be overwithheld each year globally. Considering the effects of Statutes of Limitations, this figure would give rise to an extant tax value of nearer $1.6Tn a year on a rolling basis.[2] Of this, only a fraction is ever paid at relief at source rates or reclaimed after the pay date. It's important to note here that estimates of withheld tax and reclaimed amounts do vary widely depending on the source. What is consistently agreed by all observers of the industry however is that there is a large amount of tax over withheld each year, that a large dollar value goes unrecovered each year and that Statutes of Limitations compound this value. Here's how this number is arrived at:

---

[1] https://www.evestment.com/news/2020-ended-on-a-high-note-for-most-of-hedge-fund-industry/.

[2] An entitlement arising in one year can remain validly claimable for a period known as the Statute of Limitations. $1.6Tn represents a rolling up of claims across the average statute of limitations of five years.

Assets under management[3]	$145.5 trillion[4]
Average Proportion held cross-border	25%[5]
Cross Border assets under management	$36.375 trillion
Average long-term yield	10%[6]
Yield subject to tax	$3.6 trillion
Average reclaim (statutory rate-treaty rate)	15%
Annual claim value	$540 billion
Average Statute of Limitations	5.2 years
Extant recoverable tax	$2.8 trillion

So, it's self-evident that those receiving cross-border income streams, and the industry in general, have an issue to address unless, of course, they are confident that they fall completely inside the recovered element or are eligible and gain relief or exemptions.

For institutional investors, who have substantial assets invested internationally, and who therefore derive significant income streams liable to be subject to withholding, it is critical to know enough about the management of their investments and the economic, regulatory, and political environment in which they exist, to make intelligent decisions.

The way in which an investment portfolio is deployed, managed and maximised must include a serious concern with the effects of withholding taxation and appropriate benchmarking of this activity. While every portfolio is different, a typical valuation of a portfolio of investments across just five countries can show a difference of up to 30% dependent on whether this issue is addressed or not. Most funds these days are invested in between 13 and 25 countries. Exhibit 3.1 shows the effect on a portfolio spread for a typical institutional investor. The effect of understanding this issue can clearly be seen in the difference between the net received—which is what you get if you do nothing, and the adjusted net received—which is what you get if you take action.

It's worth noting that these figures represent only a generalised picture of the effect between the statutory rate and the treaty rate. Certain kinds of investment structures e.g., pension funds, can benefit from even further reductions including to 0%, if they are deemed exempt, where all withholding tax can be recovered.

[3] https://www.pwc.com/ng/en/press-room/global-assets-under-management-set-to-rise.html.

[4] https://www.pwc.com/ng/en/press-room/global-assets-under-management-set-to-rise.html.

[5] https://www.bis.org/publ/qtrpdf/r_qt1403y.htm.

[6] https://www.nerdwallet.com/article/investing/average-stock-market-return.

Country	Dividend	Taxes Withheld (%)	Dividend Received %	Recoverable Taxes (%)	Dividend Received (%)
Asutralia	100	30	**70**	15	**85**
Asutria	100	25	**75**	10	**85**
Canada	100	25	**75**	10	**85**
Finland	100	28	**72**	13	**85**
France	100	25	**75**	10	**85**
Germany	100	21.1	**78.9**	6.1	**85**
Italy	100	27	**73**	12	**85**
Netherlands	100	25	**75**	10	**85**
New Zealand	100	30	**70**	15	**85**
Spain	100	18	**82**	3	**85**
Sweden	100	30	**70**	15	**85**
Switzerland	100	35	**65**	20	**85**

Exhibit 3.1 Comparative market performance (*Source* WTAX)

These last two years have seen more movement in taxation rates than many others in the last twenty years. The data in the table above was correct at the time of research but may have changed since then.

Exhibit 3.2 shows the effect of these new treaties combined with changes to existing treaties. There are two noteworthy aspects to this chart. First, most changes take place in January each year. Second, given a database of tax rates that must contain the changes as they may apply to types of beneficial owner, types of income, year of income (the change may be retrospective), any given single change is likely to affect more than one data point. The combination of these effects on custodians and other intermediaries is that resources need to be increased in December and January to assess and implement the changes to internal databases and more importantly assess the effects on clients. A single change by a single country can mean several hundred changes to database points and again several hundred impacts on clients.

Despite this, the effects of taxation in this regard have, for many years been ignored or, at best, treated as a necessary evil involving complex administration, much form filling and long-winded follow-ups with tax authorities.

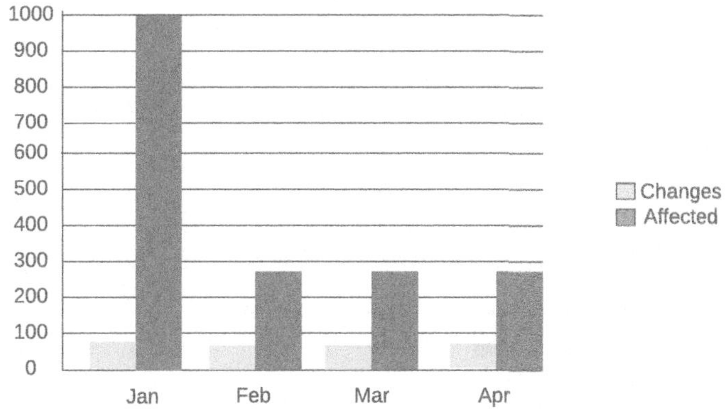

Exhibit 3.2 Changes to tax treaties and their effects (*Source* Author's own research)

However, more recently, following some notable changes, withholding tax has been rising up the investment and, as a result, the management and custodial agenda. These changes fall into three categories—commercial, geopolitical and technological.

Commercial

Two major commercial factors have been at work to bring withholding tax issues to the fore. They are:

- Increasing proportions of portfolios invested cross-border and
- Increasing pressure on custody margins.

Recent years have seen major increases in the degree to which funds are invested cross-border. In 2000 a typical fund would have invested between 15 and 25% of its value across international boundaries. The most recent research shows that this figure is now above 33% average. Exhibit 3.3 shows the rate of increase in investment cross-border (dotted line) compared to the overall rate of increase in AUM.

Between 2008 and 2021 while the absolute value of assets under management increased, the proportion held cross-border also increased but at a lower rate. Since 2009, these trends have changed. The value of assets has been hit hard by the global recession, while the proportion held cross-border has increased as a percentage since many investors are increasing the spread of their portfolio to mitigate and spread risk.

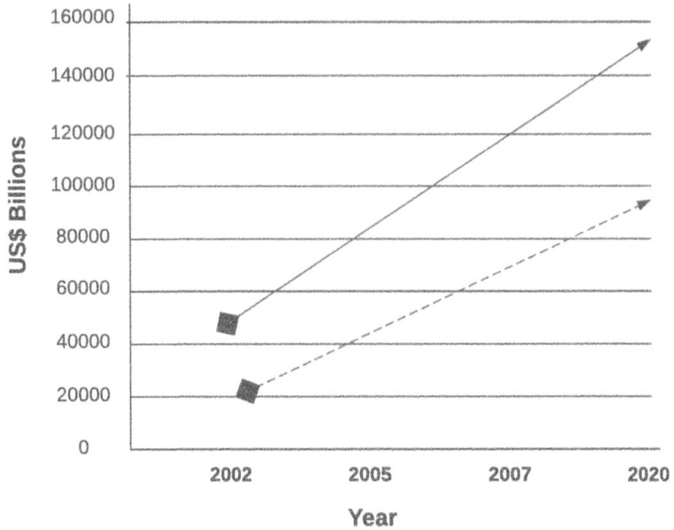

Exhibit 3.3 Growth is cross border AUM (*Source* Author)

Number of Treaties for Regional Jurisdictions

Country	Outbound Treaties
India	77
Singapore	58
Hong Kong	4
China	88
Australia	42
New Zealand	34
North Korea	8
South Korea	69
Vietnam	37
Taiwan	16
Indonesia	57
Malaysia	67
Thailand	52
Philippines	35
Japan	56
Total	700

Exhibit 3.4 Treaties of the Asia Pacific region (*Source* Author)

Of course, most of those assets are held by custodians in safe keeping accounts or with ICSDs. So, it's equally important to understand not just that the market is growing but where the assets are held. Exhibit 3.4 shows the top 10 custodians in terms of their cross-border portfolios.

Data on withholding tax is fragmented even at the custodial level. However, if we assume that the general proportion of cross-border business, for those who report both numbers, is consistent for those who don't then we see that across 54 custodians who reported global assets under management of $113,069 billion, the value of cross-border assets under custody at the beginning of 2009 can be estimated at $41,982 billion or nearly $42 trillion—37.13%).

The reality is however that there are over 25,000 financial firms worldwide managing assets, some of which are cross-border. If we assume that the data available from the top 54 custodians represent 80% of the market, which seem reasonable since they are the largest custodians, then the total estimate for assets under management globally would be in the region of $141 trillion of which $52.5 trillion would be held cross-border. Under that scenario, using the same assumptions as before of a 5% yield and 15% reclaim, the annual tax recoverable would be in the region of $393.6 billion and the total extant at any one time, around $2.05 trillion.

These are *very* rounded numbers. I have considered and balanced the mitigating factors that some pairs of countries in which the assets are held will have no treaty and therefore the claim values will drop. On the other hand, there will be many investor types that are entitled to much more than the average 15% recoverable. Either way, the numbers are truly enormous and the area worthy of close scrutiny.

The majority of custodians do have relatively sophisticated processes in place for minimising tax, from relief at source services to outsourced or semi-automated tax recovery systems. It is likely therefore that much of it will be reclaimed or have been subject to relief at source. Even so, while this book has value for those custodians who are not reclaiming at all, I hope it will still serve as a useful source of ideas for those already fully engaged in the process. As cross-border trade increases year by year, and new markets emerge, the scale of this issue will continue to rise.

Increasing volatility in markets and massive drops in fund performance have also led to increased risk and focus on previously "marginal" added value issues. Put simply, when the times get tight and the yield from the fund decreases, the proportionate impact of tax becomes a statistically significant factor. This has also led to a more intense focus on portfolio planning based on the relative friendliness of the tax regime in the invested country. Secondly, increasing pressure on custodial margins has led to a business focus by fund managers and custodians alike, on ways in which to add value for investor clients and thus exploit opportunities for enhancing margin delivery and remain competitive. This pressure has created new services for investors including, for example, contractual tax, where the fund manager/custodian agrees to pay income gross (for a small fee), based on his knowledge of the tax reclaim market and his ability to reliably predict his receivables from those markets. When I first entered the industry contractual tax was very much the exception. In recent months I've come across custodians offering contractual tax in up to fifteen markets as a matter of normal business practice. The complexity and cost of the process itself have also led to a degree of "unbundling" of fees from fund managers and custodians so that they can clarify the added value they are providing over and above normal custody operations and maximise their profit potential.

Geopolitical

Increasing levels of inter-governmental liaison, fuelled by concern over abuses of tax law increases and anti-terrorist activities, has led to (i) an increasing acceptance of the need to share information about citizens across international borders and (ii) recognition by tax authorities of the long-term benefits of moves to electronic handling of data.

The market is also not homogenous across the globe. The mature markets of investment, where over 95% of claims are currently filed have historically been the key focus. But today, the emerging markets are becoming more important. Financial power is seen to be moving towards China. The Asia Pacific region generally is more likely to have short and shallow recessions. Its historic trend has been to invest predominantly intra-regionally, but it is starting to see major fund flows inwards. However, the number of treaties on which almost all tax reclamation depends, is relatively small. There are currently just over 5000 treaties globally. Exhibit 3.4 shows the number of treaties that Asia Pacific markets have with other jurisdictions. With a total of just 700, the region represents, currently, only 14% of the active global treaties.

Increasing regulatory pressure on compliance and risk management functions together with the recent spiralling of global corporate mismanagement scandals, has increased current and historical legal exposure of custodians to investors, for failure to adopt (or have adopted) best practices or explicitly communicate gaps in service which an investor may reasonably have presumed were being performed. It has even been seen as questionable whether a custodian or fund manager can rely on a Service Level Agreement (SLA) with an institutional investor which specifically excludes or limits responsibility for tax reclaims. The argument is that these exclusions or limitations are usually hidden away in the small print of an SLA. The scale and scope of the effect of withholding tax is so fundamental and potentially large that, in the absence of the investor knowing about the issue, the fund manager or custodian must make the investor more explicitly aware of the implications of his decision simply because the fund manager or custodians role so fundamentally revolves around maximising fund value.

Technology

Increasing availability of technology-driven or specialist solutions has meant that previously very high administrative costs have, or can be, reduced significantly.

Industry moves towards Straight Through Processing (STP) and shorter trade cycles ($T + 1$) have, overall, demonstrated a clear business model for trade settlement and clearance. The industry is now beginning to address "back-office" administrative functions to truly deliver STP. Yet even now, the ISO standards for messaging between custodians related to this important area are very fragmented and have yet to be integrated into an effective model. SWIFT consistently reports in its research findings that corporate actions automation is one of the key topics and perceived benefits of automation, yet in the same surveys efforts to deliver it are not just fragmented, they have been lamentably slow to pick up any momentum.

Technology has been applied however not just to the movement of withholding tax information and to the ISO standards which will underpin it. Technology has increasingly been deployed by a variety of interests to improve the efficiencies of most, but not all parts of the process. There are basically four ways in which technology can be deployed in this area either directly or indirectly. They are:

- Buy—third party software solutions
- Outsource—to third parties who have technology solutions and significant operational experience
- Build—an internal system to automate processes or
- Bureau—buy solutions to those parts of the process that are either difficult or expensive to handle in-house.

There are some commercial companies offering technology solutions in this area. Custodians will also, for a variety of often internal political or policy reasons, choose to build their own system in-house and many have done so in recent years. Bureau solutions have offered custodians the ability to selectively buy those elements of the process that are either the most expensive to perform internally or the most difficult, leaving the remainder of the process to be integrated internally.

Finally, outsourcing allows custodians to "focus on core business" while ensuring that someone else, who has integrated their systems, takes on the full role. There are ups and downs to all these technology-based solutions, which I will discuss later, but the fact remains that technology has the capacity to make these tax processes more efficient. The degree to which it has succeeded has been influenced by history and by the various commercial interests involved. Its future capability to address this issue is becoming clearer as the tools available begin to encompass the full breadth of the taxation process rather than elements of it. Exhibit 3.5 shows a Venn diagram to explain a common occurrence. There are certain elements of the tax process that are more amenable to automation than others. At the same time, financial firms tend to treat their tax operations in different ways. Often one branch or arm of the firm will have automated processes while another, operating almost independently, will deal with the issues manually or not at all. On top of that, there may be an internal decision or strategy which provides the solution only to selected accounts, perhaps proprietary vs client accounts or large vs small accounts. The effect of this complexity is that, for any given firm, parts of that same firm, in different places, may have any one or more of the available solutions in place working simultaneously. Whether this is the result of a deliberate and well-thought-out risk management strategy, or more likely the result of historical development will be individual to the firms concerned.

The issue with all technology-based solutions is that of cost, a factor that, internally must be weighed against the return provided through fees (as any reclaim value or minimization of tax is of course the property of the investor).

Why Should We Care?

Because it's important. Because it is an entitlement. This is not some application for a benefit or, like class actions, an attempt to get part of a legal claim. The sums involved are the rightful property of the investors and anyone or any firm that chooses to manage assets should have a clear and customer-facing view of their attitude to maximising returns for investors.

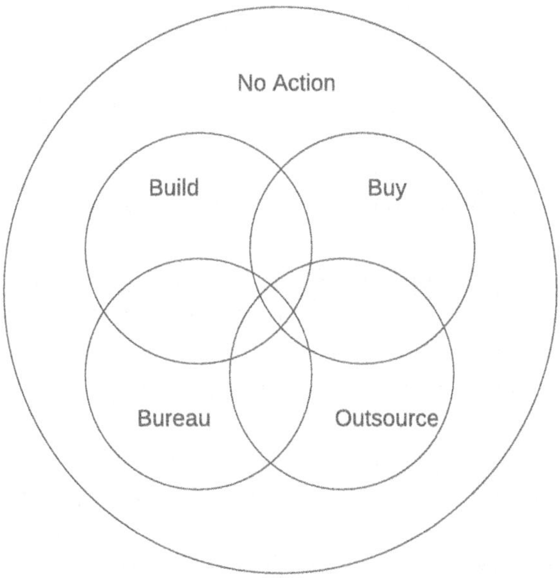

Exhibit 3.5 Solution options (*Source* Author's own)

All these factors, alone and in concert, have contributed to a much more focused attitude by many, but by no means all, investors, and custodians to leverage every possible piece of value.

Technically, the cost/benefit for the withholding tax issue has now become firmly established on the benefit side, not least because of the scale of difference that can be achieved in yield when different attitudes to tax are considered. A UK higher rate taxpayer receiving income from a Swiss investment, without any attention to the tax issue, could see a massive drop in net income after tax from his investment (Swiss withholding tax is 35% and the recoverable could be either 20% or even the full 35%). However, knowledge of the general business principles and appreciation of the importance of the issue is still extremely fragmented at all but the highest levels of custody.

There are many investors who are not receiving the benefits of professional attention to this issue. The problem is that many don't even know that they are missing out or have a problem. Most of the texts available to date are highly technical or are not aimed at the investor or concerned custodian from an operational perspective. They assume a level of knowledge of the tax systems involved that most investors, fund managers and custodians at the business point of contact, do not have.

As a result there has been no explanatory text in this area to date which brings the threads of this important issue together so that investors and custodians can consider all the factors in one place.

Institutional investors in particular, often outsource or contract either indirectly or directly with third parties—fund managers, custodians et al., to undertake some or all of the "back-office" or "corporate actions" activities that flow from their original investments (e.g., dividend announcements, bonds, rights issues, proxy voting). So, to a large extent, institutional investors are often unaware of withholding tax, or if they are aware of it, it's only to the extent of knowing basically what it is and that someone else purportedly does it for them. The question is—who? See Exhibit 3.6.

However, even these first-line fund managers also often outsource upwards of what they consider to be "non-core" elements of their service. The primary investor may not even know that this has been done as the fund manager/custodian may have contracted to perform the function but has a "back-to-back" vanilla contract with a third party. So there comes into existence a chain of assumptions about who is taking on the ultimate responsibility, and thus liability for this issue.

Even knowing that your custodian does perform tax processing should not be enough to satisfy investors. Many custodians apply a "lower threshold" to their tax operations based on their own internal estimates of cost of administration. This means that any recoverable amount below the threshold will not usually be reclaimed because the cost of doing so is administratively more than the reclaim itself. The more enlightened investor would be aware that some custodians, for these small reclaims, will credit the reclaim value to the investor anyway as a customer relations benefit even though

Exhibit 3.6 The investment chain (*Source* Author)

they do not pursue the reclaim itself. Others would be aware that some markets allow aggregation of small reclaims together. These are the types of the issue discussed in this book, allowing the investor to ask pertinent questions and gauge more accurately, the efficiencies or otherwise that lies behind the statement "yes we do tax reclaims".

Institutional investors often believe that this is a non-issue. It seems obvious that the scale of the benefit of dealing with withholding tax is so great that everyone must know about it and deal with it as fundamental to their service offering. It goes to the issue of what is "management" and what is "custody" and what can I reasonably expect from my fund manager or custodian in this area.

The business reality is that a great deal of over-withheld tax goes unreclaimed. Ipso facto, not all fund managers and custodians are maximising their investor's fund performance. An investor needs to be able to assess the performance of his incumbent custodian (and also competitive submissions by custodians) in terms of whether or not a custodian understands and/or deals with taxation. Custodians in the most general sense, for their part, operate in a thin margin, highly competitive business. They must make commercial decisions about their product and service offering and they are being increasingly driven by technology and the need to make economies of scale and reduce transactional costs. In this environment, tax, as a labour-intensive, predominantly manual activity, is an area not usually focused on for adding value. However, in any commercial and marketing environment, it's important for those at the business end of custody to understand enough of the back office detail and of the investor issues, to make intelligent decisions about the value any of their services might bring to an investor. Some custodians, for example, exclude tax reclaims from custody contracts or limit the extent of their services in this area because of the perceived complexity and cost. What should concern the investment community is the extent to which the custodian has explicitly informed the investor of this extent and if so, what the likely loss in funds will be based on the mix of the portfolio.

In 2001 Global Investor published an article in which a hypothetical example of two managers in different institutional investment firms was cited to show the effect. Both invest their own money in pension funds as well as professionally manage the funds of their firms. They both retire on the same day and compare notes about the value of their respective personal retirement funds, only to find that one is 30% larger than the other, even though the investment portfolio and spread were both pretty much the same. The article successfully personalised the issue—how would you feel if your pension fund dropped 30%, because you didn't reclaim or minimise withholding tax. Whether it's your own money or your firms, or your client's, that scale of difference deserves serious attention. Of course, the example was hypothetical, since the assumption made was that all of the investments of the fund were cross border whereas in most cases the proportion of funds held cross-border is actually nearer to 30%, but the principle is still valid. We also now know the reaction that people have to a 30% drop in fund values from the collapse of 2008.

If that isn't enough, given the global economic slowdown it seems self-evident that, in the absence of significant market growth, maintaining the value of what growth *is* generated becomes increasingly important. At its core, this book is about three things:

- understanding what withholding tax is;
- the business and process issues that surround it, the impact it can have and, most importantly;
- it's designed to give both investors and custodians enough information about the process to define, in their own framework, best practice and performance benchmarks.

This book is not written as a detailed technical description of any individual regime, in terms for instance of the rates applicable to various types of income in different circumstances. It is more concerned with increasing the level of general knowledge of the process in terms that a non-expert will find useful. Those who should be concerned to read this book are those that are in the chain of responsibility for ensuring best practices. Ultimately the investor bears the ultimate responsibility—it's their money after all.

While this book primarily focuses on withholding tax from a custodial and investment perspective, there are several different scenarios under which this tax is applied. One important one, discussed later, is withholding tax on cross-border royalties. This is not an insignificant area and most obviously would concern those accountants dealing with sectors such as pharmaceuticals, music, literature and publishing, and tobacco. If major investors and custodians, whose specialty is to know and apply best practices in the financial arena, only manage to reclaim a fraction of reclaimable tax, it is more than likely that corporate enterprises and their accountancy firms may need to be more aware of the issue also.

We've spoken so far about some of the contextual issues relating to the overall market in terms of size. However, the most interesting thing about withholding tax is the dichotomy between its simplicity as a concept on the one hand and its complexity in delivery on the other. Exhibit 3.7 makes this point eloquently.

In order to understand this diagram, we must first understand that an entitlement endowed by a treaty is based on a number of variables. How long it takes to get back an entitlement will also depend on several variables as will the process that must be followed. All these variables can act alone or in concert with one or more of the other variables. The result may be a failure or inability to recover at all, a successful recovery, or a delayed recovery. These factors are discussed in more depth in this chapter. However, to give some flavour, Exhibit 3.8 shows the market average recovery time and statutes for a range of jurisdictions.

For most investors the key variable is the length of time it will take to get money back and many are surprised to learn that it can take weeks, months or even years, up to ten years in some cases, to get claimed funds back. There are however two edges to this sword, the other being the statute of limitations. This is the amount of time after the pay date of the original income, that you have before you essentially make a free donation of your money to a foreign government.

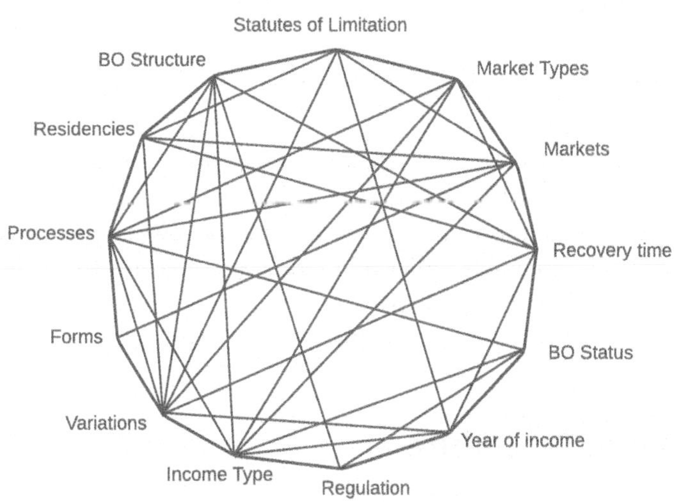

Exhibit 3.7 The Tax Cat's Cradle (*Source* Author)

Country of Issues	Deadline for Filing Claims	Indicative Times to Recovery
Asutralia	No Deadline	9 Months
Asutria	5 years from end of year div. Paid	6 Months
Belgium	3 years from end of year div. Paid	2 Years
Canada	2 years from end of year div. Paid	14 Months
Denmark	20 years from Pay Date	3 Months
Finland	5 yeras from Pay Date	3 Months
France	2 years from end of year div. was Paid	1.25 Years
Germany	4 years from end of year div. was Paid	10 Months
Ireland	10 years from Pay Date	6 Months
Italy	4 years from Pay Date for div. With record date after 7/1/99 prior div, 1 year from end of year div. was paid	5 Years
Luxembourg	2 years from Pay Date	6 Months
Mexico	5 years from Pay Date	6 Months
Netherlands	3 years from end of year div. was Paid	2 Months
New Zealand	8 years from end of year div. was Paid	6 Months
Norway	3 years from Pay Date	2 Years
Spain	2 years from Pay Date	1.25 Years
Sweden	5 years from Pay Date	3 Months
Switzerland	3 years from end of year div. was Paid	14 Months
United Kingdom	6 years from end of tax year (ending April 5) that the div was paid	6 Months

Exhibit 3.8 Statutes and recovery times (*Source* Author's own)

Non-Treaty Based Entitlements

In most cases, withholding tax optimisation is based on the existence of a treaty. The principle is that if there is no treaty, there is no claim since there is no entitlement. Well, it depends! In some cases, even where there is no treaty, there can be an entitlement under domestic law. Typically, this will be where the jurisdiction concerned has enacted law that essentially promises to treat all investors equally, irrespective of whether they are resident or non-resident.

Process and Procedure

That cat's cradle diagram hides still more complexity. Each jurisdiction has both a given process or processes and different procedures. As these will be discussed in much more detail in subsequent chapters, it's enough for the present to understand that there can be different processes, even within one jurisdiction, that may apply.

Documentation and Forms

The basis of all withholding tax lies in documentation and forms. To establish an entitlement, a beneficial owner, or their intermediary will have to provide evidence of that entitlement. While there is a core of information that is common across jurisdictions, many tax authorities have different ways of structuring the information.

Proof of residency establishes that the claimant is resident in a treaty country and that therefore one of the two required components of entitlement exists. This can be done either using a self-certification of residency (e.g. W-8BEN form for the USA), a formal residency certificate issued by the claimant's local tax authority, or it can be a stamp put onto the claim form by the claimant's local tax authority. Different jurisdictions, different requirements. It is also true that this type of documentation will be naturally included in an account set-up package of a custodian or broker under its domestic Know Your Customer "KYC" rules. Some authorities will not accept a self-certification of residence unless the KYC rules of the beneficial owner's jurisdiction have been pre-approved by the foreign jurisdiction.

Proof of Income

This will usually be generated by a custodian on behalf of a beneficial owner in the form of a tax voucher or credit advice. SWIFT messages, where the beneficial owner is another financial institution and receives confirmations by this method, are also acceptable.

Forms are the acts of the claim. Some of the information above, such as certification, can be included on these forms, but, as always, it depends. The forms vary by jurisdiction and within a jurisdiction, may vary depending on the type of income. Some will allow multiple income items on one form; some are even in English—but some are not. Most have multiple parts or copies which must be distributed correctly. An increasing number of foreign tax authorities also require a tax identification number to be issued for their own jurisdiction before they will accept a claim. For example, a Swiss claim can't be filed unless the beneficial owner has applied for and been granted a Swiss SRD number. This also supports the principle of cross-governmental information sharing. Some tax authorities will require a list of underlying investors to be attached also, for many pooled investment vehicles. Finally, the forms can vary by year as tax authorities change the fundamental information requirements for their forms.

Corporate Governance

This area has received little attention in the past and we deal with this later in this book. However, from a contextual perspective, corporate governance has two aspects. The first and more obvious is the responsibility of issuers to their shareholders. Typically, on tax matters, issuers, those corporations making corporate distributions of dividends or coupon payments of interest, have maintained a discreet distance from their shareholders. Their usual stance is that a shareholder's tax affairs are just that—the shareholder's affair. However, it is becoming more obvious that issuers have not just a moral obligation but a rapidly increasing commercial interest in trying to leverage the funds of investors. In the same way that governments have established treaties to encourage inward investment rather than just tell foreign investors that the tax is their problem, issuers also have the opportunity if not the commercial requirement to create a better inward investment profile for their business. Not only do they now have to compete with other issuers in the same industry sector or market for investor's funds, but they can also no longer rely on the banks for loan funding which has, historically, been the counterpoint of their fiscal planning. It's likely therefore that issuers will be launching more aggressive investor relations programs in the future and that these will include some provision of either education or facilitation for shareholders.

The second area of corporate governance is not so obvious and relates to those financial institutions that are also listed businesses. It applies also to those who are private, but the latter is more difficult to regulate on this topic. The issue is like the Sarbanes Oxley scenario where the market has an expectation that anything about the firm's business that could affect the share price, should be made known to the market under the principle of full disclosure, which prevents, to a certain extent, insider trading and fraud. While this may not have made many waves in the past, tightening of finances at many funds is making institutional investors much more aware of the tax problem. There is also an issue of banks not informing their customers in an appropriate way, of the degree to which their operations support their clients. This is called proportionality and is based on both the legal and commercial presumption that the role accepted by a custodian has at its core, the idea of having the interests of the client as paramount. If I have a tax entitlement to \$150 and I find that my custodian knew about it but failed to make a claim, I might be disappointed but not upset. If I have an entitlement to \$500,000 and I find that no claim was filed, even though my custodian knew that such an entitlement exists, now I'm upset, especially if someone shows me some small print that gives the bank a disclaimer. If it's not a legal issue, it's certainly a commercial one. I expect my financial adviser to keep an eye on such issues and at least keep me informed. That information should at least be in proportion to the effect on my portfolio value. This occurs also at the fund level. I've seen many fund managers dismiss an entitlement without considering that they may have an obligation to inform their investors, based on the size of the entitlement and whether the entitlement is at the fund level or at the investor level. Both these issues are likely to come to the fore in the form of regulation in the not-too-distant future, requiring fuller disclosure of "material failure". We are already seeing this from the US both in terms of Sarbanes Oxley and the current changes to the US Section 1441 NRA withholding tax regulations.

So now, after understanding the guiding principles of withholding tax, hopefully its contextualisation has given the reader a good enough understanding of the complexity involved to see that while this is an extremely valuable and important subject, the industry and investors are very far away from addressing it sufficient well and that a deeper understanding will hopefully give enough people ideas to make changes that can change that 7% recovery figure to something more like 93%.

4

Variability

This chapter builds on the previous chapter by explaining the number and type of variables involved in a cross-border investment scenario from a tax perspective. 5700 double tax treaties, each with their own rules, forms and processes are the start point. The legal availability of one or more of the tax processing models comes next (relief, quick refund and standard claims). The key data and documents necessary, the time frames and the nexus of these to provide correct taxation is explained in order that the reader has a good grasp of the complexity faced by financial institutions and investors when processing cross-border transactions.

In this chapter, having established the basic principles and context of the issue, we come across that first "it depends" scenario that pervades the industry. How do various factors impact any given decision or entitlement?

Some of those factors affect whether a claim is ever made, especially if the factor concerned makes the process so complex that the cost of obtaining the entitlement is more than the value of the entitlement. Others affect the efficiency of a claims process.

To set the scene, Exhibit 4.1 shows a typical withholding tax process as used by most custodians. Since we'll be thinking about automation later in the book, I've shaded those activities that are essentially manual, in grey and those processes that are manual as dotted lines.

R. K. McGill, *Cross-Border Investment Withholding Tax*, Finance and Capital Markets Series, https://doi.org/10.1007/978-3-031-32785-8_4

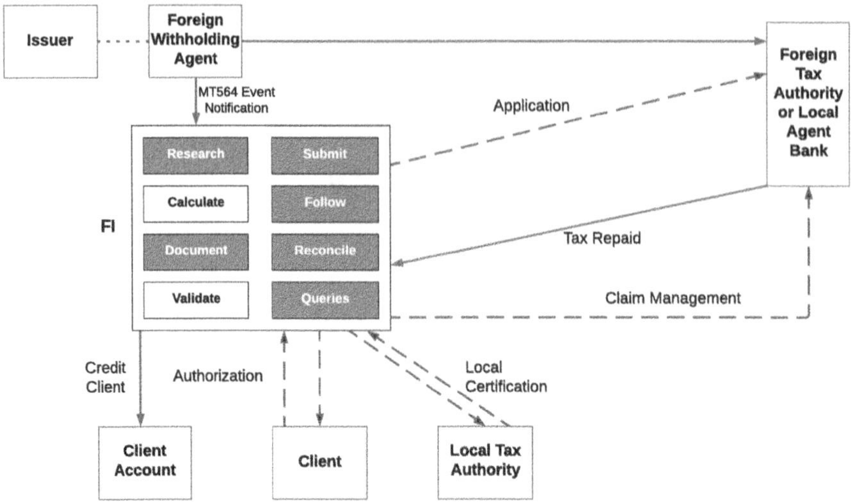

Exhibit 4.1 Typical withholding tax process (*Source* Author)

Documentation

The single biggest factor that affects entitlement to a favourable rate of tax is documentation. Documentation sits at the heart of the process, irrespective of whether it's relief at source, quick refund, or long form. Documentation has three segments to it that all investors need to be aware of and all FIs need to follow. Within each area, documentation is necessary to allow other parts of the process to take place efficiently.

Relationship

This form of documentation establishes the relationship between investor and financial firm. Most often it will set the price for any service offered as well as, in some cases, the service benchmarks. Even if the price is "bundled" into a single fee for the whole of custody, there will be an element that is attributable to withholding tax processing. More of that later. For investors, this is the primary document that makes sure that what is promised is not delivered. Yet, in many cases, the custodian will have no way to know what proportion of their custody fees is actually attributable to the withholding tax function—which leads to bad decisions on scale and scope of services. Also, the investor will have little or no way to hold the custodian or broker to account for any failure in service levels, since most custody agreements do not have any detail in this area.

Treaty

Many people forget about the treaties as documents, even though they are fundamental to the process in most, but not all cases (it depends!). The treaty is the source of entitlement for many investors. There are, at present 234 tax jurisdictions in the world. If each had a treaty with the other jurisdiction, there would be a potential 54,522 treaties. There are around 5000–6000 treaties in existence. As many of the forms needed to file claims require the investor to assert the treaty Article under which they are claiming, there is a need to have up to date and historical research on treaties, when they came into force and what their terms are.

Many custodians have this information in soft assets—people, employed because they have knowledge and experience of market practice. This is a risk as people leave or, at current time, are made redundant, the knowledge base under which a particular institution can maintain its expertise can be degraded severely.

It's true that many treaties now follow a common model—the OECD model a copy of which is provided in the Appendices to this book. That said, several treaties have variances based on local law and intent. One such is the US treaty which with all countries includes a limitation of benefits clause or "LOB". So, it's important not just to have copies of all the relevant treaties on hand, nor to have people who know what's in them. It's important to have the treaty documents available in an automated way (searchable) to allow the right decisions and updates to be made.

Status

We now move into the core of documentation. To establish an entitlement, there are two basics that a foreign tax authority is interested in. Can the claimant prove that they are who they say they are, and can they prove residency (see below)?

As far as status is concerned, there are several ways in which this can be done. The documentation that a foreign tax authority will accept as evidence of a beneficial owner's status varies by market. In many, but not all, cases beneficial owners or their appointed agents can obtain a certificate of residency from their own local tax authority. Equally, many, but not all foreign tax authorities will accept these certificates as evidence of the beneficial owner's status as a tax payer in their local market. This is generally a key factor for a tax authority receiving a claim. However, usually a foreign tax authority will require additional documentation where the beneficial owner is not an individual. For a corporate this may be the company's certificate of incorporation. For other types of non-individual entity, the documentation requirement helps the receiving tax authority understand and decide whether the claimant is, for their purpose, the beneficial owner. This introduces the concept of fiscal transparency and opacity.

Fiscal transparency can be exemplified in the case of a US resident hedge fund. For the most part, US resident hedge funds, unlike most of their non-US counterparts, are deemed to be fiscally transparent. The documentation of the hedge fund at the top of this structure makes it immediately obvious to foreign tax authorities that the fund is, to all intents and purposes, a partnership. From an operational perspective this means that one of three possible claim models might be appropriate, depending on the market concerned. The tax authority might choose to allow claims at the fund level, even though the fund is a partnership. The tax authority might allow the claim at the fund level but require additional information about the investors in the fund, typically their names and confirmation that they are all, or predominantly of the same residency as that of the fund itself. Finally, the tax authority may decide that the fund itself is not the beneficial owner at all and require that any claims made are filed at the underlying partner level.

This same principle applies to many of the more exotic investment vehicles. Any form of collective investment vehicle is currently subject to additional scrutiny to avoid "treaty shopping". As new types of vehicle emerge, the tax authorities have to make judgements on a case-by-case and market-by-market basis as to the real nature of these vehicles, their purpose and ultimately a decision on who the real beneficial owner is.

For the most part of course, many of these documents will have been obtained when the account was opened. That in itself can cause compliance issues. In current times the degree of compliance required in documentation is set out in "Know Your Customer" or "KYC" rules which most markets now have. The problem is that these rules are changed, and the documentation requirements are amended from time to time as, usually, stricter controls are identified as being necessary. So, you may have an account opened some time ago using KYC rules valid at the time, but which may now be out of date and inadequate for the task of evidencing status to a foreign tax authority. However, it gets more complex still when we consider the changes currently being discussed at the trading block level. The US 1441 NRA regulations are based on documentation that includes not just KYC level documents but also assumes additional documentation designed by the tax authority themselves. In the case of the US, this is the W8 or W9 series of documents which are essentially self-certifications of residency, status and claim of entitlements. If the QI regime is extended, it's likely that there will need to be some discussion about the degree to which self-certifications are acceptable, since, by definition, the new tax rules are aimed at finding those investors who are engaged in treaty shopping. It's not entirely unreasonable to expect an investor engaged in treaty shopping, essentially tax evasion, to file a self-certification which supports that activity. While the US regulations are clear that a custodian should use both the W8/W9 documentation and KYC documentation, this adds yet more burdens to the document management requirements.

Residency

As noted above, residency can often be determined by the use of a certificate of residency, however, this is not, as one might have presumed, the ultimate panacea for this issue. In some markets, the certificate will not be accepted and only the original tax reclaim form, stamped by the beneficial owner's local tax office will suffice. For custodians this can cause a major problem. Of all the potential elements in the processing chain, the weakest is the link between the custodian and the beneficial owner. Part of this is due to the low level of awareness at the beneficial owner level of the importance of the documentation requested, the impact it can have on their portfolio value and finally the impact that any delay can have on their custodian's operations. Suffice it to say that any one client being a bit tardy in getting their tax forms stamped by their local tax authority would be annoying but not of major concern. When you're running a department processing 20,000 claims in fifteen markets for several thousand beneficial owners' resident in several markets, this issue can create major systemic problems. New systems for tracking and monitoring claims at different stages are required which for the most part are dealt with using spreadsheets.

Authority

I touched indirectly above on the issue of who has the responsibility to make certain process elements happen. Clearly, for a custodian or broker or third-party provider to do an efficient job, they need to be in control of as many aspects of the process as possible, even the manual ones. To that extent, many custodians require their clients to sign powers of attorney granting the custodian legal rights to act as the agent of the beneficial owner. These powers of attorney can be used at several points in the tax reclamation process. Sometimes they can be used to obtain certificates of residency and sometimes they can be used to file claims to foreign tax authorities. The trick is to know which markets allow delegated authorities to be used. But that's not the end of the story as far as creating an efficient process is concerned. I have mentioned on several occasions that one of the biggest issues blocking an automated process is the lack of standardisation. The issue of whether any given market accepts delegated authority is only one half of the problem. The other half is whether the beneficial owner is prepared to give that delegated authority. In my travels, I have found that the percentage of clients providing delegated authority to their custodians varies from 40 to 60% but is rarely above 70%. Again, this creates a problem when constructing or managing a tax reclaim function. The custodian now must manage a matrix as shown below (Exhibit 4.2).

To make matters worse of course, this matrix can change over time giving the custodian a major headache for tracking systems. This also affects the time to recovery since if the market does not accept delegated authority OR if the client refuses to provide one, the time needed to process the claim can increase significantly because only the client's signature will be seen as valid. This increases postal costs and time delays.

It's also important to know that each tax authority can decide whether the wording of any particular delegated authority is, in its opinion, sufficient to allow the agent to act on behalf of the beneficial owner in a claim. So, it's important to have verified and maintain knowledge of what wording is acceptable to each tax authority.

There is also little consistency across types of beneficial owners. A greater proportion of individuals are likely to agree to such delegated powers however, the more complex corporate types of beneficial owners are often more sensitive about such delegation of powers and some even have constitutions that forbid such delegation. Custodians are therefore faced with a very difficult and complex task of document management.

PoA from Client	Market accepts PoA	Impact
Yes	No	Client must sign claim forms
Yes	Yes	Custodian or vendor can sign claim forms
No	Yes	Client must sign claim forms
No	No	Client must sign claim forms

Exhibit 4.2 Manging PoAs (*Source* Author)

Validity

Finally, if the above is not enough to exemplify the difficulties involved in documentation, many of the documents required have definite periods of validity. This of course is a core part of the custody process and so most custodians have established processes to monitor and re-validate account documentation.

Statutes of Limitation

Another key factor, unfortunately as we'll see, is the "Time Bar" or "Statute of Limitations". In relief at source processes, the Statute of Limitations is essentially the pay date. For all other entitlement types, each market has its time period during which a claim can be filed. These vary from months to many years and in one case, currently, a market with no Statute of Limitations.

The effect of a statute of limitations is that, for any given payment made net of statutory rate tax, the jurisdiction concerned will allow a certain period during which any claim can still be filed and paid (if valid). This may sound simple, but there are several issues surrounding this principle.

Of course, the most obvious is that the scale of managing the issue, for a custodian or broker it is directly proportionate to the number of markets in which they file claims.

Some markets have more than one statute of limitations, usually varying by claimant type.

By far the largest issue surrounding statutes of limitation of course is what happens when the statute is approached or breached. The latter is simple, once the statute has been passed, the claim will probably not be honoured by the receiving tax authority. In the chapter on benchmarking, I identify the benchmark: Statute Risk. This benchmark exists because, in manually driven processes used by most custodians, there is a risk that the identification and preparation process may take up a significant proportion of the statute period. As the statute is approached, the risk increases that a claim even if filed, may not get there in time to be allowed by the receiving authority. This leads to the practice of "protective claims" frowned upon when discovered.

What's more important, but less obvious is the implication of the statute of limitations on investors where custodians are operating in a manual environment. A manual environment is inherently inflexible. Changes in trading volumes or in the coverage of investment markets are difficult to respond to quickly. The natural inclination of operations and HR staff are also to staff minimally most of the year and staff up for critical periods, typically the dividend seasons. The problem with that approach is that you must have greater monitoring in place on relatively untrained staff which results in a build-up of claims. In other words, for any significant custodian, the number of possible claims builds up far faster than their resource can manage. The net result is that most custodians operate in a backlog. Some of those backlogs are extremely large. Departments often end up in a major scramble at year end trying to get claims filed that are about to go out of statute i.e., and this is important to understand, claims that could have been filed many, many months ago but weren't.

This is brinkmanship of a scary kind when you consider that its client's money at stake. But that's not all. There is another consequence of approaching but not breaching the statute of limitations. Tax authorities are also very manual, but they know that banks do have more technologically advanced resources. When it comes to paying money out again, their approach can easily be one of "well if they took two years before they filed their client's claim, they can't be that worried about it" which has the effect of putting your client's claim to the bottom of the pile while they serve the people who were on top of their game.

To make matters worse, there are also three types of the statute of limitation. The effect of this is that custodians must not only look to the date-based validity of their documentation of client's residency and status, but also to the dates on which they were the recipients of taxed income. It's a generally accepted if unwritten rule that if a client gets to within 90 days of a statute, the chance of preparing and filing all the documentation, with relevant approvals, successfully, is almost nil. The different statute types are:

- Pay date based—a given number of years calculated from the actual date on which payment was made to the beneficial owner
- Tax Year based—a given number of years calculated from the end of the tax year in which the income was received (e.g., April 5)
- Calendar Year based—a given number of years calculated from the end of the calendar year in which the income was received (i.e., December 31).

Year of Income

Following on from statutes of limitation both literally and figuratively is the issue of the year in which the income is received. Investors rarely look backwards, but they do change their advisors and agents from time to time (more frequently recently of course). The degree to which any given investor was having their income analysed and optimised for tax purposes can mean that at any given time, there are entitlements in existence that are not current but historic i.e., the income was received at some point in the past but either no claim was identified, or no claim was filed. If the statute of limitations has not run out, that entitlement is still technically valid. Of course, operationally, there is a greater risk that if any given custodian did not spot or file a reclaim historically, it will not spot it in current trading. So, the issue of which year the income was received, in this context usually only comes about either when an investor finds out from some other source that there is a potential entitlement or when they change custodian, or third-party agent, to one who spots the "miss".

Of course, the other impact directly on custodians is that while they may lose customers at one end of the pipe, they will usually be gaining them at the other. So, so-called legacy claims are an issue for everyone. The operational difficulty is not just identifying if your client has entitlements from income received in previous years, it's also determining what the relevant statutory and treaty rates were at the time they received the income and what other rules of the time may apply to any claim lodged after that year. Tax authorities are, and do, change their procedures on almost an annual basis and such changes rarely apply retroactively. So, a claim for a legacy entitlement will generally have to be filed under the rules that applied at the time the income was received. This of course puts intermediaries under an enormous burden of research and is also why the cost of such research is so high.

Types of Income

The type of income received is also a factor because the processes and calculations are different. In the world of equities, straightforward dividend payments on ORD shares represent around 90% of the withholding tax market. Although it is expected that bond income as a percentage of the whole will increase in the coming years as the amount of government debt (gilts) in the form of bonds, issued to offset the global economic downturn, increase. ORDs generally are treated by either applying for relief at source, quick refund, or long form claim, but the actors concerned are primarily the tax authorities or agent banks (e.g., France) where claims are filed directly to the market. Following some of the concerns of tax authorities about trading strategies, it is an increasing requirement, as with bonds, that claimants must show that they owned the ORDs for a set length of time before receiving the dividend. This is to try to counteract the activity known as dividend washing. Derivative products, particularly Depositary Receipts or "DR"s are treated differently. There are many kinds of DR, but they generally represent several underlying securities, often ORDs. The difference is that foreign tax authorities often don't recognise the DR as a security on which a claim can exist, only the underlying security. So the market process for DRs differs in that any claim from the market must be made to the bank that issued the DR in the first place, as they hold the underlying securities. For American Depositary Receipts, these are JPMorgan Chase, Bank of New York Mellon, Deutsche Bank and Citi.

Bond, or fixed, income is treated differently with many more complex calculations being necessary both because the security is a more complex instrument and also because there has always been concern over the use of tax arbitrage—the trading of securities on the basis of tax advantages as the basis for profit. In most cases, with the notable exceptions of Italy and Portugal, most bond distributions are exempt from withholding tax. In the case of Italy and Portugal, the jurisdictions operate an insanely complex system called "pro rata temporis". This means that the amount of tax due is based on a complex calculation with respect to the length of time an investor held the bond. The calculations can be made forwards or backwards from the next or previous coupon date to the date on which the bond was bought or sold. This is only the beginning of the story.

Pro Rata Temporis

Most tax calculations are relatively easy, being based, in the case of dividends, on the number of shares held on record date and the rate per share distributed by the Issuer. While bonds are usually exempt, there are a couple of outliers, notably Italy and Portugal.

Interest paid on Italian bonds is exempt from tax when paid to a resident of a "White List" country. Normally the bonds are held in a tax-exempt account. The interest paid by Italian bonds held in a *taxable* account is subject to tax on a "pro rata temporis" basis and is called a substitute tax. Bonds, which are issued at a discount, are subject to "scarto" tax based on the number of days of the life of the bond.

On the purchase of an Italian bond, if an investor has not provided the correct documentation (or is not resident in a "White List" country) the bond is held in a taxable account, the investor will be credited with an amount that represents the tax on the accrued interest when the bond is bought.

On pay date the investor will receive the interest net of withholding tax on the whole amount and because a credit was received when the bond was bought, the net effect is that the investor has suffered withholding tax only for the period the bond was held.

On the sale of an Italian bond, the investor is debited with withholding tax on the accrued interest calculated from the previous pay date up until the sale.

Original Issue Discount (OID)

The difference between the redemption price and the issue price is deemed to be interest. Scarto tax applies to the discount over the life of the bond. The calculation of the accrued interest is therefore slightly different as there is no "previous pay-date" to use as a reference point. Generally, it is calculated as follows:

$$Accruedinterest = \frac{\text{Redemptionprice} - \text{Issueprice}}{|\text{Issuedate} - \text{purchasedate}|}$$

The accrued deemed interest is again subject to tax and would be *credited* to the account.

Exception: short-term zero coupon government debt securities ("BOT"s).

For BOTs, the method to calculate the tax amount due is the opposite of the one mentioned above.

When you buy a BOT for your taxable account, you will be debited with an amount that corresponds to the substitute tax due on the total amount of the issue discount. In summary, the bond interest and OID is subject to tax only for the period the bond is held.

In Italy, the legal basis for pro rata temporis is Italian law (Law 239 1996, Law 239 as amended by Reform 138/2011 Net Paying Accounts and Law 239 as amended by Reform 138/2011 Gross Paying Accounts). These require that a non-Italian financial institution (second-level bank) must hold Italian bonds via an Italian resident financial institution (first-level bank). The overall requirement is based on the understanding that there are two obligations (i) withholding and (ii) reporting. The second-level financial institution operates a single "conto unico" (single omnibus) account at the first-level Italian bank.

The withholding calculation for fixed rate bonds, is based on whether the purchaser of an Italian bond is resident in a "white list" jurisdiction or a "black list" jurisdiction. In the former there is no withholding required. In the latter, the withholding tax is based on a percentage of the accrued interest on the bond in the period that the purchaser held the bond since the immediately preceding pay date. The first level bank must credit tax on the whole period from the purchase date to next payment date into the conto unico account and must then debit tax on the sell date so that the total tax paid by the beneficial owner represents the pro rata temporis calculation of tax due for the holding period.

The reporting obligation is in two monthly files (i) a Modelli file which reports all non-Italian beneficial owners and (ii) a Contabile file representing all trades eligible for exemption. In addition, there is an annual tax return for the first-level bank on Form 770 into which the monthly summary of the conto unico is included.

Different calculation rules for withholding apply for fixed rate bonds, short-term zero-coupon government debt (BOTs), OID, variable-rate bonds and indeterminate income bonds. As you can see, this is an incredibly complex set of rules, calculations and reporting obligations. I am reliably informed that one central securities depository has fifty people whose sole job is to do these calculations for their clients.

As you can also see, documentation in the form of certifications of residency are critical to this process as these will be used to determine whether the investor's assets are held in a taxable or non-taxable account by their financial institution.

Forms

If the foregoing is not enough to indicate to investors that this is a complex area, or to custodians that the process is fundamentally riskier than one might at first think; the issue of forms takes us to an entirely new level. So far, we have talked about factors that affect whether a claim can be filed and if so when. Forms addresses the issue of how claims get made. The forms are the primary communication that establishes a claim of entitlement between one party and the tax authority concerned. For custodians the problem is that each jurisdiction has its own forms and within each jurisdiction, those forms can change depending on time as well as the type of income. Custodians need to make sure that they file the correct forms for the correct year of income and for the correct type. Notwithstanding all this, some of the forms may not be in English especially if the two jurisdictions concerned do not have English as a primary language.

The forms used also differ in the information that is required. All have a common core of information of course, albeit it will be in different places and different formats for different forms. That will be the position in the security, the amount paid and the amount claimed. Each jurisdiction however has other information that is requested and this varies by market making it virtually impossible to create a standardised model.

Adding complexity, custodians need to be aware that some jurisdictions allow multiple claim items to be included on one form. Some allow a separate "schedule" of claims to be appended to a form up to a given limit. Others do not allow aggregation of claims per beneficial owner at all.

Its also well known that tax authorities are very particular about the accuracy of forms. Anecdotally, some tax authorities will reject claims for even minor typographical errors or missing information.

As you can imagine, for custodians this is going to be difficult enough to manage with their resources, even when scaled up to take account of many markets. For investors themselves, this issue is pretty much impenetrable.

Recovery Time

I've spoken a lot about identifying claims and filing them. Getting the money back is of course what it is all about. Tax claims are not like claims under securities class action suits. In the latter, a claim for damages is being made and the amount of any award is not certain, nor is the proportion of the distribution attributable to any given claimant. In the case of a tax claim, there is an entitlement created by the treaty between a pair of jurisdictions. So there is a greater degree of certainty, as long as the claim is identified correctly, filed within the statute of limitations and there were no other factors that might cause the tax authority to believe that the claim was false, duplicate, protective or otherwise should not be paid.

That leads us, and of course all investors to ask the obvious question: How long will it take to get my money back? The answer always surprises people, that claims payments will take different amounts of time to get paid, even within one jurisdiction. In other words—it depends.

Some of these delays are caused by the fact that most tax authorities are much more manually oriented than the custodians. So they are dealing with paper from a large number of sources, completed to different quality levels (many are hand-written). They are not generally, as many people think, trying to hold the money, they are generally genuinely trying to meet their treaty obligations since the benefit of meeting those obligations is to encourage inward investment. That's a much bigger prize than payment of any one claim.

It is also important to make sure that we understand what we mean by recovery time. As I mentioned earlier and explained in more depth in the chapter on benchmarking, most of the figures quoted for recovery time start the process from the point at which the claim is filed to the tax authorities. Relief at source claims of course have a zero-recovery time since the correct provision of documentation results in payment of income at the correct rate on pay date. For long form claims the real start of the process starts when the income is paid net of statutory rate tax—the pay date. If one wanted to be even more accurate, for a custodian who has good documentation systems in place, the point at which they know that a claim will exist is on the record date, usually a few days before the actual pay date. The reason that recovery times are not cited from this earlier base is because it would highlight the differences between custodian's performance. Since custodians have very different approaches to an equally manual process and different allocations of resources and money, each custodian can take very different amounts of time to get from knowing that a claim exists for one of their clients, to filing the claim to the tax authorities. I have seen management reports of major custodians that show backlogs of over three years. In other words, they still have claims that were identified internally over three years ago, that have not yet been filed to the market. So, if the market average were 6 months, while the tax authority might take 6 months to repatriate tax, the reality is that it is taken 3 years and 6 months for that process to take place. This is one of the hidden inefficiencies in tax reclamation that investors are rarely told about.

Tax Information Reporting and Audit Oversight

The USA as an investment market has created a new paradigm since 2001 when US Section 1441 NRA regulations came into force. Prior to that year, the relief at source processes, except for DTC's Elective Dividend System ("EDS"), and long form reclaim processes were all relatively stand-alone. In other words, the activities of a custodian or other intermediary on behalf of their customers did not have any reporting requirements associated with the activity in the preceding year. Nor were there any oversight constraints, again except for DTC Participant banks, imposed by tax authorities on financial institutions, other than on a case-by-case basis.

The 1441 regulations changed all that. The basic QI contract between an institution and the IRS laid out certain benefits, in return for which the institution had to submit to certain new oversights. The two primary ones being the requirement for aggregated tax reporting at the FI level, plus an oversight requirement defined in terms of two audits of compliance undertaken during the six-year term of the QI contract.

Two issues flow from this new paradigm. First, the net effect after seven years of this single-market regime, is that the IRS is proposing to further enhance the constraints of both reporting and oversight, as we'll see later on. Second is that the European Union, in the guise of Mr. Giovanini, as well as other groups such as FISCO and G30 have adopted the principle of the 1441 regulations (i.e., documentation backed relief at source) as the model for addressing Giovannini's Barrier 11—withholding tax across the whole of the EU. So, where before, we could restrict ourselves to operational factors that affect our industry, we now have also to consider broader regulatory factors that will have an enormous impact on custody costs.

The implied costs of tax information reporting and audit oversight cannot be underestimated. The IRS alone expects fines on non-US financial institutions to rise to over $300 million in the next few years for non-compliance. Already there has sprung up a new industry sector aimed at helping firms deal with these additional burdens because its clear from the results of the last few years of the US regulations, that "foreign" (in this case non-US) banks have and continue to experience major problems in compliance that not only impact themselves as banks but also their customers.

The essence of the two factors is described below, although there is a longer explanation of the detail and implications in the chapter on relief at source as well as reference to the same issue in "the future of withholding tax". The reader may infer from this the level of importance that should be attached to these factors when thinking about how to structure withholding tax services and/or solutions for the next decade.

Tax Information Reporting is a consequence of a tax authority delegating the job of documenting and assessing a client's entitlement to a favourable rate of tax in a relief at source environment. Essentially, in many regimes, such documentation must flow up or include the tax authority themselves in some way before any investor can access a relief at source process. In the qualified intermediary system, the role of documentation is entirely adopted by the QI, however, the tax authority as a result requires the QI to provide some end of year reporting that enables the tax authority to reconcile the amounts withheld under the system, to the amounts of tax actually deposited. In the case of the US as an investment market, that is primarily a regulatory requirement to report all US persons using forms 1099 which are a series separated by income type e.g., 1099-DIV reports dividends paid to a US person whereas a 1099-INT reports interest. For non-US persons who are customers of a QI, reporting is "pooled" and within the 1042 series of forms e.g., 1042-S, 1042-T and 1042 each having a different function, with the 1042-S being created based on different variables e.g., withholding rate pool, income type etc. It quickly becomes easy for a QI to exceed 250 of these forms, at which point the operational imperative is for the QI to file such forms electronically, which is a whole different process subject to its own compliance and penalties. Reporting is also complicated by the way in which the tax authority manages such reporting. In the case of 1099 reporting for example, forms cannot be downloaded from the internet (www.irs.gov) but must be requested directly, whereas the Forms 1042 series can be downloaded.

The reason for describing these issues, which are only a very small part of the picture, is that tax information reporting as an activity, is new to most financial institutions in the way that the IRS, and presumably many other tax authorities in the future, envisage. What's happening in the industry now, which is very frustrating, is not that institutions are not responding to the changes, but that the response is neither integrated nor consistent. In the face of knowledge that tax information reporting will almost certainly extend beyond the US QI regime, there is no real way that institutions can develop new systems to cope with the generality of TIR; they must perforce react individually to each new set of rules as they come out. Clearly, this is not optimal for the industry, but it seems that until tax authorities work more effectively to design and implement regulation in an integrated way, custodians and therefore investors will be impacted by the costs associated with fragmented change.

The audit oversight is also an outgrowth of the principle of having the industry be the implementor of relief at source procedures. In addition to the processes themselves for documentation, withholding, deposits and reporting, the IRS has oversight capability indirectly through the contractual requirement for QIs to undergo audits. In their latest consultation paper, they propose to increase the controls on QIs by having audits performed not by one auditor, but by two, one of which must be in the US, each taking joint and several liability for the results of the audit. When taken in conjunction with the procedures and new tax information reporting requirements, it is clear that costs will rise significantly.

If the basic QI type regime is adopted across Europe, to say nothing of the Middle and Far East, Scandinavia, etc., and TIR and multiple audit oversight are also implemented, the average custodian managing investments into say 13 core markets, would be compiling over 26 sets of tax information reporting and undergoing over 52 audits in each six-year rolling period. With the banks in their current financial position, the cost of complying with these types of regulations will become disproportionate to the benefits to clients. This will manifest itself in higher thresholds, meaning that more investors will lose out on entitlements and in a consolidation of service offerings into a small number of banks that can afford the compliance costs for given markets. The latter will also mean less choice for investors. Together, while they may help tax authorities with an increasing burden of outsourcing administration of withholding tax, it is likely that there will be a "sea-change" in investment activity as the tax advantages of investment wither away.

So, in this chapter, we have seen that there are several primary factors. The key word here is "primary". There are a great many more factors to consider and we'll come across many of these in subsequent chapters. They all however share a common trait—that the application of the factor has many twists and turns. These are not simple rules or "on/off" switches that can be applied scientifically to come to the perfect solution. Each, as we've seen, has elements that complicate and add cost for everyone in the investment chain.

5

The Pace of Change

This chapter frames the rate of change in the industry to highlight the increasing pace of change. In the thirty years between the first OECD Model Tax Convention and the second one, we landed a man on the moon, invented the internet, mobile phones, touch screens, databases and spreadsheets. In the last ten years anti-tax evasion has become the predominant driver of tax policy, tax relief at source is being adopted as the primary accepted processing model and we have digital documentation being accepted instead of paper.

The pace of technological change in our world has been rapid. Around a hundred years ago, the Wright Brothers conducted the first powered flight. Today, we send rockets to the Moon and Mars, and we can fly almost anywhere in the world in comfort in just a few hours. There are less than sixty years between these two technological ages. The history of change in the tax world has, by comparison, been glacially slow.

The Model Tax Convention created by the OECD on which most Double Tax Treaties are based, was first published in 1963, the second was published almost thirty years later. In that interim technology made one or two advances:

- Landed humans on the moon (1969)
- First mobile phone (1973)
- Apple 1 computer launched (1976)
- Spreadsheets were invented (1979)

R. K. McGill, *Cross-Border Investment Withholding Tax*, Finance and Capital Markets Series,
https://doi.org/10.1007/978-3-031-32785-8_5

- Space Shuttle maiden voyage (1981)
- The internet was invented (1983)
- World Wide Web was invented (1989)
- Graphene discovered (2004)
- iPhone launched (2007).

Comparatively

- US launches qualified intermediary program (2001)
- US passes HIRE Act (FATCA) legislation in Congress (2010)
- First FATCA Intergovernmental Agreements (2012–2014)
- EU publishes Tax Barriers Business Advisory Group Report (2013)
- OECD releases TRACE IP (2013)
- US issues second QI Agreement (2014)
- US Issues Third QI Agreement (2017)
- Finland becomes the first country to adopt TRACE I.P. (2021)
- US issues fourth QI Agreement (2023).

This glacial rate of change is to have been expected given the interests of the different parties in the chin of payment. The advent of financial technology companies, "fintechs" and regulatory technology companies "regtechs" in the mid-2000s has led to an expectation that the rate of change will be much more rapid due to new disruptive technologies such as blockchain.

These disruptors have had a significant effect in the payments industry but so far very little in the securities industry, mainly due to the complexity of the latter compared to the former. The problem is that withholding tax, as I have described, is an ecosystem with many moving parts. In some cases, despite the best efforts of key players in the industry, some of the components just do not share the same view of the trends going on. Some tax administrations continue to take the view that they would prefer to have the statutory tax taken at source rather than support a tax relief model. This approach is based on the belief that most investors will either not notice the tax being taken, assume there is nothing they can do about it or that they will be just apathetic and never claim their money back because it's too hard. They are not wrong in their presumptions, but increasingly, through the efforts of the OECD and others, the legal and regulatory frameworks are beginning to change to favour tax relief at source and it is becoming more difficult for the outliers to withstand the obvious argumentthat having an inefficient tax system damages foreign direct investment.

While the tax administrations wring their hands over matters of principle, the fintechs and regtechs have already spotted the future opportunity and are investing heavily in creating solutions for which there is currently little or no legal framework.

Most notable is the trend towards digitisation of documentation. Documentation is the single largest drag on efficiency. It does not matter whether we are talking about relief at source or standard post-pay date refunds. In all cases, the investor must provide evidence of their jurisdiction of tax residency. There are two types of tax residency evidence (1) a tax residency certificate issued by a tax administration or (2) a self-certification of tax residency. The former is paper-based, manual and takes weeks to obtain. In some cases, an apostile is required i.e., a separate certificate to confirm the validity of the signature on the first certificate. This also can take weeks to obtain.

The latter, self-certifications, also known as investor self-declarations or ISDs are becoming more acceptable. The IRS has accepted self-certifications of tax residency since 2001. The OECD and EU proposed a standardised ISD for the purpose of CRS and for TRACE IP. However, each of these "standards" is published only with respect to the framework for which it is acceptable. So, the legal wording on the OECD ISD for CRS is different from the legal wording on the ISD under the OECD TRACE IP. Only one company has so far created a co-compliant ISD i.e., where the legal wording on the form complies with more than one regulatory framework.

So, now we are getting closer to a single concept of a self-certification. This immediately leads us to the concept that if an ISD is acceptable, surely this can be delivered electronically. This then leads us inexorably to the concept of tokenisation of these documents as non-fungible tokens or NFTs. Unfortunately, none of the regulators is currently drafting a framework for withholding tax that includes NFTs, but it is clear that tokenisation of documentation will revolutionise the withholding tax industry—provided financial institutions have also developed a mechanism for verification and transmission in the small window provided between record date and pay date in a typical securities transaction.

In this latter area KPMG led the way in 2021 with a laboratory test of distributed ledger technology (DLT). DLT would, in principle, offer an excellent way to transmit information, including documentation, quickly and securely to many participants. Many large financial institutions are already looking at DLT solutions for withholding tax. All that's required is for regulators to understand the technologies well enough to allow them to be used. The only downside to this paradigm is the damage to reputations that has been caused by the use of DLT in the cryptocurrency space that, in the minds of the tax administration, presents a risk of abuse or fraud on a massive scale.

The risk of increasing the pace of change in an area where change has been resisted for so long is that tax administrations will need to be convinced of the security and fraud prevention characteristics of any new solution before they will even allow it to be trialled.

Nevertheless, it is certain that the pace of change is quickening and the drivers for change are becoming stronger.

Part II

Operational Models

The next four chapters deal with real life withholding tax processing. They explain in detail, the different types of processing environment—relief at source, standard refund *claims which together account for over 95% of all withholding tax processing, together with chapters showing how these processes sit in context to current practice as well as some optimisation issues that custodians should be aware of if not deploying.*

Part of the issue with real-life practice is that it does not always follow theory. It depends on the perspective from which we view the issue. For example, if we described withholding tax from an investor's viewpoint the picture would look like this Part V:

The difficulty with this view is that it mixes several different issues in a way that makes the process look homogenous. The exemption will be a market-specific opportunity available based on a case-by-case basis and derived from treaty, custom and practice. Relief at Source will be available in those markets where the tax authority has established this as an available process. Quick Refunds may only be available in markets where the investor's particular custodian supports such a process commercially, which in turn will depend on the payment requirements imposed by tax authorities on their domestic withholding agents (see later). Long Form claims again are a tax authority-based processing (as opposed to treaty-based) opportunity.

So, the problem that an investor has, is not just to establish what his or her portfolio's tax position might be, but also to establish what tools are available to mitigate tax and from where. It does not stop there, however, and this is usually where the communications problems start. If the investor is not aware of the source of a given market practice, they naturally assume that all elements of available process are theirs to choose from or worse, theirs by right. For example, I meet regularly with investors who claim that, in given markets, they are entitled to a quick refund. They are surprised to hear that "it depends". It depends on whether, in that market, there is a process and also who is responsible for that process—its not always the tax authority and whether they have a relationship with that institution.

To make matters worse, one would naturally expect that if there's a treaty, there would be a process and vice versa. This is not so. There are some markets where there is a treaty between two jurisdictions, but no process. In these cases there's no official documented way to get your money back.

So, again we see that most investors do not understand the difference between *having* an entitlement under treaty and the act of *getting* that entitlement in the most efficient way possible.

The largest chapter by far in this section is related to relief at source processing. This is only partly due to the fact that relief at source is set to become, for a large part of the world, the default primary withholding tax process. It is also a common fallacy, certainly in the investment community, that relief at source is a simpler process than the other available processes. These chapters will hopefully disavow readers of this belief. While in some cases (but by no means all) relief at source may be easier in processing element terms, relief at source suffers from different and particularly stringent timing requirements. To a large extent transparent to investors, this makes a huge difference to custodian's costs and infrastructures. The latest expected developments in terms of adding tax information reporting to the mix will also see relief at source as not only complex but also more complex than other processes. To that extent, I make no apology for spending a significant portion of this section, if not the book, on this topic. The first chapter in this section, on the current context will add detail to this.

As was outlined in the preface, most over-withheld tax is never returned to its rightful owners. Different people may have different views on the amounts, but all agree that the numbers are extremely significant. If my research is anything to go by, the amount of unrecovered tax would, if recovered, more than cover the losses declared by all the financial institutions in 2008. It would also increase custody fees by over $4.2 billion a year, making those same financial institutions more stable as well as more competitive. Fund performance would rise by between 150 and 250 basis points at a conservative estimate. While in 2007, those 250 basis points were often derided by fund managers as "of no consequence" or "not material", today, we see those same fund managers scrabbling for every basis point they can find.

Also, as has hopefully been amply demonstrated, the processes currently in place are 60% manual. Individuals have virtually no chance of understanding the issues let alone getting tax recovered by themselves. That leaves the custody, brokerage, and advisory community with a moral if not fiduciary or contractual obligation to educate investors as well as put programs in place to change that 7% into something substantially higher

Even without the global financial turmoil of 2008, the world of withholding tax, stagnant for many years, is seeing an enormous amount of change that was set in motion in the last five years. To what extent the events of 2008 will exacerbate those changes already in progress or change their direction or create the need for new changes, is unclear, although, if history is anything to go by, we can make some educated guesses. But that's for a different chapter of this book.

Today, we have a massive legacy of unclaimed tax, an increasing number of pairs of jurisdictions entering into double tax agreements or amending existing ones—to mitigate global financial issues. We have a range of procedures that have mostly manual elements to them that create cost, risk, and liability for intermediary institutions. We have a radically more educated and aware global institutional investor base who are more activist on behalf of their underlying investors. Several of these forces lend themselves to a common objective of making the process more efficient and this book seeks to explain and contribute to some of these, not least the issue of automating filing processes so that many of the obstacles can be removed and the markets allowed to work for the benefit of investors. However, the question before us at this stage of the book, before we try to fix the problem, is to understand where we are now. The next chapters in this book focus on specific types of process – relief at source and long form claims as the most prevalent ways to mitigate tax. However, there are other issues we need to consider, for their effects on our current status.

Entitlements and Their Place in the Macro Economic Cycle

At the global level entitlements establish the principle of an entitlement. See Appendix 2. The reason for the entitlement is a recognition at governmental level, that differential and double taxation of investors is not conducive to cross-border trade and for the countries concerned, to inward investment.

What started in the US domestic debt markets as "the sub-prime crisis" rapidly spread to the general global debt market, which in turn lowered the confidence of the banks (and confidence in them) and subsequently hit the equity markets, evidenced in increasing market volatility in early 2008. The failure of some financial institutions also heralded a reduction in lending and borrowing which, on top of already excessive personal debt, triggered the global recession.

The recession as it bit deeper, also affected the foreign exchange markets with differentials between the Euro and Sterling being extremely marked. Also a result from these factors is an anticipated change of emphasis between yields delivered by equities and those delivered by fixed income instruments. As companies see the global recession bite, fortress mentality is already setting in. This was evidenced first by the banks as they scrambled to borrow from their governments but failed to pass on these borrowings to customers (as loans) as was the intention. Instead, in the face of unknown levels of risk purchased in a loosely principles-based regulatory environment, they took the money at low interest and put it straight onto their balance sheets to improve their capital adequacy.

Similarly, we are already seeing this fortress mentality in the open market. The number of companies declaring or intending to declare dividends is dropping substantially. So even where firms do declare dividends, it's likely that the dividends will be much smaller than before. Asset allocations are also changing in favour of the fixed interest instruments. Although, one of the results of the enormous amounts of money being pumped into the system by governments is a massive increase in government debt instruments (gilts). The problem here is that, because of low confidence in governments (to understand, let alone deal with such issues), the risk associated with government debt has risen above that of corporate debt as has the price. One of the key questions for 2009/2010 is whether the headline amounts governments are pledging to solve the economic crisis, are sustainable from debt they can acquire in the markets.

The reality is that is a knife edge as to whether anyone is going to invest in government debt when the risk is high, and the price is high. All of this of course is a self-fulfilling prophecy. These are the signs of recessionary forces still gathering pace but equally, it's clear that taxation in absolute amounts of money, as well as a percentage of income, is going to become increasingly important in the performance mix.

Procedures

As has been referred to, each jurisdiction has many rules and procedures which determine how any given entitlement can be realised.

Exemption is clearly the most efficient model, but this option is open really only to a select few types of investor, normally where there is a State based "interest" in allowing an exemption. Common occurrences of this are pension funds. Another less common occurrence is with types of investors known as "sovereign immunes". These are typically governments themselves or funds controlled by governments which can, due to their status, negotiate immunity from tax with specific partners. There is no general model here and each such immunity agreement is negotiated between the parties. It's likely that, outside the parties and their close advisors, no-one even knows that such an arrangement exists. That said, unless the withholding or paying agent has specific knowledge of the arrangement, they would normally have to apply the normal rules. In a practical sense of course, exempt entities are aware that they are exempt, sovereign immunes make their own specific arrangements, but in both cases, the amounts that they are investing are typically in a relatively small number of instruments but in very large amounts. Such entities therefore make sure that they have in place specific arrangements so that, in addition to having the entitlement, they are often not taxed at all on the income.

Relief at Source comes in many flavours ranging from the extremely simple "address rule" based models through to the extremely complex USA "qualified intermediary" model. The address rule-based model is generally falling rapidly out of favour since it presents too many opportunities for abuse. In today's paranoic world of identity and fraud concerns, assessing someone's entitlement to a favourable tax rate based solely on an address on a utility bill is just not a sustainable model. However, the alternative currently being presented, as will be discussed later, is almost equally unsustainable in terms of being overly prescriptive on documentation and deadlines while adding significant new onerous obligations on the custody community for tax information reporting and audit oversight. They to all relief at source is the presentation up the chain of custody of either documentation or confirmation that any given beneficial owner is evidenced to an entitlement for a favourable rate of taxation and that this evidence or confirmation is provided before the income distribution is made.

Quick Refund

Where a domestic withholding agent has deducted tax at a statutory withholding rate but has an agreement with its tax authority to remit those funds in aggregate at specified times and frequencies, rather than item by item, this leads the path open to a quick refund process. While the tax has not yet been remitted to a tax authority, a claimant can, if the withholding agent offers such a service make what is essentially a market claim i.e. a claim to a market participant such as a financial institution, rather than a claim to a tax authority. The times for payment, documentary requirements, the terms and the procedural requirements are then set by the withholding agent on a commercial basis. As such, for example, an investor with accounts at two Italian institutions may be offered quick refunds through one institution but not through the other. So, from that perspective it's difficult to describe quick refunds as a market level procedure.

Standard Refund Claims

Standard refund claims, sometimes called "Long form claims" are really the back stop procedure of the industry. They are used in two circumstances. Either they are the only method to get back an entitlement e.g. Switzerland OR they are a secondary process supporting a primary relief at source procedure e.g. France. The number of occasions where this process has to be used in either methodology is extremely large.

Inter-Relationship

Of course, at present, most tax authorities apply one or more of the preceding models to their relationship between themselves and other jurisdictions. Most people expect that a given tax authority will have a given "position" on procedure with respect to another jurisdiction. Would that it was that simple. Some tax authorities will allow relief at source for some investor types but not for others. On the other hand, some tax authorities agree special procedures with certain custodians based on the number of claims the custodian represents. This in turn of course varies by market depending on the number, residency, and type of customer the custodian has on its books at any one time. The fact is that each tax authority makes case-by-case judgements based on several factors. One of the principles to which interest groups such as FISCO and G30 are working, is the concept of a single homogenous model. While laudable, the fact is that even with a homogenous model, even with some level of automation and standardisation, the proportion of procedures that are "special" and outside the general rules, may be significant either in volume and/or value.

In addition to the above, some tax authorities offer "combination processing". In other words, there may be a relief at source process which is expected to be the most prevalent, but if the deadlines for relief at source are not met and statutory rate tax is deducted, the jurisdiction concerned has a post payment long form process that can be used to obtain the entitlement.

Standards, Automation

Standards are noticeably lacking in the industry. The ISOguardian for the industry, SWIFT, has a few ISO15022 level MT messages that contain some tax qualifiers, but there is no consistent business process within ISO15022 to allow for the development of such a message set. ISO20022 has the capacity to establish such business processes but has not yet addressed this corporate action sub-type. While related distantly, there is also very little automation surrounding withholding tax. There are one or two software companies that have created solutions for some parts of the process but by no means all. Custodians who historically designed and built their own systems are rapidly diversifying out of this model as the true complexity of an in-house solution becomes clear (quite apart from their need to reduce costs).

Technology solutions generally work best when automating complex processes within a set of pre-determined rules. While this sounds like what withholding tax is, it is so complex, with so many variables that even the pre-determined rules have variables. The tax authorities are only recently starting to engage in the concept of automation having been for many years, and most still are, reliant on manual processes based on different forms and data for each market. Without standards, automation has no real chance to succeed. Without automation, the number variables and paper processes can't be eradicated and thus without these two issues "in-play" in the community, there is no real short-term efficiency solution deliverable in-house.

Legal

As I noted, there are some initiatives that are changing the face of withholding tax. "initiatives" of course imply some guiding force or thought process with a defined objective. However, most of the initiatives surrounding withholding tax are either accidental, reactive to a given set of circumstances or the result of a narrowly focused group of players in the market. There is recent legal activity, brought by some institutional investors, to try to force a favourable rate of tax even when the treaty entitlement does not allow it. In these circumstances, the investor cites domestic law rather than the treaty to establish that, under domestic (European) law, an investor must be treated the same way irrespective of which EU State they are resident in. Under those circumstances, if the domestic law provides an exemption from tax, then a non-resident of one EU State can claim the same exemption when investing in another EU State. This kind of application of law is currently not widespread.

Initiatives

Firstly, there are no truly global initiatives when it comes to withholding tax. It may seem like it sometimes but apart from the US in 2001 and the EU currently, there are many areas where there is no major change. It is true that historically the EU markets and the US represented 95% of all the long form claims made on an annual basis, but with economic power moving towards Asia-Pacific, these regions are now entering a new phase. Historically their investments have been more oriented to intra-Asian markets where the number of treaties is much smaller. However, there is currently a significant increase in interest in withholding tax. So, our status in the industry is that:

- most investments are subject to over-taxation.
- entitlements to a lower treaty-based rate of tax are commonplace.
- the issue, scale and scope mean that the amounts, concerned typically up to 250 basis points, will continue to become proportionately more "material" for investors.
- jurisdictions, complex enough in the past, maintain a variety of possible models for returning entitlements of inbound investors.

- the inconsistency and unfairness inherent in having so many disparate rules and processes is currently being challenged either through the international courts, to assure homogenous treatment of domestic and non-resident investors, or through the efforts of a small number of pressure groups, some commercial e.g. G30; some governmental e.g. FISCO.
- despite the long history of withholding tax in a commercial environment that spends over $1 trillion a year on automation, there are currently no standards for communicating tax-related issues between counterparties and little or no automation that could leverage such standards.

6

Tax Relief at Source

This chapter explains the principles of tax relief at source in which tax documentation, certifications and positional data must reach a nexus between the record date and pay date of a securities distribution before tax relief can be granted. It also highlights the fact that future changes in digitisation and legal frameworks (covered elsewhere in the book) will make this operating model increasingly the de facto preferred model for tax authorities. So, investors and financial intermediaries need to get ahead of this curve in their planning. This chapter also compares some of the current tax relief models which will be described in more detail in Part III.

In the interpretation of double tax agreements, I've already mentioned that there are three implementational methodologies. These are tax relief at source quick refund and standard refund.

Of the three available methodologies, tax relief at source is probably the simplest to understand. For any given corporate action, dividend, for example, provided the beneficial owner/investor can prove their eligibility and entitlement to a lower rate of tax, then the entity distributing the dividend, typically a paying agent bank, can withhold the correct amount of tax prior to the dividend being distributed. The key to this is of course timing. There is often only a short space of time between the record date, when ownership is crystallised and the pay date—sometimes a matter of a few days. It important to understand that tax relief at source can only be granted by a financial institution.

R. K. McGill, *Cross-Border Investment Withholding Tax*, Finance and Capital Markets Series,
https://doi.org/10.1007/978-3-031-32785-8_6

So, if Bank A is acting as a withholding agent for Corporation B and I hold shares in Corporation B, if I can get all the proper material to Bank A in time, Bank A will take tax at the appropriate treaty rate from my dividend so I will not be over-taxed.

The question is—how did I get to know that Corporation B was going to pay a dividend in the first place? At the single investor level, this might be something I keep track of, but Bank A may have thousands of customers with hundreds each holding a different number of shares in different companies. Expecting every investor to continuously monitor their investments for potential tax benefits is unrealistic. Of course, it is also unlikely that I am holding my shares at Bank A. I am holding my shares at a different bank, Bank C. Bank C is holding my shares (known as safe keeping or custody), co-mingled with all its other customer's shares in Corporation B, at Bank A in an omnibus account. So, for Bank A to support tax relief at source, it must have a method to inform Bank C and Bank C must have a method to get the relevant information from me so that it can tell Bank A about my eligibility and claim. Interbank communications are most commonly affected using a computer system operated by the Society for Worldwide Interbank Telecommunications ("SWIFT"), so Bank A would tell Bank C about the upcoming dividend using a SWIFT message MT564. Bank A's role is also to tell Bank C what information is required (and when) from Bank C in order for it to be able to tax at a treaty rate.

The most common operating model in custody banks is to have this all sorted out upfront in the account opening process where I would have agreed that Bank C would monitor my investments and take automatic action if tax relief could be claimed on any dividend (Exhibit 6.1).

That means that when Bank A tells Bank C about the upcoming dividend, Bank C already knows how many shares I hold in Corporation B. That's called my record date position. Now Bank A is withholding tax on this dividend based on domestic income tax law and it generally bears strict liability for any mistakes. Bank A is told by its tax administration, what information is needed. RAS documentation will include at least:

- A claim form with the name and address of the investor
- A statement of their record date position and
- A certificate of residence issued by the investor's tax administration.

So, my Bank C, will check its records for this information and complete the necessary claim form and send it for my signature with a request that I provide a certificate of residence. Once I have those documents, I can send

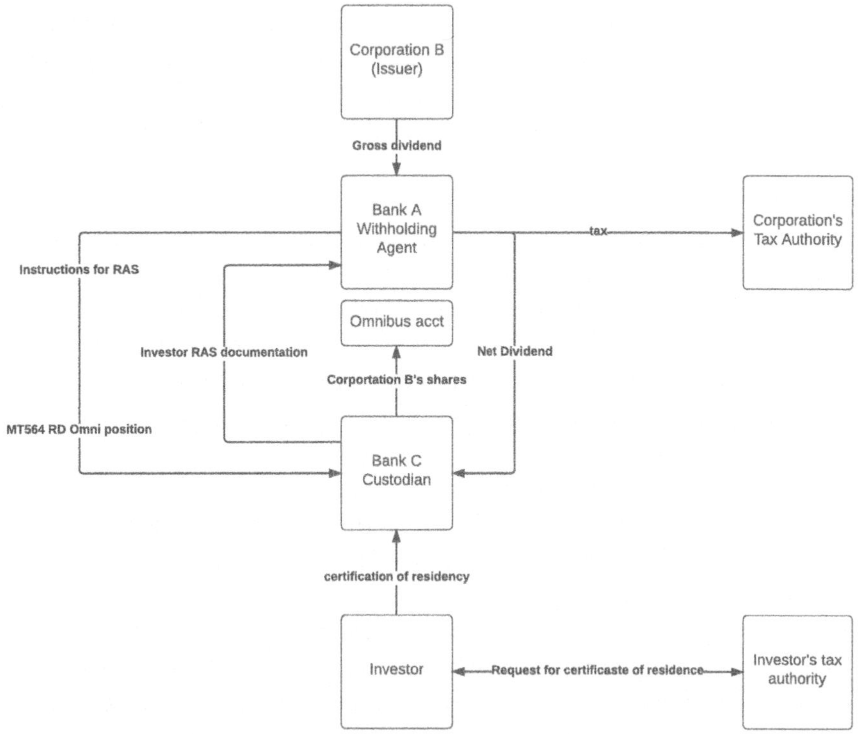

Exhibit 6.1 Relief at source process (*Source* Author)

them back to my Bank C who can then combine these with other customer's claims and send them to Bank A. Bank A checks all this information and withholds the correct amount of tax from my dividend when it pays Bank C. Bank C can then credit my account with the dividend minus the tax that was withheld by Bank C.

This all sounds very simple however when done at scale it becomes increasingly difficult without some level of automation and standardisation to support it. Financial institutions struggle with the manual components and the paper components of these processes are costly and error-prone.

I've described a situation in which there is only Bank A and Bank C. However, there is often a significant chain of payment involved with multiple financial institutions holding positions in securities through a number of omnibus accounts. I may be an investor with an account at a custodian bank. However, that custodian bank may be commingling my assets along with its other clients' assets in an omnibus account at another financial institution or counterparty. That came to the party in turn maybe commingling its customer's assets in omnibus accounts at another financial institution further up in the payment chain. This can be repeated many times. So, while I may believe that I am holding my assets at a custodian bank, the reality may be that those assets are registered in omnibus accounts in a chain. In all jurisdictions where tax relief is legally permissible, the tax administrations hold the withholding agent in that jurisdiction to have strict liability for correct withholding.

The withholding agent in the jurisdiction of the investment must inform its customers, and financial institutions, of the way in which it supports tax relief at source. Because it takes on the legal liability for correct withholding, this means that it must ensure that any investor seeking to be taxed at a right other than the statutory rate has provided sufficient evidence of their entitlement, and that the withholding agent holds no risk when withholding tax from the payment.

There are therefore two components of processing in tax relief at source jurisdictions. The first is the way in which the withholding agent, at the top of the payment chain, informs the other financial institutions in the chain of an impending corporate action event and of the tax consequences associated with it. This would typically be a notification of an impending dividend together with a list of the documentation required for any financial institution in the chain of payment. This documentation list would need to consider all the possible variations and permutations of types of investors and jurisdictions of investors. The second component is the transmission of all this data and documentation to the withholding agent. The job of the withholding agent in this operational model is to review all the documentation validate the documentation and use the data to establish how much tax to withhold on the payment it is making to its customers.

So ultimately the problem is one of timing. If there is insufficient time for the downstream financial institution to gather documentation and data and pass that up the chain to the withholding agent, then tax will be withheld at the statutory right by the withholding agent who does not want to accept the liability associated with granting a treaty rate of tax without having specific evidence of entitlement and eligibility. When we consider this in context to the number of jurisdictions, the number of corporate actions and dividend payments that are being made on a daily basis around the world and the number of financial institutions holding those assets through chains of omnibus accounts, the net result is that many financial institutions simply do not have the resources or the desire to do all of the work of cross-checking all of the documentation and data that other financial institutions might provide. They, therefore, do not support tax relief at source simply because they are unable to meet the timing constraint associated with the process.

We find therefore in the market an apparent paradox investors may do their own investigations and come to the conclusion that they should be granted tax relief at source however, the reality is that even when tax relief at source is legally allowed to be available in a market that does not mean that tax relief at source will be granted in that market because there are a number of variables that get in the way of delivery.

The model that I have described here is the simplest model for tax relief at source. The most complex tax relief at source model is operated by the United States of America. The US operates tax relief at source under US Internal Revenue Code Chapter 3 which is section 1441 of the US tax regulations. The most important component of the US tax relief at source system is that it allows non-US financial institutions to contract with the US government to withhold tax at treaty rates. These financial institutions, when contracted, are called qualified intermediaries. Qualified intermediary contract, and undertakes obligations to document its clients withhold tax, deposit tax with the US Treasury, and report annually about its withholding activities. The second important component is that, For the purpose of documentation of clients, the US permits self-certifications of tax residence for the purpose of claiming tax treaty benefits whereas most other countries require certificates of residence. A certificate of residence is a certificate that is issued by a tax administration. The US self-certification which comprises forms in the W8 series allows investors to self-certify under penalties of perjury that they have a particular tax status and to claim tax treaty benefits where applicable. The third component of the US tax relief at source regulations allow the use of omnibus accounts and a withholding statement. A Withholding statement is generally simply a statement, often a spreadsheet, provided by One Financial institution to another that allocates a proportion of the securities within a given omnibus account to a particular tax rate. The combination of self-certifications and the use of withholding statements within the structure of qualified intermediary status makes the US a complex area. The US allows digital versions of the self-certifications which makes it much easier for financial institutions to document the status of their clients.

7

Quick Refunds

This chapter explains the principles of quick refunds in which, if legally permissible, a financial institution can grant tax relief after a payment has been made (net of statutory rates of tax) by deducting the tax from funds it is due to remit to its tax authority. The chapter explains the process and the legal framework necessary to allow this operating model which provides an additional window of opportunity to investors in certain jurisdictions.

As we saw in Chapter 6, where it is legally permissible and operationally applied, tax relief at source is the most desirable outcome for the investors. The consequences of withholding tax at source means that the withholding agent will ultimately be depositing tax to the relevant tax administration. However, in practice, withholding agents are not submitting tax payments to administrations on a daily basis. It is more typical that withholding agents make single payments on a regular basis e.g., monthly. In many jurisdictions, it is common for the withholding agent to make a payment to its tax administration 30 days after it has collected the tax from the investors at the time, but it made the payment to them. This means that for that period of 30 days, the withholding agent is the one who is holding the tax. This leads to the opportunity of a quick refund. A quick refund is a situation in which tax relief at source was not granted on the pay date, but the tax has not yet been submitted by the withholding agent to the tax administration concerned.

R. K. McGill, *Cross-Border Investment Withholding Tax*, Finance and Capital Markets Series,
https://doi.org/10.1007/978-3-031-32785-8_7

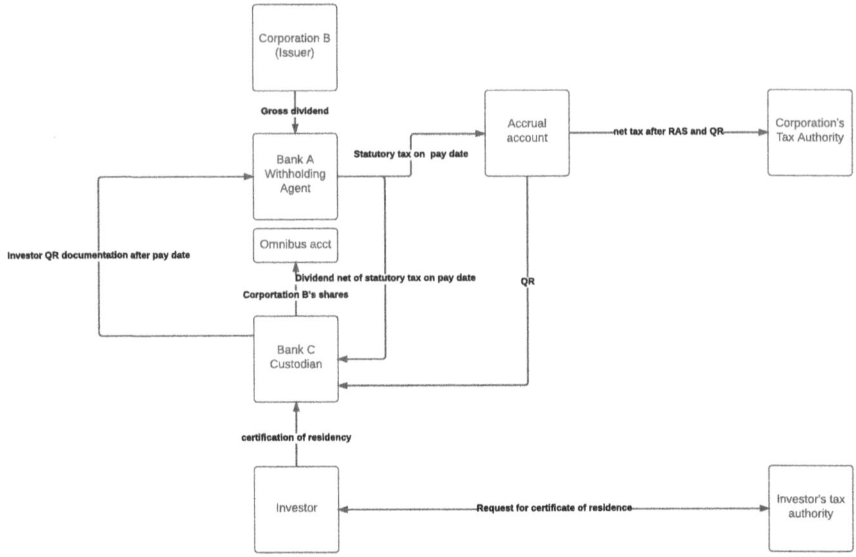

Exhibit 7.1 Quick refund process

If, in its communications to its market participants, the withholding agent announces its support for a quick refund process, this means that investors and their financial institutions get two bites at the cherry. The first is providing documentation and data for an entitlement between the record date and the pay date. However, if the financial institution an investor cannot get the documentation and data insufficient time for tax relief at source, under the quick refund principle, the claim can still be made to the withholding agent after the pay date but before the withholding agent has submitted the tax to its tax administration. The refund is therefore made by the withholding agent from the pot of tax that it withheld from the original payment.

Tax relief at source and quick refunds therefore represent two windows of opportunity for investors. Given that standard refunds can take years to be received, it's clearly in the best interests of investors to obtain tax relief at source or quick refunds wherever they can. The effect on the performance of a portfolio of investments can be substantial.

In Exhibit 7.1, following a relief at source process, tax is withheld on any payment for which relief at source documentation was not provided. That position then has statutory rate tax withheld. However, this tax is not immediately sent to the tax authority. It is first kept in a separate holding account for a period until the date that it must be sent to the tax authority, most commonly on the 15th day of the following month.

This gives the withholding agent, Bank A the ability to continue to receive tax relief documentation after the pay date and before the tax is due to be remitted to the tax authority. If any investors submit quick refund claims, their refund is taken from the holding account. This means the investor does not have to send a tax reclaim to the tax authority. The tax authority gets the correct amount of tax, being the statutory rate tax withheld on the pay date minus any quick refunds processed in between.

8

Standard Refunds

This chapter explains the "backstop" process of standard refunds in which withheld tax is in the possession of the tax authority. The chapter explains how the process of tax reclamation works and establishes the various documents and data requirements as well as the nuances. This chapter also references other chapters to highlight that while standard refunds were the main operating model in the past (tax relief being uncommon), they will become "boutique" in the future, reserved only for the most complex of transactions, as the industry moves towards a primary tax relief operating model. Key concepts include use of certificates of residence, self-certifications, problems associated with chains of intermediation in the payment chain, lack of standards, lack of automation, inaccuracies in data, limitations of custody tax offerings and cost–benefit calculations.

This chapter provides a basic overview of withholding tax reclaims. It is not intended as a detailed guide, nor is it a how-to manual. The complexities involved would fill two books at least. This chapter is designed to give the reader a basic understanding of the level of complexity involved, the scale of the problems faced by custodians in this area and enough understanding to enable the institutional investor to ask intelligent questions relating to his portfolio that will enable him and his custodian to provide the best possible return.

Exhibit 8.1 reminds us of the simple reclaim process using the taxation principal thread. At the point where we most effectively join the process, links one through 4 have already taken place.

R. K. McGill, *Cross-Border Investment Withholding Tax*, Finance and Capital Markets Series,
https://doi.org/10.1007/978-3-031-32785-8_8

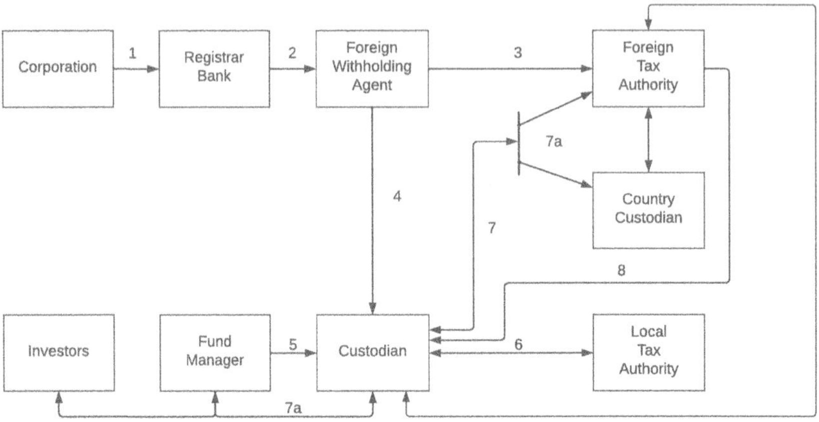

Exhibit 8.1 Standard Refund process (*Source* Author)

The income event, in this case a corporate dividend, has been administered (1) and (2) the withholding agent, in the absence of information about the investor, has withheld tax at the maximum rate possible (3) in order to protect itself from any financial liability and to meet its own domestic law requirements and the investor's custodian has received the dividend net of statutory rate tax (4).

The custodian now realises that the investor, in this example, a fund, has paid too much tax. This may seem like a simple act. In practice most custodians are dealing with a client base in the hundreds if not thousands, where the tax profile of each client is different, often in very subtle ways. This is why, traditionally, withholding tax has been a very expensive process to implement. Before step six can take place in the process diagram a number of factors need to be assessed including:

- The client's legal status may prevent or affect his ability to reclaim the over-withheld tax.
- His documentation proving his status may or may not be out of date
- The time delay between the sufferings of over withholding and the date of the tax reclaim may mean the investor has fallen out of the statute of limitations
- The type of income instrument may have special rules applying that change the amount of reclaimable tax
- If the security was lent over the ex-date there may be issues over who is entitled to the tax reclaim amount

- The investor may not have supplied a power of attorney to the custodian which will delay the process by an unknown amount of time.

All these factors have to be weighed, for each and every income event, if the investors best interests are to be served. Overriding all of this of course, the DTAs themselves change from time to time as do the procedures that the authorities use to implement the DTAs.

Step (5) in the process diagram represents the fund manager or investor providing information to the custodian and the custodian evaluating the availability of a tax reclaim.

Step 7 represents the custodian requesting from each tax authority and acquiring a supply of the relevant tax reclaim forms. This raises a benchmarking process that should ensure that the custodian has sufficient forms for its expected volume of tax reclaims. Failure to do this will result in time delays which in turn will affect the custodian's overall performance against a benchmark of time to receiving the tax reclaim funds. In many cases, these forms are now provided by tax administrations online. However, finding those forms at the appropriate website can often be difficult as the websites may not be rendered in English or a jurisdictional language of the custodian. Most solutions on the market today have these forms pre-built into them so they can be populated and printed easily.

Step (6) represents the custodian requesting proof of domicile from the local tax authority i.e., the tax authority in the country where the investor is resident for tax purposes. In order to do this, the custodian must have already identified the nature of the tax reclaim available. This is not because the local tax authority needs to know this information. It's because the most efficient way to expedite the process is to have a stamp from the local tax authority citing domicile, actually on the tax reclaim form that the foreign tax authority receives. So, the custodian normally will complete the tax reclaim form as far as possible, then send it off usually by post to the local tax office of the investor with a covering letter requesting a stamp of authority to demonstrate that the investor cited on the form is indeed resident in the country for tax purposes.

Step (7). Once the custodian has received the tax reclaim form back from the local tax authority it is free to send it to the foreign tax authority. It is usually from this point that most benchmarking takes place for the purpose of costing a contractual tax service. The most efficient method at this stage is for the custodian to have been given a power of attorney to sign the tax reclaim form on behalf of the client. This is a very fragmented process in practice. Some clients, whether from a control perspective, a monitoring perspective or simply because of internal risk management policy, may not provide power of attorney for this purpose. In addition, as a result of the several tax fraud scandals in recent years, many tax administrations no longer permit tax reclaims to be submitted on behalf of an investor by a third-party vendor. They will instead only accept tax reclaim forms signed physically by the investor. Either way from a benchmarking perspective there are delays involved with power of attorney driven tax reclaims and tax reclaims that must first go back to the investor. It is not unknown in the vendor community foreign investors to sign a tax reclaim form, understand the process that is being undertaken, and then try to do the tax reclaims in future years by themselves thus disintermediating third-party vendors. Trust the following options press one if you know the name of the hospital person or department in trying to read. step seven in the diagram is not a simple submission to a tax authority. There are some tax authorities, most notably the French, where a tax reclaim is not recognised by a tax authority unless it has been delivered through an approved in-country agent bank. So, the custodian or investor must know to which jurisdictions this rule applies and ensure that an inappropriate relationship is in place with an in-country agent to file tax reclaims on their behalf. As an added irritation these in-country agents will often charge fees for receiving and processing the claims to their domestic tax administrations.

Step (7a) is therefore only applicable if claims must be submitted via a sub-custodian. Given the chain structure of the custody process, the claim may have to pass through more than one set of hands and be sent back through the same route, before the tax authority is in possession of a properly completed and duly signed valid tax reclaim form.

Step (8) represents a tax authority approving a tax reclaim under the appropriate DTT and remitting the refund to the applicant. This is most frequently done with an actual cheque in the post. Of course, if the reclaim was submitted via an in-country agent, the refund will follow a similar path back through the in-country agent to the investor or custodian concerned.

The rule is that any tax reclaim that is filed is subject to the rules that applied at the time that the over withholding took place. This is particularly relevant in ECJ claims.

ECJ Claims

ECJ claims are a peculiarity of the European Union. The EU has many principles which affect withholding tax. One of these is the non-discrimination case law. This means that within European Union Member States any one

Member State must not discriminate against the investors of another Member State. This is the principle of objective comparability. In recent years there have been several cases where a fund resident in one member state has been treated differently from a withholding tax perspective from a fund resident within that other State. What has happened is that the fund has taken legal action in the European Court of Justice ("ECJ") against the tax administration of the other Member State claiming that the fund is being discriminated against when compared to a fund that would be resident in that other Member State.

In almost all cases the plaintiff in such legal actions wins their lawsuit. What happens next is complex. The tax administration will have had procedures in place for processing tax reclaims which were the subject of the ECJ case will stop having lost the case the tax administration must now re-evaluate its procedures in order to ensure that future claims do not discriminate against other member states investors. This process of re-evaluation can take several years. At the end of that re-evaluation process the tax administration will issue new procedures to be followed by foreign investors.

Now, in the absence of any class action, it is quite likely that the plaintiff will not be the only fund that is being treated in a discriminatory way. However, what's news of the ECJ case becomes public those other investors would naturally seek to reclaim what they consider to be tax overwithheld due to discriminatory behaviour. The problem is that the tax administration being the defendant has not yet evaluated and issued new procedures.

The difficulty is that a fund seeking to leverage and ECJ finding would need to both file a claim and demonstrate an equivalence between their situation and the situation of the original plaintiff. This led to an entire industry founded on ECJ claims. So, it's important to understand what we mean by an ECJ claim. There are two possibilities. The first is that an ECJ claim is the activity of bringing a lawsuit to the European Court of justice as the first plaintiff in a case. The second meaning of ECJ claims is that of a fund or other institutional investor who seeks to leverage the benefit of a previously determined ECJ case. As the author is not a lawyer, this book will not go into the details of how to bring an ECJ claim for discrimination.

With respect to the second scenario, the problems faced by the fund have not yet disappeared. They may well be able to take legal advice to determine that their circumstances, structure, and investments are essentially equivalent to those of the original plaintiff. That being the case they would only be able to file a tax reclaim to the tax administration based on the original procedures and documentary requirements which the ECJ had found to be discriminatory. It's important to note that the claim that's being filed in this circumstance is not a claim whose legal basis is a double tax agreement the legal basis for the claim is the ECJ case. Therefore, while much of the documentation including attacks reclaimed forms and the supporting documentation would be effectively the same as if the claim was being filed based on a double tax agreement, there would need to be a covering letter explaining the basis of the claim and establishing the equivalence of the claimant to the original plaintiff. it goes without saying that the legal teams within tax administrations would be looking for any minute difference between the circumstances of the plaintiff and the circumstances of the new claimant to find a reason to deny such claims. In addition, there is a difficulty with the potential for a statute of limitations breach. As we have found each jurisdiction has a statute of limitations. This is the period starting on the pay date during which a standard refund can be filed. The average statute of limitations across a normal portfolio of 13 markets would be around 5.2 years. It is therefore entirely possible that a claim filed based on an ECJ decision may not be reviewed by a tax administration until after the statute of limitations has passed. Such a claim would then be denied on the basis that it was filed too late. The normal process therefore is to file what is known as a protective reclaim. In other words, the claim is filed as quickly as it can be, and the covering letter notes specifically that this is a protective claim being filed so that the receiving tax administration must record in its books of record that a claim had been received. Ultimately, this may mean that once the tax administration has evaluated the ECJ case and made necessary changes to its procedures that new documentation is necessary or new data is necessary for a claim to be passed at that point, because the protective claim had been filed the tax administration has the obligation to go back to the investor and request additional information in order that the claim can be assessed.

Beneficial Owners

A beneficial owner is the ultimate owner of the benefit in an income event. So, a private investor is also a beneficial owner. It's important to understand at this stage that beneficial ownership of an asset is not necessarily the same as beneficial ownership of the income from that asset. This matter is discussed in later chapters when we talk about cum-ex scandals In which the ownership over security can't change between the record date and the ex-date leaving one of the two parties entitled to the income from the asset but not actually owning the asset.

Different withholding rates can apply depending on the tax status of the beneficial owner and these must be researched in depth if the correct withholding and any reclaim is to be pursued successfully.

Financial Instruments

There is clearly a large range of financial instruments, income from which can be affected by withholding tax and these do change from time to time. It must be said, however, that the vast majority of withheld tax falls into the two categories of tax on corporate dividends and tax on royalties.

However withholding tax can also apply in certain circumstances to a variety of securities including, as well as ordinary shares, government stocks, debenture stocks, convertible and bearer bonds, fixed-term deposits, bank interest and unit trusts.

The Role of Sub-Custodians

So, custodians play a vital role in the reclaim process and it's important for investors to be aware of this. Dealing with custodians who have not only a wide network of sub-custodians, but also where those sub-custody locations fit with the investor's portfolio, is an important element of the custody selection process. A global custodian may provide a globally based asset management and safe keeping service, but this is often underpinned by a network of smaller custodians who have specialist knowledge of their particular market or a particular area of the business. This is analogous to outsourcing, although not structured in the same way. A sub-custodian will provide in-country services which would otherwise be difficult or expensive for a global custodian to provide.

There are also some circumstances where an in-country custodian is also the route for a tax reclaim to be submitted rather than directly to attack authority.

The Role of Investors

The investor only has a role in the relief at source or tax reclaim process if he has not derogated his responsibilities to a custodian under a power of attorney or to a third-party vendor. The nature of the power attorney granted is often an issue for investors as their financial affairs are complex and the requirements of internal policy for institutional investors and compliance may make it difficult for an investor to provide a blanket power of attorney to a custodian. While abuse may be unlikely, since the custodian will have access to extremely sensitive information about the investor, it's more often the case that a limited power of attorney is given to a custodian or third-party vendor solely to provide specific services. This limits the liability on both sides and makes operational compliance and thus risk lower.

Operationally, this is further complicated by the fact that many investors subdivide their portfolios in different ways. Some may wish to take direct responsibility for certain markets and outsource or derogate responsibilities for others to the custodian. Again, for reduction of risk and compliance powers of attorney may be limited not just by the process empowered but also by the jurisdictions in which that process is derogated.

However, if no such derogation has taken place, the investor has the ultimate responsibility for ensuring that the information on any tax reclaim form is correct. The investor will be supplied with completed tax reclaim forms on a regular basis which he will have to sign and return to the custodian to facilitate efficient filing.

This area is one of the most aggravating for custodians. Investors, many of whom don't understand the process or the tax itself usually have other priorities. Best practice would require that all parties recognise the scale of the value that tax reclaimed can represent and make best efforts to facilitate the process. Unfortunately, investors often fail to make adequate provisions of resource to deal with and turn around tax reclaims affectively. In my recent consultancy work, I've often had to make note of the fact that a service level agreement should be just as much about what the investor is committing to as what the custodian is committing to.

In many areas, investors can cause problems and indeed failures in the SLA by not understanding the process is that custodians engage in and where they fit into the equation will stop if the benchmark starting point for a tax reclaim is the income event notification, then if the investor has not provided a power of attorney to the custodian, many days can be added to the process simply in order to get an investor's signature on the required forms. The benchmarking process described elsewhere in this book makes note of the fact that the benchmarking process should be directed, not just at the custodian but also at the investor who can materially affect the time taken to recoup refunds for reinvestment.

The resource required includes personnel with a combination of the knowledge to be able to assess accuracy to a given level and the authority to sign and return the forms to the custodian will stop the most common mistake of course, particularly for an investor new to the issue, is that he wishes to see everything. The only way this can be achieved in the tax reclaim arena is for no power of attorney to be granted thus requiring Paul forms to be submitted to the investor. While this solves the process well the investor's hopefully temporary insecurity, it makes the investor liable for any errors. If the investor knows enough to make this judgement, he probably doesn't need the custodian for this purpose anyway.

The role of the investor is therefore much more effectively focused on establishing the level of competency of his custodian through detailed benchmarking. Having established the scope of competency, a properly constructed service level agreement should define how the custodian operates the SLA will define, in turn, the exact nature of the power of attorney that is granted to the custodian will stop that's the way it should be done. unfortunately, in practice, investors don't always perform this process and hand over too much power to a custodian in a generic power of attorney which can leave the investor exposed.

Certifying Residency

Historically tax reclaims have involved 2 tax administrations. Firstly, the tax administration is in the jurisdiction of the residence of the investor. Secondly the tax administration in the jurisdiction of the issuer of the securities. As far as the tax authority of the issuer's jurisdiction is concerned it will only approve a reclaim or a reclaim if there is documentary evidence of the tax status of the beneficial owner. In some cases, this is achieved by getting a stamp placed by the tax administration of the investor onto a completed tax reclaim form. In other cases, there must be a request made to the tax administration of the investor to obtain a certificate of residence. In some cases, these certificates of residents even need to be validated, such a process is called an apostille. Finally, in more advanced markets the investor can provide a self-certification of tax residency provided they accept the risk and liability associated with making any kind of false or fraudulent statements on such a certification. This latter scenario is likely to become the norm simply because it offers the opportunity for automation and standardisation as well as digitisation.

Responsibility for Accuracy

Fundamentally, whoever is shining attacked reclaimed form is accepting responsibility for its accuracy and truthfulness and completeness. If the investor has not given the power of attorney to a custodian or a third-party colour then the custodian or third party will be sending him completed tax reclaim forms for signature on a regular basis.

The reality is that tax authorities have limited technology in place compared to custodians and it's entirely possible common given the volume of reclaims that are filed annually to some markets, for duplicate reclaims to be filed ie., two reclaims for the same single over-withheld amount. Clearly not an acceptable situation. The investor is ultimately responsible for making sure that not only is this particular reclaim correct in every respect but also that it is the only reclaim filed for this particular purpose. This place is a great responsibility on investors who may have withheld the power of attorney for entirely subjective reasons.

If an investor has provided a power of attorney to a custodial third party, that custodian or third party can then complete the reclaim form and it. However, the signature must be appended to the words on behalf of. So, as you can see that race still goes ultimately back to the investor or beneficial owner. The degree of liability accepted by the custodian with respect to the accuracy of a tax reclaim is determined by the wording on the power of attorney and in the service level agreement. Legally, the issue goes to whether in this respect the custodian is contracted to provide reasonable efforts or best efforts in conducting calculations of validity eligibility and value. In risk management terms, for the best interests of both parties, it is important to make the allocation of responsibility explicitly clear.

Tax administrations have a particular view of the role of third-party vendors in tax reclamation. Third-party vendors themselves tend to take the view that there are merely providing a processing service IE an administrative role and that the risk and liability are solely with the investor. The tax administrations on the other hand do not necessarily follow that view. They take the view that the vendor or custodian is providing some level of knowledge and skill in the process. Yes, there is an administrative component, but the investor is essentially relying on the skill and knowledge and expertise of the vendor or custodian concerned. This can be very important if claims are rejected or found to be fraudulent or abusive of the double tax agreements in general. The risk for custodians and for third-party vendors is that if their clients are indeed engaging in abusive or fraudulent activity, the affected tax administrations are likely to take up legal considerations on the basis of unlawful enrichment. In other words, the fees charged by the custodian or third-party vendor have, as a component, expertise and knowledge i.e., their service offering is not just an administrative activity.

Service Level Agreements

Service Level Agreements do not usually address tax reclaim issues beyond defining whether or not such processes are offered, the markets in which they are offered, whether contractual tax is offered and the basic reporting on such activities that will be provided.

As seen in the last section, best practice in this area can be greatly improved by investors taking a more direct interest at the beginning of their relationship with a custodian. The later chapter on Benchmarking gives some good guidelines for the types of questions and standards that an investor can ask of a custodian's tax operations department.

Also, as I've said already, I firmly believe that SLAs should be two-way and that each part of the process should be understood by an investor to the extent that a custodian can show the investor how their actions can impact the efficiencies of the processes involved.

The Role of Tax Authorities

Tax authorities have two hats in the withholding tax process. From one perspective they are "local" tax authorities with respect to beneficial owners/investors resident for tax purposes in their jurisdiction. From the other perspective, they are "foreign" tax authorities receiving claims for refunds from foreign investors and custodians.

Proof of Tax Residency

For residents of their country, tax authorities provide proof of domicile for tax purposes. A custodian or investor who submits a completed reclaim form or a request for relief at source must ask their local tax office to stamp the form or provide some other documentation to attest that the subject of the tax form is indeed, as far as they are concerned, a resident of that country for tax purposes. This is basically what will establish eligibility for treaty rate benefits as far as the foreign tax authority is concerned.

Sources of Reclaim Forms

Tax authorities, in the main, process tax reclaims manually. That is they receive printed forms from custodians or investors. The source of these forms is usually, of course, the tax authority themselves.

When the IN countries in the European Union each lost their currencies and adopted the Euro, this caused a problem because all the tax authorities in those countries had their own forms all of which showed their previous domestic currency.

The opportunity to harmonise these forms across Europe was lost, which would have been a major step towards ultimately allowing automation of these forms. However, each country did take a different approach to the provision of the many thousands of forms required by custodians and investors on almost a daily basis.

In particular of course, some custodians already had large stocks of these forms and decisions on what was to be done at the changeover weren't made clear until very close to the deadline. Some countries allowed custodians to cross out and replace the domestic currency symbol with the Euro symbol, the pragmatic approach. Others required all previous forms to be used up first before they released new forms.

While this is history now, it serves to highlight the fact that, however politically desirable harmonisation may be across Europe, its administrative systems, particularly in tax, are a long way behind in capability.

While the basic source of original forms remains the tax authorities, both internal IT departments and also external solutions providers have not been slow to realise that being able to reproduce such forms from an electronic template, is a way of improving the efficiency of the process. This of course must be done with the knowledge of the relevant tax authority whether directly or indirectly.

Receipt and Assessment of Reclaims

As there is no network of linked tax authorities nor a unified system currently capable of transmitting and receiving tax reclaims, however, the tax reclaim forms are produced, they must still be delivered, once fully and properly completed, by normal mail. In relative terms this is a very small cost in the process. However, in operational terms it does include an element of risk both in the internal processing of reclaims through the post room and of course the larger risk that the reclaim will get lost somewhere between the custodian and the tax authority.

Custodians generally have a labour-intensive process to follow up filed reclaims, precisely because there is so little connectivity between tax authorities themselves nor between tax authorities and custodians. This labour-intensive process begins with the original filing. In a best practice environment filing would either be recorded on delivery or be followed up a few days after sending so that the client record could be updated.

Proof of Identity

One of the keys to successful tax reclaims is the demonstration of identity. Fundamentally the tax authority in receipt of a claim for recovery of tax must be assured that the entity making the claim is who they say they are. This tends to be much more onerous in Relief at Source regimes (e.g., USA) since the tax authority will be granting relief from tax based on advance documentation i.e., it will not have the cash. On the other hand, in a reclaim process, the tax authority already has the cash and so it can afford to adopt a different approach. In most cases, proof of identity can take several forms. For instance, to have opened an account with a custodian, most investors, institutional or otherwise will have had to follow money laundering control regulations, known as Know Your Customer or "KYC" rules. These will include some evidence by the investor of their identity and particularly their status. There may also be room for a self-certification of identity. Finally, since the investor is undoubtedly registered with its own tax authority, this latter body can effectively certify that the applicant for a reclaim is known to them as a resident of their jurisdiction.

Proof of Sufferance of Double Tax

Proof of sufferance is often a difficult area, which may seem strange to many readers. Of course, the tax authority receiving a reclaim is facing several questions. Is the person making the reclaim, the person they say they are? Did they receive the income they say they received and was tax actually withheld on that income as it is represented on the reclaim form? In most cases, particularly where, for instance, withholding agent and custodian are members of the financial network SWIFT, the custodian can use a SWIFT message to demonstrate that it has been advised by a withholding agent, of an income event on which tax has been withheld. More details of the SWIFT messages involved can be found in a later chapter. However, this can often be relied upon to demonstrate withholding. Separate from this the investor may of course be in possession of a hard copy dividend voucher which will show the details of the income and any tax deducted. This also can be used as proof of sufferance. Finally, there is a level of trust that can be applied. If there is no other documentary evidence to hand, the custodian can produce on its own headed paper, effectively a statement of withholding to indicate to the receiving tax authority that the custodian knows that the income event has taken place and that recoverable tax has been deducted.

Powers of Attorney

Powers of attorney are common in this area of back-office operations, although not ubiquitous. Most powers of attorney are strictly limited to the process of tax reclaims, and investors would not have it otherwise, nor for liability purposes would custodians. For good reason, it is also sensible for investors to consider whether a power of attorney should be limited in time as well as scope. If a service agreement is in place that has a fixed period, presumably so that the investor can negotiate a review or change at some agreed break point, then any power of attorney granted should be similarly limited in time. The power of attorney is used by a custodian to represent the claimant. Often this will not just be representation to a tax authority. As we have learned, there are many entities involved in this process. The best powers of attorney are thus limited in time to coincide with any time limits on service provision, limited in scope to tax reclaims and broad enough to give the custodian authority to deal with all the various entities they may meet on behalf of the investor.

The power of attorney has two effects. The first is clearly to remove from the investor much of the onerous work involved in signing each tax reclaim form. The second is to allow the custodian to pursue the tax reclaim without further recourse to client contacts. Both are desirable if they are properly controlled.

Benchmarking

I've devoted a whole chapter to benchmarking later in this book. However, I felt it important to precursor that chapter with some words on the tax reclaim process itself.

Investors have an absolute interest in this process not just as bystanders watching custodians' process reclaims, but as we've seen, their actions can inhibit as well as enhance the efficiency of the process.

To that extent, there are some areas of the process that attract risk and it's as well to have a clear picture of these as Compliance Officers and Risk Managers will also be paying attention to how well these issues are addressed. Tax reclaims are one of the first areas where any failure to correctly identify certain aspects of an investor's profile, will appear.

Validity

Not all income events create taxable issues.

Exhibit 8.2 shows that, from the universe of all income events, the first filter that must be applied is whether the event is valid or not. In other words, on its own, is the income of a type that would normally fall within the definition of an income type that would attract withholding tax.

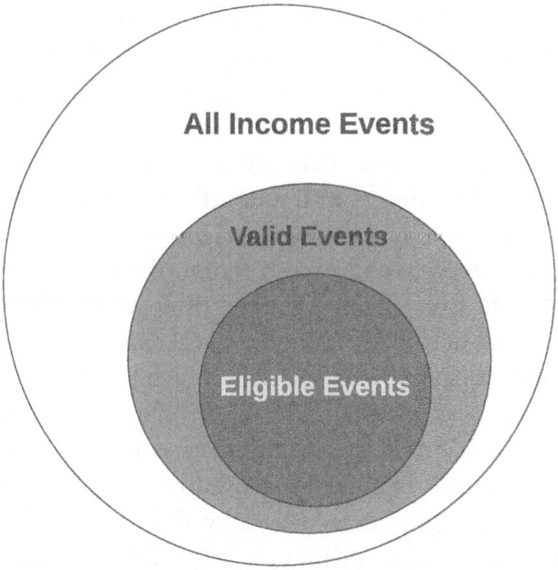

Exhibit 8.2 Validity vs Eligibility (*Source* Author)

Establishing Validity

Validity is a function of the income event and the treaty regulations covering the country of issuance and the countries of residence for which the custodian represents clients. An event is *valid* if, for the market m, a DTA exists which would create a withholding tax rate greater than the treaty rate for any income type I. This sets the scene for custodians or those processing reclaims.

The risk here is clearly that either some events will be thought to be valid when they are not or vice versa, resulting in either technically fraudulent reclaims or a failure to make reclaims when they are available. Actually, in practice this risk is fairly small. Custodians are very good at establishing valid events and withholding agents, for the most part, are able to notify correctly. There can however be problems associated with validity, particularly identifying where the income was technically sourced. This was highlighted at a conference recently when a US withholding agent asked how US source income could be reliably identified. True, in most cases, the answer is obvious. Either the company is well known to be US and/or the security identifier is reason to presume a primary indicator of being US source. But there are occasions when the answer is not quite so clear and where, ultimately, the withholding agent and/or the custodian have to perform more research in order to establish their view of where the income is technically from. Clearly, again the risk here is that one entity may view the set of research and come to one conclusion while another may come to a different conclusion. As I've said, this does not occur often, but it's as well, from a tax perspective to have knowledge of the income source country as firmly identified as possible.

Once valid income events have been found, the key is to find those who are eligible to benefit from them. The flow from validity to eligibility is, for most custodians both automatic and usually electronic these days. The status of clients is usually documented manually but held electronically. The risk involved here is the way in which the client's manually documented status is transferred to an electronic medium. There is obvious potential for data entry errors at this stage. Exhibit 8.3 shows the risk profile of this element of the process. This can be exacerbated by the continuing risk associated with *maintaining* correct documentation. Some forms of documentation are valid only within certain time limits. If they are to be used as proof of eligibility, then the custodian concerned must make sure that their systems are capable of tracking document validity. If a client's data record is not updated, then, while in all eventuality the client's status has probably not changed, in a best practice environment, the compliance department should hold that the client's status is effectively "undocumented". Therefore, there can be no eligibility for a treaty rate of withholding and thus no reclaim. This is found to a much higher degree in the US 1441 NRA relief at source regulations where documentary evidence rules are more strictly defined and applied. If a client's record is updated but is in error, the same risk would apply. The compliance function has the greatest interest in how these processes should work most efficiently and be monitored. The eligibility of a particular client is however not just dependent on status data. There are many other factors that may have a bearing on whether any client is eligible for a reclaim or not. Some are defined absolutely by their status while some are optional and may be selected by the client as a preferred instruction to the custodian. All are usually stored either manually or electronically. Where there are information elements held in both types of systems, clearly the integration risk is highest with the likelihood that the manual information will be missed or inaccurately assessed.

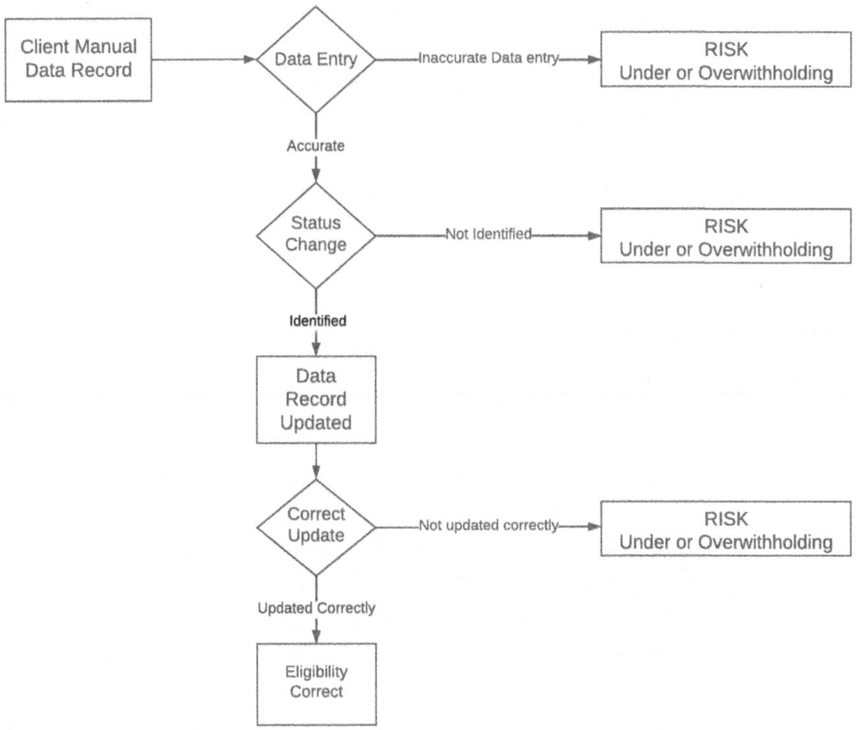

Exhibit 8.3 Risk profiling eligibility (*Source* Author)

Calculating Value

Once valid income events have been applied to the custodian's client base to identify eligible recipients, the next stage of the process is to calculate the value of any reclaim. This is probably the simplest part of the process, being a straightforward calculation. It is also the most expensive to maintain. However, this calculation is made, it is based on information about the client's status, the income event and the rates of withholding and treaty between the two countries concerned. Of course, from a custodian's viewpoint the set of permutations is limited to the scale and cope of his client base and their portfolio spread. Even so, the cost of researching and maintaining such information sources is not small. For those custodians employing third-party software or outsourcing solutions, the information is often provided as part of the product or service offering and thus the cost and effort are spread across the supplier's entire client base for the most part. The risk in the process is clearly that the calculation may be incorrect. If the reclaim process is entirely internal, the liability will end internally. If there is an external element, say the provision of tax data, then liability may be attributable elsewhere depending on what and where the error was. A tax authority is likely to merely reject the reclaim as incorrect, after which it can be re-submitted in correct form, unless during the process, it crosses the Statute of Limitations. In most circumstances, this will be a rare event.

Filling in Forms

So, now we have a valid event, an eligible client with correct information and a correct calculation of the recoverable. The next stage is completing the tax reclaim form. These forms are relatively simple but appear very complex, are often multi-part and usually, but not always are at least double language—the local language and English. Forms are completed either manually or electronically. Most custodians with internal solutions are still filling forms in manually. Conversely, those employing third-party solutions either software or outsourcing, are almost always able to complete forms electronically and automatically. From a risk perspective, one would assume that manual completion is more risk prone than electronic. On the assumption that the electronic data is somehow more likely to be accurate than the manual, this is true. Compliance officers should risk assess the manual to electronic interface to establish the reality of this in practice. Either way, if the form, once completed is incorrect in the smallest degree, it is likely to be ultimately rejected.

Getting Local Tax Authority Approval

Having got this far in the process, the foreign tax authority is still not able to receive the reclaim forms. First, the forms must be sent to the local tax office of the claimant. Here, the tax office is asked to verify that the person named on the form as the claimant is indeed a resident of the local country concerned. There is little risk here, other than the usual loss of forms in the post or tardiness by the local authority to verify, stamp and return the forms to the custodian. From a protective position, the custodian should of course have retained copies of all documentation sent, so that the reclaim can be re-created if it's lost.

Filing to Foreign Tax Authorities

As has been said elsewhere, tax authorities themselves have something of a dilemma to cope with. Their primary function is to deal with tax affairs and the structure of withholding tax regimes. However, the existence of Statutes of Limitations also gives them access to an income source from those investors who fail to make reclaim submissions on time or make inaccurate reclaims that are not subsequently re-filed. A smaller proportion is accounted for by investors whose proof of domicile or other documentation is found to be invalid for the date of the income, in which case a withholding agent if he's aware of such a lapse, must withhold at a higher rate.

As can be imagined from the relative amounts of over-withheld tax reclaimed, various countries around the world benefit from these failures to a very substantial degree.

While quality assurance would of course be a natural element of any claim for the return of over-withheld tax, it is known that many tax authorities are particularly strict when it comes to assessing the validity of tax reclaims. Its therefore incumbent on the custodian to ensure that all the documentation provided, including the tax reclaim itself, is accurate and valid as of the date of the income event. This can affect relief at source regimes just as much as reclaim regimes. The US tax authorities require, as part of their QI Agreements, that if a QI is relying on a Form W-8BEN to self-certify its beneficial owner for treaty rate benefits, that W-8BEN must have been valid on the date that the income was received. The problem for custodians is that W-8BENs are valid for three years after the year in which they were signed. This means a major administration operation consisting of cross-checking each income event for an investor as it occurs with the validity dates for the supporting documentation. Similarly in jurisdictions such as Spain, Certificates of Domicile must be lodged every 6 months to be able to claim benefits. In other jurisdictions, fresh supporting documentation must be filed each time a reclaim is made. While this poses obvious problems for custodians, who have the potential for automation within their grasp or the ability to employ staff to do the job manually, tax authorities receiving this mountain of documentation from all over the world sometimes have difficulty managing rapid funds turnarounds. Some tax authorities are however recognising that automation is good for business. Rapid return of funds gives investors greater assurance and makes them more prepared to invest.

The Role of Sub Custodians

Many of the global custodians, those largest custodial banks in the world, access local markets by appointing sub-custodians rather than setting up operations of their own in each jurisdiction. This is the same effect as having a "specialist country desk".

Chasing for Payment

This is one of the critical areas which is predominantly manual. Failure to perform it can significantly lengthen time to recoup funds. Many custodians have "country desks" which are staffed by people who know not only the language of the country they specialise in, but also the procedures and the people involved in the process. This is raised as a key benchmark. The length of time taken to recoup funds for each market is a standard benchmark which assumes no chasing of refunds after the tax reclaim has been submitted. There are therefore significant opportunities for custodians to demonstrate how their investment in people and systems can improve on this factor.

Refund Payments

At the end of the process, a tax authority will pay out refunds to the person authorised to receive them. In the case of reclaims where the investor had to sign the form i.e., no power of attorney, there will usually be a cheque in the name of the claimant. However, a substantial number of claims are filed by custodians or third-party specialists on behalf of investors. This often leads to bulk refunds being issued.

When these are made to third-party specialists, the receiving firm will have to identify whether any one specific claim has been paid. This usually means that when the claims are filed, each line item on a claim form is given an identification reference number and the tax authority is asked to quote this when making payments. That doesn't always happen so when that happens, the receiver must reconcile the bilk payment against all the claims they've made to that tax authority. The other reason this is important is because most third parties charge based on a percentage of funds received. They receive the whole refund from the tax authority, usually in an in-country bank account. They will then deduct their fee and transfer the net into their client's bank account.

It is not unknown for tax authorities to over-pay refunds which makes reconciliation of bulk payments more difficult and it is notoriously difficult to send money back to them for payments not related to a refund.

As you might expect, tax authorities are starting to move to electronic payments, but many still issue paper cheques.

So, the basic reclaim procedure has elements:

1. Pre-Reclaim Activity
   a. Notification of overwithholding
   b. Receipt and management of documentary evidence
   c. Establishing eligibility and validity
   d. Acquisition and maintenance of a stock of tax reclaim forms
2. Reclaim Process
   a. Completion and submission of standard tax forms
      i. To local authorities
      ii. To foreign sub-custodians (if applicable) or
      iii. To foreign authorities
   b. Chasing for payment
3. Post Reclaim Activity

Crediting Client Accounts

Variations to the basic process take two primary forms. The first is a variation by instrument type, and the second by market. The latter is more extensive than the former simply because there are more markets involved and of course, the political influences on those markets make variations more likely.

Of particular note, in terms of income type variations, is the process of Depositary Receipts. Depositary Receipts are instruments that are often used to enable residents of a country who would otherwise be prohibited from owning shares in foreign companies, to do so. This doesn't stop anyone else from purchasing DRs. The Depositary Receipt is denominated in the currency of the resident's country. So for example, an American Depositary Receipt (ADR) is denominated in US dollars. The depositary receipt represents several underlying shares in a foreign (in this example non-US) company. From a withholding tax perspective, the variation to the process is that, for American Depositary Receipts, the tax reclaim, if any, must be processed through the sponsor/issuer for example Citibank, JP Morgan, Deutsche Bank and Mellon ADR issues must go through them. The DTC, which is described in more detail elsewhere, has processes that support the underlying banks that sponsor and promote these issues.

There are several markets that have variations in procedure which can have a marked effect on the ability of a custodian to deliver good results.

Italy, for instance, is renowned for taking sometimes up to ten years to make tax refund payments, mainly because of the way in which it manages approvals and budgeting in the reclaim process.

Australia has dividends that can be "franked" or unfranked" which affects the availability of a tax reclaim or relief at source. The process is described here to show the type of effect and the type of complexity that custodians must deal with on an everyday basis. While we're on the subject of Australia, this serves as a useful point at which to highlight the application of withholding tax to other forms of income than dividends, which make up most of the custodial work.

The Australian Tax Authority withholds over $1.43Bn of tax from non-resident aliens. Of this, the following income types are represented:

- Interest 39%
- Dividends 22%
- Royalties 25%

The Tax Office ("ATO") will provide Certificates of Payment to non-residents whose Australian-sourced income is subject to interest, dividend or royalty withholding tax.

A Certificate of Payment is a document issued by the ATO to non-residents (whose Australian sourced income is subject to Australian non-resident interest, dividend or royalty withholding tax) who require proof of payment to comply with their resident country's taxation requirements.

A Certificate of Payment will only be verified for those payees whose country of residence has a comprehensive double taxation agreement with Australia.

The ATO will issue one Certificate of Payment per payee, per year, for each type of withholding tax. That is, only one Certificate of Payment will be issued for each total annual amount withheld for interest, dividend or royalty withholding tax.

Payers, in other words, custodians, request a Certificate of Payment for their payees, at the end of the financial year of the country requiring the Certificate of Payment. Most of the countries that have a double tax agreement with Australia have a financial year ending 31 December.

Before a custodian can ask the ATO for a Certificate of Payment for a payee, he must first obtain a request for a Certificate of Payment from the payee, the investor, for each year that a Certificate of Payment is required.

The next step, for the custodian, is to gather the following information:

1. The country of residence of the payee who requires a Certificate of Payment
2. The start and end dates of the financial year of that country
3. The name of the payee, and
4. The type of withholding tax applied. That is, was the amount withheld for interest, dividend or royalty withholding tax?

The custodian must also gather the transaction details for the financial year specified, including:

1. Each amount subject to withholding tax by the payee
2. The total annual amount subject to withholding tax by the payee
3. Each amount withheld and paid to the ATO
4. The total amount paid to the ATO, and
5. The date each amount was paid to the ATO.

Franked dividends are payments made to shareholders or to holders of non-share equity interests on which the company has already paid tax.

Unfranked dividends have had no Australian company tax paid on them before they are paid to shareholders or to holders of non-share equity interests. If the dividend is unfranked, there is no imputation credit.

From 1 July 2001, certain interests which are not shares began to be treated in a similar way to shares for tax law purposes. These interests are called 'non-share equity interests'.

A dividend statement is sent to shareholders and to holders of non-share equity interests by companies to advise the dividend amounts and whether they are franked or unfranked, the amount of imputation credit and TFN amounts withheld (if any).

A distribution statement (also called a taxation statement) is sent to investors in managed funds or unit trusts. The statement can include unfranked dividends, franked dividends, tax file number amounts withheld and imputation credits.

In Thailand, the Nominee structure here means that Thai beneficial owners can make their investments through nominee vehicles thus hiding their identity behind the nominee. This, as we will see, is increasingly coming under scrutiny by tax authorities, particularly those that are developing advanced relief at source regimes where transparency to the beneficial owner is one of the building blocks.

Singapore and Malaysia share a similarity with the UK because they have a system that permits an "imputation tax credit". This means that if there is withholding in one country at say 30% and the recipient in the UK is a 40% taxpayer, then, as far as his accounting goes, he can claim an imputation credit, effectively saying that he has already paid 30% and is therefore liable only for the difference, 10%. While this is all very well and good, one thing comes about. The imputation credit leaves the actual cash in the hands of the foreign tax authority, so the local tax authority, while giving the benefit of the tax already withheld to the beneficial owner, is not in possession of the tax concerned. This may be of more interest to the patriots who would prefer that if any tax is withheld, at least it should be their government that gets it and not some other foreign government. These are just a few examples and, as with most things, by the time this book is read, some of these areas may have changed.

So, in this chapter we have learnt about the way in which tax reclaims are dealt with, and some ideas on best practice, but most of all, the reader is probably more aware than ever before now, just how complex an activity tax reclaims are. Indeed, there should be significant respect for the expertise of tax reclaimers generally. In the last part of the chapter, we looked at some of the variants of the basic pattern. But to be honest, these vary both in time and in scale. It's much more important to understand the basic process and particularly the risks associated with it, than it is to apply knowledge of variations to your own circumstance. It does raise the question for investors that they should be aware of the level and depth of country-specific knowledge that is available from their custodian. This is not just about a simple form-filling exercise.

9

Reporting

In this chapter I will explore the new field of tax reporting. Cross-border investment withholding tax has, historically, not been the subject of reporting. Once a tax reclaim or claim of relief had been granted, there was no further action needed by intermediary or investor. The advent of anti-tax evasion regulations has had an effect on this and begun a trend towards reporting of tax relief and tax reclaim reporting so that tax authorities can effectively "join the dots". The US began this with 1042-S reporting and is generally included as a concept in the TRACE framework as well as the EU Code of Conduct. Financial institutions spend enormous resources gathering and checking data for reporting to their domestic and now foreign tax authorities. This raises important questions about legality of collection and data protection, both of which will be explored in this chapter.

One of the most curious things about cross-border withholding tax is the relative absence of oversight through reporting. If you are taxed on a Swiss dividend and you claim those funds overwithheld back, that's the end of it. There is no reporting component that will be a check or balance on the process. However, as we move from a post pay date tax processing world to relief at source world, financial institutions become an integral part of the process. Where generally a standard post pay date refund claim can be filed directly to a tax authority, tax relief at source can only be granted by a financial institution authorised to do so by a tax administration. This is the foundation of the US and OECD tax relief frameworks.

R. K. McGill, *Cross-Border Investment Withholding Tax*, Finance and Capital Markets Series,
https://doi.org/10.1007/978-3-031-32785-8_9

The US framework allows for pooled reporting where the withholding agent is a qualified intermediary. Non-qualified intermediaries are not trusted, so reporting is at beneficial owner level. This presents some problems, not least of which is data protection. These reports are information returns. They contain personally identifiable Information ("PII") of data subjects. For all European and UK-based NQIs, the GDPR data protection regime dictates what can and cannot be done with PII. In addition, the transfer of data is dependent on whether the source jurisdiction considers the US to be. Safe jurisdiction for data protection. The problem is that data protection laws are fragmented in the US between federal, state and municipality. The US used to have a framework called Safe Harbor under which transfers could be allowed to be registered. The Safe Harbor fell in 2016 and was replaced with the Privacy Shield. The Privacy Shield fell under legal scrutiny and so, at present, there is no legal basis of equivalence between the US and the UK or EU. In the UK, firms would have to perform a Transfer Risk Assessment ("TRA") before they could take on the role of data processor for an NQI.

Now, this is only an issue because the US regulations require reporting by non-US financial institutions across national boundaries. In many markets, the withholding agent is a sub-custodian in the same jurisdiction as the Issuer and the withholding agent. So, under EU rules, there is no transfer across boundaries.

The US framework also has a reporting obligation under anti-tax evasion principles—FATCA. FATCA reporting is different, albeit not less controversial, because it requires any non-US financial institution that operates accounts for Americans, to report said accounts to the IRS annually. The basis of this reporting is a finding by the IRS that wealthy Americans have found ways to hide their taxable assets outside the US and thus evade US taxes. This is controversial for several reasons.

First, the US applies citizenship by birth and taxes the global income of its citizens based on that citizenship. The only other country to apply citizenship-based taxation is Eritrea, a very small elite club indeed. Every other country applies residency-based taxation. The problem is that the US has some complex rules surrounding citizenship that leads to many people being tripped up by these rules and being unknowingly "Accidental Americans[1]". The FATCA reporting rules are underpinned by complex due diligence obligations, so most financial institutions, from 2014 onwards have

[1] https://en.wikipedia.org/wiki/accidental_american.

chosen not to allow Americans, accidental or otherwise, to have accounts. It has also led to a record number of US citizens renouncing their citizenship simply so that they can open a bank account.

The reporting itself is clearly influenced by the purpose. The prior 1042-S reporting discussed, was focused on taxation of US-sourced income paid to non-US recipients. FATCA is more interested in the value of the account of US persons. So, for example, to reduce the imposition on financial institutions, FATCA allows an exemption from due diligence and reporting for account holders that are US but have an end-of-year aggregated balance in their accounts of less than $50,000. FATCA reporting also wants to catch any financial firm that is not meetings its due diligence obligations (non-participating FFI) and any account holder that effuses to give their FATCA status of their financial institution (recalcitrant). So, recalcitrant account holders are also reported in FATCA even though they are probably not American. The US is taking a risk-averse approach to tax evasion.

Now these cohorts of Accidental Americans, recalcitrant account holders and non-participating financial institutions may well have US investments that distribute FDAP income such as dividends or interest. This is where the relevance to withholding tax occurs because if these accounts receive income, that income must be reported on forms 1042-S and a tax penalty of 30% applied. So, from a reporting perspective, its entirely possible that n account holder could be penalised under FATCA with a 30% withholding, reported under FATCA as an American, yet also have their income reported under the 1042-S reporting rules.

What is clear is that reporting is not as simple as it might sound. Other jurisdictions are moving towards similar systems. Finland requires Authorised Intermediaries to report at beneficial owner level when tax relief at source is applied. This is also electronic, as is the US system in both 1042-S and FATCA.

The US is also changing its reporting systems with upgraded identification and security. So, if you are a non-US firm trying to report for tax year 2022 in 2023, you'll need an Employer Identification Number ("EIN"), a transmitter Control Code ("TCC") a verified ID.me account and a registration at the IRS Modernised efile portal ("MeF") as well as a registration at the underlying Filing Information Returns Electronically ("FIRE" portal). We expect major problems with their systems in 2023–2025 simply because they've made their systems too complex.

Other jurisdictions have reporting requirements, but these are usually for domestic withholding agents acting as sub-custodians. They will generally have the purpose of allowing a tax administration to reconcile tax receipts to the withholding agents. Since the withholding agents assume strict liability for the tax they withhold, it is up to them to have systems and records that can account for any individual transaction on which tax was withheld.

10

Governance and Enforcement

As tax relief becomes the predominant tax processing model for cross-border investment, which effectively transfers tax withholding and reporting obligations from a tax authority to a financial institution), tax authorities increasingly want some level of oversight and enforcement capability. This chapter looks at how tax administrations require the appointment of a Responsible Officer to oversee specific compliance to their regulations, annual reporting, auditing, certifications and penalties —all tools of governance that tax administrations are starting to impose to ensure proper compliance.

It's one thing to have law, treaties and regulation to provide for the opportunity to avoid double taxation or, indeed, double non-taxation. However, tax administrations are increasingly sensitive to the fact that these frameworks are becoming so complex that investors and, in some cases, financial institutions, can find ways around them for their own benefit. In some cases, the benefit is directly financial. In others, it's the avoidance of cost or effort that would otherwise have to be employed.

The most regulated market in this respect is the US with its qualified intermediary program. Following close behind is the OECD TRACE Implementation Protocol that provides the opportunity, but not the mandate of enforcement for those jurisdictions adopting the framework.

Exhibit 10.1 shows how the US withholding tax system integrates operational obligations with governance obligations. The essence of the US system is three cycles, the contractual cycle is six years long with the most recent QI

R. K. McGill, *Cross-Border Investment Withholding Tax*, Finance and Capital Markets Series,
https://doi.org/10.1007/978-3-031-32785-8_10

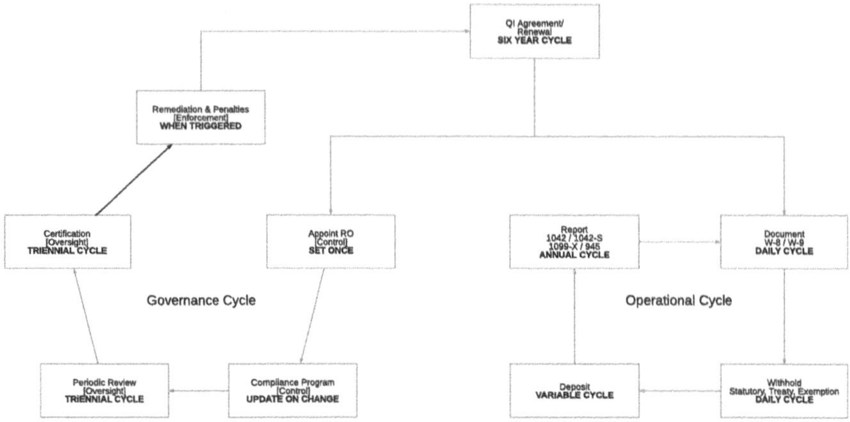

Exhibit 10.1 Governance and Enforcement cycle of the US market

contract being issued as Revenue Procedure 2022–2043. This is the fourth version of the contract, the earlier versions being Revenue Procedure 2000–2012, Revenue Procedure 2014–2039, Revenue Procedure 2017–2015. So, it can't be said that this governance and enforcement framework for withholding tax is not mature and tested.

This contract establishes the operational cycle under which a qualified intermediary must document its clients, withhold the correct amount of tax based on that documentation (and tests of its validity), deposit tax with the US Treasury and submit information returns and a US tax return each year.

The contract also defines certain terms e.g., under-withholding and over-withholding, material failures and events of default together with procedures for disclosure to the IRS if these events occur (and they all too frequently do).

The other key characteristic of the non-operational elements of the QI framework is the requirement for QIs to make certifications of compliance to the IRS every three years. These are called "certification periods". There are two types of certifications (i) certification of effective internal controls and (ii) a qualified certification. Each certification requires a QI to update the factual information it provided to the IRS when it first applied for QI status. This gives the IRS a level of oversight over the financial institution with whom it has these contractual obligations.

As if that weren't enough, the QI contract also requires the financial firm to appoint a responsible officer ("RO") to make sure that the contract terms are adhered to. Two of the primary obligations of an RO, in contract, are to have a written compliance program that explains how the firm will operationally meet its contractual obligations. The second is a requirement for the RO to have an independent, competent person review conducted using one of three years in each certification period, to make sure that the firm is meeting its obligations. This is called a Periodic Review.

Once these governance and oversight components are in place, the IRS can use the definitions of material failure and events of default to create processes to control the quality of a qualified intermediary's conduct of withholding tax operations.

There are some rules that apply to mitigate the level of work that a QI needs to do. This is designed to make sure that the workload on smaller firms is not disproportionate to the benefits of QI status. So, for example, a small QI with gross receipts of US-sourced FDAP income less than $5 million, can apply for a waiver of the Periodic Review obligation and the IRS can counter-propose alternatives such as a correspondence review. I have rarely seen a Periodic Review cost less than $60,000. So, while they only occur twice in six years, they are still something to be budgeted and planned for. The Periodic Review itself is supposed to be of all accounts in any given year, that received US-sourced income. The IRS has provided some relief inasmuch as, if the number of accounts to be reviewed is impractical, then a sampling method can be used instead, and the IRS graciously provides a Safe Harbor Sampling Methodology in one of the Annexes to the QI Agreement. So, if a firm does not qualify for a waiver, it can limit the effort to sample of its accounts.

Now, clearly, everyone hopes that their firm will get everything right. Sadly, in my experience, this is rarely the case. The most common approach among financial institutions is to the absolute minimum that they can get away with. This leads to some bizarre situations that can lead to the enforcement component of governance being used. Without naming names, here are the top failures we see.

1. Using the wrong form to certify your firm's status to another financial institution.

   This happens a lot more than you would think. Financial institutions usually certify their status to their counterparties with a form W-8IMY. However, we see a number that use the W-8BEN-E instead. The problem is that the W-8BEN-E is, like all the other forms in the W-8 series, signed under penalty of perjury. So, providing the wrong form places the signer in significant legal jeopardy. The only occasion that a financial firm should use a W-8BEN-E is if the assets in the account that the form refers to are the proprietary assets of the firm itself and not those of its clients. The causes of this vary. Some fill out the form because they were told to by their counterparty. This is particularly egregious because of the effect. It simplifies the counterparty's reporting obligations, and it means that the firm itself cannot submit reports to the IRS. Others fill out the form inadvertently due to a lack of knowledge or misinterpretation. As the saying goes "ignorantia juris non excusat". Ignorance of the law is no excuse.

2. Applying a 30% withholding even when clients have correctly claimed a lower rate.
   This is a common response, even though one of the benefits of QI status is to be able to provide tax treaty benefits to clients that are eligible. The reason is usually that it costs money to set up the tax rate pool omnibus accounts with a counterparty and effort to make sure that the result of W-8 validation is the correct placement of US assets into those tax rate pool accounts. It's easier just to operate. Single omnibus account and have everything taxed at a single rate. The problem is that, if the firm is in possession of a valid W-8 with a treaty claim, the correct tax rate will be the relevant treaty rate. A blanket 30% will be overwithholding which is a material failure of the QI agreement. In addition, even with the right account structures, the forms that create the entitlement are only valid for three years or earlier if there is a material change in circumstances. In the absence of valid documentation on pay date, the correct tax rate reverts to the 30% statutory rate. So, if a change gets missed and the assets are not moved to the correct account until a new valid form is received, there will be under-withholding. This is a more serious issue than overwithholding and, if done on a systematic basis, would be an event of default rather than a material failure.
3. Filing information returns and/or tax returns late
   So, as we've seen, there are a number of ways things can go wrong ranging from accidental to deliberate. The third most common failure that will lead to enforcement action is a failure to meet a deadline. Most firms are familiar with this concept and have plans in place to make sure that their obligations are met on time. In the case of the US, for qualified intermediaries that receive US-sourced income and for non-qualified intermediaries that receive US-sourced income but do not disclose their clients to a qualified intermediary, these types of firms must submit information returns on forms 1042-S by March 15th each year and a US tax return on form 1042 by the same date.

US information reporting, as it is generally called, is the most common cause of actual financial penalties. There are a number of different ones that can apply and even the late filing penalties vary depending on how late the submission is.

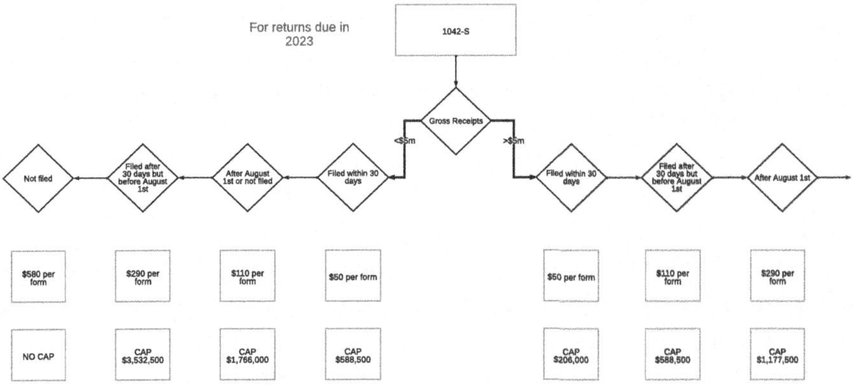

Exhibit 10.2 US reporting penalties

Exhibit 10.2 shows how this works. Most firms use the right-hand portion of this diagram as they have gross receipts of more than $5 million. A qualified intermediary generally has little exposure because its reporting is pooled by income type. So typically a QI might have 20 forms to file. The risk and exposure are for non-qualified intermediaries because they cannot pool their reporting: (i) they must report each beneficial owner per income type and per withholding agent and (ii) they must provide a copy of the 1042-S to the beneficial owner within 30 days. So, if an NQI has 1000 clients receiving dividends and portfolio interest in a tax year through one withholding agent, that will mean they must submit a data file to the IRS by March 15th of the following year with 2000 data lines and provide a copy of each to the beneficial owners. That's 4000 documents with a. deadline.

As you can see from Exhibit 10.2, failure to file by the deadline of March 15th exposes this NQI to a $50 per form penalty. If they submit their file within thirty days, the fine they will receive will be $200,000. If they fail to file within 30 days but do file before August 1st, their penalty will be $110 per form or $440,000. If they miss the August 1st deadline, when they eventually file, the penalty will be $290 per form or $1,160,000. When firms are presented with this scenario, they usually ask "but how will the IRS be able to catch us?". The answer is simple. The reporting system is electronic and cascade in nature. The firm above in the payment chain to a QI or NQI will report the payments it made to that QI or NQI to the IRS in their 1042-S submission. So, the IRS has all the information it needs (i) to know what any financial institution paid to any other financial institution including what tax was withheld and (ii) whether to expect information returns and a tax return from that lower level institution.

So, overall, there are a number of different enforcement actions that can be taken against a financial institution if it fails to meet its regulatory obligations. Under-withholding is the most serious, but outside of that, failure to meet other obligations such as compliance obligations, can lead to censure or loss of status. In the case of the US, there are around 250 QI each year that either revoke their QI agreement or are kicked out of the system for compliance failures.

The OECD TRACE IP framework provides opportunities for tax administrations to create similar governance and enforcement frameworks but, unlike the US system, these are voluntary. Finland, for example, has not adopted the requirement for a QI agreement or even a Periodic Review, but it does mandate reporting obligations.

Finally, many of these withholding tax regulatory frameworks take, as their basis, the obligation to Know Your Customer ("KYC") imposed by domestic regulators. In many cases cross-border regulation leverages this domestic obligation to make sure that, if a firm fails to meet its cross-border obligations, it's the domestic regulator that will likely take action. This is, for example, the case with US anti-tax evasion regulations ("FATCA") that allow for substantial non-compliance to be reported by the US to any of the over 100 jurisdictions with whom it has an inter-governmental agreement ("IGA"). This includes the UK which have published penalty rates for late reporting under both the FATCA and Common Reporting Standard ("CRS") frameworks.

Part III

Practical Implementations

11

United States of America

This chapter describes and updates the US withholding tax regime characterised as the Qualified Intermediary Program. The US market represents 55.9% of all global securities by value. Significant updates include new form revisions, impending new Chapter 1 Section 871(m) regulations coming into force in January 2023. The chapter describes the operational processes of documentation, withholding, depositing of tax and reporting together with the governance cycle of periodic reviews and certifications. The chapter will also highlight common problems that lead to penalties.

The US is the largest securities market in the world by a large margin. In fact, the US represents 55.9% of global stock market value. It is therefore difficult for any financial institution to avoid the US in its market offering to clients. This means that the US withholding tax system is very difficult to commercially avoid (Exhibit 11.1).

The US is a combination jurisdiction. This means that it operates a primary tax relief at source mechanism, but also has a quick refund model as well as the traditional standard refund process. Both the EU and the OECD TRACE framework were built on the basic principles of the US system.

In the US system, the tax administration, the US Internal Revenue Service (IRS) permits non-US financial institutions to sign a commercial contract allowing the financial institution to be an appointed and qualified withholding agent—a Qualified Intermediary or "QI". There is no formal signing process. The agreement itself is available as a Revenue Procedure.

R. K. McGill, *Cross-Border Investment Withholding Tax*, Finance and Capital Markets Series,
https://doi.org/10.1007/978-3-031-32785-8_11

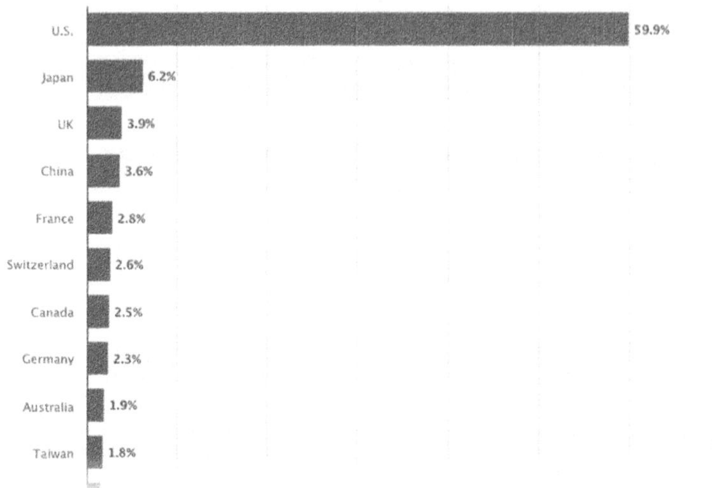

Exhibit 11.1 Proportion of global equity by market (*Source* Statista.com)

There have been four QI Agreements. The first was issued in 2001 as Revenue Procedure 2000–2012. The second was Revenue Procedure 2014–2039, issued shortly after FATCA was implemented. The third was Revenue Procedure 2017–2015 and the latest, Revenue Procedure 2022–43, became effective on January 1, 2023.

The US framework essentially splits all non-US financial institutions into one of two categories—(i) those that have signed a QI agreement and (ii) those that have not—so-called "non-qualified intermediaries". By default, any financial institution that has not signed a QI agreement, is an NQI.

There are currently around 5000 QIs globally. The QI Agreement is a six year contract that obligates the financial institution to undertake certain tasks in an operational cycle—documentation of clients, withholding of tax, depositing of tax to the US Treasury and reporting to the IRS. In return, QIs are the only non-US financial institutions outside the US that can grant tax treaty benefits to account holders.

The QI Agreement brings together several sections or "Chapters" of the US Internal Revenue Code ("IRC"). These are:

Chapter 1 Section 871(m) deals with a financial institution's obligation to determine whether a transaction is a Dividend Equivalent Payment ("DEP") or an Equity Linked Instrument ("ELI") that represents a US withholdable transaction due to its underlying exposure to US securities.

Chapter 3 Section 1441 deals with the due diligence, tax withholding, tax depositing and reporting of US Sourced FDAP[1] income (and DEPs) paid to non-US recipients and the application of exemption from withholding on portfolio interest paid to non-US recipients.
Chapter 3 Sections 1446(a) and (f) deal with the taxation of income paid to partners or realised gains by a transferor relating to publicly traded partnerships where such amounts are paid to non-US persons.
Chapter 4 Section 1471 deals with anti-tax evasion by US Persons including penalty withholding on US-sourced FDAP income (including DEPs) with respect to recalcitrant account holders and non-participating FFIs. This is an overlap (and addition) to a firm's general exposure to FATCA via domestic law (in the case of an IGA[2] jurisdiction) or an FFI[3] Agreement in the case of a non-IGA jurisdiction. Chapter 4 is a negative proof system. All FFIs must document the Chapter 4 status of all customers, irrespective of whether they receive US source income or not, to determine Chapter 4 status and reportability of account holders.
Chapter 31 Section 3406 deals with backup withholding and reporting of US (or presumed US) recipients of US-sourced FDAP income.
Chapter 61 Section 6041, 6042, 6045, 6049 and 6050N deal with the identification and reporting of US non-exempt recipients on forms 1099-X.

These Chapters basically identify all those types of US-sourced income that is FDAP in nature i.e., being fixed, determinable, annual or periodic. Th components of tax relief at source for the US market have two "cycles", the operational and the governance cycle. The operational cycle consists of documentation, withholding, depositing and reporting. The governance cycle consists of Responsible 'officers, Compliance Program documentation Periodic Review and triennial certification as shown in Exhibit 11.2.

Documentation

The basic principle of the US tax system is the documentation of beneficial owners in order to determine whether they should be subject to US withholding tax and if so, at what rate. Unlike many other jurisdictions, the US allows the use of self-certifications of tax status to allow beneficial owners to certify their tax status and residency. These are called *withholding certificates* and there are different forms for different kinds of beneficial owner. W-8BEN is for individuals. W-8BEN-E is for entities such as corporations and certain

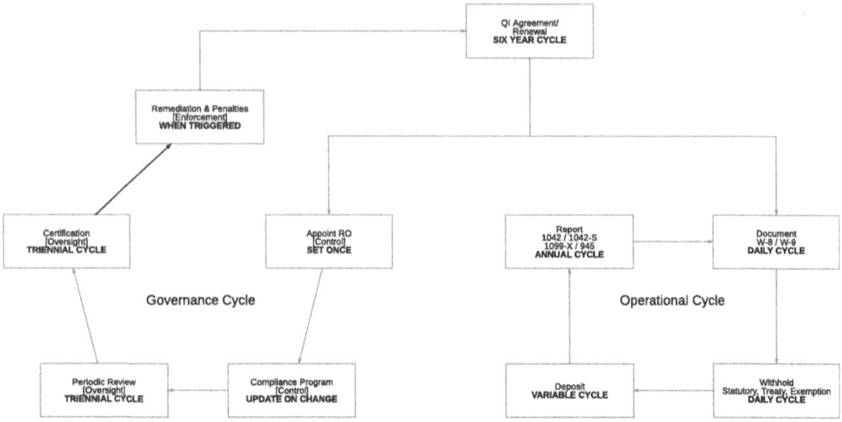

Exhibit 11.2 Cycles for tax relief at source (*Source* Author)

kinds of trust. W-8EXP is used by exempt entities and international organisations. W-8ECI is used by those who have income that is effectively connected with a US trade or business. W-8IMY is used by financial institutions. Finally, the form W-9 is used by US individuals and US entities. These forms are all signed under penalty of perjury and, apart from the W-9 and W-8IMY are valid for three years from the end of the year in which they are signed. Importantly for the tax relief component we are looking at, the W-8BEN and W-8BEN-E contain a claim of treaty benefits which, provided the financial institution validates the form correctly, can be relied upon by a QI to grant a lower rate of tax. For QIs the requirement is also to obtain documentation under approved KYC rules. In fact it is one of the eligibility criteria for a QI that they be subject to KYC rules that have been approved by the IRS. Essentially, any financial institution offering access to the US securities markets will need to document their client for Chapter 3 purposes so that they can allow that client to obtain tax treaty relief at source. Many firms take steps to guide their clients into which form they should be completing. I have seen Asian retail brokers with boxes of blank W-8BENs on their counter-tops and other firms that direct clients to specific forms. This practice may make it easier at an operational level, but, because there is a claim of treaty benefits and a perjury statement on the form, firms that engage in this guidance are effectively providing tax advice to their clients and almost certainly do not have the relevant authority to do so. A financial firm receiving one of the W-8 forms must conduct three tests (1) is the form valid on the face i.e., is the form complete, signed, dated and are the statements made consistent with each other (2) dos the information on the form match the information gathered under the firm's KYC regulations and (3) does the firm have any other "*reason to know*" or "*actual* knowledge" that the statements on the form are, or may be unreliable. Only when these three tests have been performed and documented with respect to each form, can the form be used as reliable for the reduction in US tax. In some cases, firms have developed or licenced a digital substitute form with an electronic signature to make the client experience easier. Over 50% of the W-8 forms we see are not fit for purpose because these tests have not been performed and the firms that use them are systemically underwithholding tax.

The forms used by entities are more complex and contain a limitation of benefits ("LOB") clause. Most US double tax treaties have an LOB clause that limits the degree to which a non-US entity can claim treaty benefits. The W-8BEN-E contains a selection of these and the representative signing he form, must select the correct reason why the LOB clauses do not apply. The LOB clauses have some connections to the OECD Base Erosion and Profit Shifting framework ("BEPS") designed to prevent an entity from moving profits around in order to get a lower tax rate ("treaty shopping"). Other LOB clauses relate to the structure of the entity and its owners which is a common feature in anti-tax evasion regulation.

Many clients of financial firm are not happy about these forms and sometimes refuse to provide them. The IRS has taken this into account with *presumption rules* that must be applied by a financial firm if a client does not provide requested documentation. These presumption rules apply for Chapters 3 and 4 of the US Internal Revenue Code. These rules are vigorously avoided by most banks because of the negative effect on the financial institution's compliance and on the client too.[1]

Each financial firm in a chain of payment of US-sourced FDAP income must also document itself to its upstream counterparty(ies) with a form W-8IMY. While this form does not contain a claim of treaty benefits, because the financial institution may be acting for many different beneficial owners, they can attach a withholding statement to the W-8IMY that provides their counterparty with instructions for how to withhold.

[1] https://link.springer.com/book/10.1007/978-3-030-23085-2.

Withholding

The US tax relief system also recognises that financial institutions generally comingle the assets of clients into omnibus accounts in which the upper-level financial institution has no knowledge of the account holders whose assets are comingled in the account.

So, when a US corporation, for example, distributes a dividend, it will do so by making a payment to an omnibus account. The owner of the omnibus account will then make a payment to its client which, if its another financial institution will also be to an omnibus account and so on through a chain of financial institutions each of which holds a record of the assets in an omnibus account.

This, of course, creates a problem, in that the US Issuer holds the strict liability for collecting the tax on such distributions i.e., it must have evidence on hand on the pay date that any portion of the assets in an omnibus account can be taxed at a lower treaty rate. This problem is solved by the US through the use of "withholding statements". A withholding statement is a document, often a spreadsheet or a table that identifies the tax rate to be applied to an omnibus account for a particular kind of income. These omnibus accounts are also known as "tax rate pool accounts" due to the fact that they are comingling assets of account holders that have the same categorisation for US tax purposes. Exhibit 11.3 shows how this typically works. In this example, each financial institution in the chain has three clients that each hold 300 shares in a US corporation. FI1 holds these shares in an omnibus account at FI2. FI2 comingles these assets with its own three clients into an omnibus account it holds at FI3. This continues until we reach the withholding agent appointed by the Issuer to distribute the dividend.

The withholding statements are underpinned by the concept of documentation. It's the documentation that results in a client's US assets being recorded in a given omnibus account. Each financial institution must document itself to its counterparty. So, this documentation principle applies not just to the customers of financial institutions, but also to and between the institutions themselves. In fact, the W-8IMY, which is the certification provided by one institution to another, is signed under penalty of perjury and that certification under penalty, also applies to the withholding statement.

Exhibit 11.4 shows how this comingling of assets occurs, on the left side of the diagram, while the right side shows the flow of documentation to support it. Now, most financial institutions can only apply one rate of tax for one kind of income per omnibus account. So, in this case, if a financial institution has a client that is not entitled to tax relief and must be taxed at the full 30% US

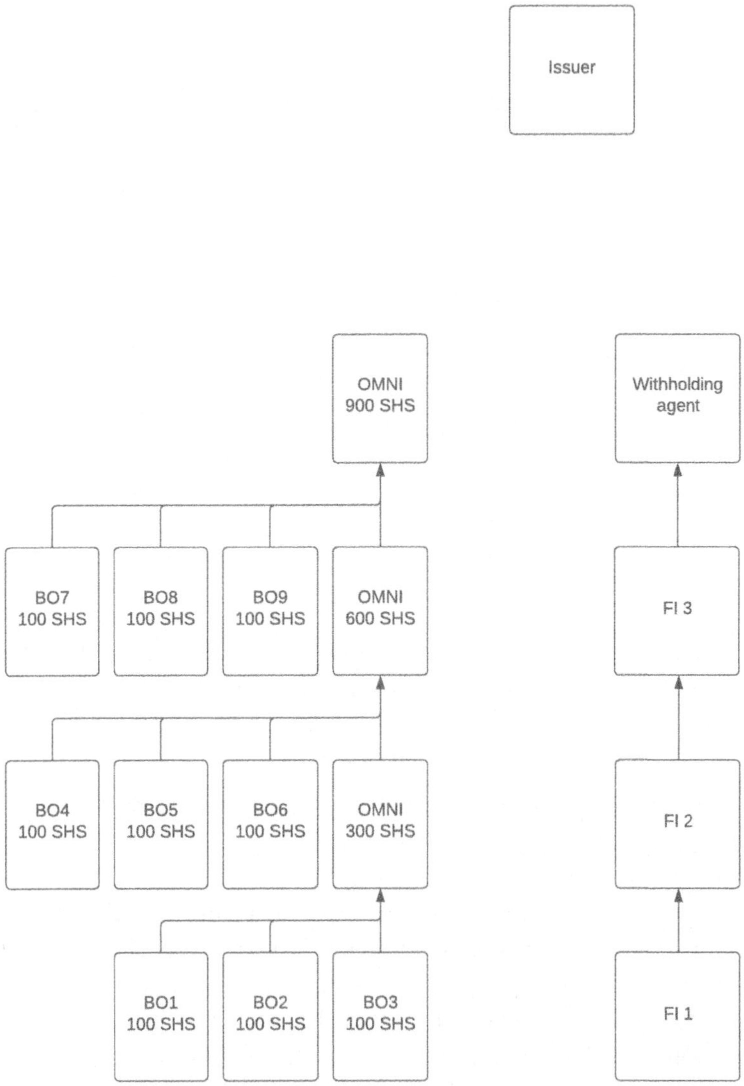

Exhibit 11.3 Use of omnibus accounts to comingle assets (*Source* Author)

tax rate, they would need a second omnibus account in which to place those assets, and a separate withholding statement for that account.

From a withholding tax perspective, as I have said, there are QIs and NQIs. In the above model, FIs 1, 2 and 3 are technically non-withholding, because the tax is actually withheld from the payment made by the withholding agent to FI3. As each payment is made down the chain, each financial institution can credit its client's account (including the omnibus account)

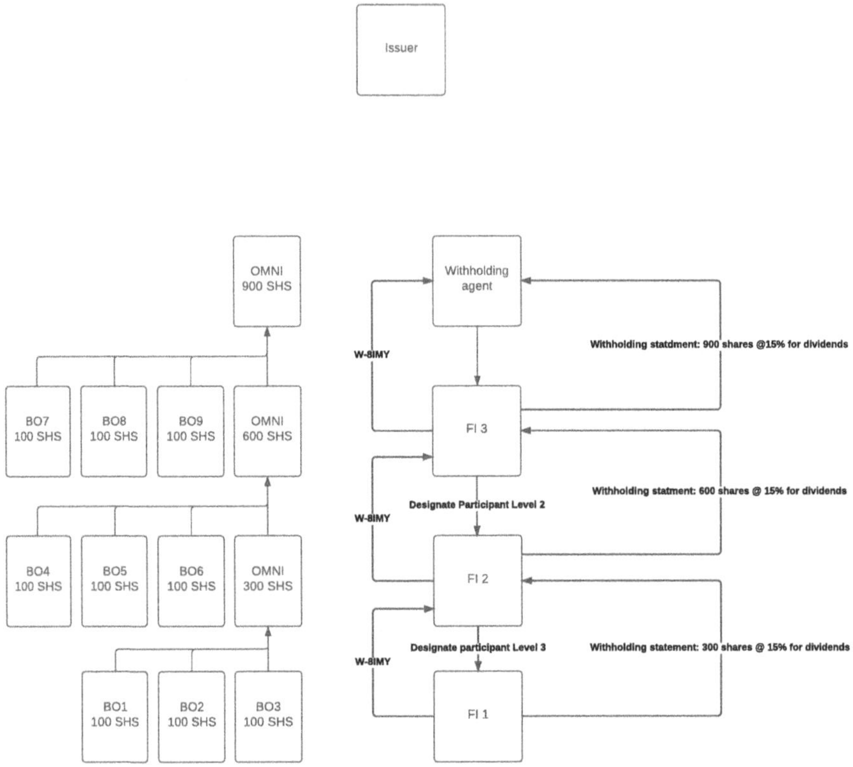

Exhibit 11.4 Use of withholding statements for US tax relief at source (*Source* Author)

with the correct net dividend payment because it can reconcile it to both the withholding statement and the documentation collected from the client.

The relationship between financial counterparties in the payment chain for US-sourced income is very important because it defines how each counterparty will act. The first component is the operating model. Qualified Intermediaries are allowed to pool their clients for the purpose of withholding and reporting so that no client information is disclosed. Non-qualified intermediaries can adopt disclosing or non-disclosing status, the former being the only way that an NQI can access lower double tax treaty rates for its clients. When applying for QI status, a firm will be asked whether they intend to be a withholding QI or a non-withholding QI. The difference is that a withholding QI will be paid gross by the counterparty above them in the payment chain and the withholding QI ("WQI") will be responsible for deducting the tax component from the payment and sending it to the US Treasury. A non-withholding QI must instruct their counterparty how to withhold using a withholding statement. A withholding QI typically operates a single omnibus account with its counterparty, because all payments are received gross. A non-withholding QI will typically operate a number of omnibus accounts into which it will place the securities assets of its clients based on the documentation it receives from them, including any claims of treaty benefits. The "rate pool" accounts comingle assets based on the tax rate for dividends. Other securities can be held in these accounts e.g., bonds and a withholding statement specifies the tax rate for each income type. The counterparty will then tax the income on any assets in a given account, based on the withholding statement.

Exhibit 11.5 also highlights that the W-8IMY certificate is account specific and that a QI does not always have to act as a QI. In this diagram the types of documentation are specified for each type of relationship. To express the possibilities the diagram shows a financial institution that is a QI. They operate three accounts at a counterparty. The first is a proprietary account where the bank is the beneficial owner so they document themselves with a W-8BEN-E. The second is an account where the firm has decided to act in the capacity of a QI because it is acting on behalf of its clients. The third account is an account where, for whatever reason, the firm has decided to act in the capacity of an NQI—for that account. On their W-8IMY, they will have to tell their counterparty whether they will disclose their clients or not. If they do, the counterparty will need to receive all the client documentation and subsequently submit 1042-S information returns to the IRS at the beneficial owner level. If they do not disclose, all the income will be taxed at the statutory rate of 30% and the firm itself will have the obligation to report its clients to the IRS. It is rare for a financial firm to act in different capacities with counterparties. The permutations of withholding and reporting obligations re just too complex for most firms o handle effectively.

Exhibit 11.6 shows how a withholding QI need only operate a single omnibus account to receive US-sourced income gross, and pay the Treasury. Some firms prefer the withholding QI model because it means they retain full control of the process. That said, there are some peculiarities of withholding QI status, not least in reporting. A withholding QI must report on a pooled basis, that's the good news. The bad news is that they must report the withholding in time slots based on when the tax liability arose and not when they paid the Treasury. This means a further 59 boxes on the 1042 tax return must be completed by a WQI, while a Non-Withholding QI does not have to do that.

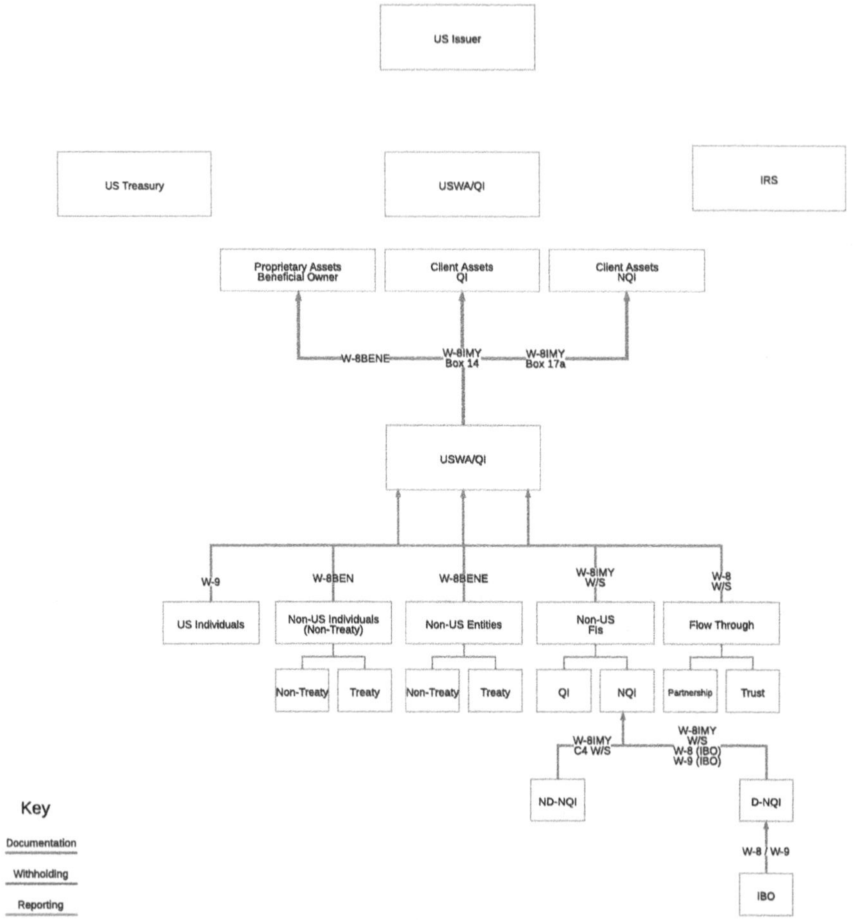

Exhibit 11.5 QI documentation model (*Source* Author)

Account number	Income type	Description	Tax rate (%)	Allocation (%)
XXXXXXXX	06	Dividends	0	100
XXXXXXXX	01	Portfolio Interest	0	100

The withholding statement for a withholding QI, as shown above, is very simple because the tax rate on all income types will be 0%.

Exhibit 11.7 demonstrates that a non-withholding QI operates rate pool accounts. The assets of clients are placed into the accounts based on their

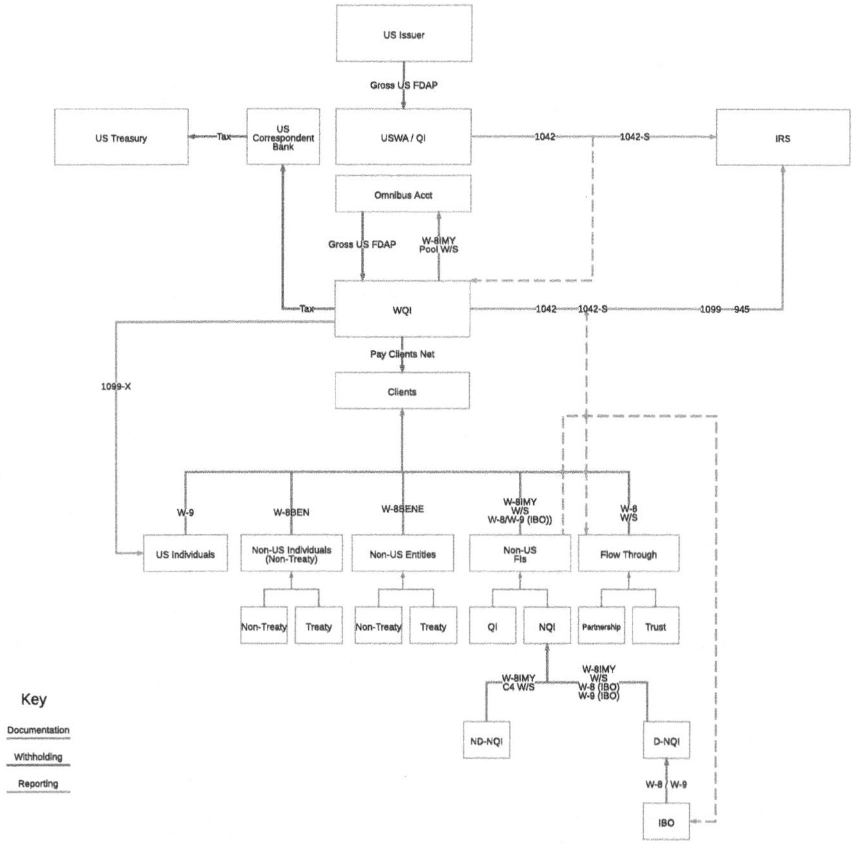

Exhibit 11.6 QI operating model—withholding (*Source* Author)

certifications on W-8 forms. The key feature of this model is its "fire and forget" from the QI's perspective.

Account number	Income type	Description	Tax rate (%)	Allocation (%)
12,345	06	Dividends	15	100
23,456	06	Dividends	30	100
12,345	01	Portfolio interest	0	100
23,456	01	Portfolio interest	0	100

The withholding statement that is presented with the W-8IMy is slightly more complex. In this simplified case, the QI operates two rate pool accounts 12,345 and 23,456. Account 12,345 contains the US assets of non-US clients that have documented themselves and claimed a treaty rate of 15%. Account 23,456 contains the US assets of non-US clients that either did not claim a

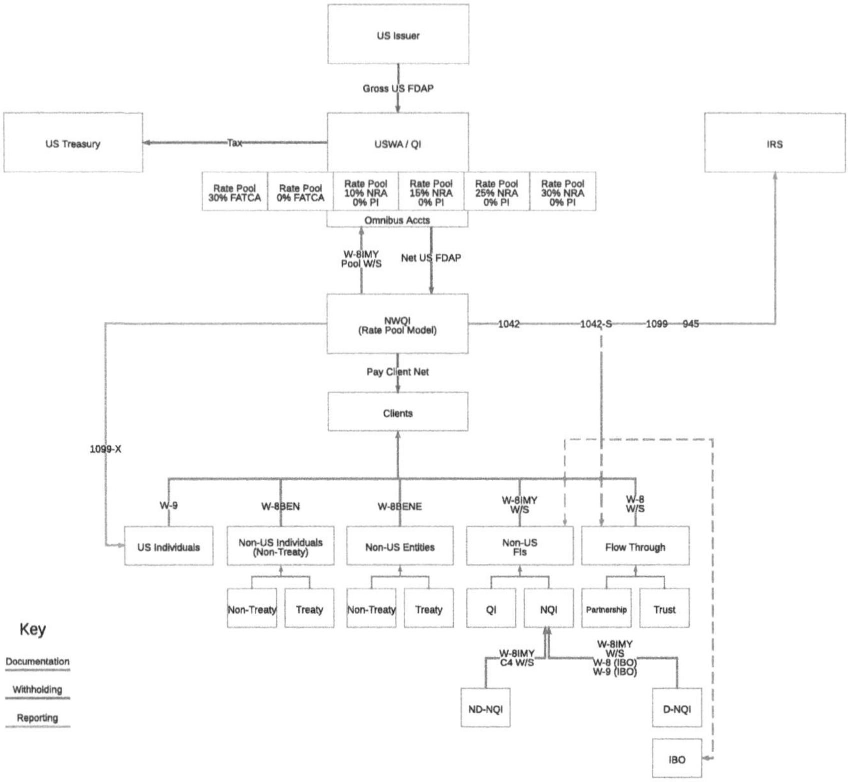

Exhibit 11.7 QI operating model—non-withholding—rate pool

treaty rate, did not provide a W-8 form or whose W-8 form had expired—all of which triggers a 30% withholding. In both accounts any corporate or government bonds are taxed at 0% because these accounts only hold the assets of non-US clients. The US has an exemption—the portfolio interest exemption that exempts this income type from withholding *as long as the recipient is not a US person.* A separate omnibus tax rate pool account would be needed for any additional tax rates that should be applied. The US has several tax rates applicable to dividends—10, 15 and 25% being the most common.

Exhibit 11.8 demonstrates the rarest operating model that combines a single omnibus account with a withholding rate pool statement. This means that the QI must instruct its counterparty on how to withhold for each income event. In order to do so, the downstream counterparty will need to be informed on an event by event basis of impending payments. For each record date, the QI will need to prepare a pooled withholding statement for that specific payment. These information flows are most frequently conducted using SWIFT messages, MT564 pre-record date and MT564 record date notices.

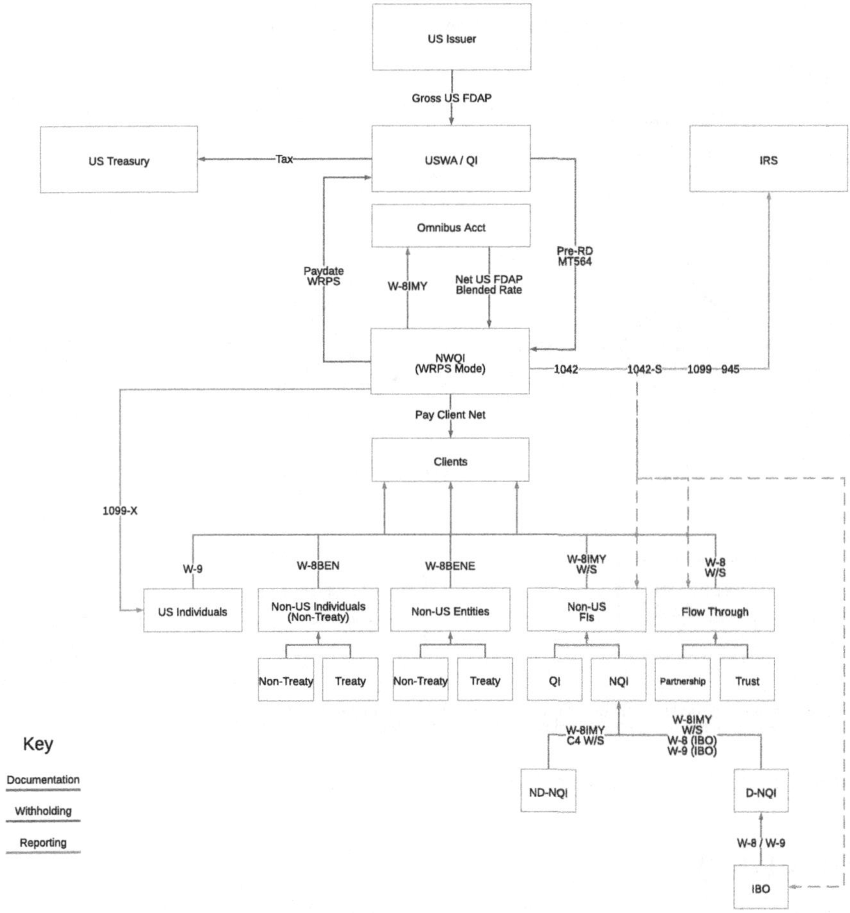

Exhibit 11.8 QI operating model—WRPS

Deposits

Tax relief at source does not mean no tax, it means the correct tax is collected on the pay date. Financial institutions collecting tax must deposit the tax with the US Treasury on a regular basis according to a formula published by the IRS. See Exhibit 11.9.

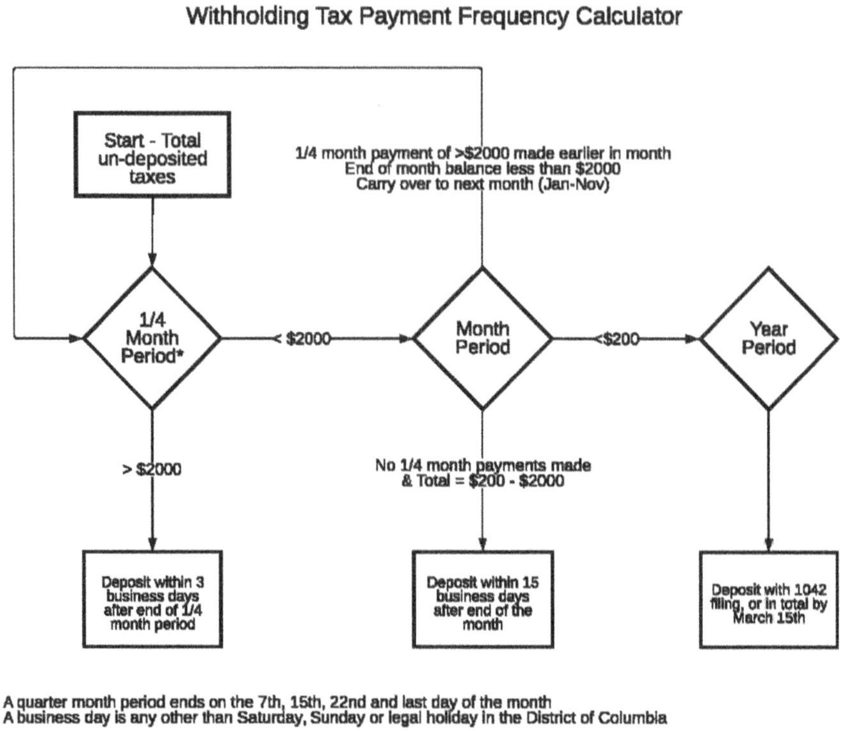

Exhibit 11.9 Tax deposit calculator (*Source* Author)

Reporting

The US, unlike many other jurisdictions, having provided "foreign" financial institutions with the opportunity to become QIs, wants to make sure that these institutions are correctly implementing their regulations and withholding correctly. They do this through information reporting, tax returns and through control and enforcement procedures.

The kind of reports required depend on the type of recipient, since this is about the taxation of investment income. All reports and returns submitted by financial institutions must be done electronically. Where the income is not pooled, recipient copies must be generated and provided to beneficial owners, usually within thirty days. As the system is a cascade and uses omnibus accounts and withholding statements, these all connect up together so that the IRS has full knowledge of the payment chain in terms of what any given financial institution paid to another financial institution.

US-sourced income paid to non-US recipients is reported on Information Returns 1042-S. The deadline is March 15th of each year with respect to income received in the prior calendar year. One of the benefits of being a QI is the ability to report on a pooled basis so that no account specific data is shared with the IRS. All financial institutions receiving US-sourced income on behalf of clients must submit information returns. If the financial institution is an NQI, this reporting cannot be pooled. So, each recipient must be reported individually, per income type with a copy of the return being provided to the recipient within 30 days.

Financial institutions must also submit a US tax return—form 1042. You can consider the 1042 to be a summary of all US-sourced income received from all sources—some financial institutions maintain multiple omnibus accounts at different financial institutions. The IRS has an online portal system for the delivery of these reports. In 2023, that system has been upgraded to the Modernized eFile system ("MeF"), access to which is restricted to people who have verified identity through the ID.me system.

US-sourced income paid to US recipients must be reported on Information returns 1099-X where X is the abbreviation for the type of income being reported. So, dividends would be reported on form 1099-DV for example.

The US reporting system is cascade in nature as Exhibit 11.5 shows.

In Exhibit 11.10 there are three financial institutions in a chain of payment for US-sourced income to an ultimate beneficial owner (BO). The QI at the top of the chain submits a pooled 1042-S with a separate 1042-S identifying the amounts paid to the lower-level QI. That lower-level QI submits its 1042-S, again on a pooled basis, with a separate 1042-S identifying an NQI as its customer. The NQI cannot submit pooled reports and must file a 1042-S for each recipient and provide the recipient with a copy. In this way, the IRS received information returns from each layer in the chin of payment and can this match what each layer is reporting to what each lower layer is reporting. This represents the first component of control in governance. If there is a mismatch in any reporting, the lower-level FI will receive a penalty notice.

This information return process takes a total of nine months each year. Exhibit 11.11 shows the elements involved. Most notably, while the reporting deadline is March 15th each year, all financial institutions generally apply for extension of time to file—30 days for the 1042-S and 6 months for the 1042. This difference is because some US Issuers can re-classify income after the end of the US tax year. For example, a mutual fund dividend (withholdable and reportable) may be re-classified as a return of capital (not withholdable but reportable). The six month extension gives everyone enough time to file their first submission and then submit amended filings to account for these changes.

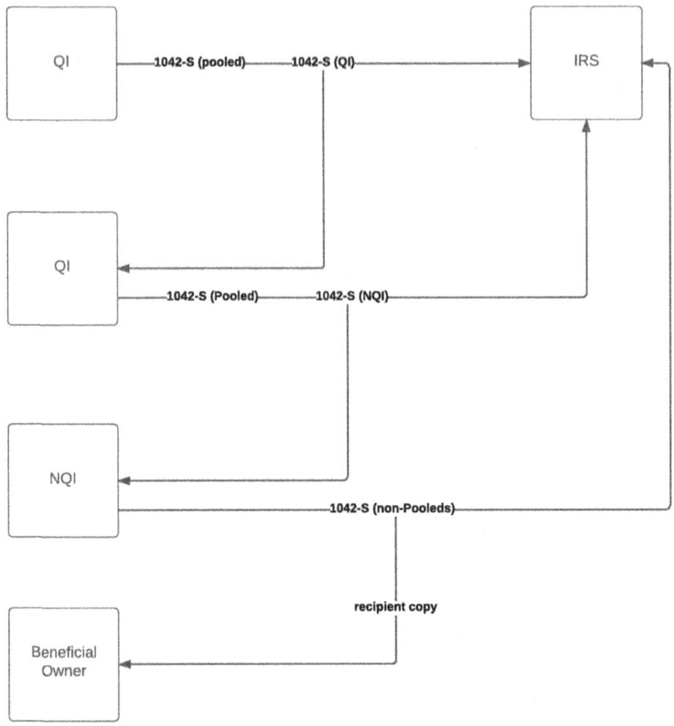

Exhibit 11.10 Cascade nature of US reporting (*Source* Author)

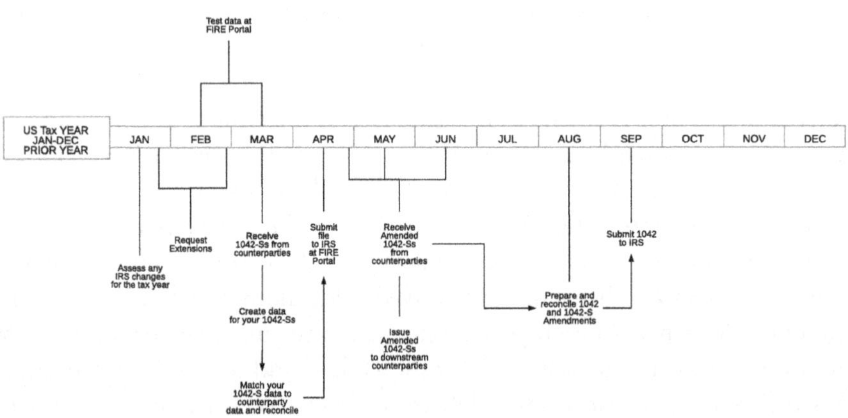

Exhibit 11.11 US Information return and Tax Return cycle (*Source* Author)

NQIs

I mentioned at the start of this chapter that there are around 5000 QIs registered with the IRS and the IRs will be publishing a list of registered QIs in due course. This makes the number of NQIs roughly 50,000. The rules are different for NQIs. NQIs cannot grant treaty benefits to their customers directly. To obtain tax relief at source, they must disclose their clients to a QI. NQIs can use omnibus accounts and withholding statements i.e., they can pool their clients for the purpose of withholding, but they cannot pool their clients for the purpose of reporting. This leads to the concept of an NQI that discloses its clients to a QI in order that these indirect clients of a QI can gain access to treaty benefits. Disclosure in this context means that an NQI must collect W-8 self-certifications from its clients and provide these to a QI together with a W-8IMY on which they certify the capacity in which they are acting, and a withholding statement that lists each beneficial owner for whom documentation was disclosed. The. Receiving QI must now validate the certificates before it can apply a tax treaty benefit to the disclosed clients. For withholding purposes, the NQI is permitted to comingle the US assets of its disclosed non-US clients i.e., NQIs can pool for the purpose of withholding and thus gain treaty benefits.

When it comes to reporting, however, the act of disclosure effectively transfers the reporting obligation from the NQI to the QI. So, a QI receiving documentation from an NQI for indirect clients will be required to report those clients on information returns 1042-S annually. However, it doesn't end there. Because these indirect clients were customers of an NQI, the QI cannot aggregate these indirect clients with its direct clients i.e., a QI can only pool its direct clients and must report each recipient separately on a 1042-S. So, in the edge case, if an NQI discloses 100% of its clients to a QI, the NQI will have no information return obligation and therefore also no tax return obligation. This is because the withholding statements and the supporting documentation will all match up to what the QI withheld.

Governance

The big difference between the US and other tax relief markets that are active today, is that the US tax relief system has a governance component consisting of compliance obligations, oversight activities and enforcement. Qualified Intermediaries have effectively signed a commercial contract, the QI Agreement, with the IRS. The Agreement text is provided in Revenue Procedure

2022–2043. That contract has a six year term that is divided into two "certification periods" of three years each. At the end of each certification period, a QI must certify to the IRS that they have met all the obligations of the contract. In order to make that certification, the QI Agreement also obligates the QI to have arranged for the conduct of a Periodic Review of the QI's compliance to the contract by an independent and competent person. The Periodic Review is a very mechanical process defined in the Annexes to the QI Agreement, so there is really no room for manoeuvre.

In order to force the QI to conduct this review, the contract also obligates the QI to appoint a Responsible Officer of sufficient authority to be able to make any necessary changes to the QI's operating model in order to ensure compliance and to have a written compliance document demonstrating how the contractual obligations are met.

This probably explains why the US withholding tax system is viewed as the most complex in the world which, given its dominance of global equity markets is perhaps unsurprising. As we will see in the following chapters, this has formed the basis of other tax relief models and is likely to become the pre-eminent model over the coming years.

12

871(m), 1446(a) and 1446(f) Withholding

In this chapter, I will explain some of the more recent changes in withholding tax in the US securities market. In particular I will address Chapter 1 Section 871(m) that deals with the tax treatment of derivatives, Chapter 3 Section 1446(a) that deals with distributions of partnerships and finally Chapter 3 Section 1446(f) that deals with gross proceeds withholding on publicly traded partnership trading.

871(m)

Some years ago, it was found that some investors were evading US taxes by investing in derivative instruments that had an indirect connection to a US security or basket of securities. Because the derivative was not a US security, no US tax was applied.

IRC Chapter 1 Section 871(m) was crafted to stop that. This is a continuing theme in withholding tax. One regulatory framework is circumvented leading to another set of regulation to close the loophole. The EU DAC6 regulation was created to close the loophole of investors circumventing CRS reporting. Section 871(m) is truly complex. It establishes the concept of an Equity Linked Instrument ("ELI") being the derivative. When the underlying US security distributes value, the derivative re-distributes that value on some calculated basis. The US considers this to be a Dividend Equivalent

R. K. McGill, *Cross-Border Investment Withholding Tax*, Finance and Capital Markets Series,
https://doi.org/10.1007/978-3-031-32785-8_12

payment ("DEP") and therefore subject to US withholding tax. The tax itself is withheld and reported under normal Chapter 3 rules. 871(m) establishes a set of tests to be conducted, rules for who conducts those tests and when. The result of those tests determines whether a transaction is withholdable and reportable. It also tries to close obvious loopholes by making sure that some combinations of transactions are withholdable even if the individual transactions are not. The primary principle of the tests is to determine the delta of a transaction that is the relative volatility between the price of the derivative and the price of the underlying US security.

Now all this may seem relatively simple to implement, but while 871(m) was drafted in the year 2010, it has still not been fully implemented in 2023, thirteen years later, due to concerns from the industry about its complexity and the systems needed to manage this withholding tax. The latest Notice from the IRS has, again, deferred the implementation of many aspects of 871(m) to 2025.

Exhibit 12.1 shows the basic principles of 871(m) in any transaction. The tests to be performed in order to determine whether withholding is necessary, are performed either by the short party to a transaction or by the party acting as a broker dealer. The second phase is a determination of whether the transaction meets the definition of an ELI or a notional principal contract ("NPC") or a sale repurchase agreement, all of which are potential 871(m) exposed products. If not, then the transaction is not 871(m) and no withholding or reporting is required. If yes, then one of two tests need to be conducted to determine if the transaction or combination must be treated as 871(m) withholdable. This is done by determining if the contract is simple or complex. Helpfully, the IRS defines a complex contract as any contract that is not simple. In most cases, a financial institution will refer to the instrument's prospectus to see if the Issuer has already done this test or has published the delta of the instrument. At present, if the delta of the instrument is greater than 0.8, the transaction is exposed to 871(m) and must be withheld upon. For a complex contract, the delta test is not sufficient, so the IRS has defined a Substantial Equivalent Test ("SET") that looks at the standard deviations applicable to the price of the derivative compared to the price of the underlying US security and compares it to a benchmark. If the SET result is less than the benchmark, the transaction is 871(m) exposed.

As you might expect, there are exemptions and exceptions. Generally, if the underlying security is a tracker index, the derivative will be exempt. However, there are issues even here. One particular concern is over Exchange Traded Funds ("ETFs"). Normally, an ETF would be considered exempt, but there are legal opinions out there that indicate this might not be as simple as it

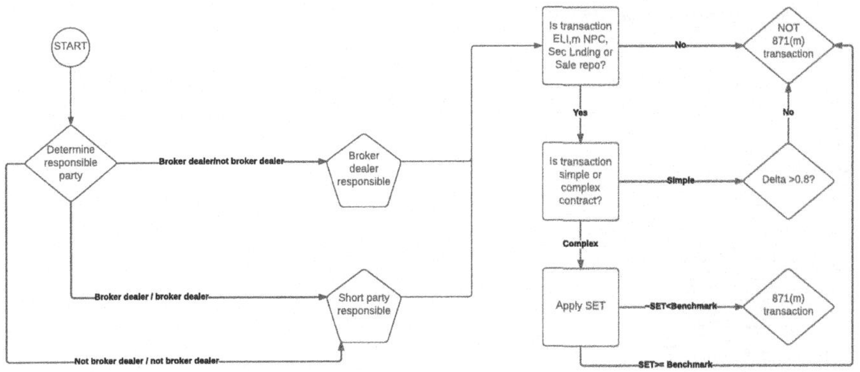

Exhibit 12.1 871(m) tests

looks.[1] An ETF consists of an invested portion and a cash portion. If the ETF presents itself as exempt because it is tracking a US index, the problem is that only the invested portion can track an index, the cash portion cannot. There is a great deal of analysis that needs to be done to get any definitive advice on what level of cash in an ETF is the trigger to stop the fund from being considered exempt from 871(m).

As you can clearly see from Exhibit 12.2, this withholding tax regulation has a long and complex history. The industry has been consistently pushing back to the IRS with the argument that the proposed system is too complex and would require substantial investment in systems that, in context to the problem it is trying to solve, is disproportionate. The compromise is the Good Faith Efforts standard required to be met in order that the IRS for their part, defer implementation of the major parts of the regulation while the industry continues to develop systems.

CEDEARs

There is a particular problem that we think exists with CEDEARs. CEDEARs are Argentine securities that act like ADRs i.e., they are an Argentine security representing an underlying US security.

CEDEARS are a popular financial instrument in Argentina. They are similar to a reverse ADR, with certain exceptions notably that they are freely convertible to the underlying US security, and they pay in US dollars. CEDEAR Issuers, typically brokers, buy US securities in their street

[1] https://www.sullcrom.com/files/upload/Publication-Hochberg-The-Tax-Lawyer-2018.pdf.

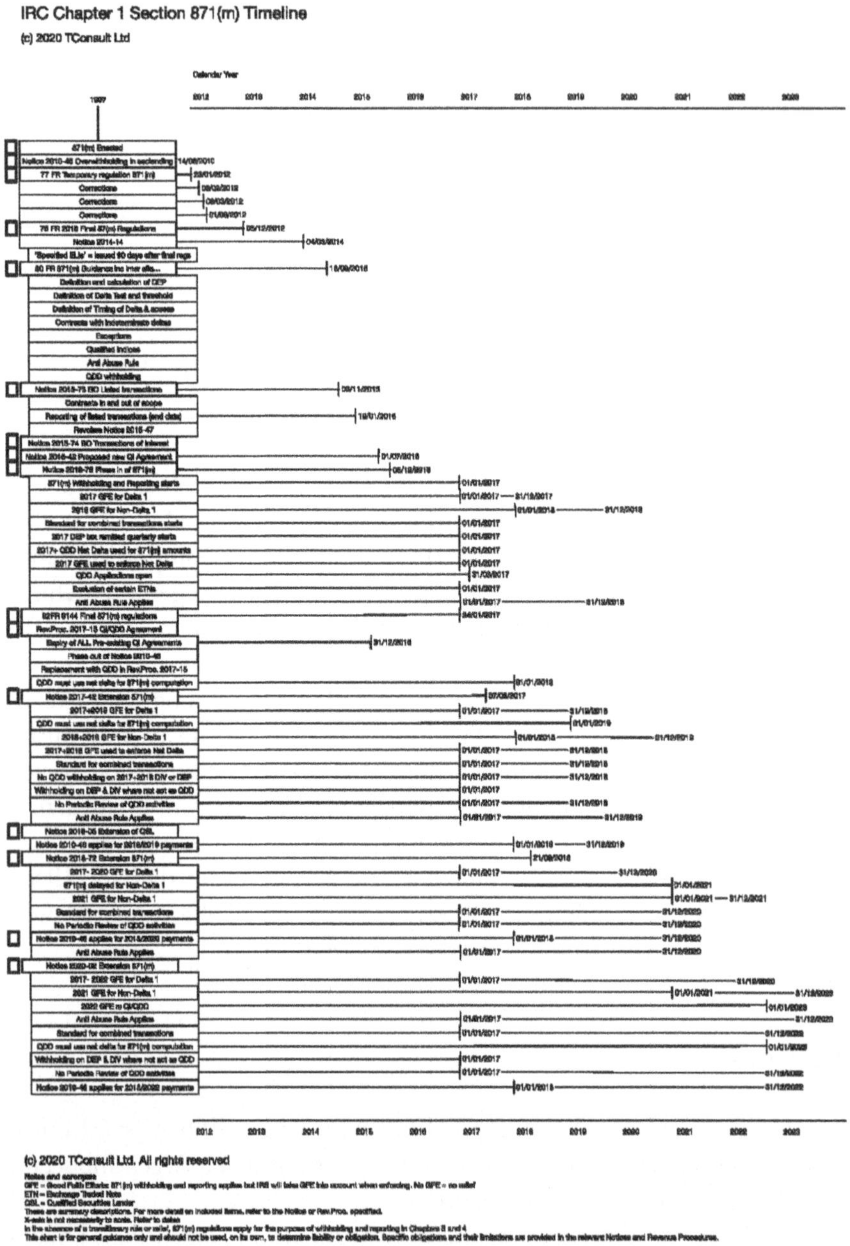

Exhibit 12.2 871(m) timeline (*Source* Author)

name, then create and sell a CEDEAR to their customers to represent the underlying US security. As such, in our opinion, these are equity linked instruments (ELIs) and are subject to Section 871(m) regulation because dividend payments on the CEDEAR are dividend equivalent payments (DEPs). This includes withholding and reporting wherever the delta is greater than 0.8. The delta is a measure of the difference in price volatility between the ELI and the underlying US security and for CEDEARS its usually 1. Anecdotally, many US investors buy CEDEARs to circumvent Argentina's strict currency rules and gain a better exchange rate. An Argentine investor receiving a dividend on a CEDEAR should expect to receive a 1042-S information return from their broker to report payments under income codes 40 or 56. As noted above, this information will eventually be provided back to the Argentine tax administration by the IRS as part of its reciprocal IGA commitment to anti-tax evasion.

Its not clear whether this information reporting is happening today, because many of the CEDEAR Issuers believe that they are the beneficial owner of the US securities which means that all reporting stops with them and no contingent payment to their CEDEAR holders is reported on. In reality, as the wording on a W-8BENE makes clear, the certification of beneficial ownership is in regard to the income from the asset, not the ownership of the asset itself. As there is a connection between the CEDEAR and a US security, in our humble opinion, Argentine CEDEAR Issuers are NOT the beneficial owners of the income from the US securities they are buying—because they make DEPs to underlying clients when the US security pays out.

1446(a) and 1446(f)

The US Internal Revenue Service (IRS) announced in 2022 that a new QI Agreement would come into effect on 1 January 2023. The proposed changes were described in full in Notice 2022–2023.[2]

The new QI Agreement provides the rules for implementing a new tax—1446(f).

It was effectively telling all financial institutions outside the US that they must not only look at income as a reason to apply US withholding tax, but also at the proceeds from the sale of securities. This was an entirely new playing field for non-US financial institutions. The industry was provided

[2] https://www.irs.gov/pub/irs-drop/n-22-23.pdf.

with around 6 months to understand the implications of allowing heir customers to own publicly traded partnership interests ("PTPs") and what happened when they sold those interests.

For financial institutions, it all comes down to whether they are a QI or NQI. Operationally, the IRS connected the new PTP regulations to the new QI agreement that came into force on 1 January 2023.

The new QI Agreement introduced new withholding and reporting obligations for qualified intermediaries that allow their customers to trade interests in publicly traded partnerships (PTPs) with income that is effectively connected to a US business or trade.

A publicly traded partnership (PTP) is a type of a limited partnership managed by two or more general partners, including individuals, corporations, or other partnerships. PTPs are capitalised by limited partners who provide capital but have no management role in the partnership.

Interests in PTPs are either traded on an established securities market or are readily tradable on a secondary market.

Where the new QI Agreement refers to PTPs, it specifically means PTPs that are engaged in a trade or business within the US or have some component of their business related to the US.

Qualified intermediaries that allow their account holders to trade interests in PTPs must ensure that the correct amount of tax is withheld and deposited with the US Treasury when:

1. There is a distribution by the PTP
2. There is a gain on the disposition of an interest in a PTP that would be treated as effectively connected with the conduct of a trade or business within the US.

Section 1446(a) of the US tax code describes the rules governing the tax on distributions by a PTP.

Under 1446(a), the QI is required to withhold at a rate of 37% for individuals and 21% for entities on an amount paid to an account holder that is non-US unless an exception applies because the account holder is a non-US entity described in Section 501(c) (3) or because the account holder has claimed an exemption from withholding under an income tax treaty. This withholding and amount realised should be reported on Form 1042-S using income code 27.

Section 1446(f) of the US tax code describes the rules governing the tax when there is a gain on disposition of an interest in a PTP.

Under 1446(f), the seller or transferor of the partnership interest must withhold 10% of the amount realised on that sale if any portion of the gain would be treated as effectively connected with the conduct of a trade or business within the US, unless the transaction qualifies for a full or partial exemption.

The withholding and amount realised should be reported on Form 1042-S using income code 57.

Operating Model Options

The new QI Agreement set out several options that allow qualified intermediaries to comply with their new obligations from an operational perspective.

Withholding QI

QIs can choose to assume primary withholding responsibility under Section 1446(a) and (f). If they choose to assume primary withholding responsibility under 1446(a), they must also assume primary withholding responsibility under 1446(f) and vice versa. This decision is not dependent on whether they choose to assume primary withholding responsibility under Chapters 3 and 4.

Non-Withholding QI

If they choose **not** to assume primary withholding responsibility under Sections 1446(a) and (f), they must provide sufficient information to their upstream counterparty so that they can apply the correct rate of withholding to the payment. They can do this in one of two ways:

1. **As a Disclosing QI**: Disclosing their account holders to their upstream on a payee basis
2. **As a Non-Disclosing QI**: Disclosing their account holders to their upstream on a pooled basis.

Exhibit 12.3 provides a comparison of the requirements for these two options.

While the new QI Agreement allows QIs to choose how to act, the upstream counterparty may restrict the available options for commercial reasons of their own (Exhibit 12.4).

	Disclosing QI	Non-Disclosing QI
Client Documentation Disclosure to Upstream	✓	×
Payee-Level Withholding Statement	✓	×
Pooled Withholding Statement	×	✓
1042-S Reporting	×	✓

Exhibit 12.3 Requirements for Disclosing QI vs Non-Disclosing QI

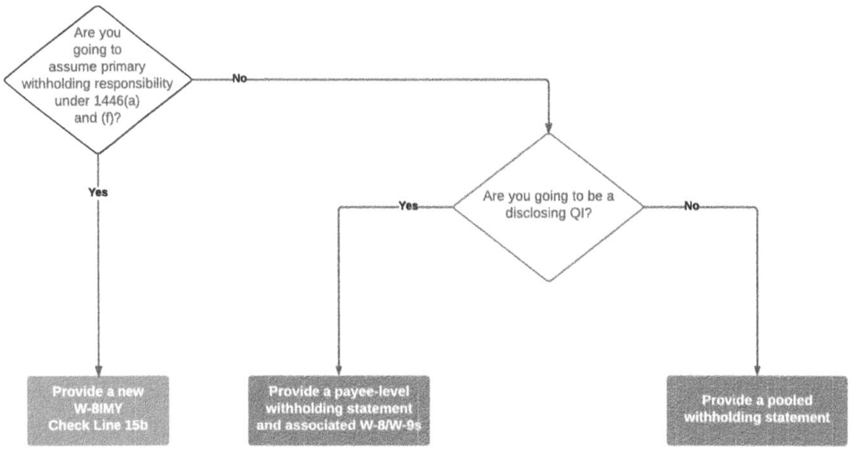

Exhibit 12.4 Operating models for 1446(f)

Most financial institutions that we've spoken to took the decision in late 2022 to shut down ownership of PTPs to their clients because, like 871(m), they lacked the systems and data necessary to determine whether they should withhold. The failure of the IRS to consult with the industry meant that the only source of knowledge was the IRS Notices on the subject and the QI Agreement itself which was only published in December 2022.

Exhibit 12.5 shows how a financial institution should address 1446(f) withholding. As the diagram explains, 1446(f) imposes an obligation to withhold a 10% tax on the gross proceeds of a sale of a PTP when paid to a non-US person. The big difference is that gross proceeds is related to trading activity while most other withholding is concerned with the taxation of passive income. There are a number of exceptions and exemptions in Section 1446(f) and its that most financial institutions found difficult to understand and/or implement.

Key among these is the concept of a Qualified Notice. A Qualified Notice is a notice issued by the partnership itself and defines whether any proportion of the partnership's income in a given year should not be treated as taxable. The problem is that there is no standardised way for these notices

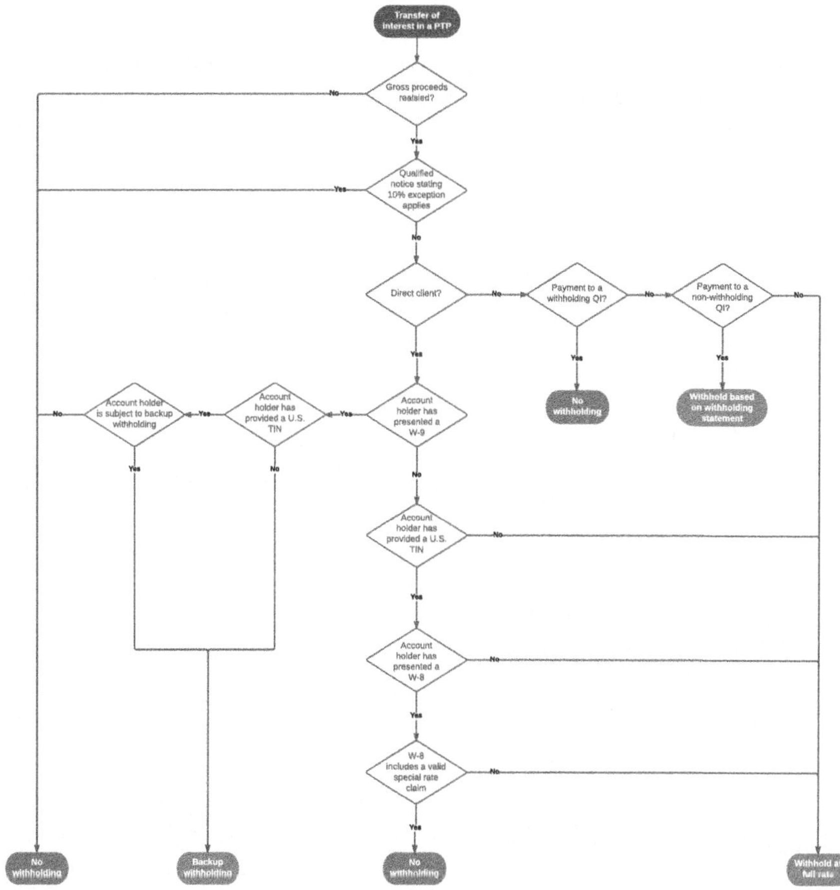

Exhibit 12.5 1446(f) withholding (*Source* Author)

to be communicated through the industry and no way to know when these notices have been issued. The other main exemption si if a double tax treaty provides for an exception to withholding on gross proceeds that can then be claimed as a special rate on a W-8 form. The problem with this is that it assumes that an investor will have knowledge of the terms of his or her relevant double tax treaty with the US and/or have time to research it, then be able to properly claim the exemption on their W-8 form.

The IRS did update the W-8 forms in October 2021 to provide for 1446(f) claims, but overall, most of the industry has just thrown up its hands and said "how do we avoid having to deal with this?" The answer is not to allow clients to trade PTPs at all or, if so, to only allow US Persons to trade them.

Otherwise, the effort required simply to keep track of PTPs is seen as disproportionate to the benefit gained by the financial institution, which typically runs on very thin margins.

13

EU Withholding Tax Code of Conduct

This chapter describes the history and the current state of the European Withholding Tax Code of Conduct that parallels the OECD TRACE initiative and had its roots in the work of Alberto Giovanini, the European Commission FISCO group and latterly the European Commission Tax Barriers Business Advisory Group. The Chapter describes the ten principles of the Code focusing on issues that can lead to automation and standardisation of tax policy in Europe.

The story of the journey of the European Union begins in the nineteen nineties with Alberto Giovannini whos was tasked with identifying the barriers o the free movement of capital, a principle that underpinned the EU's political structures. Of those he identified, two were related to cross-border withholding tax. There began a multi decade process of committees being formed to further analyse these two barriers—why did they exist, what was the solution to them. I came into this picture between 2006,[1] 2007[2] and 2010[3] when I was asked to be an expert witness to one of these committees the fiscal compliance experts committee or FISCO. My contribution was to the 2010 report, but the overall nature of the committee was to delve deeper and deeper into the morass of withholding tax procedures, policies and rates that exemplified the problem—no systemic approach, manual paper-based

[1] https://finance.ec.europa.eu/system/files/2016-12/fact-finding-study-19042006_en.pdf.

[2] https://finance.ec.europa.eu/system/files/2016-12/fisco-report-23102007_en.pdf.

[3] https://finance.ec.europa.eu/system/files/2016-12/booklet-fisco-09022010_en.pdf.

R. K. McGill, *Cross-Border Investment Withholding Tax*, Finance and Capital Markets Series,
https://doi.org/10.1007/978-3-031-32785-8_13

processes that had different rules and time periods associated with them all unco-ordinated between Member States.

Following the 2010 report, another committee was set up basing its work on the foundations of the 2010 report. In other words, the next committee, originally called CESAME 2 and re-named the Tax Barriers Business Advisory Group or T-BAG aimed to provide practical solutions to the issues identified in the 2010 report. This on the basis that if someone came up with practical solutions, the easy bit would be implementation. How wrong they were!

The T-BAG committee came closest to an all encompassing and workable solution. Their report was published in 2013.[4] It established ten principles which, if adopted by Member States, would remove the barriers that Albert Giovannini had identified. These were:

1. Member States agree a common standardised "Authorised Intermediary" Agreement ("AIA") which may be entered into between a financial intermediary and a Member State.
2. AI Agreements would provide rules for the conduct of (i) documentation of beneficial owners, (ii) application of relief at source on payments, (iii) withholding, (iv) information reporting and (v) control and oversight.
3. Member States agree a common form and distribution mechanism (e.g. web site) for Guidance on the application of treaty benefits to different types of a beneficial owner on which an AI may rely, subject to the understanding that such guidance does not over-rule a Member State's ability to question any specific case for a claim of treaty entitlement. It is envisaged that existing mechanisms for clarification of individual cases would still be available.
4. The identification of beneficial owners to be permitted by AIs through the mechanism of (i) Taxpayer Identification Numbers (TINs) issued by the beneficial owner's home State, (ii) application of the KYC rules of the AI's home State, to the extent that the source State accepts the degree to which, in its view, KYC rules establish beneficial ownership and (iii) agreement by Member States to the development and use of a common and electronically transmissible self- certification of residency ("Investor Self-Declaration" or "ISD"). To the extent possible, the system should permit the use of Powers of Attorney ("PoA") to allow AIs and authorised third parties to facilitate any additionally required documentation.

[4] https://finance.ec.europa.eu/system/files/2016-12/tbag-report-24052013_en.pdf.

5. Provided the documentation and identification rules are met, AIs would be permitted to make (or instruct) payments to eligible beneficial owners net of the appropriate treaty rate of withholding tax on pay date.
6. Liability for under-withholding and/or incorrect documentation of beneficial owners should lie (i) with the beneficial owner (for incorrect or fraudulent representations), (ii) the AI for processing errors and (iii) the Source Member State for technical issues related to treaty eligibility, the latter being minimised through the clear Guidance proposal.
7. AIs servicing beneficial owners directly would provide annual information reports (i) to the source State at the beneficial owner level of disclosure and (ii) upstream at pooled level (by withholding rate applied) to other AIs in the payment chain. Such reports to be electronic and to a format standardised between Member States e.g. XML.
8. Where a source country receives information reports from an AI and wishes to query the eligibility of any beneficial owner, Exchange of Information rules would be applied to permit the source country to apply directly to the home country using the TIN of the beneficial owner.
9. Under the terms of an AI agreement, AIs would be subject to a choice of internal review, certified by a responsible officer and subject to appropriate penalties, or external oversight by an approved independent third party by means of an Agreed Upon Procedure" ("AUP") whose report would be available to the Source Member State. Governments would retain the right to undertake spot checks in both cases.
10. For those beneficial owners who were unable to meet the relevant documentation standards prior to pay date, but where they can still prove eligibility under a treaty, Member States agree to develop a standardised, machine readable tax reclaim form capable of being delivered electronically.

The reader will quickly see how these 10 principles bear a striking similarity to the way in which the US tax relief system works. Just replace QI with AI and there you have it. I was in one committee meeting and made this observation. To my surprise, the chair observed that, in Europe, we don't like to be seen to be following America, so, the "idea" was communicated as a development of the Irish QI model. This is humorous only because the Irish QI model is known to have been founded on the US model. No escape.

Now that a solution or set of solutions had been identified by the committee, the question became one of implementation. As a novice at such senior-level meetings, including as they did members from major banks, tax administrations and political appointees, I assumed that the most logical step would be a European ‘union Directive that would force all Member States to adopt this Utopian ideal. Sadly, that was not to be the case.

An EU Directive must be unanimously agreed by all Member States. As you can imagine, these can take anywhere from five to ten years to negotiate and, by the time the final negotiated solution is agreed, it looks nothing like the originally recommended model. The alternative was “voluntary adoption” in which the committee’s report is circulated to Member States who can then determine, if, when and how they may or may not adopt the proposed principles. If you want any evidence for the glacial pace of change in the withholding tax industry, this is it.

A Directive would have the advantage of enforced unanimity, but would take a great deal of time. A voluntary adoption process would be quicker, but would not guarantee full or homogenous adoption. The EU decided on the latter course, it is made clear that the Member States were particularly sensitive to devolving tax matters into central hands of the European Commission. What resulted was the Withholding Tax Code of Conduct.

The Code of Conduct

The Code of Conduct was issued in 2017[5] as a response the European Commission’s initiative to build a capital markets union (“CMU”). It is, by their own admission, a compilation of approaches that Member States can *consider* and amend as appropriate to their national needs. This ignores the problem that while double tax treaties are bilateral, the same issues occur again and again between different Member States Italy, for example, has a tax relief at source model. However, it incredibly difficult to administer and, if you are unlucky enough to not to meet the documentary evidence deadlines, the standard refund procedure can easily literally take decades. The refund time for Switzerland or Netherlands on the other hand is a few months.

The Code has 8 principles. They are:

1. Who gets to claim?
    - Tax administrations allow non-resident beneficial owners to submit claims or apply for relief on their own behalf.

[5] https://taxation-customs.ec.europa.eu/system/files/2017-12/code_of_conduct_on_witholding_tax.pdf.

- Tax administrations allow non-resident financial institutions or other representatives of the beneficial owners, within the limits of what is currently allowed by law, 5 to claim relief on behalf of their customers.
- Tax administrations do not require non-resident beneficial owners, institutions or other representatives to maintain a resident fiscal agent and/or representative or to use resident tax advisory firms to claim relief, within the limits of what is currently allowed by law.

2. How are claims submitted?

- Tax administrations identify which forms need to be filled in and publish them online.
- The whole reclaim process can be completed online through a user-friendly portal. To ease the submission of supporting documents, tax administrations allow file upload easily.
- Permits global custodians and other financial institutions to submit claims in respect of multiple beneficial owners at once.
- To receive data quickly and efficiently, tax administrations implement a system to system option for qualified intermediaries.
- Tax administrations ensure that the external IT systems (i.e. the approach described in this section) are connected to their internal IT systems (described in the following section).

3. Using what IT systems?

- Effective and make the best possible use of data, allowing tax administrations to easily retrieve, cross-check and match data gathered from various sources and those already available to the tax administrations;
- Connected to the online e-filing system used by beneficial owners and/or financial intermediaries to reclaim WHT;
- Smart in the sense that automatically alert tax administrations of possible risks in the refund claims, to minimise the likelihood of fake or fraudulent claims being processed;
- Able to keep its data secure;
- Able to allow tax administrations to simply and rapidly create statistical reports on claims processing; and
- Are cost effective.

4. Centralised and standardised information

- Tax administrations publish on their websites documentation requirements, description of the law and the deadlines, if any, that taxpayers need to respect for submitting their claims.

- Effective IT systems (described in the previous section) available to taxpayers and tax administrations.
- Tailored forms, easy to fill in online.

5. Use of Digital Forms

- Strive to provide electronic forms, which are tailor-made, interactive, comprehensive and self-explanatory;
- Provide proactive, transparent and comprehensive guidance to different types of taxpayers (small retail investors, pension funds, insurance groups, transparent funds and their investors etc.) on different incomes (dividends, interests etc.) or key definitions (beneficial owner etc.) and communicate in a tailored-made way (considering for instance the applicable tax treaties) to meet the needs of these target groups, so that taxpayers can quickly find the forms they need to fill in and reduce mistakes in doing so;
- Make forms and guidance available in addition to the national language in at least one foreign language customary in the sphere of international finance;
- Ensure guidance is kept up to date as treaties and domestic law changes; and
- The European Commission provides and keeps up to date a single webpage listing all links to national websites where forms and guidance can be found.

6. Claim Documentation

To simplify documentation requirements, yet within the limits of what is currently allowed by law and in particular tax treaties, tax administrations:

- Publish online clear and comprehensive documentation requirements for different entity and income types, when applicable;
- When appropriate, simplify documentation requirements for cases of minor risk;
- Allow supporting documents in electronic formats, as far as legally possible;
- Avoid requesting excessive information from taxpayers;
- Avoid requesting documents that it is not possible for the taxpayer to obtain with reasonable effort;
- Avoid excessive, ad hoc, non-standardised requests to taxpayers for information, unless necessary for compliance, relying on risk assessment;
- Avoid recurrent documentation requirements, if the information is already available to tax administration;

- Accept certain valid documentation to support a series of different claims, when appropriate;
- Accept tax residence certificates in the format provided by the residence country of the beneficial owners as proof of their tax residence;
- Allow proofs of the beneficial owners' entitlement to treaty benefits other than tax residence certificates in relation to the amount(s) in question issued by the residence country, for example such as:
  - Allowing claimants to use self-certification of tax residence, where enough information is available possibly in combination with
  - Allowing claimants to rely on financial institutions' "know your customer" (KYC) procedures to certify tax residence; and
- Set up a central information platform (example: the European TIN Portal) which provides information about WHT reclaim and refund procedures and on the different formats used for tax residence certificates in the EU.

7. Single Point of Contact

- Identify a single point of contact for refund claims and applications for relief.
- Single point of contact is the point of reference for providing easy to understand and accessible guidance to taxpayers, also in one additional foreign language customary in the sphere of international finance.
- Single points of contact are easy to find on the websites of the tax administrations.
- The European Commission provides and maintains a single webpage listing all links to Member States' single points of contact.

8. Relief at Source

- Tax administrations try to carry out tax relief at source systems in the least burdensome manner for investors and financial intermediaries, balancing however the need for simplification with the necessity of ensuring compliance.
- For example, tax administrations may grant WHT relief at source relying on a system of authorised information agents and withholding agents, in which the information agent closest to the beneficial owner:
- Verifies whether the beneficial owner is entitled to tax relief;
  - Passes to the next information agent in the custody chain pooled WHT rate information;
  - Reports investor-specific information to the source Member State when needed; and

  - And the withholding agent applies WHT relief at source on the basis of pooled WHT rate information.
- Another way to grant relief at source is a system where the tax authorities verify whether the beneficial owner is entitled to tax relief:
  - The beneficial owner applies for full or partial exemption from WHT before the underlying payments are made;
  - If the conditions are met, the tax authorities issue a certificate of exemption; and
  - The beneficial owner hands this certificate to the payor and the latter applies WHT relief at source accordingly.
- Tax administrations cooperate to ensure that information agents and withholding agents comply with their obligations.

Much of this bears a striking similarity to the more detailed 2013 Tax barriers Report. The differences are that (i) these are not mandatory obligations, but just *ideas* on how a Member State *might* want to *consider* improving its withholding tax procedures, (ii) not one Member State since the report was issued in 2017, has implemented the Code and (iii) unlike the 2013 report, there is no "how" in the Code, just top-level ideas.

There is a factor that might explain this—self-interest. Elsewhere in this book, I have noted that one of the biggest factors leading to lost entitlements is apathy or lack of awareness. This works both ways. It is, on first view, in the self-interest of tax administrations to have many investors not claim their entitlements. They will receive tax at a high statutory rate. To have to give it back is anathema to their purpose of gathering tax revenues. The more apathetic and unaware an investor is just means more free money for the tax administration once those entitlements pass the statute of limitations. This may also explain why tax administrations implement such archaic procedures for reclamation. My view on this is that those administrations that create barriers to effective and correct taxation at source, merely deter foreign direct investment. They may win some free cash in the short term, but in the long term, investment strategies will change once recoveries become more difficult.[6] This is highlighted in the London School of Economics paper The Impact of Double Taxation Treaties on Foreign Direct Investment: Evidence from Large Dyadic Panel Data published in Contemporary Economic Policy, 28(3), 2010. Bathel, Busse and Neumayer.

[6] https://eprints.lse.ac.uk/28823/1/__Libfile_repository_Content_NGU0XH-S_TC7W1N-Q_The%20impact%20of%20double%20taxation%20treaties%20on%20foreign%20direct%20investment%20evidence%20from%20large%20dyadic%20panel%20data%20%28LSE%20RO%29.pdf.

While the EU initiative is important for its acceptance of modern general principles, it is less developed than the OECD model and it is less clear how one would tell if an EU market were "adopting" the model as opposed to cherry picking.

14

OECD Tax Relief and Compliance Enhancement

This chapter describes the OECD Tax Relief and Compliance Enhancement protocol in general terms. TRACE is a framework that allows tax administrations to adopt a standardised tax processing model with primary focus on relief at source. TRACE uses the concept of authorised intermediaries to allow tax administrations to outsource tax determinations under AI contracts. This is supported by the principles of using self-certifications of residency to replace certificates issued by tax authorities and annual reporting. The system has many similarities to the US QI Program but has been adapted by the OECD to simplify and standardise the model for global use.

At around the same time that the European Union was working on its 2013 report, the OECD had a parallel initiative in progress. The Tax Relief and Compliance Enhancement framework known as TRACE. The TRACE implementation package ("TRACE IP") was approved by the Committee on Fiscal Affairs in 2013.

Now, for context, its important to understand two components of regulatory tax compliance. The US FATCA regulation, the OECD Automatic Exchange of Information ("AEoI") and its subordinate control framework, the Common Reporting Standard ("CRS") are all about anti-tax evasion. So, they have a commonality of purpose—to detect those natural persons who may be evading tax by holding assets in a foreign jurisdiction.

In contrast, the US Qualified Intermediary Program ("QI"), the OECD Tax Relief and Compliance Enhancement Implementation Protocol

R. K. McGill, *Cross-Border Investment Withholding Tax*, Finance and Capital Markets Series,
https://doi.org/10.1007/978-3-031-32785-8_14

("TRACE IP") and the EU Withholding Tax Code of Conduct are all about the correct taxation of passive investment income when paid to a non-resident i.e., cross border. Again, these have the commonality of purpose, but its not the same purpose as the anti-tax evasion frameworks.

The OECD committee that worked on TRACE took their deliberations one step further than the EU and created an implementation protocol i.e., how it would work in practice.

The basic principles of TRACE are the same as those of the US qualified intermediary program:

1. The primary mechanism is tax relief at source
2. Financial institutions can contract with a tax administration to act as an Authorised Intermediary ("AI")
3. These AIs could use digital self-certifications of residency known as Investor Self-Declarations ("ISDs") to document the tax status of their customers an record claims of treaty benefits
4. Financial institutions that did not become AIs are automatically Contractual Intermediaries ("CIs")
5. AIs must have ISDs to be able to grant tax treaty relief at source on any payment
6. An annual reporting system can be adopted as part of control and oversight of the AI agreement
7. TRACE tax administrations can impose a requirement for AIs to undergo regular audits (Exhibit 14.1).

The legal basis of the TRACE framework is similar to that of the Automatic Exchange of Information (AEoI). Once the framework has been published, a potential adopting jurisdiction will have to assess its legal structures and put in place primary and secondary legislation. The purpose of that legislation is to set the basis for regulation that gives financial institutions, particularly non-resident financial institutions with the ability to contract with the State. That legislation will also specify the regulation—new or amended, that codifies the controls, due diligence, the oversight, reporting and the penalties that will be applicable.

The OECD has also provided a publication called the implementation protocol, now in its second edition, that gives both tax administrations and financial institutions general guidance on how to implement TRACE in their jurisdiction. This can of course be adjusted depending on which components of TRACE are being adopted and which are not.

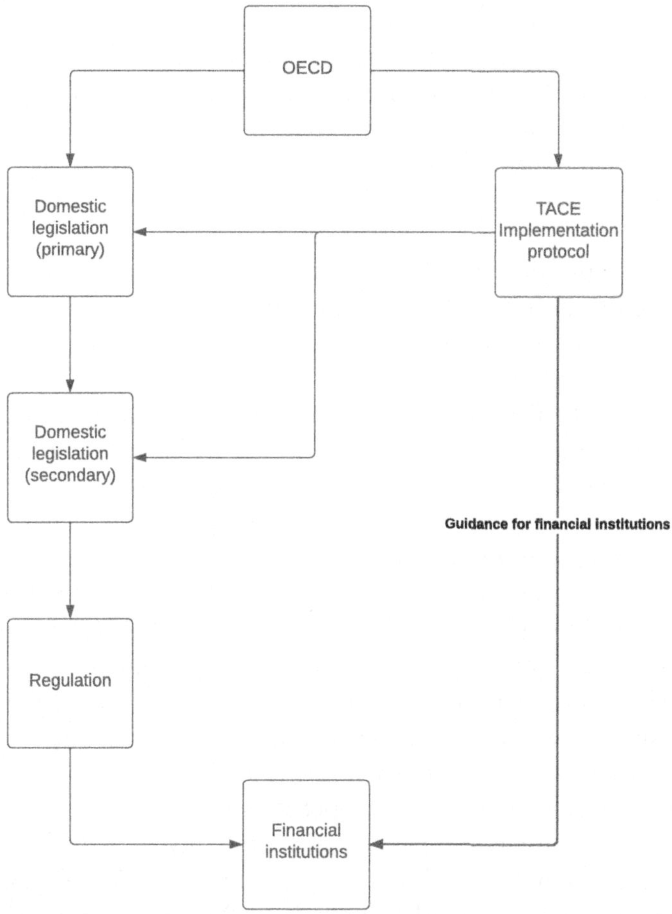

Exhibit 14.1 TRACE framework (*Source* Author)

As might be expected, given that the protocol includes the application of treaty benefits, the protocol provides detailed guidance for investor self-declarations. The legal basis is founded on changes to domestic law that allow a financial institution to rely on a self-certification for the purposes of granting treaty benefits. This is an obvious change from the more administratively difficult certification process that other jurisdictions use. The legislation will also make sure that liability is clearly defined. This is usually that the liability for errors depends on where the error occurred. mIf the financial institution follows the guidance for validation and the investor made. Statement or certification that was later found to untrue, but could not have been forseen by the financial institution, then the liability rests with the investor. If the error occurred as a processing error of the financial institution, then the liability rests with them. This is why so much store is placed both in the US system and in TRACE, on the proper validation of a self-certification.

Now, unlike the US QI system, which is essentially bilateral, The OECD had to recognise that its equivalent could only work if several countries adopted the framework. This led to a fundamental compromise in which the framework was published but OECD member states could choose

i. whether to introduce it,
ii. when to introduce it and, most importantly,
iii. which components of it were to be included.

To that extent, TRACE has the same problems as the EU Code of Conduct namely, adoption and consistency. In principle, OECD members can make a rapid assessment of how close their existing tax system is to the proposed TRACE system and then make some decisions about changes to legal structures necessary to implement TRACE.

That done, they need only decide which components of the basic framework they want to implement and over what period of time. This assessment process can take a couple of years, with another couple of years for legal changes. This generally means that, from the announcement of the protocol, it can be expected to take 4–5 years before any country could go live—as was the case with Finland as we will see in the next chapter.

The one difficulty that arises is operational. Given that each adopting jurisdiction can adjust the implementation, the way in which investor self-declarations are implemented becomes critical. In principle an investor investing in Finland may need to provide an ISD to an Authorised Intermediary and claim the treaty benefits between their home jurisdiction and Finland. The same investor investing in another TRACE adopting jurisdiction may find themselves completing a slightly different ISD for that jurisdiction. The only firm, so far, that has successfully addressed this issue in advance of a second TRACE adopter, is TConsult with their co-compliant ISD platform. This platform allows an investor to specify which TRACE adopting jurisdictions they wish to claim treaty benefits in. The resulting ISD provides all the required legal language on the form before being electronically signed by the investor.

15

Finland

Finland is the first country to have adopted the TRACE protocol, having spent two years adapting its legislative framework to allow it to change to a tax relief at source model. The chapter will draw heavily on contributions from the Finnish tax authority, Vero Skatt, to provide context to the challenges faced by tax administrations seeking to follow their lead. The chapter will also look at the participation rate of the Authorised Intermediary system in Finland and some of the practical challenges and opportunities for financial institutions.

Finnish corporations paying certain types of income are required to apply a 35% withholding tax on payments to non-residents. Bilateral double tax treaties are most often set at 15% for dividends. Payments of interest to non-residents are usually exempt.

On January 1, 2021, Finland became the first jurisdiction to formally adopt the TRACE IP for withholding tax relief at source. As noted in the previous chapter, TRACE IP's fundamental weakness, is that it is not a law, but a framework. The framework, published by the OECD, allows for each adopting jurisdiction to make choices about how it wishes to implement the framework. In the long run, this will lead to exactly the same situation in which we find ourselves a day. There may be many adopters of TRACE IP, but they may not implement in the same way.

The journey began with Finland adopting primary and secondary legislation to give legal effect to the necessary components. The main one was to

R. K. McGill, *Cross-Border Investment Withholding Tax*, Finance and Capital Markets Series,
https://doi.org/10.1007/978-3-031-32785-8_15

allow non-Finnish financial institutions to adopt withholding agent status on the distribution of income from Finnish securities.

The EU makes up almost 65% of Finland's total trade. Finland's largest bilateral trade flows are with Germany, Russia, and Sweden. Finland's key export sectors are transportation, electronics, forestry, machinery, and chemicals.

In 2021, the US was the third-largest market for Finnish exports and Finland's sixth-largest source of imports. Two-way trade in goods and services between the US and Finland was about $11.6 billion. Two-way trade in goods totalled around $7.4 billion, with US goods exports to Finland totalling $2.5 billion, chiefly computer and electronic products, minerals and ores, transportation equipment, chemicals, and non-electrical machinery. Finnish goods exports to the US totalled $4.9 billion, chiefly chemicals, non-electrical machinery, petroleum and coal products, paper, and transportation equipment. Two-way trade in services totalled $1.7 billion.

Its these bilateral trade flows that create the drivers for bilateral double tax treaties. The Finnish implementation of TRACE contained two important departures from the framework model.

The first was the concept of an Authorised Intermediary. This is a fundamental concept in TRACE that allows a non-resident financial institution to adopt withholding agent status for Finnish securities. The TRACE framework assumes that this status will be adopted using a contract in much the same way as the US QI program. The Finnish tax administration, Vero Skatt, opted for a simple registration model in which a financial institution submits an application online and is assigned an Authorised Intermediary Number ("AIN"). The AIN list is public domain, whereas the US QIEIN list is not. Following this, provided the AI has a valid ISD for an investor, dividends can be paid out at tax treaty rates, usually 15%. The only obligation on the AI, is to make sure that the ISD and treaty claim are valid.

The second departure was in the use of investor self-declarations ("ISDs") for the purpose of granting treaty benefits. This is analogous to the US W-8 series of forms. To their credit Vero Skatt does allow these ISDs to be digital and electronically signed, thus allowing an opening for financial institutions to create substantial automated solutions. The difference here is that the validity period for these ISDs is five years from the end of the year in which they are signed. While TRACE does allow for flexibility here, the US certificates only have three-year validity period. This does mean that a financial institution with clients exposed to the US *and* Finnish securities markets will have an operational problem to solve in terms of renewing forms that are about to expire. On its own, this should not be insurmountable, but if more jurisdictions adopt TRACE and choose different validity periods, this could become an issue.

Unlike the US, the Finnish tax administration has provided very clear guidance on the validation of these ISDs at its web site. This is not to say that the US has not provided guidance, it has. However, the US securities market is much larger and more complex than the Finnish market. Guidance on the application and use of the W-8 forms is extremely complex and, not always consistent.

In its first year of operation, Finnish corporations paid 81% of dividends at the lower treaty rate, at source based on TRACE and AIs processing the payments.[1]

In Finland, if you're not an AI, then you will be a "CI" or contractual intermediary. This is analogous to the QI and NQI model in the US. A CI will need to disclose its clients to an AI in order to obtain tax relief for its clients. These will then be reported by the AI.

An AI must meet certain eligibility criteria to be registered. They must be (i) authorised to perform custodial activities, (ii) have a permit or equivalent to undertake custodial activities, (iii) be domiciled within the European Union or a country with which Finland has a DTT and (iv) be subject to KYC and AML regulation in their home market. The application to register as an AI can be found at https://www.vero.fi/en/About-us/contact-us/forms/descriptions/application-for-entry-in-the-register-of-authorised-intermediaries-6920e-and-6921e/.

An Authorised Intermediary can only take responsibility for dividends paid by publicly listed companies to non-residents where the underlying shares are nominee-registered. In other situations, the primary tax liability and reporting responsibility is with the dividend paying company, also referred to as payor.

The statutory withholding tax rate on Finnish securities when paid to an undisclosed non-Finnish person increased to 35%. A reduced rate of 20% is available to non-resident entities who provide an investor self-declaration that contains a claim of treaty benefits. The rate for individuals that provide an ISD is 30%. It is important to understand that these rates are enshrined now in local legislation and not in double tax treaties. So, the benefit to be gained by making such claims in an ISD can be substantial.

---

[1] https://www.vero.fi/en/About-us/newsroom/news/uutiset/2022/reduced-tax-at-source-was-applied-to-over-50-of-the-dividends-paid-on-nominee-registered-shares-last-year--small-investors-also-benefitted-from-the-introduction-of-the-trace-procedure/.

Company	World rank	Market capitalisation (July 2022)
Nordea Bank ABP	390	$49.6 Bn
Neste OYJ	519	$39.1 Bn
Konye OYJ	560	$36.7 Bn
Nokia Corporation	582	$35.6 Bn
Sampo OYJ	744	$27.8 Bn
Fortum OYJ	805	$26.2 Bn
UPM-Kymmene OYJ	994	$20.9 Bn
Stora Enso OYJ	1,341	$15 Bn
Kesko OYJ	1,565	$12.6 Bn
Elisa OYJ	1,919	$9.8 Bn

Exhibit 15.1 Top 10 Finnish securities (*Source* https://www.value.today/headquarters/finland)

Exhibit 15.1 lists the top ten companies in the Finnish securities market. Nokia is probably the best known of these, attracting investment from many global pension funds and other institutional investors.

Also, somewhat analogous to the US system, the Finnish system has some control and oversight through annual reporting. In this scenario an AI must submit an annual report detailing the tax that it has withheld and paid. However, unlike the US system, an AI cannot pool their reporting.

The Finnish TRACE system also departs from the OECD TRACE Framework in that it does not obligate an AI to undergo any form of audit or Periodic Review. This may not be the kind of problem that tax purists may think it is. In the US QI system, reporting is a component of oversight, while the Periodic Review is a component of Control. In a complex system such as the US QI program both control and oversight are necessary. However, the relative simplicity of the Finnish securities market means that Vero Skatt essentially took the decision that it was an unrealistic burden to place on an AI. If history teaches us anything, as long as here are no major fraud and compliance failures, this approach will continue. As soon as there is a problem, it is likely that additional control tools will be implemented.

The Finnish implementation for TRACE also allows for quick refunds and standard post pay date refunds if too much tax was withheld at source. For a quick refund, after statutory rate tax has been withheld, a beneficiary would need to request a tax-at-source card from the Finnish tax administration and present this to their custodian bank (AI).

The standard refund process uses an .xml submission[2] including for bulk submissions. Bulk submissions are only available to corporate entities. Finally, as a last resort, the beneficiary can use a QR-coded form available from the Finnish tax administration when electronic methods are not available.

For corporations, refunds are processed using forms 6163e, 6167e and 6165e.[3] The application form for tax-at-source card is 6211e. For natural persons the refunds are processed with forms 6164e, 6167e and 6166e[4] while the tax-at-source card is applied for with form 5057e.[5]

So, the reader can clearly see that it doesn't matter how simplified an approach is taken, decisions are taken that create some level of complexity.

The Finnish tax administration has been very pleased with its first year of operating this new system and many other tax administrations are now looking at adopting TRACE IP. I expect we will see three or four new adoptions over the next three to five years, bearing in mind that it took two years for Finland to put in place the legal changes necessary to allow TRACE to proceed.

The challenges faced by AIs in Finland are similar to those of a QI under the US regulations—proper documentation of clients, correct application of withholding and timely and accurate reporting. Of these, documentation is the most challenging. Only one company to date, TConsult, has created a digital ISD for use in the Finnish market.[6]

---

[2] https://www.vero.fi/en/About-us/it_developer/data-format-specifications/specifications__direct_data_transfers_a/.

[3] https://www.vero.fi/en/About-us/contact-us/forms/descriptions/application_for_refund_of_finnish_withh2/.

[4] https://www.vero.fi/en/About-us/contact-us/forms/descriptions/application_for_refund_of_finnish_withh/.

[5] https://www.vero.fi/en/About-us/contact-us/forms/descriptions/application_for_a_nonresident_taxpayers/.

[6] https://taxcompliancetoolkit.com.

Part IV

Impacts of Tax Evasion and Fraud

This part of the book describes current frameworks whose purpose is to deter, detect and prevent cross-border tax evasion. This is the use of the financial system to move and hold assets outside an investor's home jurisdiction and where such assets and income deriving therefrom may go unreported and untaxed. This portion of the book is important because it parallels the matters discussed in Parts 2 and 3. Where parts 2 and 3 focus on the correct withholding of tax on cross-border transactions, Part 4 shows how tax administrations have responded to other ways in which investors can "game the system" of international treaties by establishing the principles of mutual assistance in tax matters.

In the previous parts of this book, we have focused on the way in which tax on cross-border investment income is calculated, withheld and reported. This is complex enough in its own right, but, as any average reader will know, the tax space has been subject to enormous scrutiny over the last few years and there is no sign that scrutiny is going to get any less. I have no intention of going into any depth about the causes of this scrutiny. Suffice it to say that major geopolitical issues such as the COVID-19 pandemic, Brexit, the rise of populism, the increasing wealth gap and climate change, have all contributed to a social pressure that expresses itself in an anti-elite and anti-science attitude together with a very high focus on the issue of taxation and, more particularly, tax evasion.

The result of these factors is that tax policy, from a cross-border perspective, focuses on two major pillars. The first is an effective international system that taxes income correctly, according to the DTTs. The second is an effective deterrent and detection mechanism for tax evasion. Whenever I'm asked to describe our subject matter expertise, I am at pains to explain by example. Effective taxation regulations are grouped together as, for example, the US qualified intermediaryregulations, the OECDTRACE framework and the European Union Withholding Tax Code of Conduct. All three have, at their heart, the purpose of facilitating, in a controlled way, the proper taxation of cross-border income, with appropriate control and oversight through reporting and contractual obligations. On the other hand, tax evasion regulations are grouped together as, for example, FATCA, AEoI/CRS and DAC6. These are focused on forcing financial institutions and intermediaries to report any non-resident financial accounts to their home jurisdictions in order to facilitate scrutiny by domestic regulators.

Jurisdiction(s)	Taxation of Income paid to non-residents	Anti-tax evasion
USA	US Revenue Code Chapter 3 ("QI" regulation)	US Revenue Code Chapters 4 ("FATCA"), 31 and 61
OECD	TRACE	AEoI/CRS
EU	Withholding Tax Code of Conduct	

While there does not appear to be an overlap, As we will see in Chapter 15, the US system provides for FATCA rules to apply within the QIcontract. So, one set of FATCA rules applies to accounts that do not receive US-sourced income and another set applies to accounts that do receive US-sourced income.

It is, therefore, in my opinion. Entirely logical that a discussion of cross-border withholding tax should now include an explanation of the anti-tax evasion strategies being adopted and how they overlap.

16

FATCA

This chapter describes the framework Title V of the Hiring Incentives to Restore Employment Act (2010), usually referred to as FATCA. FATCA imposes obligations on all non-US financial institutions to report accounts held by US Persons (or presumed US persons). The FATCA framework is enforced using intergovernmental agreements (IGAs) and has had a significant impact on the ability of Americans to open or maintain financial accounts outside the US. FATCA includes due diligence rules for financial institutions to establish. Reportable accounts, IGA terms that establish what data is to be collected and how it is to be transmitted to the IRS. The nexus to withholding tax is created by the enforcement and deterrence component of the regulation that forces financial institutions to penalise anyone not complying with FATCA by withholding 30% of USA-sourced income paid to such accountholders and reporting such through the US tax system.

I observed once to a colleague in the industry that it seemed counter intuitive that the Americans would find it attractive to have accounts outside the US from which they made their US investments on the basis that they would be subject to a 30% withholding tax. The response was quite surprising to me and it was this: given that a US tax payer that's wealthy would likely to be subject to marginal tax rates as high as 49 or 50% or even more, if you can offer a US tax payer a way to invest in US securities and *only* be paying a 30% tax you'll have them queuing up at your door.

R. K. McGill, *Cross-Border Investment Withholding Tax*, Finance and Capital Markets Series,
https://doi.org/10.1007/978-3-031-32785-8_16

In 2010, this came to a head as the US government decided to go on a crusade to tackle what it considered to be tax evasion by its citizens. The net result was the enactment of the HIRE Act (2010), more formally known as the Hiring Incentives to Restore Employment Act. The HIRE Act contained Title V. There were previous attempts to implement a law in the US equivalent to what we now know as FATCA but these failed to gain sufficient traction from the Senate. In the end what we now know as FATCA was copied and pasted from previous bills into Title V of the HIRE Act. In itself the HIRE Act was a short-term measure to grant US companies tax breaks and incentivise them to employ more people. All of the tax breaks that were in the HIRE Act have long since passed.

Unfortunately the acronym that was applied at the time that the HIRE Act was passed was the foreign account tax compliance act. Due to the failure of the bills that directly applied FATCA in Congress, the actual act on US statute books is still the HIRE Act (2010). As a purist therefore, I continue to point out to people that there is no (and never has been) a US law called the foreign account tax compliance act or FATCA.

All that being said the term FATCA Has now entered the general lexicon of terms to describe components of the US withholding taxation system in Chapter 4 Section 1471–1474 of the US Internal Revenue Code.

Apart from the law that is represented by the higher Act 2010, the implementing regulations are contained in Chapter 4 of the US Internal Revenue Code.

FATCA has 2 pillar components. Overall, the purpose of FATCA is to enshrine measures to deter and detect tax evasion being conducted by US persons through foreign accounts. The first pillar of FATCA, is therefore a requirement on US persons to disclose any non-US financial accounts they may hold. They do this using what is called FBAR or foreign bank account reporting. The second component is by far the more contentious. This component obligates all financial institutions located outside the US to have the Chapter 4 status of all of their clients and to report any US accounts to the IRS. In 2010 this was seen as the most outrageous form of overreach conducted by a tax administration. However, given the size of the US securities market, the rest of the industry essentially for the most part gave up and sought ways to acquiesce to the US government demands.

When I use the term "Chapter 4 status", essentially what is being asked for here is a tax determination of the tax residency of an account holder. For this purpose the US Internal Revenue Service created definitions of financial institutions and accountholders and a number of other different terms. In order to comply with Chapter 4 of the US Internal Revenue Code every non-US financial institution was and is required to determine whether the account holder is a US person or not. For an individual this is relatively simple and the Chapter 4 status is either US reportable person or non-US person. As soon as the determination is made that the account holder is not US, Chapter 4 no longer applies.

It's important to understand here that, because the purpose of FATCA is anti-tax evasion, the IRS essentially comes to the conclusion that tax evasion is only likely to be materially undertaken by Americans who are wealthy. The due diligence rules in the IGAs therefore also create different rules for due diligence dependent on the value of an account operated by an account holder. Typically, accounts that are valued less than $50,000 at the end of each reporting year do not have any due diligence required and no reporting of these accounts is necessary even if the account holder is definitively a US person.

Equally accounts valued at over $1,000,000 are generally subject to enhanced review each year—the financial institution must obtain a tax certificate or self-certification, check all of its electronic records and interview the relationship manager responsible for the account. The purpose of the enhanced review is to make sure that this high value account is not being used by an American and that no information has materially changed during the year. As an aside, FATCA rules also require the aggregation of all accounts owned by one beneficial owner. So you can't get around FATCA reporting simply by opening a number of small value accounts to hide your true wealth. All this does of course, is create increasing levels of complexity as financial institutions must annually aggregate and establish the value of accounts in order to determine what level of review is required before deciding which accounts are reportable and which are not. These account values are called thresholds.

The net result between 2012 and 2019 is that rather than have to cope with the due diligence obligations and additional workloads most financial institutions chose not to accept US persons as accountholders will stop which created an enormous backlash from financial institutions particularly in Europe. Today it is still common to find financial institutions who will not accept US clients. Part of the problem associated with these due diligence problems is that there are account holders at foreign financial institutions who do not necessarily know or understand whether they have tripped over US tax regulations and are, in effect for the purpose of FATCA, reportable US persons. For example there are a number of tests which can be used to establish that an account holder is actually or should be treated as a US person.

The green card test. There are many people who have visited the US, often for an educational reason, and while they are there they get a part time job for which they require a green card under which they become a resident alien. However resident aliens have an obligation to file a US tax return from FATCA's perspective that makes them a reportable US person for a financial institution outside the US.

If an apparently non-US account holder has a US telephone number or a mailing address in the US or regularly transfers funds from a non-US account to a US account, these are all indicators of potential US tax status. The obligation on the financial institution is to identify these US indicia and to cure them. In the absence of a cure the financial institution is required to treat the account holder as presumed you US and report them as such. If no response is required is received from the account holder, they would be deemed to be recalcitrant with your S indicia.

Substantial presence test. Most countries have rules that create an obligation to file a tax return based on the length of time that the person is in the country. For the US this is 183 days. There is a formula that needs to be applied in full which information needs to be sought from the account holder. If the account holder has stayed in the US for a total of 183 days or more over the previous three years and they are not subject to any exemptions, then they are deemed to have failed the substantial presence test and must be treated as a US person.

Place of birth test. In the US, if you were born in the US, then you automatically granted US citizenship. However it is not uncommon for a person to be born in the US a yet then be removed from the US within a few days of the birth. This means that they will have your S citizenship but will not have a Social Security number or ssn associated with them when the birth is registered. We see this in pockets around the world notably in Malta where substantial portions of the population in Gozo effectively have US status because of this rule even though they have never been to the US and have no interest in US and have no securities trading in the US. Curing this test is more difficult. The only way to effectively cure place of birth test issues is for the person to obtain a certificate of loss of nationality from EU S government, to do which they must ironically, first apply for a US Social Security number. The process is not free and the association of accidental Americans has made representations to the IRS and has a legal case pending that the cost of revoking your S citizenship is unrealistically high.

Part of the problem that the financial services industry outside the US has with FATCA is firstly, that it is extra territorial and secondly that it is a negative proof system. In other words it doesn't matter where you are in the world if you are a financial institution you must meet US withholding tax regulations and FATCA in particular. This leads us to discuss two of the major problems associated with FATCA.

There were two big problems with implementing Chapter 4—data privacy and withholding. The first problem was that the regulations in Chapter 4 required that any account holder that was determined to be a US person must be reported to the IRS on what was then form 8966. The principle behind the US government's thinking, was that The US person themselves through FATCA had an obligation to report the accounts to the IRS separately using FBAR. Therefore, you could consider FATCA to be the most enormous join the dots exercise conducted by a tax administration. If a US person operated an account in, for example, France, the account holder, an American, would be expected to report that French account on the FBAR form. The financial institution at which this American held their account would also report this account on their form 8966. So as long as the dots joined up and the IRS can associate accounts disclosed in FBAR with accounts disclosed by a financial institution, the IRS has all of the information it needs to assess whether this American may be in a position to evade US taxes.

The problem was that many financial institutions outside the US were, and are subject to a number of domestic and regional regulations. In particular this includes data protection. The first wave of push back against the US government's FATCA regulations was based on the principle that a financial institution that had an obligation to protect the data of its account holders could not disclose that information to another government because by doing so, they would essentially be breaking domestic law in order to meet the terms of US law. This led to a major realignment of the principles of FATCA by establishing a number of intergovernmental agreements or IGAs.

As the name implies these agreements were made between the US government and the IRS as its agent and a foreign government. The purpose of entering into these IGAs was to establish the requirement on the foreign government to implement domestic law that would have the effect of creating an obligation on a domestic financial institution to report US accountholders, where no such obligation existed before. Between 2010 and 2012 over 100 governments signed up to IGAs. Now, given that the purpose was deterrence of tax evasion many of these governments had concerns in the opposite direction. In the example cited before, the French government would have a natural concern that they may be French citizens operating bank accounts in the US which were not being reported to the French government. This would provide a French citizen with a mechanism to potentially evade French tax. Many foreign governments therefore pushed back on the IRS and ask for reciprocity in the IGAs. By the time they did this many intergovernmental agreements had already been signed and translated into domestic law.

The IRS response was to create two types of intergovernmental agreements—Model 1 and Model 2. The main reason that there are two different model structures for intergovernmental agreements is to allow for different reporting processes to take place. The IRS established their own system for submitting reports called the international data exchange system (IDES). Financial institutions located in a jurisdiction that had a Model 1 intergovernmental agreement with the US, would not be required to report to the IRS directly. Instead as FATCA had been translated into domestic law, these financial institutions would be reporting to their domestic tax administration the personal details of US accountholders. It would then be for the domestic tax administration under the terms of the intergovernmental agreement, to send that data two the IRS using the IDES system. By this rather circuitous mechanism, foreign financial institutions would not be required to break domestic law since they would be reporting US account holders to their own domestic regulators. The tax administrations themselves would, under the terms of intergovernmental agreements, then be able to pass that information on and so data protection laws would not have been broken. This has been repeatedly challenged and is currently still being challenged particularly in the European courts as a breach of EU citizens' rights under GDPR.

The IGAs are also subdivided into model 1A and model 1B IGAs. The difference between the two types is differentiated by the principle of reciprocity. A model 1B IGA contains wording that establishes the principle that the US will enact domestic regulation to force American financial institutions to collect Chapter 4 status of their account holders and report those to the IRS who, in principle, would then pass that information to their foreign counterparts.

The end result of all of these activities is an anti-tax evasion framework based on the principle the financial institutions will document the US tax status of their account holders and report any US account holders to the IRS either directly or indirectly. This model has been to a large extent copied by the OECD in the framework known as the automatic exchange of information or AEoI.

The second problem is that of withholding. Now unlike the OECD framework, US regulations generally include provisions to penalise anyone who fails to comply with the rules. Now, the IGAs contained all of the rules for the financial institutions to complete due diligence on their account holders in order to establish Chapter 4 status. Of course, as many people noted at the time on the day that FATCA came into force most financial institutions already had large numbers of account holders who of course had not been documented for the purpose of Chapter 4. The IRS calls these pre-existing accounts. The text of each IGA therefore had different rules that would apply to accounts that were pre-existing as opposed to accounts that were being newly opened. These rules were called due diligence rules and they created an enormous amount of complexity because now, what was originally seen as a simple set of documentation rules became bifurcated with different rules applying to pre-existing accounts than those which applied to accounts which were being newly opened.

I can't overstate the extent of dissatisfaction that the financial services industry has towards FATCA. As a regulatory framework it has so many flaws, you could drive the proverbial truck through it. But as many have observed, without teeth regulations tend to be ignored or circumvented in one way or another. The IRS's response was to require a withholding of 30% on any US-sourced FDAP income received by a US person or an account holder that had to be presumed to be US if they had not provided their financial institution with sufficient information required under the intergovernmental agreement. For this purpose, the intergovernmental agreements also include definitions such as account holder deemed to be *recalcitrant* i.e., having not provided required documentation within 90 days, and non-participating FFI. A nonparticipating FFI is a financial institution that has not met the extra territorial obligations of FATCA.

Now, at this point I should make the observation that while over 100 governments have signed intergovernmental agreements with the US, not all governments have done so. For those jurisdictions which have no IGA in place the IRS created a contract called the FFI agreement. Instead of relying on domestic regulation resulting from an intergovernmental agreement, financial institutions in non-IGA jurisdictions could sign the FFI agreement instead, indicating that they agreed to the due diligence and withholding obligations in FATCA.

The effect of all of this on the financial services industry has been substantial. Financial institutions generally are highly risk averse. They see the withholding obligation in fact as being a penalty. In order to avoid the penalty most financial institutions will not accept other financial institutions as customers unless they meet certain criteria.

There is a concept within FATCA that helps these financial institutions achieve this. In order to demonstrate that they have accepted FATCA principles, they must obtain a special identification number from the IRS a global intermediary identification number or GIIN. So, the basic rule being implemented in the market is that if you are a financial institution seeking to open account at another financial institution, if you do not have a global intermediary identification number your application will stop right there.

The US tax regulations also deal with how financial institutions handle the issue of FATCA withholding penalties. Most financial institutions operate omnibus accounts with their counterparties. The IRS has therefore adopted a mechanism called a withholding statement. Withholding statement is simply a message passed from One Financial institution to another financial institution that specifies whether and at what rate any tax should be withheld on the contents of an omnibus account held by one party at the other.

At this point, Chapter 4 of the US Internal Revenue Code has some overlap to Chapter 3 of the US Internal Revenue Code. Chapter 3 deals with the taxation of income paid to non-US recipients. In Chapter 3, a financial institution will generally either be a qualified intermediary—QI or a non-qualified intermediary—NQI. Since Chapter 4 is about anti-tax evasion and financial institutions are unsurprisingly highly risk averse, the purpose of a withholding statement is for one financial institution to certify to its counterparty whether any of its account holders should be subject to a FATCA penalty. Since most financial institutions cannot apply more than one rate of tax to any given income type within an omnibus account, it is more common that if one financial institution does have account holders that must be penalised, they will open a segregated omnibus account purely for the purpose of applying a FATCA penalty. This particularly affects non-qualified intermediaries since generally NQIs do not disclose their clients to their counterparties so, they are obligated to provide, at least once per year, a Chapter 4 withholding statement. This serves as confirmation that a non-qualified intermediary has met its due diligence obligations under FATCA.

For the purpose of providing a rounded and more complete picture, I should highlight some of the differences between the FFI agreement and being subject to FATCA through an IGA.

The original regulations implemented by the IRS are, by most people's judgement, draconian. Some of these draconian measures still exist in the FFI agreement today.

For example, in a non-IGA jurisdiction if an account holder is able to assert data protection law with the intent of preventing their financial institution from reporting them to the IRS, the FFI agreement requires but the financial institution to obtain a waiver of the account holders data protection rights in order that the financial institution can comply with the contractual obligations.

Another example still seen to be egregious, is that of account closure. In an IGA jurisdiction, if an account holder fails to respond to a reasonable request for a tax certificate that provides Chapter 4 status, that account holder will be classified as recalcitrant either with or without US indicia. However, in a non-IGA jurisdiction, a financial institution that has signed the FFI agreement is required to obtain the Chapter 4 status of its account holder and if it fails to do so after six months it must close the account.

There are another couple of oddities about FATCA that are worthy of note here. If a FATCA penalty is applied to any account holder that penalty must be reported by the financial institution within its normal reporting obligations in Chapter 3. This means that a Chapter 4 penalty would be reported on a form 1042-S and amounts included in the financial institution's U S tax return on form 1042.

It was also noted in the early days of FATCA that any FATCA penalty applied would not be subject to recovery, reduction or reclaim. That has since changed and today if a non-qualified intermediary receives a form 1042-S from another financial institution further up in the payment chain on which a Chapter 4 penalty is reported, the receiving financial institution, which has an obligation to provide its customers with recipient copies of forms 1042-S, is able to re-classify what was reported upstream as a FATCA penalty into a Chapter 3 withholding. There are certain rules governing how and when this can happen. However, in circumstances where this occurs it does lead to the opportunity for the financial institution to reduce the level of that penalty if they can provide sufficient evidence that the penalty should not have been applied in the first place.

To say that FATCA has been controversial would be a massive understatement. The association of accidental Americans continues to lobby for the removal of FATCA or for its substantial revision. It has been successful, especially in the context of reports by committees of US Congress which seemed to indicate that although staggering amounts of money have been spent both by the US administration and by foreign financial institutions, very little is available as evidence that this anti-tax evasion regulation has been effective in any way.

The only argument that seems to me to be valid against FATCA is that of reciprocity. The US has still as of today not met its obligations under reciprocal IGAs to implement domestic law to force American financial institutions to conduct due diligence reporting and withholding on account of non-US persons. Instead the IRS has said that it has met reciprocal obligations by providing 1042-S reports two it's counterparty's. This seems to me to be a way of wriggling around the question without answering it. Form 1042-S returns are provided by foreign financial institutions to the IRS in the first place with respect to non-US persons receiving US-sourced income. That's simply not the same as, for example, a French person operating an account at a US bank. There is no current legislation that would force a US bank to report that French person to the French tax administration.

17

AEoI/Common Reporting Standard

This chapter describes the way in which OECD has developed a framework for its member states under which tax administrations can share information about each other's financial institutions and accounts held at those institutions by their partner jurisdictions tax residents. Where AEoI is the mechanism by which partner jurisdictions share information, the Common Reporting Standard (CRS) describes the method by which the financial institutions in partner jurisdictions must go about identifying and reporting their foreign resident account holders to their domestic competent authority. This chapter describes the legal framework of AEoI and CRS as well as the due diligence and reporting mechanisms used.

AEoI and CRS are not the same thing. AEoI or the Automatic Exchange of Information is similar in concept to the IGAs in FATCA seen in the preceding chapter. The AEoI framework provides information sharing between tax administrations for the purpose of detecting and preventing tax evasion. The key term here is "automatic". Prior to AEoI, if a jurisdiction was concerned about tax evasion by one of its citizens, it would have to present that evidence to the other jurisdiction with a request for additional information. The US was particularly aggressive in this methodology with the Swiss tax administration, to the extent that the Swiss accused the US of "fishing" i.e., requesting information without supporting evidence. The Swiss, renowned for banking secrecy were not amenable to these kinds of requests.

The situation blew up in 2007, when Bradley Birkenfield, a UBS banker disclosed client information that he believed was evidence of tax evasion

R. K. McGill, *Cross-Border Investment Withholding Tax*, Finance and Capital Markets Series,
https://doi.org/10.1007/978-3-031-32785-8_17

by US citizens. UBS was fined $780 million and reached a deferred prosecution agreement with the US Department of Justice. In the narrow view, this was what triggered FATCA as the US response when it figured out that Switzerland wasn't the only place that such tax evasion might occur. Ironically Birkenfield was later charged with abetting a felony by one of its clients and sentenced to 40 months in prison after pleading guilty. Of the $780 million fine, $400 million represented US taxes that UBS failed to withhold.

This was the beginning of the end for bank secrecy of this kind in Switzerland and the start of discussions at the OECD to formalise a framework whereby participating jurisdictions could rely on information collected automatically by partner jurisdictions from their financial institutions that disclosed non-resident account holders.

It was quickly recognised that, while the principle of information sharing was useful on a bilateral basis, each jurisdiction would need to create domestic legislation, sometimes both primary and secondary, to force the financial institutions to do the required due diligence necessary to identify such account. Once that concept was understood, it became obvious that within that legislation, there would need to be common set of definitions to describe the types of account holder that were seen as tax evasion risk, the types of account that could be used for tax evasion. These were subsequently published by the OECD as the Common Reporting Standard ("CRS").

So, where AEoI describes the obligations of pairs of participating *governments* to share information automatically each year with each other, CRS describes the due diligence and reporting standards to be used by *financial institutions* in each jurisdiction, that flow from domestic legislation, that is then submitted to each jurisdiction's competent authority so that it can meet its information sharing obligations of AEoI.

Exhibit 17.1 describes this separation of principles. The relationship between jurisdictions is manged through Competent Authority Agreements ("CAA"s). If these are bilateral, they only have effect between the two specified parties. If they are multi-lateral ("MCAA"), they have an effect between any other jurisdiction that has also adopted the multi-lateral approach. There are two sub-types of MCAA depending on whether the jurisdictions already have either a double tax treaty in effect or a tax information exchange agreement ("TIEA") in place. Its worth noting, for the avoidance of confusion, that the TIEA is the non-fishing version of anti-tax evasion, in which one party has prima facie evidence and requests cooperation from its partner.

Once the CAA is in place, this gives the impetus for both jurisdictions to put in place domestic legislation to force their respective financial institutions

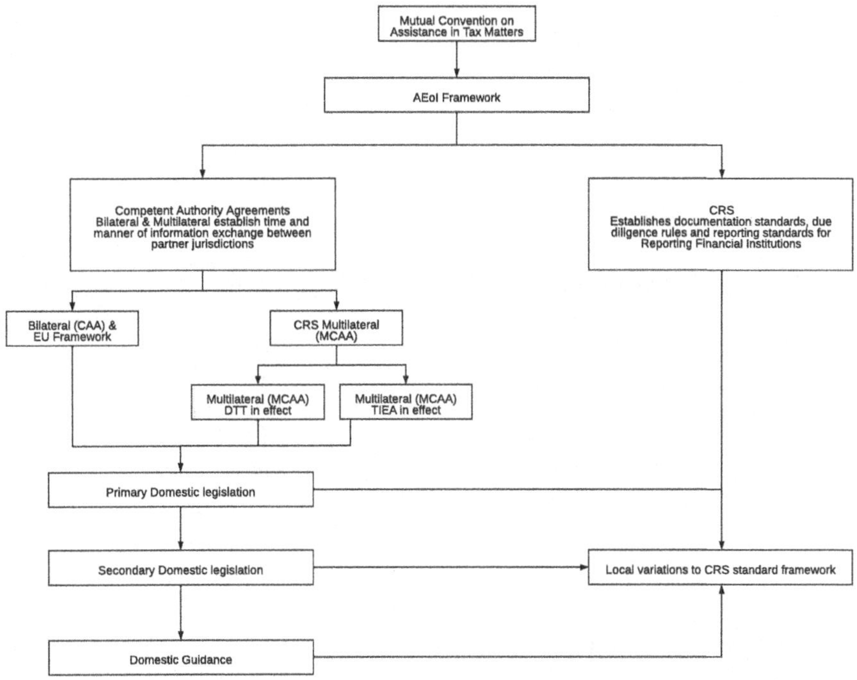

Exhibit 17.1 AEoI and CRS legal context

to provide them with data files representing accounts held by non-residents. This is represented on the right side of Exhibit 17.1.

As I have already noted with OECD frameworks, until the CAAs are in place, the framework is not legally binding. This opens the way for variations to CRS to creep in over time.

Exhibit 17.2 provides an overview of how CRS operates within the AEoI framework.

Financial institutions review financial accounts to identify reportable accounts by applying the CRS due diligence rules and then report these to their Host Country Competent Authority ("HCTA"). The HCTA collates the reports from all financial institutions, re-packages the data on a country-by-country basis and submits it to its partner Competent Authorities according to the terms of the CAA. If the partner jurisdiction identifies any issues, they can raise these, under the terms of the CAA as a matter of substantial non-compliance. Any such non-compliance would then be handled by the domestic regulator for the application of any penalties laid down in the implementing primary or secondary legislation.

As of October 2022, there are over 4900 bilateral exchange relationships activated with respect to more than 110 jurisdictions committed to the CRS,

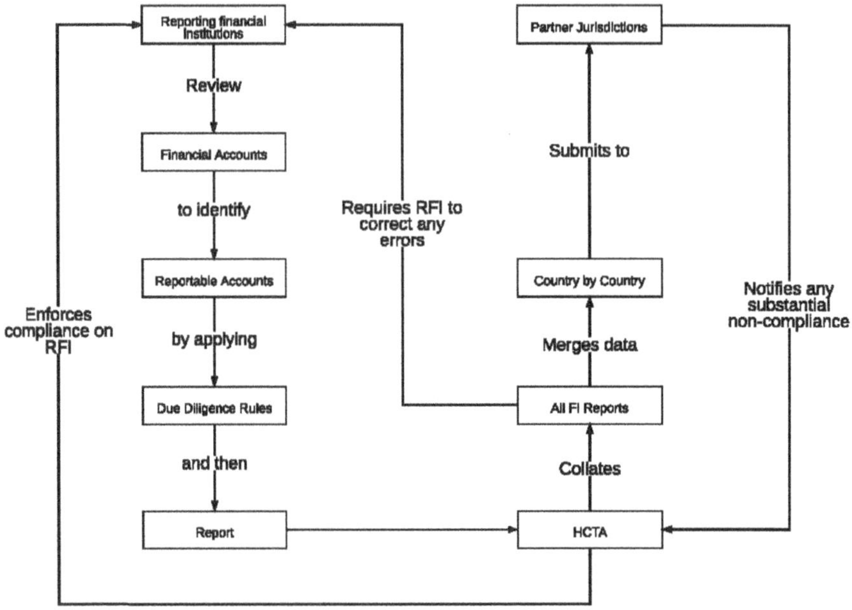

Exhibit 17.2 CRS process flow

with next exchanges between these jurisdictions set to take place at the end of September 2021. The relationships include those under the framework of Article 6 of the Multilateral Convention and the CRS MCAA, as well as exchange relationships based on bilateral agreements and the EU framework.

As of October 2022, there are over 3300 bilateral exchange relationships activated with respect to jurisdictions committed to exchanging Country-by-Country ("CbC") reports, and the first automatic exchanges of CbC reports took place in June 2018. These include exchanges between the signatories to the CbC Multilateral Competent Authority Agreement (CbC MCAA), between EU Member States under EU Council Directive 2016/881/EU and between signatories to bilateral competent authority agreements for exchanges under Double Tax Conventions or Tax Information Exchange Agreements, including 41 bilateral agreements with the US. Jurisdictions continue to negotiate arrangements for the exchange of CbC reports and the OECD will publish regular updates, to provide clarity for Multi National Enterprise ("MNE") Groups and tax administrations.

From the perspective of a financial institution, doing business with account holders who want to hold assets cross-border, the regulatory landscape is extremely complex. Very large sums of money have, and continue to be spent on systems to automate and streamline the due diligence required by CRS.

The OECD publishes guidelines for financial institutions, now in its second edition.[1] Much of this document is taken up with definitions allowing financial institutions the opportunity to create rules and systems to deal with potentially very large numbers of accounts to be reviewed and aggregated in order to come up with a much smaller number of reportable accounts.

Unlike FATCA, AEoI/CRS does not have any withholding component. FATCA can impose a 30% penalty, applied via the withholding tax system, on any US-sourced income received by a non-compliant financial institution.

As with any oversight system, the more complex it is, and this is complex indeed, it does not take long before some find the loopholes and weaknesses and seek to exploit them. In essence, this is why DAC6 was created—to find those who try to evade CRS, as we shall see in the next chapter.

[1] http://www.oecd.org/tax/exchange-of-tax-information/implementation-handbook-standard-for-automatic-exchange-of-financial-account-information-in-tax-matters.htm.

18

DAC6

This chapter describes the European Council Directive (EU) 2018/822 of 25 May 2018 amending Directive 2011/16/EU more commonly known as DAC6. DAC6 is intended to catch those cross-border arrangements that could be used to evade CRS. DAC6 defines the hallmarks of a cross-border arrangement that might represent evasion and thus be reportable. DAC6 also defines those parties who must report such arrangements if they become aware of them. This chapter describes the hallmarks and the procedures that firms and practitioners must be aware of to avoid liability and risk.

Causes

One of the common themes of withholding tax is the propensity for any system to be abused. The more complex the system, the easier it is to abuse it. There is a constant tension between the efforts of the regulators to second guess what tax evaders will do and the efforts of tax evaders themselves—who are usually smarter, better funded and more nimble.

It became clear that, in the same way that FATCA has many flaws, CRS also had weaknesses that allowed certain unscrupulous investors to get around the CRS disclosure obligations. Both FATCA and CRS are what are called "rules based" regulatory frameworks. They seek to define a rule for what to

R. K. McGill, *Cross-Border Investment Withholding Tax*, Finance and Capital Markets Series,
https://doi.org/10.1007/978-3-031-32785-8_18

do in any given set of circumstances. As the reader can imagine, in this space, the number of possible variables and therefore permutations requiring a rule, is very large. It was also clear that focusing solely on the financial institutions where accounts were held, would not be enough.

Purpose

What was needed was something that was broad enough and general enough that it could catch tax evaders without having to figure out every possible way they might achieve it. This led to DAC6 which, unlike FATCA or CRS, is a "principles-based" regulatory structure.

DAC6 basically is trying to catch people who are trying to evade AEoI/ CRS. Evading CRS can be done in a number of ways. The most common include setting up accounts for complex nested-and-chained legal structures in different markets with different financial institutions. This makes it difficult to trace the ultimate underlying investors and so they evade being reported to their home jurisdiction. Another method used by financial institutions, is to onboard clients into a business unit in one jurisdiction (A) and move the assets to another financial institution, in omnibus accounts, in another jurisdiction (B). If the residency of the investor is not on the CRS partner list of jurisdiction (A) but is on the CRS partner list of jurisdiction (B), the investor will have effectively evaded CRS reporting because the financial institution in jurisdiction (A) will not report them (because they aren't on the partner reporting list) and the financial institution in jurisdiction (B) will not report them (because they don't know who they are).

Intermediaries

DAC6 also recognises that its not just the investors who are doing this. They are usually facilitated by people who understand how all these frameworks and regulations work and who can advise them on what structures to set up, in which markets and how to structure the movement of assets. These structures are called "arrangements" and the facilitators (as well as the financial institutions) are called "intermediaries".

So, one of the ways that DAC6 differs from CRS is in (i) the definition of an intermediary i.e., a person responsible that is aware of an arrangement and (ii) the concept of legal professional privilege ("LPP") that some intermediaries might use to avoid reporting an arrangement they are involved in or aware of.

The definition of an intermediary has been widened to include *anyone* that designs, markets, organises or makes available for implementation or manages the implementation of a reportable cross-border arrangement. It also means any person that, having regard to the relevant facts and circumstances and based on available information and the relevant expertise and understanding required to provide such services, knows or could be reasonably expected to know that they have undertaken to provide, directly or by means of other persons, aid, assistance or advice with respect to designing, marketing, organising, making available for implementation or managing the implementation of a reportable cross-border arrangement. The effect to understand here is that for any given arrangement, assuming it to be reportable, it might get reported by more than one intermediary, perhaps by several.

It must also be remembered that DAC6 is a European Union Directive, it has no force outside the EU. However, as the UK found out after Brexit, while they are no longer in the EU, they have made similar commitments to the OECD so that the UK, while not directly affected by DAC6 any more, is still required to report under Hallmarks D1 or D2.

So, in order to be an intermediary, one or more of the following four conditions must be met:

a. be resident for tax purposes in a Member State;
b. have a permanent establishment in a Member State through which the services with respect to the arrangement are provided;
c. be incorporated in, or governed by the laws of, a Member State; and
d. be registered with a professional association related to legal, taxation or consultancy services in a Member State.

This means that, in either of the two examples I cited earlier, whoever has knowledge of the arrangement or facilitated the construction or implementation of the arrangement, would have an obligation to report it. Now, this leads to two more concepts. First, what is a reportable arrangement? How is this defined so that an intermediary can decide whether they should report. Second, what to do if the intermediary is a lawyer or other person who could refuse to report an arrangement by relying on another legal basis, such as legal privilege.

Legal Professional Privilege

So, if for example, you're a lawyer and a client asks you opine or help with an arrangement that trips one of the Hallmarks you would expect that lawyer to not report and claim client-attorney privilege. This would, of course, create a situation where reporting could be avoided and thus the arrangement may not get caught.

So, DAC6 provides that "Each Member State may take the necessary measures to give intermediaries the right to a waiver from filing information on a reportable cross-border arrangement where the reporting obligation would breach the legal professional privilege under the national law of that Member State. In such circumstances, each Member State shall take the necessary measures to require intermediaries to notify, without delay, any other intermediary or, if there is no such intermediary, the relevant taxpayer of their reporting obligations.... Intermediaries may only be entitled to a waiver [...] to the extent that they operate within the limits of the relevant national laws that define their professions".

In effect, this means that, if a lawyer is involved with or becomes aware of a reportable arrangement, they must either report the arrangement or rely on a waiver provided a Competent Authority. Now, if a jurisdiction provides a general waiver to certain types of intermediary, this will work well. However, if the intermediary is required to request a waiver on a case-by-case basis, this rather dilutes the privilege since the Competent Authority will be made aware that there is a reportable arrangement for which the intermediary is claiming a waiver of reporting. The last part of this clause however, provides the catch-all, in that, if an intermediary is able to rely on a waiver, they must take action to tell someone else, either another intermediary or, as a last resort, the taxpayer themselves that what they are doing is reportable.

Hallmarks

Exhibit 18.1 provides an overview of the hallmarks that DAC6 defines. The reader will notice that the descriptions of these hallmarks is very general, speaking more to intent and effect than specifically how an arrangement is constructed.

The Hallmarks are grouped into five categories A–E. Hallmarks A and B are linked to a concept called the Main Benefits Test or MBT. The MBT is designed to flush out arrangements where the main benefit of the arrangement can be determined to be for a tax purpose and not primarily for another

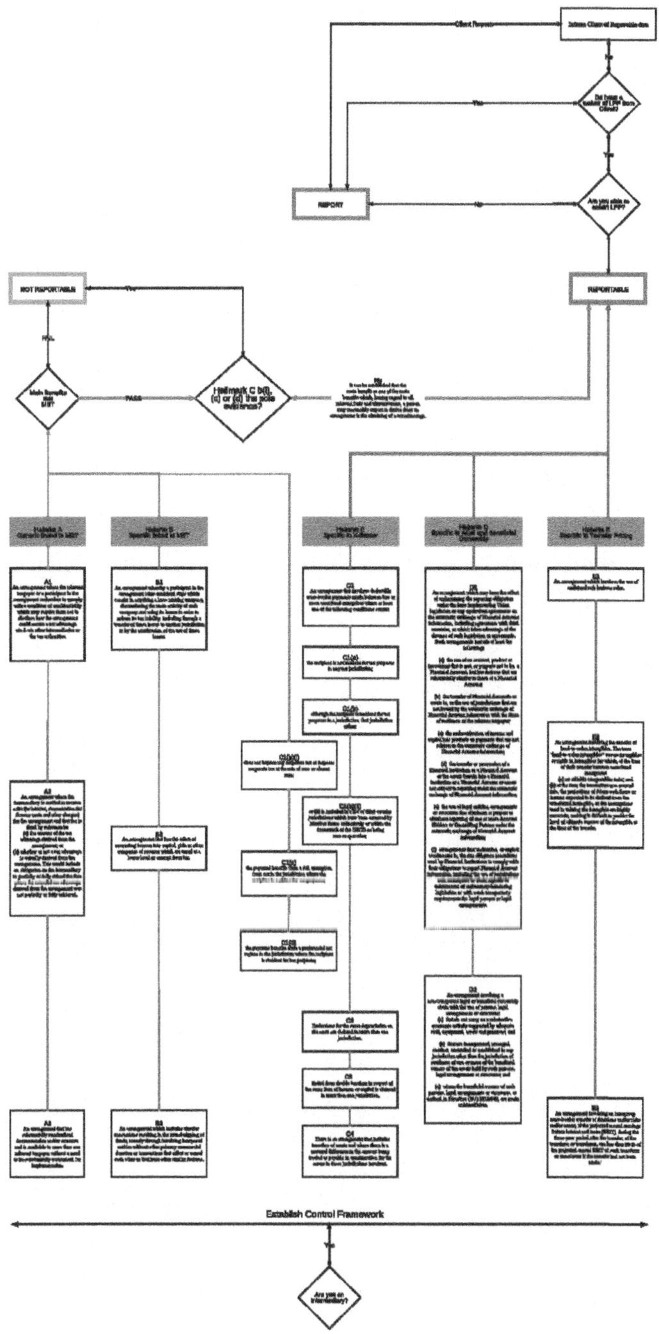

Exhibit 18.1 DAC6 decision tree

economic purpose. Hallmarks A and B do not have to relate to cross-border arrangements. Hallmarks in category C are specific to arrangements that are cross border in nature. Hallmarks in category D are specific to arrangements based on beneficial ownership and Hallmarks in category E are related to arrangements based on transfer pricing. Now, it's important to understand that just because an arrangement becomes reportable, because it trips one or more Hallmarks, does not mean that it is a tax evading arrangement. It merely means that it has characteristics that mean it could be used for tax evasion. The ultimate decision on these matters will be the Competent Authorities to who the reports are submitted.

Framework

The obligation in DAC6, to have a compliance framework, applies to anyone who fits the definition of an intermediary. This means policy and procedure to detect, gather and report on any matter that fits the description of a Hallmark.

19

Tax Fraud

Denmark

The Danish tax authority has filed several lawsuits since 2018 claiming $2 billion of fraudulent withholding tax claims were made and paid to over a hundred defendants in the period 2012–2015. These fraud claims highlight weaknesses in the tax system. This chapter shows how these scams worked and what the tax authorities have done about it since (i) in chasing them perpetrators and (ii) changing the rules of tax reclaims in response. The chapter also discusses the wider implications of this type of fraud on the reputation of financial institutions and tax administrations. This chapter is also useful for investors to understand the degree to which tax planning can easily cross a line into tax evasion and even fraud.

I mentioned earlier that double tax treaties essentially set the framework for entitlements that result in the tax processes implemented by tax administrations. To this extent the tax treaties are intergovernmental, while specific tax processes are implemented by department of tax administrations. However, while governments can establish wide-ranging frameworks, the task of implementing specific procedures for tax reclaims is much more difficult. The tax administrations must decide what form the tax reclaims must take, when such reclaims can be filed and by whom as well as what evidence is required for each reclaim to be processed before a refund cheque is issued. This is one of the complications referenced by both the OECD and by the European Union when researching the barriers to the free movement of capital between

R. K. McGill, *Cross-Border Investment Withholding Tax*, Finance and Capital Markets Series,
https://doi.org/10.1007/978-3-031-32785-8_19

member states. Tax administrations are typically not well funded by governments. Therefore, they are restricted in manpower and processing capability and often lack oversight since withholding tax particularly with respect to foreign investors is not at the top of the agenda.

The Danish case centred around Mr. Sanjay Shah, former CEO of Solo Capital. Solo Capital was cited in the Panama papers as having an almost impenetrable ownership structure. The nature of the alleged fraud had two components to it. The first was that it became clear that the Danish tax authorities only had one person responsible for receiving tax reclaim applications and processing these through to refund cheques. It was alleged that false claims were filed through third-party vendors using securities lending and borrowing techniques in a tax arbitrage model.

In a tax arbitrage model there are typically two or more parties, one of whom is a securities lender, the other a securities borrower. The key to the abuse is that the borrower is an investor resident in a jurisdiction with a favourable tax treaty with the target jurisdiction. Typically, the investor would also be eligible for favourable treatment. If the investor is exempt from withholding tax, they would be able to claim 100% of any tax withheld in a reclaim. So, as an example I may enter into an agreement with an investor such that prior to the record date I buy a very large number of shares in a particular company. If I kept the shares over the record date, statutory withholding tax would be applied and I could, in principle, file a tax reclaim to claim back the difference between the statutory rate applied, say 30%, and the treaty rate to which I was entitled say 15%. However, if I agree with my partner that I will sell them the shares just prior to the record date and my partner agrees that they will sell the shares back to me just after the pay date, this means that my partner is entitled to file a reclaim because they were the owner of the shares on the record date. However, because they are tax exempt instead of claiming back the difference between the statutory rate and the treaty rate, my partner can claim the whole amount of tax withheld back. That which makes this an abuse of treaty is the agreement between me and my partner in which he agrees to split the profits of the reclaim with me after the claim is paid. This model tends to work best when very large positions in securities are held and transferred. In the Danish case, the total size of the refunds made was in the region of €2 billion.

Mr. Shah was targeted by the Danish tax administration in numerous legal cases the most recent of which was a request for his extradition from Dubai. Mr. Shah has consistently denied the allegations against him citing that he was merely exploiting loopholes in the tax system. The Danish administration also took action in US courts against the third-party vendors who had assisted

Solo Capital in filing the claims. The position being taken was that the third-party vendors we're guilty of unlawful enrichment by receiving fees when they should, in the view of the Danish administration, have had sufficient due diligence on the activities of Solo Capital to have been able to raise red flags about the pattern of activity being undertaken. The attempt to extradite Mr. Shaw by the Danish tax authorities suffered a setback in September 2022 when a judge in the United Arab Emirates rejected the extradition request.

There was however not just one loophole that was being exploited. Another loophole involved US investors who had set up 401K arrangements. There are rules in the US about the funding of 401K arrangements which are essentially personal pension plans. In US court papers, it became clear that just prior to engaging in substantial Danish investments these 401(K)s were funded for the purpose of buying the shares to an extraordinary level. This level of fraud became unsustainable when some simple calculations were made. Those calculations showed that for any given fraudulent reclaim, the funds required to purchase the shares in order to file the reclaim we're often larger than the capital value of the target companies themselves.

Finally, it was also alleged that Mr. Shah bribed the Danish tax official in order to speed up the payment of the fraudulent reclaims.

Germany

Cum-Ex Dividend Scandal

Over a hundred German banks are currently reported to be under investigation for their part in illicit tax refund claims totalling €12 billion between 2001 and 2011. This section describes the history and nature of these transactions together with commentary on how effective the remedial measures have been and the effect this has had on other reclaims.

Following the financial crisis of 2008, many tax administrations became suspicious about the nature of certain trading activities that were leading to tax reclaims. Germany was concerned with a type of trading called cum-ex. It's reported that German tax administration may have been subject to illegal tax refund applications totalling €12 billion.

In a normal dividend there are two dates of note. The first is the record date. This is the date on which the ownership of the shares is crystallised for the purpose of withholding of tax. The second date is the pay date which, as the name implies, is the date on which the distribution of the dividend is made to those investors holding the securities on the record date. However, the trading in these shares can continue all the way up to the record date and across the record date. There are two more terms that are relevant to this type of fraudulent activity. The first is cum dividend. A security is cum dividend meaning that the company has declared that there will be a dividend in the future but has not yet paid it out. The second term is ex-dividend. The ex-dividend date for stocks is usually set one business day before the record date. If you purchase a security on its ex-dividend date or after that you, will not receive the next dividend payment. Instead, the seller gets the dividend if you purchase before the ex-date, you get the dividend. This leads to the opportunity for a fraudulent transaction in which an investor is aware of a security that is cum dividend. In other words, the investor is purchasing the shares at a point in time when the company has already declared that it will be paying a dividend. Securities can continue to be traded and will continue to trade with a dividend entitlement until the ex-dividend date. After the ex-dividend date the stock can still trade but without its dividend rates. This means that when the dividend is actually paid out the seller receives the dividend, because the buyer is no longer entitled to the dividend having purchased after the ex-date.

However, in the German case investors were claiming back tax based on the double tax treaties both as buyers and sellers. As soon as this loophole had been identified, the criminals involved in the transactions would typically engage in trades of extremely high volumes of German shares and in some cases it was claimed the German banks were complicit in organising these kinds of trades knowing that the tax administration would pay out on tax reclaims simply on the basis of who owned the shares.

The German authorities established a parliamentary inquiry committee of the German Bundestag to investigate the scandal. In general terms this type of trading is an abuse of tax treaty. The net outcome is that the German tax administration when receiving standard refund applications has increased its level of scrutiny. This includes, for example requesting evidence of trading history of the security with the investor up to and including the record date. Another effect is that, because the illegal activity was generally on extremely large positions in these German securities, that German tax administration will audit tax reclaims above a certain value almost automatically. This can obviously delay the payment of a claim. It can also result in additional questions being asked of the claimant all their agent and generally this has the effect of slowing down the tax reclaim process in Germany.

The scale of this fraud in Germany was so large that is said to have affected almost every German bank to some level. At the end of 2016 for example UniCredit Hypovereinsbank brought claims for damages amounting to €140 million against three former board members for their personal roles in shaping bank policy on this type of trading.

The industry ends up in a difficult situation. It's clear that there are significant drivers for improvements in what were and to some extent still are overly complex procedures. However, tax administrations are generally not well funded enough to afford the latest technology or even the latest innovations in approaches to the use of technology. This means that as other drivers such as digitisation, distributed Ledger, tokenisation and increase the use of standards and automation all the subject of substantial investments by financial institutions, tax administrations are substantially left behind. As with all things, when you make things more complex it becomes easier for unscrupulous investors to identify ways to game the system. The response from tax administrations has been both slow and to a large extent ineffective. Rather than engage in more robust technologies and improved procedures, they have resorted to increased manual procedures and increased manual oversight. Given the amount of data that they could request, it would have been more logical to apply artificial intelligence to these large data sets because it would have been much more capable of identifying patterns of behaviour of investors that could have, in some circumstances, detected and prevented tax fraud from occurring in the first place or failing that, stemming a flood of abusive claims after the early stage.

Part V

Technology

20

ISO Standards

This chapter explores the current state of standards in the industry, as a prerequisite to automation, in relation to withholding tax. The International Standards Organisation (ISO) appointed the Society for Worldwide Interbank Telecommunications (SWIFT) to police ISO standards in financial services. The chapter looks at what standards currently exist (ISO15022) and the transition to a new standard (ISO20022). Particular emphasis will be given to (i) how tax processing will be affected by the transition of the message-based model of ISO15022 to the business process model of ISO20022 and (ii) the specific tax tags that are available.

ISO15022 & ISO20022

The International Standards Organisation ("ISO") appointed the Society for Worldwide Interbank Financial Telecommunications ("SWIFT") as the Standards Authority for financial services. SWIFT is a Belgian not for profit organisation with over 8000 banks as members/owners. SWIFT is the ISO Registration Authority for ISO 9362 (BIC), ISO 10383 (MIC), ISO 13616 (IBAN), ISO 15022 (scheme for securities messages), and ISO 20022 (universal financial industry message scheme). SWIFT began its messaging service in 1977 and today, it guarantees that a message that leaves one

R. K. McGill, *Cross-Border Investment Withholding Tax*, Finance and Capital Markets Series,
https://doi.org/10.1007/978-3-031-32785-8_20

member will reach its destination member with a network uptime of greater than 99.99999% and s guarantee of security for that message.

In 2015 there was a reported theft of $101 million from the Bangladesh Central Bank ostensibly using the SWIFT network. This caused a major scandal, given SWIFT's claim to absolute security of content. It became clear, after investigation that the fault did not lie with SWIFT but with the security of the end points in the SWIFT network. If your SWIFT credentials can be hacked or stolen, anyone can access the SWIFT network and steal money by moving it around the network. This led to changes in security and a heightened awareness of the risks posed by the end points in the SWIFT network.

I have the honour to serve on three ISO subcommittees—corporate actions, funds management and proxy voting. The purpose of these committees is to help the industry coalesce around a single standard for financial messaging. The committees also receive and assess requests for changes to the ISO Standards Release that happens periodically. These change requests ("CRs") allow the industry to change the standard to meet changing needs. Often these will be country-specific changes. There is notably no subcommittee for withholding tax. My presence on these committees is to contribute subject matter expertise on tax that form a component of each committee's general work. So, for the corporate actions committee I am most concerned with making sure that messages for specific types of corporate actions events have the appropriate codes available to allow banks to communicate the tax elements of a dividend for example.

The current standard in the industry is ISO20022. The prior standard was ISO15022. The difference between the two is fundamental. ISO15022's focus was on messages, a different message for each purpose. ISO20022 is more holistic and is focussed on business processes. In the ISO15022 Standards Release of 2019, messages are identified by type so MT564 is a Message Type and 564 identifies the message itself as a pre-advice. The message itself is comprised of "blocks" of data, each block representing a different component of data related to the message. Within each block are fields. These data fields are specified very precisely—NUM for numeric, TXT for text, etc right down to the number of characters allowed for each field and whether the field is optional or mandatory within the Standard.

Two very important features of these messages are their associated functionalities. From a tax perspective these are //COPY and repeatable blocks. //COPY just means that when one party wants to send a message to another party, if they include //COPY, the message will also be copied and sent to a third party. Repeatable blocks is a feature only available in some message types and allows the sender to include multiple sets of data in one message. So, for example, MT564 messages can have repeatable blocks, so you can send pre-advices for more than one corporate action. However MT566 confirmation messages cannot have repeatable blocks.

Exhibit 20.1 shows how this can work, at its most basic level. A financial institution (2) with an investor as a client holds securities in an omnibus account at another financial institution (1). When the upstream financial institution learns of an impending dividend, it will issue a pre-advice message MT564 to inform its customer of the relevant details—ISIN, record date, pay date, rate per share, etc. With //COPY active, the vendor, engaged by financial institution (2) can prepare for tax reclamation by gathering documentation from financial institution (2) who in turn obtains it from its client, the investor.

On the record date itself, the financial institution will issue another MT564. This message has an additional piece of data—the record date position in the security which the financial institution holds in its omnibus account. This message also had the //COPY feature included so that a tax reclaim vendor engaged by the second financial institution, can also be made aware of the event.

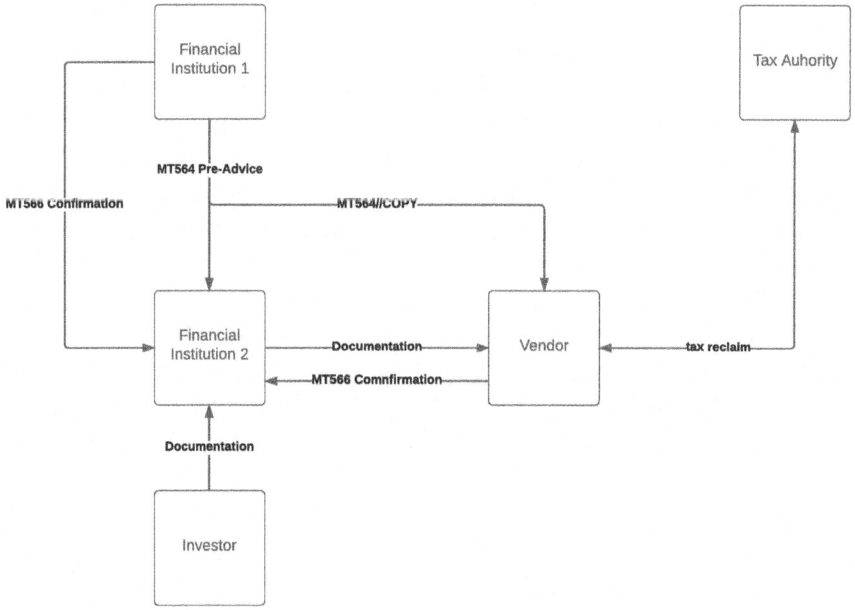

Exhibit 20.1 Basic SWIFT implementation for tax reclaims

In the background, the relevant documentation can be provided to the vendor. On the pay date, financial institution (2) receives an MT566 confirmation message indicating that a dividend has been paid with tax withheld, the code WITH is used in the message to identify the tax withheld and the amount. This provides the vendor with the missing evidence necessary to complete a tax reclaim filing to a tax authority. If the vendor is also a member of SWIFT, it can also confirm the payment of the refund using an MT566 message, this time using the code TREC meaning an event related to a tax reclaim.

As the reader can see, codes in SWIFT messages can be used with the ISO standard to automate aspects of the tax reclaim process. Similar codes can be used for tax relief events e.g., WTRC. Codes are used instead of more verbose textual descriptions simply to (i) reduce the size of the messages and (ii) to allow for further automation to be used on the messages by other systems that are capable of looking for he codes in expected locations in the message in order to trigger other activities in what is called a straight through processing ("STP") environment.

STP was all the rage in the noughties before digitisation, tokenisation and DLT had arrived. While it is still the holy grail for many corporate actions professionals, it has fallen out of usage compared to the sexier terms in the digital space.

This is a good example of how standards are the prerequisite for automation. Sadly, automation of withholding tax on the SWIFT network has not seen major adoption or substantial moves to an STP environment.

In an ISO20022 environment, while the messages themselves would remain unchanged, the consideration would be of the whole process with the *expectation* of an STP flow so that the way in which the message reacts can be modelled more effectively.

It is also important to note here that the codes used in SWIFT messages are often supported by conditional logic in the standard. So, for example, a tax code could only be used in certain circumstances where tax was a relevant function of the message.

XBRL

Another standard used in the withholding tax space is the extended business reporting language, xbrl. The first use of this standard related to American Depositary Receipts ("ADRs"). The problem that xbrl addresses is the machine readability of complex documents related to the tax component of these securities. The initiative was innovated by GlobeTax who are the back office processor for all four of the US depositary banks, JP Morgan, Citibank, Deutsche bank and BNY Mellon.

American Depositary Receipts are a derivative instrument invented by JP Morgan in 1923. ADRs were a way to sell non-US securities to Americans. The key feature of ADRs is that they are denominated in US dollars and each ADR can represent a fixed number of underlying non-US securities—the ADR ratio. When launched, and until the advent of exchange-traded funds ("ETFs"), ADRs experienced substantial popularity and growth with the US investing public and institutional investors alike. As the market liked these so much, everyone else started buying ADRs too.

So, when a non-US security distributed a dividend, if the security is also listed in ADR form, typically the ADR would pay out a dividend too. The ADR pay date may not be the same as the underlying security pay date and may be subject to different tax treatments. All of this information is set out in the ADRs prospectus.

When these programs are set up by the ADR banks, they are called "*sponsored* ADRs".

Now, anyone with access to the trading markets can buy ADRs so, if a UK resident bought a Nestle ADR (Swiss). The tax withheld on the Nestle dividend would be a Swiss withholding tax at 35%. Even though the ADR is denominated in US dollars, its important to understand that the dividend is not US-sourced FDAP income, so its not taxable under US tax regulations. As a UK resident, I would be able to claim a tax refund of 20% under the Swiss-UK double tax agreement. This scenario could play out with any number of types and residencies of investor owning ADRs when they distribute dividends.

As the final sweetener for the industry, XBRL is compliant with ISO20022 standards and effectively interoperable.

One of my major criticisms of standard in financial services has, and continues to be that a standard is not treated as a standard but as a convenient tool to be circumnavigated when necessary. There is a massive amount of replication and reconciliation going on, simply because not enough effort has been put into following the standard and leveraging the benefits it can bring. Even with ISO standard messaging, the risk averse nature of financial institutions and insistence on the "four-eyes" risk management principle means that when a financial institution receives a SWIFT message, the first response is to print it, review it, decide on any action and in many cases re-key it into another SWIFT message. This is lunacy when the very principle of interbank messaging was, and is, to provide a consistent standard by means of which manual processing can be avoided. The complexity of transaction banking has overtaken this simple principle and rendered it almost useless.

I remain however a staunch advocate of standards, in the pure sense, and their intelligent use to generate automation and digitisation opportunities for innovation in financial services.

To answer this, and highlight the role of XBRL, we need to understand the role of GlobeTax as shown in Exhibit 20.2 GlobeTax has a near 100% market share of ADR tax processing business. GlobeTax works with the underlying issuer, via the ADR bank, to gather security level information, ISIN, security name and description. It receives from the ADR bank, details of the corporate action, record date, pay date, rate per share, ADR ratio. Combining all this data, it prepares an Important Notice that also contains a description of the procedures to be followed for any combination of investor type and residency. This Important Notice is provided to DTC whose role is to distribute the Notice to its direct participants. Most direct participants in the DTC system are US financial institutions such as banks and brokers, each of whom may have direct clients such as individuals or entities as investors. However, using omnibus accounts, other non-US financial institutions can effectively be indirect participants by having an account at a direct participant. They in turn will have their own clients among which may be other financial institutions, and so there is created a cascade of omnibus accounts and a chain of payment.

The Important Notices are passed down this chain so that each level of indirect participant can figure out (i) whether any of its direct clients could be eligible for tax relief or a reclaim and (ii) whether there is another layer of financial institutions below them that could claim.

Its this chain of intermediaries that causes the problem and for which XBRL was seen as the solution. While much of these Important Notices is data, the tax component can be extremely complex inasmuch as it must specify, for each residency, whether there is a tax benefit to b gained, if so what type and if so, what documents are required and when, in order to gain that benefit.

XBRL was mandated in the US as the method for corporations to file their annual accounts, again, documents that combine data components with textual components. By the use of XBRL, a document can be rendered into an *XBRL instance* where data components can be extracted, including those included within text, by the use of standardised tags—a bit like bookmarking. The big benefit of this is that an XBRL instance is machine readable.

Before XBRL's use in DTC Important Notices, as the Notice was published and passed on, each recipient would have to print the Notice, review it, decide

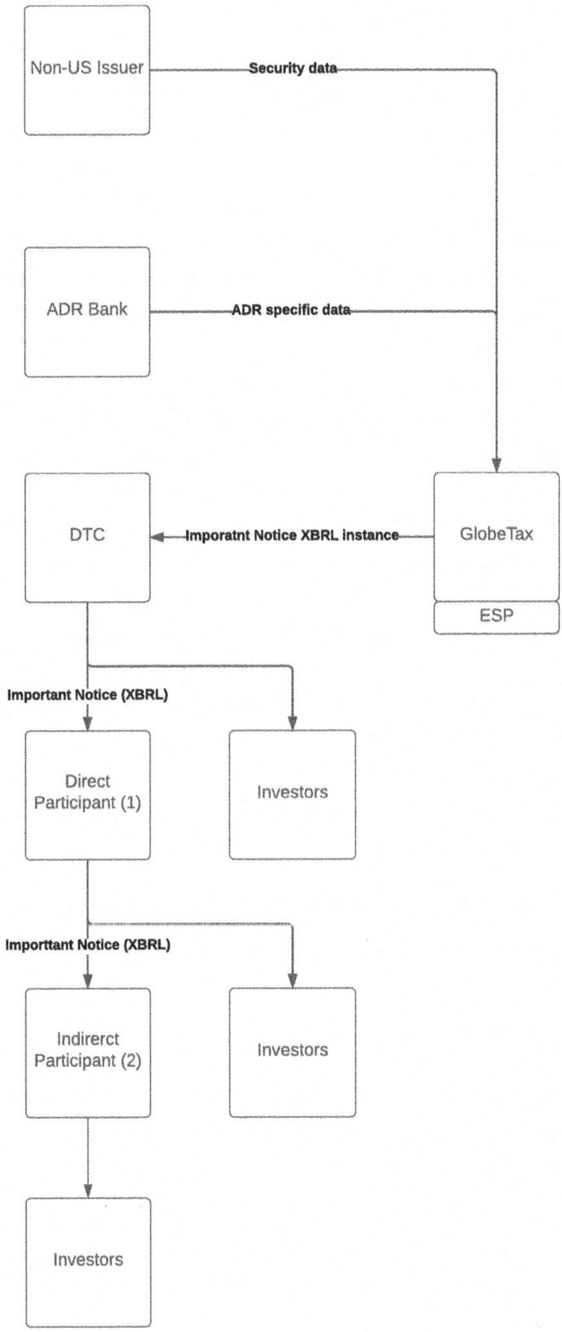

Exhibit 20.2 Use of XBRL in important notices

whether to pass it on and, where relevant decide whether any of their direct clients as investors could benefit in order to decide whether they need to do anything. After XBRL, in principle, many of these manual assessment tasks could be automated, essentially creating that sought after STP.

An after effect of this automation is also that the level of participation in the tax component of an ADR distribution could be massively increased because the financial institutions further down the payment chain would have more time to know about the event and gather the relevant documentation. To facilitate this, GlobeTax created its ESP platform that is described elsewhere in this book.

The difference here is that the ESP platform effectively sets a proprietary standard while ISO provides a generic industry standard. If you want to benefit from tax relief on an ADR, your financial institution will generally have to use GlobeTax's ESP system (and pay the relevant depositary fees).

Proprietary standards are useful because they provide targeted specific benefits. Their creators want to effectively become a de facto industry standard through the mechanism of widespread adoption. If everyone has to use a single toll-bridge, that toll-bridge becomes the standard way to get to the destination.

The increasing adoption by tax administrations of xml standards that are ISO20022 compliant does mean that those with proprietary standards will increasingly have to adopt ISO20022 components into their proprietary standards if they want to continue integration efforts with financial institutions.

21

Platforms

Many financial institutions and third-party vendors in this space now have platform-based web technology in place to provide their customers with a seamless, single and integrated source of information. Withholding tax has been late to this party, but there are now several notable platforms available that improve efficiency and compliance in withholding tax processing. GlobeTax's MIDAS platform, GOAL's Adroit platform and TConsult's Tax Compliance Toolkit™ are three that will be described.

Platforms are used by firms who want to offer high-volume processing services at a retail level. Retail in this context just means at the individual investor level, even if the platform itself is used by a financial institution. In the following sections I will provide a brief explanation of some of the more notable tax platforms.

ESP®[1]

An acronym for Electronic Submission Portal. ESP is operated by GlobeTax based in the USA. ESP is a platform deployed by GlobeTax as an agent for the four US depositary banks. The purpose of the platform is to facilitate the provision of documents and data from financial institutions in the payment chain of American depositary Receipts ("ADRs") (Exhibit 21.1).

[1] https://www.globetax.com/esp/.

R. K. McGill, *Cross-Border Investment Withholding Tax*, Finance and Capital Markets Series,
https://doi.org/10.1007/978-3-031-32785-8_21

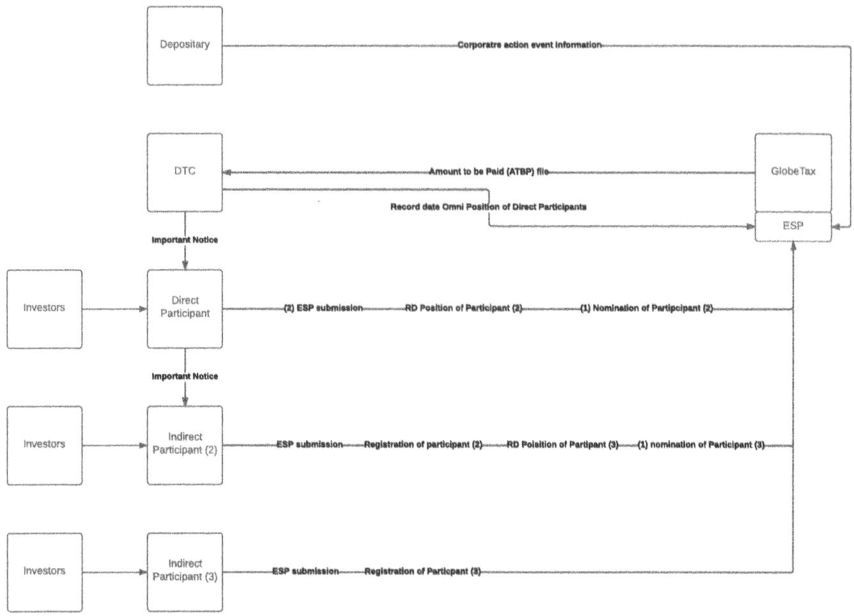

Exhibit 21.1 ESP

The portal is populated by GlobeTax in association with the depositaries, with respect to corporate actions that have some tax component. The financial institutions that are registered with ESP can see those "events" and, in particular, the tax-related information. This is called an eligibility matrix. The eligibility matrix allows a financial institution to map its own client base in terms of positions and tax residencies in order to see whether any of its clients could be in a position to claim a tax benefit when the corporate action event occurs. The matrix also specifies which documents will be required for each beneficial owner. In some cases, the portal can also automatically generate some of the documentation needed e.g., letters of indemnity.

Once the record date occurs, the platform is populated with the position of the top-most financial institutions in the chain of payment. These will typically be DTC direct Participants. That aggregated position is the maximum position i.e., number of shares, that can be claimed for any kind of treaty relief. Of course, the position on record date of the top-most financial institution, is comprised of a combination of the positions of its own direct customers and the position in any omnibus account of its customers that are other financial institutions.

These lower-level financial institutions cannot make any claim at all, unless the higher-level institution authorises them to use the platform, enters the record date position of the lower-level institution in its omnibus account.

Equally, the lower-level institution must register with the portal to make its own claim. Each lower-level institution must also indemnify the higher-level institution against liability for tax or penalties if its claims are subsequently found to be invalid. And so, as each level of financial institutions authorises its customers in lower levels, the chain of payment can be constructed as each financial institution in each level submits documentation and data for its claims, in line with the eligibility matrix. This methodology is insensitive to whether the tax is relief at source, quick refund or standard refund claim.

The benefit of a platform approach is to provide greater access to a larger number of financial institutions to participate in a corporate action. Without a platform approach, most second level institutions and below simply would not have enough time to obtain the information and then act on it. This is because the average time between record date and pay date for ADRs is around three days. That said, the platform approach still relies on communications, authorisations and registrations after a corporate actions announcement and before the record date. This still acts as a drag on the efficiency of the system and therefore the overall adoption rates. In any event, adoption and participations rates drop sharply, the lower down the payment chain you are.

The nature of the investment chain for ADRs is that transfer agents also have a role to play, and a benefit to gain from using this platform. Working on behalf of issuers, transfer agents are responsible for identifying and tracking registered shareholders and beneficial owners to ensure tax is withheld at appropriate rates. Collecting and verifying this information from shareholders—while managing the ever-changing rules and requirements—is a time-consuming and expensive task. The ESP platform operates to facilitate a transfer agent's obligations to its Issuer clients.

Of course, ultimately, this is all driven by Issuers. Historically Issuers have been noticeably absent from the tax space, due to its complexity and also because investment strategies have not needed a tax component for alpha in their performance. That all changed in 2008 when the tax component became material to alpha. The presence of a platform such as ESP provides the Issuers with a way to openly state to their market that shareholder value is important to them.

MIDAS®[2]

An acronym for Managed Income Distributions At Source. MIDAS is operated by GlobeTax. MIDAS is a system that allows financial institutions to outsource components of tax relief so that they can ultimately withhold tax correctly on pay date wherever possible.

As I mentioned earlier, positions in securities are typically held in omnibus accounts. To pay out at treaty rates, the entity withholding the tax is at the top of the payment chain and the end investor is at the bottom of the chain. There may be several financial institutions in between. Generally, the withholding agent has strict legal liability for any tax withheld. It is therefore critical that any tax rate applied in reduction from the statutory rate, has documentary evidence associated with it to support the rate.

MIDAS is a platform to be used by financial institutions to allow them to monitor potential tax optimisation opportunities. This typically means receiving a monthly data file from a financial institution representing income paid in the previous month. MIDAS can analyse that data and, where the client has given either its financial institution or GlobeTax instruction or discretion, MIDAS can make elections at DTC's elective dividend service ("EDS") or file standard refunds to tax administrations. It could thus be described as a monitoring service combined with a processing service, where conditions permit. This kind of service suits institutional investors e.g., hedge funds, more than individual retail investors. The company's website indicates in a case study that it has recovered $46 million in 18,000 tax entitlement claims, making the average claim value around $2555. The term average in this sense would be misleading. In my experience 80% of the value of tax reclaims rest in 20% of the claims. So, a weighted average would be more useful.

Tax Compliance Toolkit™

The Tax Compliance Toolkit ("TCT")[3] is operated by TConsult, based in the UK. This is the only platform that is not primarily predicated on volume processing because it is predominantly a compliance platform for financial institutions and is not investor-facing.

---

[2] https://www.globetax.com/midas/

[3] https://taxcompliancetoolkit.com.

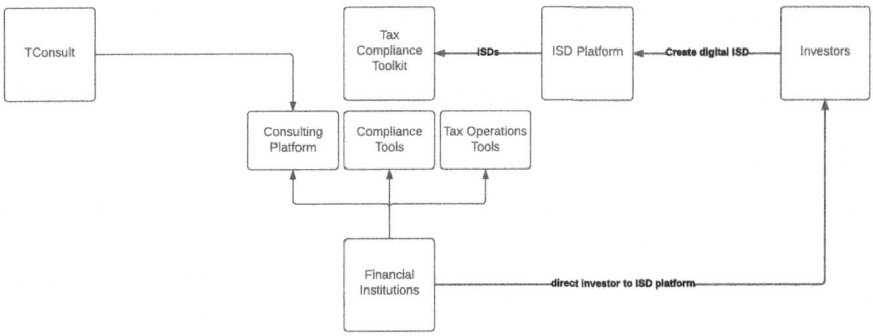

Exhibit 21.2 Tax Compliance Toolkit

All the frameworks I have described, whether they be anti-tax evasion or tax processing, all have components of control, oversight and an operational aspect. In FATCA and CRS, the purpose is anti-tax evasion and focuses on due diligence conducted by financial institutions to identify reportable accounts. In QI and TRACE the purpose is to withhold tax correctly at source when paid to non-residents. There are a number of common processes—documentation, withholding and reporting that need to be conducted and knowledge is the key. The Toolkit is an assembly of separate tools that provides financial firms not just with training materials in the form of video training material, but also operational tools such as project templates for common regulatory tasks, automated reporting services and an integrated regulatory consulting service (Exhibit 21.2).

Investor Self Declarations™

The Investor Self-Declarations ("ISD") platform is operated by TConsult. One of the most common themes in this book is about documentation and tax self-certifications in particular. Both the US and OECD have settled on the principle of a self-certification of tax status—the US with their W-8 series and the TRACE framework with its ISD. As far as the US is concerned, the ISD represents a compliant electronically signed substitute W-8 or W-9.

Over a period of two years, TConsult analysed the structures, validation rules and legal text associated with each of these tax frameworks to come up with a single self-certification that was compliant with the needs of QI, FATCA, TRACE and CRS. This so-called co-compliance means that a single ISD can be used for multiple regulatory purposes. The ISD process is triggered by a financial institution as the requestor, typically at onboarding although there is a parallel process for renewal of an existing ISD. The institution makes a url link available to its customer who is then directed to the ISD platform where the initial recognition process takes place before the ISD is completed (Exhibit 21.3).

The ISD platform itself is in a questionnaire format with underlying tax logic algorithms that ensure the data quality and reliability are high. Once the investor has completed the questionnaire and has been given the opportunity to review their answers, they can electronically sign the ISD. Once signed,

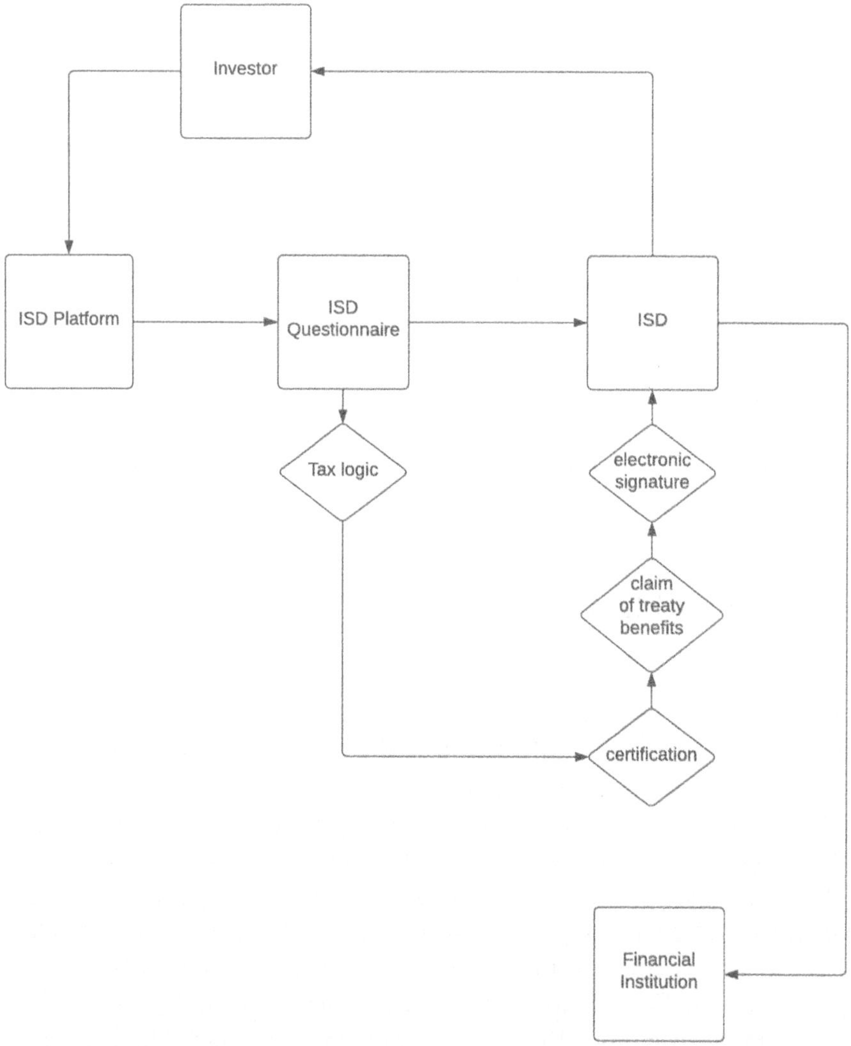

Exhibit 21.3 Investor self-declarations platform

a copy is sent to the investor for their records and another is sent to the financial institution for additional KYC checks.

This functionality comes about because, notably for the US, an ISD must, in addition to being "valid on the face" be consistent with KYC data. Between 2020 and 2023, this was achieved manually with data imported to the Tax compliance Toolkit where one of the "tools" was a manual questionnaire for bank staff to check the form against KYC. In 2023, this process was further automated with Application Programming Interfaces ("APIs"), to gather KYC data in advance from account opening data, for pre-population of the ISD (the extent permitted by the IRS). Future developments are expected to include tokenisation of ISDs to allow them to form part of a distributed ledger technology-based withholding tax solution.

Adroit™[4]

This platform is operated by the GOAL group and is targeted to compete with ESP. The platform provides all the same functionality required by an agent of a US depositary bank to support ADR processing.

GOAL collaborates with all stakeholders including custodians, issuers, tax authorities, the Depositary Trust & Clearing Corporation (DTCC), transfer agents, registered shareholders, and Participants to ensure correct and efficient withholding tax relief through relief at source, quick refund and long form reclaims, using their application, ADRoit™.

GOAL provides support during every step of the journey, from the creation of important notices, tax documentation generation and validation services, claim reconciliation, support with foreign tax authority audits, OFAC compliance support, payment and FX services.

Like GlobeTax, they also partnered with global transfer agents who utilise the same tax relief services on repatriated ordinary shares.

[4] https://www.goalgroup.com/products-services/withholding-tax-reclaims/adroit-adroit/

22

Getting Rid of Paper

In this chapter I will describe the challenges of documentation required for every withholding tax claim, whether it be relief at source, quick refund or standard refund. Any kind of claim is based on (i) evidence of who the beneficial owner is, (ii) evidence of their ownership of the securities involved, (iii) evidence that they were subject to taxation. In many cases, due to the issues described in Chapters 17 and 18, evidence is also required to prove the trail of ownership leading to the claim position. This chapter will identify each of these components and discuss the new initiatives and technologies that are being brought to bear to remove paper from the process.

Platforms, as the previous chapter exemplifies, provide the basis of high-volume transactional business when it is conducted through a chain of intermediaries. However, as the reader will have noted, these platforms have not yet eliminated the paper component of these processes. The securities industry is renowned for its reliance on paper and its reticence to get rid of it. This means that, even as automation and new technologies arise that could remove paper from the environment, the degree to which paper is embedded in tax processes, makes it very hard to make change rapidly, if at all.

For example, the US permits the use of W-8 forms to allow investors to self-certify their tax status. There are, by my estimation, around 900 million of these paper forms in circulation at any point. They only have a three-year validity period before they must be renewed.

R. K. McGill, *Cross-Border Investment Withholding Tax*, Finance and Capital Markets Series,
https://doi.org/10.1007/978-3-031-32785-8_22

The US does allow the use of substitute W-8s (being any form that is not a paper W-8) and they even allow electronic signatures. These two things on their own open the doors wide for technology providers to remove all that paper. The problem is not the paper itself. It's that the financial institutions that must ask for them and validate them have invested so much in manual processing and human resources, they find it difficult to switch the paper process off—too many people will lose their job and too much time will be spent re-writing training manuals.

The OECD frameworks and the EU also envision a tax environment without paper, all now allowing digital representations of tax status to replace paper. However, its one thing to facilitate digital replacing paper, but financial institutions are generally much closer to adopt such technology.

The most common paper document required for withholding tax purposes is a certificate of tax residency. A certificate of tax residency is a physical certificate provided, on request, by a tax administration. These certificates can be issued to legal entities as well as natural persons. In the UK, the HMRC can issue one of these within a couple of weeks. So, the first and largest problem associated with certifications of tax residency, is time delay. Normally someone won't ask for a certificate of residency unless they are told to do so. They can be used for many purposes, not just cross-border investment withholding tax. My company, as an example, deals with clients in 22 countries and, in many cases, we will be asked for these certificates before we can sign a contract. In a smaller number of cases, we will be asked to get an "apostille" attached to the certificate—to prove that the signature on the main certificate is an authorised signer. The apostille process takes another couple of weeks, which, when you're trying to get a valuable contract signed, can be very frustrating. If you're using it to make a tax reclaim, it can be even more frustrating.

The equivalent document in the US is a form 6166 certificate of US residency. Because the US has a big culture of international investing, it is also one where tax reclaims to foreign governments are big business. The US is also problematic because the US tax administration—the Internal revenue Service ("IRS") uses forms for everything. So, in order to obtain a 6166, guess what, you need to file a form 8802 at least 45 days before you need the 6166.

The 6166 is printed by the IRS on special paper using proprietary ink and each 6166 is only valid for one US tax year per US Person. So, if you're intending file for tax relief on a typical portfolio covering, say, nine markets with five investments in each, you'll need to request forty five 6166s on your form 8802. Filing an 8802 costs $85 for individuals and $185 for corporate entities, so it is not a free process either. Anecdotally, at least one large custodian bank in the US requests over 250,000 6166s annually so it's prepared for bulk processing of tax reclaims for its clients. Each year, it has to shred at least 175,000 because they cannot be used outside the year of issue. I find it quite ironic that the IRS allows digital self-certifications to be used by non-US persons claiming tax relief on US income, but requires a paper 6166 certificate issued by the IRS for a US person claiming a treaty benefit outside the US.

Both these scenarios highlight that, while the overall processing of withholding tax may seem simple, the devil is in the detail, and you have to know what you're doing if you're going to get it right. This is why many financial institutions limit the scope and scale of their tax offering to clients—it's just too much hard work.

Once you've got certificates of residence (or self-certifications), another component necessary for tax relief and reclamation is a tax voucher. This is often the only evidence that a tax administration will accept as evidence that the claimant was over-taxed. The tax voucher is often paper, but can sometimes be electronic. It must have an authorised signature and it must show the name and address of the recipient as well as the income they received and the amount of tax withheld. While these are usually issued per security, when they are issued in bulk, the voucher is known as a consolidated tax voucher. Financial institutions spend enormous amounts of money facilitating the production of tax vouchers for their clients. This represents yet another component of delay and cost.

Cost

There is another factor associated with paper—cost. For a financial institution, historically, the cost of tax reclamation has been bundled into the overall fee charged to the client for custody services. For a hedge fund that fee might be 4 basis points calculated annually based on the value of assets under management ("AUM"). The more complex and manual the process, the higher the cost to the institution. The problem is that its very rare for a financial institution to know how much the process of providing tax services to its clients is. More recently this issue has been addressed by financial institutions unbundling tax reclaim processing from their custody fees. Clearstream is a good example. Their basic service is investor-self-service, but they also offer ProAct in which Clearstream will prepare and submit the claim forms for you.[1] Clearstream's service is generally limited in scope to dividends and interest payments and is only applicable to investors resident in certain jurisdictions.

As you can imagine, there are many free models out there. Clearstream will charge €63 to get you a tax certification, €1500 if you are late providing the required forms, €26.25 per tax voucher and that before a €105 fee per dividend for the tax reclaim. So, if you're claiming on three dividends from Switzerland, you're looking at €404.25 in fees. If the claim value is less than those fees, it may just not be worth filing the claim because the cost of processing is higher than what you'll get back.[2] There can be additional fees for certain jurisdictions that have specific requirements e.g., French attestation.

Third-party providers i.e., not financial institutions generally have simpler fees and many have made those fees contingent on the success of the claim. Generally, this means that these third parties are pickier about who they take on as a client and they may do additional due diligence to make sure that any claims they do file on their client's behalf, will be successful. Prices can range from 20% of the recovered amount to 35% if the beneficial owner is a flow-through entity such as a partnership or trust. Now, you may think that 20% or 35% is an outrageous fee for processing a claim form to a tax administration, but, in context to the complexity and the amount of paper being handled, its perhaps not as expensive as you might first think. All providers, whether they be third parties or financial institutions reserve the right to not process a claim if it is not profitable to do so. These are called thresholds. They are typically in the range $100–$250 where the price can go as high as 50% if you insist on the filing.

You might think that this is a perfect argument to get rid of paper, and you'd be right. Cost reduction through automation is well established in financial services as a disruptive force. But it takes two to Tango, as they say. While technology firms can invest in automated solutions, those investments have to be based on a reasonable expectation that the environment will change over a relatively short period of time, to allow those solutions to be deployed and to compete. Until the OECD frameworks were agreed in 2013, the US was the only framework that had any component that would allow

[1] https://www.clearstream.com/clearstream-en/products-and-services/asset-services/tax-and-certification/tax-reclaim-service.

[2] https://www.clearstream.com/resource/blob/3414974/52a5f40c47c17746179ce6aa9c98e607/2303-fee-schedule-en-data.pdf.

such automation. Then, once there is confidence in the evolutionary framework, you have to give time for adoption. As we've seen, the 2013 OECD TRACE IP has only been adopted by one country and that not until 2021.

There is certainly a trend firmly in place now, to replace paper with digital equivalents. The rise of the electronic signature was a necessary component of that trend and is now firmly established. Many financial institutions are trying to replace paper certificates where they can with digital client onboarding. Systems like ID.me, Muinmos and ShuftiPro have proved that simple document acquisition can be accomplished without having the physical paper in your hand. Most now have video-based identification and OCR or AI-based interpretation to verify identity. But in the tax space, these are still only just starting to be used effectively. This is because most of these systems are focused on collection and data verification. Tax documents often have an additional layer of intelligent processing that must be conducted.

For example, collecting an image of a passport is easy enough and, with API connectivity, and a video call its easy enough to verify that the passport is valid and represents the account holder—providing an extremely smooth client experience. That's not enough for self-certification where, particularly for legal entities, there must be some data processing at the document level to ensure that certain permutations of certification that are not possible under the regulations, cannot be accidentally selected by an account holder. This, so-called, verification "on-the-face" can require complex algorithms and secondary questions and explanations before a valid document can be created. Most brokers, for example, in a narrow margin low volume business, just want to onboard as many investors as they can in as short a time period as possible. Why? Because they don't care about clients. They make money whether their client wins or not because they make money from the trading activity not from the gain or loss. The result is that when these brokers come across regulatory requirements they implement "tick the box" solutions with no further checks or balances. Anything that gets in the way of onboarding is bad. This means that there are several systems out there that I've seen that simply do not meet the regulatory requirement for digital substitutes of paper documentation.

Nowhere is this clearer than in the US W-8 system. The US tax system bifurcates around the axis of jurisdiction. The advent of FATCA in 2010 has meant that US investors resident outside the US have become pariahs. Most financial institutions have adopted a blanket policy of not accepting US clients to avoid FATCA. They do this with a tick box in the onboarding process. The problem is that, from a tax perspective, many people don't realise that they have a US tax return liability—the so-called "Accidental Americans".

There are a number of tests for US tax return liability—the Green Card Test, the Place of Birth Test, the Substantial Presence Test. Tripping any of these would be a high risk of making the client a US Person for tax purposes. The regulations provide "cures" for each of these so that financial institutions can allow onboarding and treat the client as non-US. The place of birth test requires a Certificate of Loss of Nationality ("CLN")—a long and costly process for someone who just wants to open a bank account. The Association of Accidental Americans has been lobbying the European commission and the US Federal government to make the CLN process both easier and less costly and is making some progress.[3] The point here is that without asking these questions at onboarding, a financial institution exposes itself to a risk that they do indeed onboard a US person against their own policy and procedure. This opens them up to FATCA reporting and, if they receive investment income from the US, to 1099 and 945 reporting. So, there are some circumstances in which using what appear to be easy shortcuts during client onboarding, like "tick-the-box" can not only be a bad thing, but a regulatory failure too. Doing it fast does not equal doing it well or properly.

One final comment on the issue of getting rid of paper. Regulators are like banks. They tend to be extremely conservative and resistant to change. So, at present, while they have opened up the industry to the *concept* of digital versus paper, they have not yet written regulation that is based purely on the principle of digital documentation. So, again using the US as the poster-boy, all the regulation is written on the assumption that a financial institution gathers paper W-8s. The rules on the three validation processes that a financial institution must perform are based on the assumption of a paper W-8. The regulations do not make any but the lightest reference to how such validation procedures would or should work in a completely digital environment, other than indicating that an electronic signature is acceptable.

Getting rid of paper is certainly the end-game for withholding tax and we are some way along in that process, but there is still some way to go.

[3] https://americansoverseas.org/en/american-tax/?gclid=EAIaIQobChMIucrohPz2_AIViNDtCh0uBwehEAAYASAAEgJAQfD_BwE.

23

Withholding Tax on the Blockchain

In 2021 Ernst & Young announced that they had successfully trialled a proof of concept for withholding tax processing using Distributed Ledger Technology (DLT). This chapter explains how this would work in a large-scale environment, explores some of the challenges.

I have spoken on many occasions, including in this book, about the trend towards the digitisation of tax. The UK HMRC has a slogan for it: "Make Tax Digital", and they're right. There is an indisputable trend towards the removal of paper. At the corporate level, financial statements are increasingly required to be submitted electronically in the Extended Business markup Reporting Language (xbrl), in itself a subset of the extended markup language, xml. The use of these languages has a purpose. On the one hand, it allows these data to be machine readable—which provides for faster and easier analysis. On the other hand, it provides tax administrations, such as HMRC in the UK with the tools they need to do pattern analysis using artificial intelligence, which helps them identify behaviour or features of a corporation's financials that are indicative of potential tax evasion or avoidance.

However, elsewhere, such trends towards the digital can have operational benefits, none more so perhaps than the use of distributed ledger technology ("DLT"). Many people think of DLT as a solution. In actual fact, its more like an operating system. It provides as framework for the handling of digital assets. So, to understand the potential applications for, and impact of DLT

R. K. McGill, *Cross-Border Investment Withholding Tax*, Finance and Capital Markets Series,
https://doi.org/10.1007/978-3-031-32785-8_23

on financial services, we must consider DLT in conjunction with the things for which it will be a solution.

For this purpose, I want to consider a very specific situation, that of the payment of a dividend on an American Depositary Receipt. We could run the same analysis on any DR instrument including GDRs, they all work the same way. ADRs are a derivative instrument. They represent a number of underlying non-US securities, but the DR is denominated in US dollars. DRs also have some characteristics that are different from other securities. In particular, DRs have a ratio that describes the number of underlying shares represented by each DR. So, for example one depositary receipt may represent 10 underlying shares, while another depositary receipt might represent 100 underlying shares. A DR can also often have a different pay date from the underlying security. All of this is because a DR is created by a depositary bank who "sponsors" the issue and effectively makes the market for that specific security. The Depositary Bank looks for large corporations. Their "pitch" is that in addition to bonds and listing shares on an exchange, they can also raise money (and the capital value of their firm) by issuing ADRs. Once a corporation agrees to issue an ADR, the Depositary bank negotiates and agrees the terms of the issue including such things as the DR ratio. It is then down to the depositary to make the market in the ADR so that investors are aware of it and can buy it. This includes listing the ADR on the main US exchanges. There are only four American Depositary banks—Bank of New York Mellon, Citibank, Deutsche Bank and finally, J P Morgan who invented the instrument.

ADRs are very widely held both by individuals and by institutional investors all over the world. Just like normal shares, some are held "long" by investors in the expectation of dividends and some are traded short and/or quickly to leverage expected volatility in the share price on the exchange. One of the core components of the product offered by depositories to their customers is tax processing. However, it is many years since any depositary bank processed withholding tax. All four of the US depositary banks have outsourced withholding tax processing to a specialist agent, GlobeTax.

Exhibit 23.1 shows the standard model for processing of tax withholding on a dividend associated with a depositary receipt. Diagram the depositary receipt has already been created and marketed and now the issuer, i.e., the corporation that has engaged the depositary to sponsor the ADR, has decided to declare a dividend. For efficient withholding tax processing, as previously described, there are two pillars. The first pillar is the creation of an important notice. The important notice is created by three parties dash the Issuer, the depositary's agent and the Depositary. The issuer provides information about the underlying security including the ISIN, security name etc. The depositary provides information about the der itself including the ratio the record date, and the pay date of the DR. the depositary's agent provides the text expertise. This latter will include the data and documentation required for any investor to claim a reduced rate of withholding. For this purpose the depository's agent will need extensive research to determine from which jurisdictions kind investor could claim an entitlement to a reduced rate of withholding through a double tax agreement. In each of these jurisdictions the depository's agent will need to specify precisely which documents are required and which data elements are needed. Remember that for the most part investors may be at the bottom of a chain of financial institutions each of which is holding a position in the security in an omnibus account with an upstream financial institution.

So, in Exhibit 23.1, I have shown three levels of financial institution each termed a participant. The top level will be a financial institution that is a direct participant in the DTC. So to complete the first pillar of withholding tax processing after a dividend has been declared, is the creation of an important notice coordinated by the depositary's agent. Once this is done, the important notice is provided to the DTC who posts the notice and may also send the notice to its direct participants. The depositary's agent may also show the details of the DR event in its own systems.

These Important Notices Also made available in machine-readable form in xbrl. In principle this means that the DTC participant in level 1 can inform the participant in level 2 in an automated fashion. Most DTC important notices are now available in xbrl, however, the level of usage continues to be relatively low. So, while a level of standardisation and automation is available and has been for some years, there appears to be little appetite for converting this manual paper-based process into a digital one.

Exhibit 23.2 shows how the processing of depositary receipts occurs on the record date. In this diagram there are three investors who are customers of a financial institution, participant Level 3. Each holds 100 DRs. these 300 depositary receipts are commingled into an omnibus account which the participant in level three holds at a participant financial institution in level 2. The financial institution at participant level 2 also has three direct customers holding 100 DRs each, in addition to its customer participant Level 3 which is an omnibus account. This structure can be repeated as often as necessary where each financial institution comingles the assets of its customers into an omnibus account at another financial institution. Thus the DTC participant in this example at level 1 has a record date position of 900 depositary receipts. The participant at Level 1 has no knowledge of participant at Level 3.

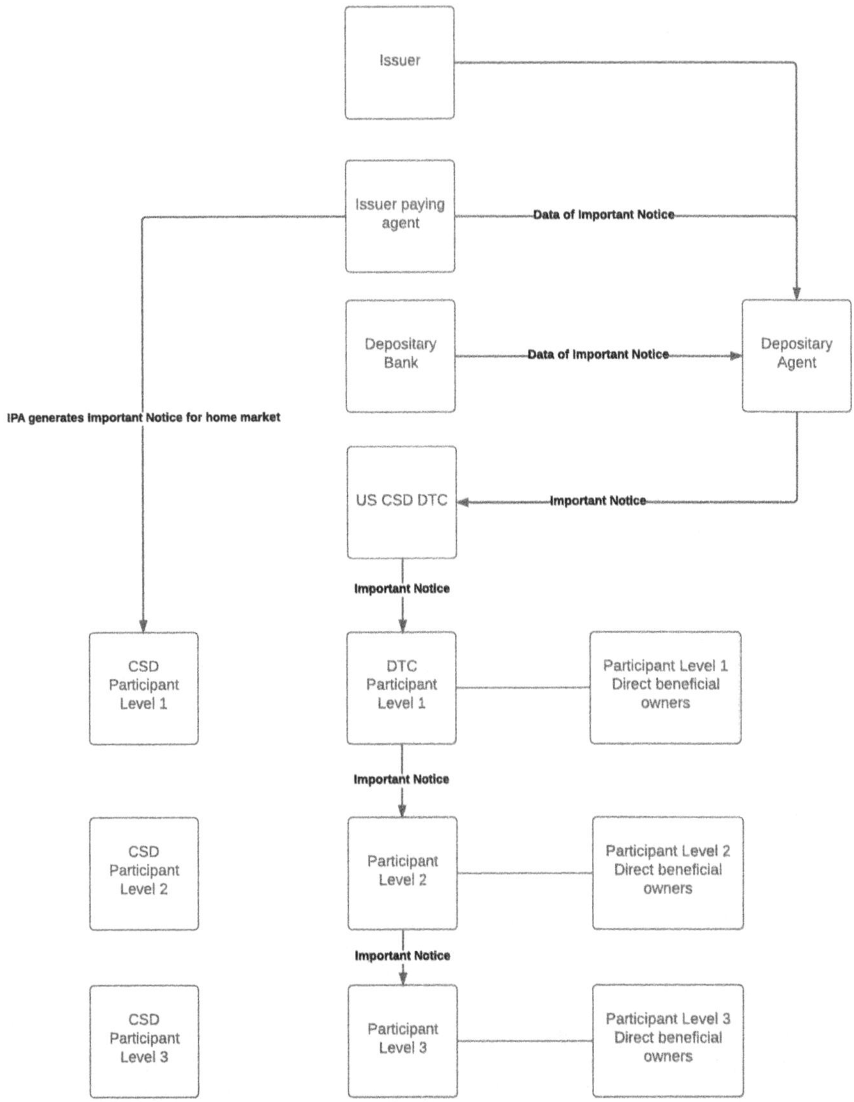

Exhibit 23.1 Standard withholding processing on depositary receipts (*Source* Author)

The depositary's agent has created a system call the electronic submission portal, ESP. The purpose of ESP is to provide a single ecosystem in which all participants can engage in one or more of the withholding tax processes available based on the Important Notice information. On the record date, which is when the beneficial ownership of the depositary receipt is crystallised, each participant in the chain of payment can designate the omnibus account of

Exhibit 23.2 Record date processing of depositary receipts (*Source* Author)

its customer in the next level. This designation will include the record date position of that omnibus account. In other words, each participant level has a door opened into ESP and a record date position established against which they can claim, provided they are able to provide the documentation and data required by the important notice.

Exhibit 23.3 shows what happens on pay date. On the left of the diagram the holding structure of the depositary receipts is shown as described within nested omnibus accounts. The delivery of the important notice between participants is shown. On the right hand side of the diagram, each participant has designated the financial institution and their omnibus account together with the record date position in that account into the depositary agent's system. I would note here that historically, all depositary receipt processing was done through GlobeTax. However, in more recent times competitive offerings from GOAL group and Acupay have meant that some depositary receipts are processed through competitive systems. All of these competitive systems operate to a similar processing model. They facilitate the gathering of documentation and data.

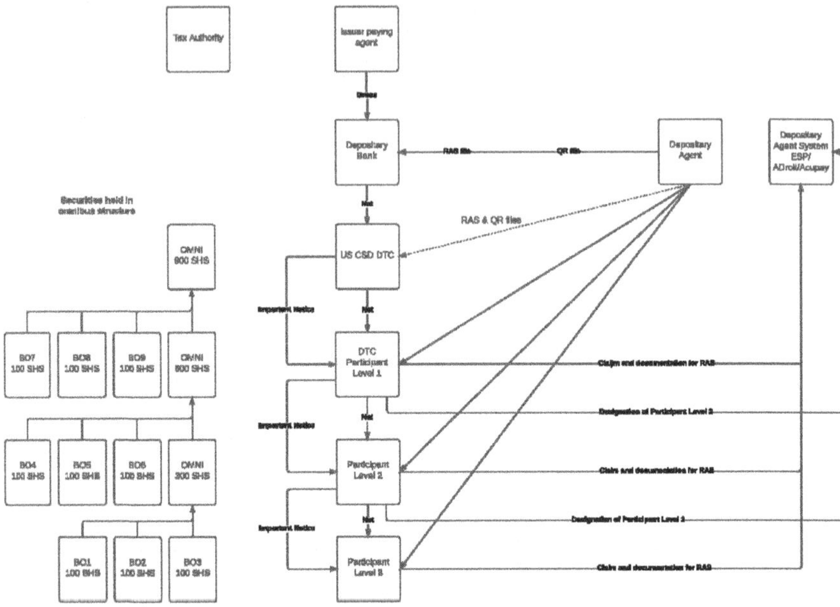

Exhibit 23.3 Pay date processing of depositary receipts (*Source* Author)

The function of the depositary agent is now to assess all of the documentation that has been provided by participants. Remember that the paying agent of the issuer hold strict legal liability for any tax withheld. It is also noteworthy that DTC has recently gained a licence from the SEC to be a withholding agent.

From all of the available documentation and data the depositary agent is able to construct a payment file. This file provides the information to the withholding agent about the amount of tax to withhold. The depositary agent's system will provide each participant with similar information. The general principles of these systems apply to all three operating models i.e., relief at source quick refund and standard refund. This means that payments on pay date can now proceed and each participant is made aware of what it needs to pay and how much tax was withheld with respect to the omnibus account it operates on behalf of its customer the participant in a level below.

There are two problems with these types of pillar processes.

The first is that these systems are all centralised databases whereas the chain of payment is as the name implies not centralised but a chain of linked intermediaries. While the depositary agent has undoubtedly processed many billions of claims in the depositary space, the participation rate is relatively low. This means that if you are an investor whose financial institution is at or near the top of the payment train, it's likely that your financial institution will be able to obtain the relevant documentation from you and make a claim of entitlement. However, if you are three or more levels down in the payment chain, it's likely that your financial institution either is not aware of the corporate action and or doesn't have sufficient time to obtain documentation from you and submit it to the depositary agent's system for processing. So, for a jurisdiction that allows all three processing models, it's likely that only a small proportion of investors will be able to participate in the relief at source process. Another proportion may be able to benefit from quick refund, but the majority may well fall into the back stop process of standard refunds. As has been described relief at source is the preferred model and standard refunds the least preferred.

So, the question is, is there a technology available that would allow information flows to be further automated, standardised and streamlined to allow a greater participation by investors in tax relief at source. I would argue that there is. Whether there is a desire to implement such a solution is an important subordinate question. I should point out this stage, the biggest difference between a normal security and a depositary receipt is that from a tax perspective, the investor does not own the underlying security, the investor only owns the depositary receipt. Therefore, claims cannot be filed directly to a tax administration, but can only be filed by the depositary or their agent. The depositary has effectively converted the depositary receipt into the equivalent number of underlying securities that it will have purchased in order to secure the receipt itself.

Distributed Ledger technology and the more commonly known blockchain concepts would, I believe, provide an exciting new evolution for withholding tax processing. The concept that can bring all of this together includes non-fungible tokens to replace paper documentation and smart contracts to automate and distribute the calculation of eligibility.

Exhibit 23.4 shows a schematic of a distributed Ledger technology architecture that could provide the basis of the next evolution of tax processing. The same actors that have roles to play in traditional processing would have nodes on the distributed network. The purpose of each node and its capabilities can be pre-defined. The use of omnibus accounts to comingle assets of investors can be replaced with the use of wallets, another common concept found with distributed Ledger technology. The Ledger itself, shown in the centre of the diagram, would be associated with a smart contract established by the depositary or the depositary's agent. A single smart contract would represent an individual payment of a dividend with respect to one security.

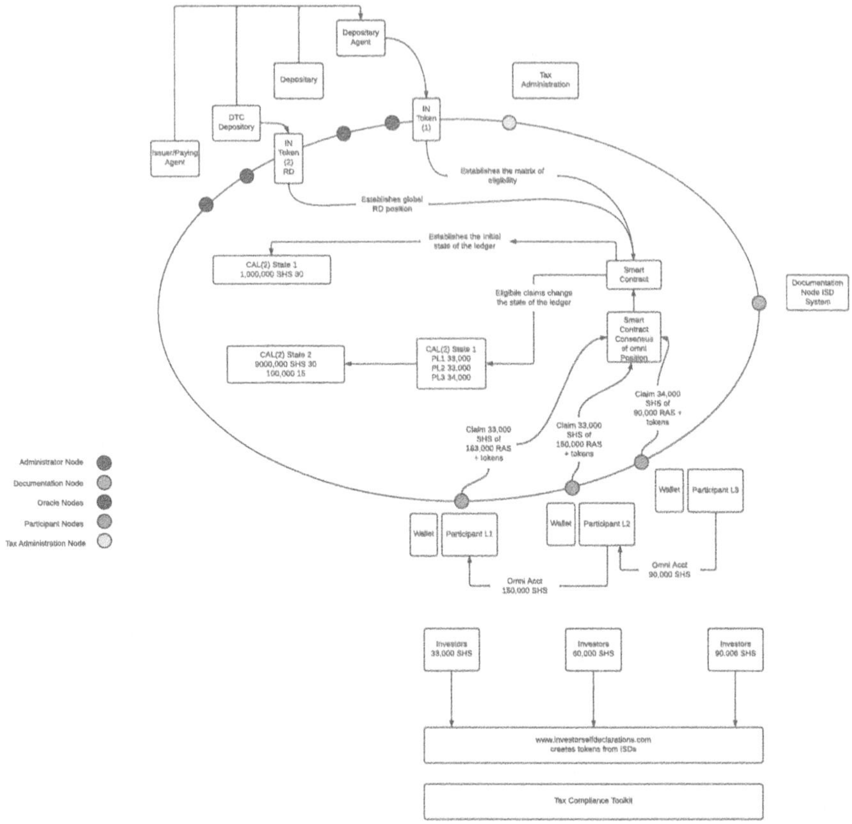

Exhibit 23.4 Suggested DLT model for withholding tax processing (*Source* Author)

On record date, the initial state of the Ledger is established as the total position of the depositary receipt i.e., the total number of depositary receipts available to be claimed. The important notice would be distributed on the network and would not suffer from the degradation associated with a series chain of linked institutions. In effect the important notice would be instantly available to all nodes on the network at the same time. This would essentially be a consensus between the traditional three parties, the depositary the issuer and the depositary agent. The depositary agent role would be to create a matrix of eligibility in data form, tokenise the data and apply this to the smart contract.

At the other end of the process financial institutions would be requesting documentation from clients if they were holding the depositary receipt on record date. The difference will be that the certificate of residence most commonly required to accompany a claim would also be digital in the form of a non-fungible token. There are a small number of third parties who have created systems for this purpose. Most notably TConsult created the platform, the Tax Compliance Toolkit, in 2020. That platform contains a component called the investor self-declaration or ISD. The ISD is called Co-compliant. This means that the ISD created will comply with multiple regulatory frameworks including The US qualified intermediary system, the OECD trace implementation protocol, the US FATCA system and the OECD common reporting standard.

So, using these new technologies, all of which include electronic signatures, the documentation needed for tax processing can be solicited much more quickly and efficiently than before. The next evolution will be the conversion of these investor self-declarations into tokenised form. This means either fungible or non-fungible tokens representing investor self-declarations of tax residency that can be easily produced and added to the smart contracts in order to facilitate tax processing.

Fungibility in this context has a similar effect to that of a consolidated tax voucher. An non-fungible token can represent one self-certification of residency valid for three years. A fungible token would have the additional attribute of being capable being assimilated with other fungible tokens. So, for example, a partnership with three partners could provide one non-fungible token to represent itself and three fungible tokens that could be used individually or together to document the underlying partners of the partnership.

At the heart of the distributed ledger concept is the smart contract. The smart contract replaces the work that would have otherwise been done by the depositary's agent when it received all of the documentation and data and established whether any given claim was valid. The algorithms in the smart contract react when new tokens and claims are added, always checking to make sure that the total position is not exceeded. This will be of particular interest to tax administrations who sometimes struggle with duplicate claims. The smart contract also knows the date parameters of the corporate action and the windows of opportunity set by the depositary. The system will also maintain wallets at each financial institution. These wallets will contain that institution's record date "state" of the ledger and act as another control over claimed positions. So, in effect, each financial institution will be able to claim directly to the smart contract by submitting a claim together with tokens to represent the documentation required. Valid claims will reduce the state of the ledger for that particular window type leaving the balance as the opening position for the next window.

The Ernst & Young trial of DLT did not use this model and also referenced that the documentation portion would be completed "*off-chain*". To me this is illogical because that's the part of the process that the most difficult. In my interpretation, the use of smart contracts and tokenised self-certifications means that the whole process can be automated and standardised.

Part VI

Performance

24

Benchmarking

This chapter describes each step of the withholding tax process and establishes methods for calculating a benchmark of performance for financial institutions. Investors will also find this useful because it highlights the questions they should be asking of their financial institution (or third-party vendor) to establish the parameters and expectations of their service offering.

The reader by now has some grasp of the matrix of factors which can have an effect on the withholding tax issue and the subsequent value of a portfolio. In this chapter, I have taken each of the issues raised during previous explanations of withholding tax processes and tried to establish the kind of benchmark that might apply. I make no apology for repeating myself in terms of explanations behind some of these benchmarks. In my experience, the issues are many, complex and inter-reactive. For investors, and others, the more often an issue is explored, each time from a slightly different perspective, the more likely that a holistic picture will emerge.

This series of benchmarks could be used by:

- an institutional investor to perform quality assurance on existing custodian's or
- internal departmental performance
- a fund manager or custodian sales team to set and monitor benchmarks in order to

R. K. McGill, *Cross-Border Investment Withholding Tax*, Finance and Capital Markets Series,
https://doi.org/10.1007/978-3-031-32785-8_24

- establish a competitive advantage
- an IT or other cross-functional improvement group to set project deliverables for an
- automation of withholding tax processes
- a board of directors to set minimum service levels for an outsourcing contract.

There are basically three parties who could perform withholding tax processing for investors. At this point, I will take standard refunds, i.e., post pay date claims made to a tax administration as the basis of benchmarking. There are three types of persons that should be interested in benchmarking: (1) the investor themselves, (2) the custodian of the assets and (3) a third-party vendor specialising in tax reclaims. Generally speaking, the only investors who file reclaims themselves are institutional investors who are familiar with the withholding tax concepts and with the procedures required. These are not common.

There is an extensive list of benchmarks in this chapter. However, in the market many custodians do not use these, preferring a more old-fashioned simplistic set of criteria for judgement of any are used at all.

An example of this is Recovery Time. Each market pays back to claimants using a different model. In some markets of course such as France and, as we've seen previously, with ADRs, there are also market factors to contend with. However, there is available a market table showing the *average* market recovery time. Now most clients look at this table and assume that this is the length of time it will take to recover their tax starting from the point at which they were over-taxed—the pay date. A completely reasonable assumption given the amount of money spent by banks on STP systems and also completely untrue. The benchmark for recovery is almost universally applied from the date that the claim is filed to the market, i.e., it leaves the custodian. This also would be reasonable (a) if the interpretation of the benchmark was made clear and (b) if the preceding part of the activity between the pay date and filing date were very short.

As we'll see elsewhere, however, even though this preparatory phase of claims filing is entirely within the intermediary's control, it is the least publicised because it is where there are more delays caused than are caused by any part of the market process.

Intermediaries actually have extremely fragmented systems that have grown up over time and usually did not start out with a strategic design or purpose, but more of a tactical need.

I have seen custody reports that show backlogs of claims going back over three years worth over $17 million. In other words, there are claims that have not been filed yet (some of which will have gone out of Statute), where the pay date was anything up to three years ago. In these conditions, simplistic reporting and lack of use of benchmarks hide the reality of the process—an inefficient intermediary and hides the effect on the client—lack of funds.

This is pretty counter-intuitive to the average client where the intermediary generates fees from the size of assets under management (AUM). You would think therefore (as a client) that it would be in the intermediary's financial interests to identify and process claims without a backlog in order to maximise both its client's income and its own. However, this is not the case. Withholding tax, for many years has been a back-of-back-office function, attracting little attention and even less investment mainly because no one could figure out, other than by throwing people at it, how to make the process efficient. Those people not only make mistakes but they work slowly and have a morass of paperwork to deal with.

Worse, the people in these functions know that they have a backlog. Internal reports often still show these amounts as "outstanding" claims that have some validity. Here are two vignettes that show the effect of allowing these backlogs to develop.

First, the claim amounts are shown as outstanding even though there is little or no chance after so much time has passed that the claims will ever be filed at all. Think about it. If you have a department that's running like crazy to keep up with the current dividend season volumes and letting claims drop back into the backlog through a lack of capacity, what chance is there that those claims, after three years, will ever get compiled and sent? Very little. So, these claims should really be written off and the client made whole (it's not their fault, their intermediary has a backlog, and after all, it's actually their money).

Second, let's presume for a moment that some claims from that far back do eventually get filed. When they arrive at a tax authority, they face a similar issue. The tax authorities generally are manually oriented and have the same kind of backlogs as the intermediaries (the difference is, they are the ones with the client's money). They take a pragmatic attitude, since they are also facing current claims from the current dividend season. They take the attitude "if you took three years before you even filed the claim, you can't be that concerned about the money", the net result of which is that, unless the intermediary makes a substantive effort (unlikely), the tax authority will not prioritise the claims over the current claims. The net result of that of course, returning to our original subject, is that the time cited as an average recovery time is an average because there are claims that take much longer than the average—guess which they are.

The use and interpretation of benchmarks therefore are critical. While individual benchmarks are important, it's equally important to recognise their limitations in the real world and their impact on other parts of the process, so that intermediaries and clients alike can have transparency on the subject of performance.

Eurobonds

A **Eurobond** is an international bond that is denominated in a currency not native to the country where it is issued. It can be categorised according to the currency in which it is issued. London is one of the centres of the Eurobond market, but Eurobonds may be traded throughout the world—for example, in Singapore or Tokyo. Eurobonds are named after the currency they are denominated in. For example, Euroyen and Eurodollar bonds are denominated in Japanese yen and American dollars respectively.

A Eurobond is normally a bearer bond, payable to the bearer. The bank will pay the holder of the coupon the interest payment due.

The majority of Eurobonds are owned in "electronic" rather than physical form. The bonds are held and traded within one of the clearing systems (Euroclear and Clearstream being the most common). Coupons are paid electronically via the clearing systems to the holder of the Eurobond (or their nominee account).

Eurobonds have historically been deemed to be exempt from withholding tax. However, in recent years things have changed. The tax authorities of an increasing number of markets including Estonia, Iceland, Ireland, Lebanon, Portugal and Spain are taking the view that an entitlement to exemption should be achieved by taxing the Eurobond in the first place and having a relief at source and/or long-form process to obtain that entitlement, which would of course, be 100%. At present around 5% of Eurobonds are taxable (Source: International Capital Markets Services Association—ICMSA).

Exhibit 24.1 provides a decision flowchart for a custodian who has clients with Eurobond income. This decision tree allows the custodian to establish whether or not it can meet the requirements of the Eurobond quick refund process and, if not, implement a long-form process to ensure that their client is not disadvantaged. In the model shown in Exhibit 7.1, the custodian will use a third-party service bureau to process any long-form claims that are not paid under the quick refund or relief at source process.

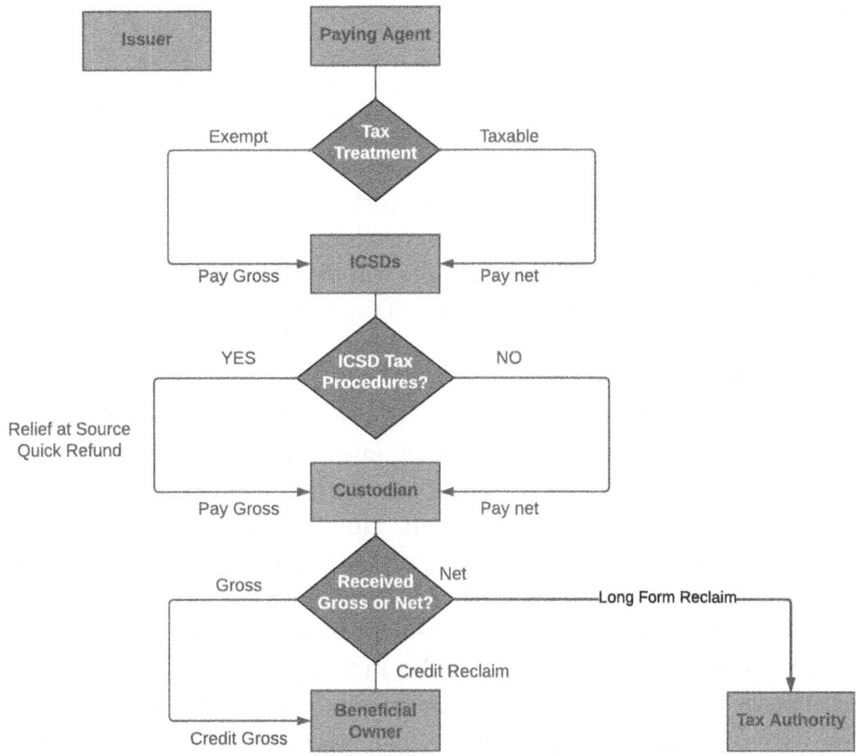

Exhibit 24.1 Optimisation of Eurobond income (*Source* Author)

In the Spanish tax environment, under Spanish law, Eurobond Notes issued by a Spanish Issuer are subject to withholding tax. No relief from this tax is available to investors who are either Spanish resident individuals or are resident in a jurisdiction deemed to be a tax haven. Since the ICSDs have a key role to play in Eurobond management, these firms manage the relief at source/quick refund process for the market, including Spain. The procedure required is based on the downstream custodians providing certificates of residency, known as Annexos, as the documentary evidence of an investor's entitlement to exemption plus the amount of interest received and details of the relevant notes.

From a different perspective, As far as Issuers of Eurobonds are concerned, the information that they should describe relating to the tax treatment of their instruments includes:

- Taxable events
- Availability of withholding relief
- Eligibility criteria for relief

- Documentation requirements
- Holding restrictions.

What's important here is to avoid the presumption that Eurobonds are tax-exempt. The answer is, as always, "it depends". Not only that but, even though the tax is deducted, the ICSD's quick refund process is complex and has several quite tight deadlines. It is therefore likely, although the scale is unknown, that some Eurobond investors will be taxed, even.

The Eurobond market in terms of taxation is affected also by which market the Eurobonds are issued in. The most complex is Spain which is described here to exemplify the issue.

By far the largest proportion of filers of tax reclaims are custodian banks. These financial institutions are providing safe keeping for client assets. It is therefore not unreasonable for investors to expect their custodians to include tax reclamation as a service component. However, not all custodians offer tax reclamation as a service. I should point out here that prime brokerages, another type of financial institution, almost never provide tax reclaim services to their clients. The custodian bank benefits by having a direct relationship with the ultimate beneficial owner and is in a better position to compile tax reclaims for their clients. Finally, there are a number of third-party vendors who have built their own systems to help investors with tax reclamation. Some of these vendors, notably GOAL group and RAQUEST GmbH, have focused on providing software. Others notably, GlobeTax and WTAX have focused on providing an outsourced service. In order to deliver an outsourced service, the vendor will need a data feed from the custodian provided under a letter of authority from the beneficial owner. Most vendors have arrangements in place with many custodians under which they receive these data files on a monthly basis. When it comes to compiling a tax reclaim, these vendors may also have an authority letter from the custodian so that they can use the letter of authority to create a tax voucher or credit advice. The tax voucher essentially confirms that the custodian paid the investor a given amount of money as a dividend and that a certain amount of that dividend was withheld in tax.

In the following section of benchmarks, I've assumed that the filer will be the custodian bank. However, these benchmarks can be applied to two third-party vendors as well.

Part of the problem of benchmarking this process of course is that, in theory and to a certain extent in practice, several parts of the process, from any given viewpoint, are out of direct control.

Below I've given a summary that shows how all these benchmarks can come together to create an overview of withholding tax issues. Following the table is a more detailed description of each benchmark, how they might be applied and what investors and custodians can learn from them (Exhibit 24.2).

Since there's no real set of benchmarks for this corporate actions area at present, rather than simply defining the benchmarks in mathematical terms, I have taken a more discursive approach. This is to ensure that both investors and financial institutions are able to understand *why* I believe that a particular benchmark should exist and what factors affected it. The mathematical endpoint is still given both at the end of the discursive element and also in summary table form at the end of the chapter.

Code	Description
PE	Process Efficiency
PF	Proportion of Fails
ADP	Age Debt Performance
F	Fit
SR	Statute Risk
RAS	Relief at Source Efficiency
PoA	Power of Attorney Index
RT	Reconciliation & Traceability Index
B	Backlog Index
C	Capacity
CR	Cost Per Reclaim
ΔN	Reclaim Rate
CB	Cost Benefit
TH	Threshold Index
CTI	Contractual Tax Index

Exhibit 24.2 Benchmark indices

Process Efficiency

This is a simple additive formula with several elements. It is market specific and can also be aggregated to provide an average ranking. Because the profile of many portfolios is different colour this latter measurement is somewhat less useful than the market-specific P index used in conjunction with the fit index defined later. The difficulty for practitioners is that there is likely to be a disparity of applied units in some of the measurements. The disparity exists because of the significant differences that can occur in different parts of the process, some can take seconds while others may take months or even years. For example, if a custodian has an automated process, the action of establishing validity, eligibility and value maybe almost simultaneous and certainly not take days. However, the activity of communicating with clients and tax authorities most certainly takes days at the very least. So, for some custodians, several of the measures included in the benchmarking process will be so close to zero as to be effectively negligible. This does not mean however that they can be ignored because they are not negligible in all cases. On the one hand, there are many custodians who have not automated process and who will take days whereas others take seconds. Separately, even if the processes are automated and deemed to be negligible from a process efficiency viewpoint these same elements each have a risk associated with them which must be considered these then are the very benchmarks that can highlight custodians adopting less effective methods.

Process Efficiency is given, for market m as follows:

$$\mathrm{PE}m = \sum\nolimits_{1}^{n} T$$

where T is the time taken for the process element n for the market m. so, for example:

- $T1$ is the length of time taken for the custodian to be made aware of an income event commencing from the pay date. Usually, this is an aggregate of the time taken from the issuance of a notification, e.g., a corporation announces a dividend, through a registrar bank to a withholding agent and thence to the custodian.
- $T2$ is the time taken for the custodian to establish the validity of the event, the eligibility of the event with respect to its client base, and finally the value of the event to each of its eligible clients. Each of these elements has a corresponding risk associated with the way in which the custodian performs this activity, which is discussed later. While from an institutional

investors perspective, this time is only relevant for the particular investments he holds, it must be recognised that the custodian is acting for many investors who will stop this measure is taken across all investors because the larger the number of clients, the more likely it is that the custodian will have efficiency business drivers in place to reduce the transactional cost of processing these three functions $T2$ is an aggregate function in itself where $T2m$ equals T_V plus T_E plus $T_{Valm.}$

This formula is a mathematical equivalent of asking the question how long did it take you to figure out that there was a reclaim? How long did it take you to figure out that I was affected by this income event?

- $T3$ is the time taken to assemble a tax reclaim. Again, $T3$ is an aggregate function $T3$ equals T_f plus T_D plus T_s for market m.
  - T_F consists of the time required to obtain the correct tax reclamation forms. Most sophisticated custodians and third party vendors request these original forms in bulk from tax administrations based on prior experience. However, some tax administrations, notably Switzerland, issue forms with unique identification numbers pre-printed on them—SRD numbers. Other tax administrations allow these forms to be downloaded from their websites. In other words, there is no one rule. However, whoever is filing the claims needs to know where these forms can be obtained, what format they have to be in before they are able to proceed and make sure that they have the correct form for the correct year.
  - T_D is the time required to acquire the specific data for each reclaim, enter it onto the reclaim form and quality cheque for errors and omissions.
  - T_S is the time required to collate supporting documentation. This will include creating a tax voucher, obtaining a certificate of residency and other documents depending on the nature of the beneficial owner, collating them in printed form and preparing them for despatch.
- $T4$ is the time taken to locally validate a tax reclaim. $T4$ is not generally market specific because all of its elements occur within the custodian or

within the local jurisdiction $T4$ consists of two additives, serial subprocesses. $T4 = T_a + T_{LTA}$ where

- T_A is the time taken to obtain approval from the client. A signature is required on each tax reclaim form. If the custodian does not have power of attorney, this signature must be that of the client or beneficial owner. If the power of attorney is vested in the custodian, the custodian may sign the form. Equally, if a third-party vendor is being used then the third-party vendor may sign the form on behalf of the beneficial owner. It is noteworthy that due to the number of tax frauds being perpetrated in recent years on tax administrations, many tax administrations are no longer allowing tax reclaims to be filed by third parties under a power of attorney. In many cases, the reclaim forms must be signed by the beneficial owner who is entitled to the claim.
- T_{LTA} is the time taken in days for the tax reclaim form to be sent to the local tax authority and returned with a valid stamp. In other words, generally speaking, once a tax reclaim form has been created and signed by the beneficial owner it must be sent to the beneficial owner's local tax administration so that they can stamp the tax reclaim form to verify that the beneficial owner named on the form is a tax resident of the jurisdiction being claimed under a double tax agreement.

- $T5$ is the time taken for the now completed tax reclaim to be sent for payment. This involves at least one and sometimes two steps. However, if there are two steps, as with France, where the tax reclaim must be submitted to a French sub-custodian who then files it to the authorities, the second step is usually opaque to the custodian from a measurement perspective. Therefore, $T5$ is measured from the date of posting by the custodian to the receipt of the tax reclaim funds.
- $T6$ is the time required for the tax reclaim to be credited to the client's account. This is not as simple as it appears. Firstly, many authorities remit cheques rather than electronic payments, which therefore involves a clearance process. Secondly, if a tax authority remits funds covering more than one reclaim, funds cannot be credited to client accounts until a reconciliation process has identified how the sum received from a tax authority has been made-up. Of course, where the clearance process occurs in parallel to the reconciliation process, $T6$ is actually just the larger of TD&T_{recon} such that $T6 = (T_{cl} + T_{recon})$ where T_{cl} Is the time taken to clear a tax reclaim payment and T_{recon} is the time taken to reconcile a tax authority payment to a specific tax reclaim. Please note here that reconciliation is not

a simple process. In my experience, Connor tax administrations are just as likely to make mistakes as the filers of reclaims. It is not unknown for a tax administration to remit a larger sum than was actually claimed. If the filer of the claims had commingled the claims in a batch, the reconciliation process can be extensive in order to determine which claims the tax administration was actually paying so that the filer can return some of the funds.

I would note here that there are significant differences in the way that some entities file claims. For example, some of the larger custodians choose to file claims only once per year. On the other hand, some third-party vendors pride themselves in filing claims within one month of receiving income data. The reason given for filing claims only once per year is usually that resource is limited and it takes nearly 12 months for income events to be analysed in order to establish that there is a claim that could be filed. This is why benchmarking is important. Any investor holding their securities with a custodian that only files once per year will be at a significant disadvantage compared to engaging an independent third-party vendor who would file on a continuous basis during each year.

So, it can be seen that a process efficiency benchmark can be established. In mathematical terms, of course, the custodian may take certain measures to minimise or even eradicate some of the elements described above. In which case those elements will drop to zero. In other cases, the time required for a particular part of the process is so small in comparison to other elements that it can be said to be immaterial to the process's efficiency. This latter is important because, while the time required to perform an element may be insignificant, the effect of its failure can be extremely significant. In the next section, we will look at the process in more depth from a risk management perspective.

Risk Management Benchmarks

In this section, we will look at sub-measurements that can be identified which either directly or indirectly point to a greater or lesser confidence in custodial attention to detail. Some of these benchmarks are obvious, some are less so. However, in a process with so many linkages, and in particular where those linkages include external bodies over whom the custodian has little or no control, an error in anyone element can cause the catastrophic failure of the whole process.

The basis of the risk management issue in withholding tax is to establish best practise and to measure performance against it. Some custodians will have minimised risk in this area of corporate actions in one or more ways. These include:

- retention of staff with appropriate levels of skill, knowledge and experience together with back up contingency and succession plans
- formalisation of manual processes to externalise the skills knowledge and experience of key staff. Essentially creating corporate memory
- automation will stop this may include in-house automation of elements of the process together with surrounding management tools to identify potential risk areas. Also included in this area would be the use of Bureau systems where certain elements of the process had been automated by third parties and their value can be purchased as and when necessary.
- Outsourcing. This moves the whole process over to a firm that has demonstrable experience in the area. They may or may not have their own internal tools, however, their existence in the market, there pricing, the volume of tax reclaims they file annually and the level of success they've had, IE that consistency will reflect their capabilities.

Of course, the final element in the risk management of this complex area is to assess the level of integration of the aforementioned elements. Custodians must decide what level of redundancy to incorporate into their systems to create a resilient process. To that extent comment the institutional investor must pay attention not just to the individual benchmarks applying to the process elements described, but also to how the custodian integrates the different risk mitigation strategies together to create an efficient system.

From a contractual viewpoint, particularly if third-party information or tools are being used attention must be given to the nature of contractual liability and the measurements required by the custodian from his supplier.

Proportion of Fails (PF)

The benchmark, PF, represents the top-level measurement of risk management. Anecdotally, a tax reclaim form must be correct in every respect if it is to be validated by the foreign tax authority. Any error in calculation or indeed completion of the correct boxes on the forms will result in a rejection. It must be assumed to some extent the custodian will have correctly completed all of the preceding steps in the process before submission to a foreign tax authority, so the preceding steps themselves are less likely to cause a failure and are more likely to cause a delay. The difficulty with this approach from a risk management perspective is of course that the statute of limitations overlays the process. If a delay is caused, if documents are lost in the post or if other delays are experienced at one or more points in the process, there is a risk that the submission will have fallen outside the statute of limitations by the time it reaches a tax administration. All these issues are separately benchmarked in this chapter. This is so that an institutional investor or custodial manager will have tools available to monitor and measure not just top-level performance but also some of the specific risk areas that go to make up the overall picture. I can tell the reader from personal experience, without revealing the identity of the institution involved, that there can be some significant impacts on investment returns when custodians fail to address withholding tax processing. I have personally seen management reports from one of the largest global custodian banks in the world which show over $300 million in claims outstanding, i.e., not yet filed, for more than 12 months because the paperwork is stuck with a sub-custodian. The same custodian had a staff of 20 people of whom only two had more than five years of experience in the industry.

PF is insensitive to the reason for the failure. It is highly likely that given the length of some statutes of limitation, sometimes years, a custodian with a failed reclaim or relief at source application, will have sufficient time to rectify the failure and refile documentation to the appropriate authorities. The intention is that this measure should be applied to the originating event.

To illustrate this, consider the following example. Of 1000 income events resulting in tax reclaims, 30 fail on the first attempt, say because of an incomplete form, but are successful on the second attempt after remedial action. A further 30 fail completely. This could occur, for example, if a custodian is applying a threshold system based on the administrative cost of reclaiming. This latter event might apply if the reclaim was for $100 and the cost of reclaiming is $80. The first failure makes the total cost of reclaiming including the second submission, effectively $160 in order to get a $100 reclaim. However, from 1000 reclaims PF in this example would be 6%. It could be argued that the figure should be 3% because 30 of the reclaims were eventually successful. However, I would disagree with this on the basis that this latter interpretation fails to identify the problem in the system, which is its primary objective. At 3%, a custodian may consider this to be an acceptable level and take no further action will stop. At 6% it's likely that a manager or someone will have to take notice and take some action. The latter course is clearly best practice, the former is an example of using a benchmark badly and not using it to identify problems and improve business efficiency.

Of course, PF can only be measured with respect to an endpoint in the system that will stop a reclaim that has been filed but not received or rejected cannot be included since, at the time of the measurement it's not known whether it has failed or not will stop this does not mean that such a reclaim will fallout of the benchmarking process, merely that it appears in a different benchmark set, a sort of work in progress.

PF can be applied on a market-specific basis and also on an aggregated basis to all markets or even to a portfolio set.

$$\mathrm{PF} = \frac{f}{l}$$

where f is the number of failed events and l is the total number of valid, eligible events which have either failed or succeeded, i.e., they must have reached an endpoint and not be "work in progress".

PF_m and PF_p would represent the same benchmark carried out for events only with respect to a particular market m or portfolio p.

It is clear also that, the lower the number of tax reclaims a custodian performs as part of its business offering, the greater the likelihood it will not have invested in risk mitigation measures as the cost will be deemed too high for the return. The consequence will be a higher level of PF will stop indeed in some cases PF as a ratio could exceed 1 even if not all reclaims ultimately fail. For example, a custodian filing 30 claims a year may have 15 failures and a further 15 which fail then subsequently succeed, in which case PF equals one. This is where interpretation is important. The result highlights a problem. It could mean that all reclaims failed, but this is unlikely. It does mean that the custodians' processes and controls are well below best practise and should be addressed.

Age Debt Performance (ADP)

Age debt is a well-understood financial measure. This tool, however, applied to this process, has two factors that must be used together to make the measure effective. Firstly, the standard age debt calculation places the receivable expected from the tax administration into a time slot, e.g., current, over 30 days, one to three months, over six months et cetera this is a good measure in itself and is useful in its own right for both tax department and treasury departments as it is effectively a cash flow forecast statement.

Of course, another element that must be considered is the point in time from which the age deck measurement is made. While the pay date of security would be an expected fixed point from an investor's viewpoint, many custodians use the date that the reclaim was filed to a foreign tax authority as their base point for calculation. This makes more sense as, until that time there is really no receivable recognised by a tax authority. While the income event may be valid and the client eligible, the custodian creates the receivable through its actions in calculating the value of the receivable and processing the correct forms.

However, this is not the entire picture. Each market has variables that affect how and when payments are made. France pays twice a year. So, from this perspective the age debt benchmark gives no indication of when the receivable will actually arrive and the reader would have to know the profile of the French market to be able to intelligently interpret and aged debt or outstanding reclaim report from the custodian.

The second factor therefore is the expected age that the debt should acquire before payment is received. So, for example, and age debt report showing half \$1,000,000 outstanding for six months from France is meaningless. If the events which created this reclaim value occurred more than six months ago, there is an issue to address as they should have been paid. If less than six months, irrespective of the date of creation of the event within that., the reclaim is well within its expected receivable date and a custodian need not be concerned. As we have to see in the discussion on process management, particularly in the French market, it makes sense to hold French reclaims until close to the date of payment. This has the effect of making the payment. And therefore the custodian looks remarkably quick it also provides added time for internal quality control cheques to make sure the reclaim is valid.

$$\mathrm{ADP} = ave\left(\frac{R_a}{R_e}\right)$$

where:

R_a is the actual time from the day the reclaim is filed to the current day or date of payment and

R_e is the expected time for the reclaim to be paid starting from the date of filing.

The overall average value of ADP is formed by attention to market-specific values. In this way, a custodian or an investor can view not only a custodian's overall performance but can also calculate performance for a particular portfolio spread based on n markets.

$$\mathrm{ADP}n = ave\left(\frac{R_a}{R_e}\right)m$$

ADP calculated for the set of reclaims where payment has not yet been made is thus a good measure of whether a custodian is performing well. ADP calculated for the set of reclaims where payment has already been received gives a good historical context to previous performance. A custodian may wish to establish this latter measure to assess the potential effects of investments in automation or outsourcing or demonstrate continuous improvement at a departmental or sales level.

Fit (*F*)

Fit is an important measure for investors. A custodian may have operations extending too many countries, for many types of income. Some of these, and the custodian's performance within them, are irrelevant to an investor whose portfolio does not include those areas. In other words, a custodian who has strengths and sub-custody network in Indonesia will be of little value to the investor whose investment portfolio focus is European. Fit is therefore a measure of the degree to which the investor's portfolio matches that of the custodian's skill set. In many requests for proposals ("RFP"), this stage is both manual and laborious. Custodians spend much time extolling the virtues of their organisational structures and reach, without making a measured statement of the fit between their activities and skills and the needs of their customers.

Of course, the fact that a custodian operates, for example, in a market which is not covered by a client's portfolio, does not mean that there is no benefit to be attributed to that fact. There will be a beneficial effect simply from the increased experience of world markets that flow from an extended market capacity. This is why global custodians are so strong. In addition, of course, the investor may at some point decide to expand the coverage of their portfolio and selecting a custard custodian with a larger capacity than the investor's portfolio spread will then have its advantages.

Fit by market, income types and client types are the three most important areas to consider. Fit by client types may seem strange but, any given client, in this context maybe representing a larger universe of sub-clients who may have a variety of statuses.

$$F = F_m \times F_i \times F_t$$

where

- F_m is the fit in markets covered and is a percentage represented by the number of markets in the client's portfolio compared to the number of similar markets in which the custodian has expertise. It should be noted that this does not give any qualitative description of how good that market expertise is.
- F_i is the fit in income types and is a percentage represented by the number of income types that the client will be receiving, compared to the number of similar income types with which the custodian has experience dealing with.
- F_t is the fit in client types covered and is a percentage represented by the number of legal entity types represented by the client compared to the number of similar client types with which the custodian has experienced.

In all these cases, we deal with the word similar. A perfect fit is of course 1. So, if a client portfolio has twelve markets and the custodian deals with twenty markets, of which only 10 coincide with the client's markets, the fit is 10 divided by 12 or 83.3%.

The other calculation that can be made of course is the actual coverage of the custodian compared to the need of the client will stop in the above case this would be 20 markets covered divided by the match need of 10. So, from a fit perspective, an investor can use this measure in two ways. The first has a measure of true quantitative fit to the current need. The second is a measure of potential future fit.

Statute Risk (SR)

The risk in any process occurs when there is a defined moment or moments at which the possibility of success for the process becomes 0. In the tax reclaim world, this moment is the last day of the statute of limitations provided by the tax administration. Set by each jurisdiction, once a tax reclaim fails to have been filed by this date, the value it represents effectively goes into the invisible earnings of the country concerned. As one of my esteemed colleagues in the industry once put it: if you allow your entitlement to go past the statute

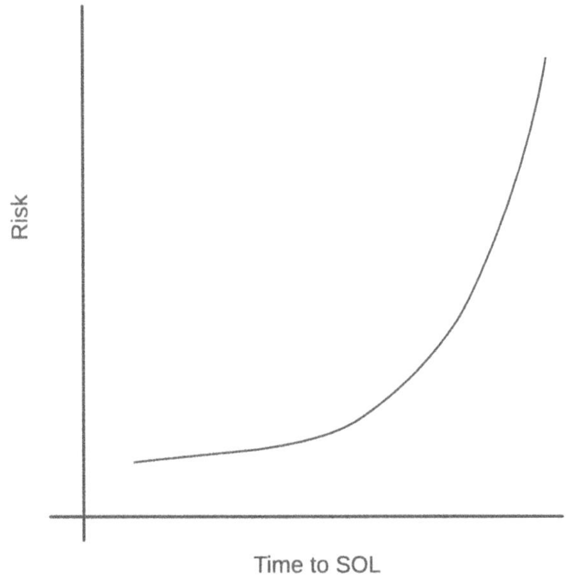

Exhibit 24.3 Statute risk (*Source* Author)

of limitations you can consider that you've just made a tax-free charitable donation to a foreign government (Exhibit 24.3).

Given the reader's knowledge of the other and preceding elements of the process, it's not difficult to understand why, in the absence of significant automation or other resources, many custodians struggle with a backlog of unfilled claims. The measurement of the risk that the reclaim will cross the statute of limitations barrier is defined by the length of time left between the end of the statute and the current date. The business principle behind statute risk is essentially that, if you are a custodian and a proportion of your claims are getting close to the statute of limitations, the risk that you will suffer further delays that take you beyond the statute of limitations is higher. The smallest statute of limitations is one year. The largest exists where the jurisdiction does not have a statute of limitations and claims can be filed at anytime after the pay date.

Statute risk, in its most fundamental form, is a measure of the funds at risk in the process. However, the funds will either be paid or not paid, so the value at risk is easy to calculate. The probability that that value will be lost is a different matter. Again, statute risk, like many other benchmarks is an aggregate measure which can be subdivided into market-specific benchmarks. This allows individual statute risk elements to be compounded together to measure the statute risk for any portfolio P or any market M.

$$\mathrm{SR} = \frac{T1 + T2 + T3 + T4}{SoL} - paydate$$

$$\mathrm{SR}m = \frac{(T1 + T2 + T3 + T4)m}{(\mathrm{SoL})\mathrm{m}} - \mathrm{paydate}$$

$$\mathrm{SR}p = \frac{(T1 + T2 + T3 + T4)p}{(\mathrm{SoL})\mathrm{p}} - \mathrm{paydate}$$

where $T1$, $T2$, $T3$ and $T4$ have the meanings ascribed earlier to the process timings.

SoL is the number of days in the statute of limitations available for a reclaim to be filed.

By ascribing a subscript of m and p to the variables in this equation, we can create alternative equations but calculate the statute risk for markets and portfolios.

RAS Efficient (RAS)

There are a number of markets where relief at source is available. Relief at source efficiency measures the degree to which the custodian is processing in the most efficient way. Clearly, if documentation can be obtained in advance and maintained in a valid form, this will save the expense of proceeding through a reclaim process. There are three measures that fall into this category. As with statute of limitations efficiency and risk, relief at source efficiency can be measured at the overall level at the market level and the portfolio level.

The issue is somewhat complicated because some markets offer relief at source, but only under certain conditions. So, for example, Germany is a reclaim market, unless you happen to be a US participant in the Depository Trust Company DTC. The DTC has negotiated special terms to allow its participants to benefit from a tax relief at the source process in Germany. So, the relief at source efficiency benchmark must reflect what the custodian is capable of treating as relief at source internally and what is available to it from the market.

$$\mathrm{RAS}m = \frac{Mac}{Mav}$$

- Where *Mac* is the number of markets where relief at source is achieved. In this context, macd would be a measure of whether the custodian achieves relief at source on a majority basis. In other words, all other things being equal does the custodian deliver relief at source for most of its clients.
- *Mav* is the number of markets where relief at source is available.

So, relief at source at the portfolio level would represent the relief at source efficiency of a custodian at portfolio level with respect to a limited data set p, representing the countries in which the investor holds his portfolio. An example would be an investor with a portfolio of 15 countries. Relief at source is say, available in five of those countries, but the custodian only offers relief at source in four of these. At this level, the custodian's relief at source efficiency is only 27% out of a potential 33%.

Of course, there is another method of calculating and interpreting relief at the source. This is because, in many instances, the ability to obtain relief at source is dependent on valid documentation. So, relief at source can also be calculated by reference to the number of occasions on which relief at source was achieved at the client level compared to the relief at source that was theoretically possible at the time, on that portfolio, if documentation was available and valid. the reader will see quickly but this is a sort of reverse way of measuring a custodian's ability to manage documentation. From a practical perspective, I prefer this method to a simple sampling system. The former is, after all, a sample whereas the latter is a direct reflection of the investor's ability to receive funds gross or with minimised withholding. In other words, achieve results. With such funds in place, the investor can reinvest or take the return but at least he has the choice.

$$\mathrm{RAS}c = \frac{I_{ac}}{I_{av}}$$

where:

- I_{ac} is the number of income events in any one period where the custodian actually achieved relief at source and
- I_{av} is the number of income events, for the same client over the same., for which relief at source was available in theory.

This may all look extremely complex. However, the fact is that most custodians would be able to calculate this ratio electronically in a number of different ways.

PoA Index

There are a number of small factors that can affect the efficiency with which some of the process elements of tax reclamation are administered. One such is powers of attorney. Without these, as has been described elsewhere, the process of a tax reclaim is extended because the custodian must obtain a signature on the form itself before sending it to the local tax authority for verification, and thereafter to the foreign tax authority for the approval of the reclaim. Investors are of course extremely efficient at returning these forms (*sic*), but delays can happen. The tax reclaim form is a statement and a claim for funds on a foreign entity. As such, from an institutional investor's perspective, it's important that the form is thoroughly checked. A power of attorney, whether limited or not, vests such authority with the custodian or third-party provider. The difficulty for custodians of course is that the decision on whether a client provides a power of attorney rests ultimately with the client and the custodian can't be held completely responsible for not getting power of attorney on every occasion. However, the PoAs index does give an outside investor a feel for how the custodian's business process is set up. A very high PoA index indicates that much streamlining and efficiency savings are possible. A very low PoA index implies this custodian will have to engage in a great deal of potentially costly and time-wasting communication with clients, some of which may be reflected in their custody fees. An index of around 0.5 indicates that the custodian hasn't even mixed however this in itself may cause operational risk problems through having to operate effectively two parallel client document management philosophies at the same time.

$$\text{PoA} = \frac{Cp}{C}$$

where:

- Cp is the number of clients for whom the custodian has power of attorney with respect to the withholding tax issues and
- C is the total number of clients.

To maintain consistency this measure should be used with similar client bases, e.g., all those clients with cross-border assets under custody. Again, if necessary, because the industry is specific in several ways, to markets, portfolios, etc. this index can be specified at any of the relevant levels. So, from an investor's perspective, he would probably want to see the global position as well as the index as it pertains to his portfolio of invested countries with SIM with clients or similar types.

Reconciliation and Traceability (RT)

Reconciliation and traceability are two sides of the same coin. An increase in traceability permits easier and cheaper reconciliation in tax operations. Measuring reconciliations is an entire area of study in its own right that I am not going to go into detail with here. However, from an investor's perspective what's important, in withholding tax issues is that:

1. reconciliation takes place
2. that it's done in the most cost-efficient manner
3. that traps exceptions effectively
4. there aren't many unreconciled items trapped and
5. all the trapped items are eventually reconciled.

Most financial institutions have large department dedicated to reconciliation. This should not be confused with matching. Matching is merely the process of ensuring that one data set is the same as another data set. So, for example, a data file from a custodian purporting to represent payments made to a client will need to match the clients' statement from the financial institution. The fact is that on many occasions these two data sets do not match. Once a mismatch has occurred the process of understanding why the two data sets don't match and correcting any errors is the process of reconciliation. With very large data sets involved and complex transactions occurring of different types among different dates reconciliation can be an extremely difficult and time-consuming process.

$$\text{RT} = \sum_1^n \left(\frac{Er}{Et} \right)$$

where

- Er is the number of exception events identified and reconciled successfully and

there is a proportionate chance that the investors reclaims may also fall into this category.

Threshold risk represents the portion of events whose tax value falls below any given custodian-applied level and which would otherwise be reclaimable and more creditable to investor's account.

$$\text{Thresholdvalue} = \frac{NTh \times Nh}{Val}$$

where:

- TH is the threshold value
- *Nh* is the number of reclaim events at all below TH
- *Val* is the total reclaim value of all events

So, if a custodian has 200,000 income events per year whose total value is $30 million of which 50,000 fall below a nominal threshold of $100, TH is equal to 0.16. A competing custodian who applies a lower threshold value is likely to have a smaller number of events falling into this category, thus TH will be a smaller fraction. The use of the term at all below in this index makes the calculation much simpler from a mathematical viewpoint. In addition, the use of this limiting factor gives an investor a view of the worst-case scenario where all this whole hypothetical events are just under the threshold value, and its portfolio would then receive the worst possible service and value.

It's worth noting here that some tax administrations allow small came claims to be aggregated together onto one reclaim form. Some custodians and third-party providers specifically allow for this in their pricing model and operational model. This means that the provider will acknowledge a claim below the threshold level and accrue this value for a period of time until other claims for the same investor take the total value of claims above the threshold. At this point, the reclaim is valued at the aggregate level and therefore submitted as the normal course of business.

Contractual Tax Index (CTI)

In many markets today the time taken to reclaim tax from a foreign tax administration can be substantial. For example, the time taken for a standard refund in Italy can easily be over 10 years. During that time the investor does not have access to the reclaim funds for the purpose of reinvestment. Contractual Tax is a commercial service offered by some custodians and some third-party providers in which the value of the refund is credited to the investor at the same time as the payment is made. This means that the investor effectively gets the benefit of tax relief at source even when that relief at source is not technically available to them. This is very similar to invoice financing in which the investor is effectively selling the tax reclaim entitlement to the provider. The provider knows how long the tax reclaim is likely to take before payment and therefore makes a calculation to provide the investor with the reclaim funds up front while they process the tax reclaim in the background. Contractual tax only really works if the provider has a sufficient volume of reclaims of a similar type to be able to statistically predict how long the tax reclaim will take to pay back with a high level of confidence. Once this is done, the provider need only calculate the cost of financing to be able to provide the investor with a price. The net result is that the investor gets their money much more quickly while the provider must go through the normal channels to process the tax reclaim. The only difficulty with contractual tax is that having made the financial arrangements, as far as the foreign tax administration is concerned it's still the investor who has the entitlement. Therefore, the investor must agree to support the provider with any information requested by the tax administration as part of the tax reclaim processing.

In the same way that other indices can be modified to apply either to the whole market or a portfolio within markets, the contractual tax index can be calculated in different ways. Since contractual tax delivers the quickest gross funds to an investor, are high convergence between the investor's portfolio spread and that of the custodian is desirable. What this index does not do is make any assessment of the profitability of such an arrangement. Since the custodians' prices for custodial tax must reflect their own efficiencies in the cost of financing as well as a profit margin, a convergence between the portfolio and the custody operations spread may not always be right for the investor.

$$\mathrm{CTI} = \frac{C_p}{C_m}$$

where:

- C_p is the number of markets in the investor's portfolio which have matching entries in the custodians spread and
- C_m is the number of markets in which the custodian offers contractual tax.

VeV Index

Validity, eligibility and value index is a Composite Index and is most important in assessing a custodian's internal systems and procedures. It reflects the three-stage internal process a custodian engages in after it becomes aware of an income event. The sub-indices which comprise the composite relate to the inefficiency with which the custodian is able to:

i. **Assess the validity of an event.** The sub-index here is the validity index, i.e., at what speed can a custodian decide whether any particular income event is likely to generate a withholding tax reclaim or relief at source opportunity or not. This will be an assessment of jurisdiction and whether the type of income is subject to withholding tax. This index can hold one of three values—2 is a completely manual process based on knowledge held in paper form or in staff experience, one is a partially automated process through the use of common tools such as spreadsheets, where a matrix has been compiled against which the in-colour event can be assessed will stop since the knowledge has been externalised, it has also reduced the operational risk in the process as well as improving the ability of management to open the oversee the tools level of accuracy and precision. 0 is a completely automated process where information about the income is held electronically and assessed electronically against information about jurisdictions. This value would also be used for outsourcing solutions.
ii. **Assess the eligibility** of a particular income event or client pairing. The eligibility index is a measure of how efficiently the custodian acquires, holds, and manages information about its clients. This can range from a fully manual system through to a completely automated and integrated system. In this element of the process, the custodian must acquire information from the client, usually from the account opening process under KYC rules, as well as documentation—irrespective of whether the client has issued a power of attorney. It must then assess in the light of the validity of the income event, whether the client is eligible for further attention whether under relief at source procedures, reclaim procedures or other procedures such as contractual tax. This will determine, under the circumstances and reporting principles, whether the client's account should be credited immediately or at a later date. The eligibility index is ranged between zero and two and is formed according to the following equation EI = AF plus SF AF is the acquisition factor being zero for electronic and one for manual. The storage and retrieval factor SF is 0 for

25

Portfolio Performance

This chapter provides mathematical modelling of tax processing to show how much value can be added to an investment portfolio as a result of tax optimisation processes such as relief at source and standard reclaims. It uses some of the techniques described in the previous chapter to identify risks and how to minimise them. It will also describe non-optimal but common tax processes that delay the delivery of portfolio value, thus providing investors and financial institutions with a guide of what to look out for.

Other than retail investors who are often choosing securities based on emotional factors, institutional investors typically have a very carefully planned strategy and portfolio of investments that suit their needs. Some of these strategies have no withholding tax impact and the investors don't really care because that's not where they make their returns.

Hedge funds and pension funds, for instance, often hold positions in securities both long (over the record date) and short (borrowed securities). Only the long positions have tax reclaims associated with them. Equally, an investment strategy that is focused on leveraging volatility will be trading very quickly, as with high-frequency trading ("HFT") in which the margin is made on the buy–sell difference. Very high-volumes of trades leveraged off extremely small differences in the buy or sell price can build up to substantial overall returns.

On the other hand, long-only fund strategies are very sensitive to withholding tax principally because part of their return is made from the receipt

R. K. McGill, *Cross-Border Investment Withholding Tax*, Finance and Capital Markets Series,
https://doi.org/10.1007/978-3-031-32785-8_25

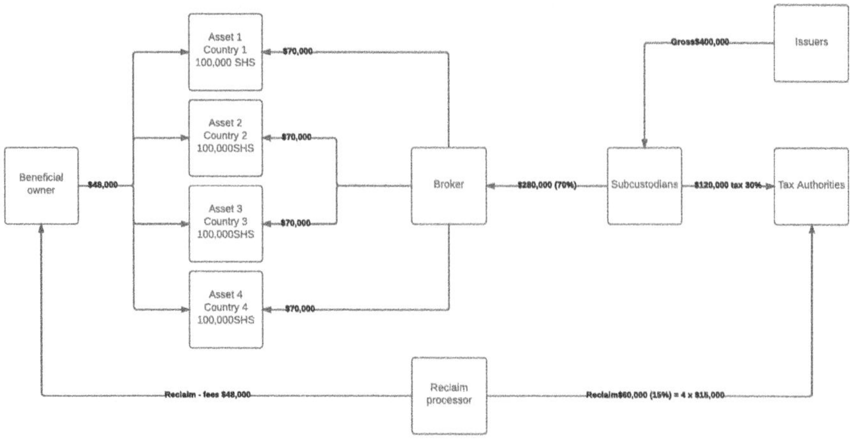

Exhibit 25.1 Portfolio performance (*Source* Author)

of dividends or interest. The logical question to ask is of course "what kind of difference can withholding tax have on a portfolio?". The answer, like so much else about withholding tax, is "It depends!".

The best way to demonstrate this is with an example (Exhibit 25.1).

Let's suppose that an investor has a portfolio of investments held through a Broker. The portfolio holds mainly equities, and the investor tends to hold those investments "long". He likes to get the dividends. An average portfolio might have securities issued by companies in, say, four countries and he invests in the top company in each country. The average statutory rate of tax across those four countries is around 30%. The typical treaty rate, to which this investor is entitled, is 15% this being the most common treaty rate in double tax agreements.

Now let's suppose that this investor holds 100,000 shares in each of the top companies in each of those four countries, a total position of 400,000 shares. Now, outside the US, there are generally two dividend seasons each year (four in the US). Now let's assume that each of those companies distributes a dividend to its shareholders and pays that dividend at an equivalent rate of $1 per share. If tax relief or quick refund is not available to this investor, the Issuer or their agent will withhold tax at the statutory rate in the country of the issuer, in this example 30%. At $1 per share, the gross amount paid by the Issuer will be $400,000 of which $120,000 will be withheld and paid to the tax administrations of each of the nine countries. The investor will receive a net dividend of $280,000.

Now, in scenario 1, if this investor does not know about withholding tax reclamation or looks into it and thinks it's too hard to figure out, that will be the end of the matter. His entitlement to the treaty rate of tax will still exist until the statutes of limitation run out, at which point, the money belongs to the foreign tax administrations. The performance of the portfolio is effectively a return of $280,000.

In scenario 2, this investor contracts with a vendor to do the reclaims for him. The claims are filed correctly and the investor, a year or so later, receives a refund of 15%, the treaty rate of tax, $60,000, back from the foreign tax administrations minus any fees applied by his agent for processing the claims. So, in this scenario, this portfolio ultimately receives $340,000. His portfolio performance increased by 21.4% by processing tax reclaims, compared to not doing anything at all.

Now the average fee rate for tax reclamation is say 20% of the recovered funds. So, to give a more realistic picture, the actual amount received by this investor would be $328,000 having paid his agent 20% of the $60,000 reclaim ($12,000). That means his portfolio performance is actually 17.1% higher compared to not doing anything at all.

Finally, let's assume that this investor has been sitting on this portfolio of securities for some years and that the same dividend was paid out by each company in each of those years. The average statute of limitations across nine EU markets is around 5 years. That means that, in addition to claiming back the tax on this year's dividend, he could also claim back the same amount for the dividends he received in each of the preceding five years. Then his recoverable is $300,000, the fees are $60,000 and his portfolio benefits from and additional income of $1.4 million in dividends and $240,000 in refunds (minus 20% fees).

Now, there are a number of variables in this performance calculation. How many securities are in the portfolio, what are the statutory rates and treaty rates involved, 15% and 30% are just the most common. What was the rate per share of the distribution? All that said, it's easy to see that acting on withholding tax can make a substantial difference to return on investment compared to doing nothing at all—which is why institutional investors are often much more aware of this issue than retail investors. In the real world where these variables will vary wildly, it's not uncommon to see portfolio, performance improvement of 150 to 200 basis points, i.e., 1.5%–2% uplift. If you're managing a $10bn hedge fund, the numbers get interesting very quickly.

The other significant variable I have not mentioned yet is the type of beneficial owner. The example above is for a wealthy US individual. However, some institutional investors get special treatment in double tax agreements, most notably pension funds and sovereign wealth funds. Pension funds and sovereign wealth funds are generally treated as tax-exempt. So, if the example had been of a pension fund, it would have been entitled to a 0% rate, but been subjected to the 30% statutory rate so this investor would have received all the tax back, a 42.8% performance uplift.

This differential between statutory rates and treaty rates can sometimes drive investment strategy, leading ultimately to a risk of tax arbitrage or fraudulent claims. The desire to leverage weaknesses or loopholes in tax policy can lead some down a dark path as discussed in the chapters on recent Danish and German tax fraud cases.

Contractual Tax

The time it takes for tax authority to refund a claimant varies too, from a few months, e.g., Netherlands, Switzerland etc. to several years, e.g., Italy. For large value claims, this can cause a problem. The uplift in performance is not realised until the claim is paid because that is the earliest point in time that the money is available for reinvestment.

This has led to a new offering from some in the industry, most often called contractual tax. Contractual tax is similar to invoice factoring in many ways. If your firm processes large volumes of reclaims, you will have a statistical basis of knowledge at a market level, to know how long any given value of claim will take to be refunded. This provides an opportunity. Some market participants can do this calculation and offer to effectively buy the entitlement. In this product, a firm will pay the reclaimed amount out of its own money straight away. This is attractive because it means that the investor has the reclaim funds much earlier than would otherwise be the case and can reinvest those funds straight away for more return on investment ("RoI"). Of course, there is a cost associated with this product—the cost to the firm of financing the money provided to the investor. Also, even when factored, the legal entitlement still remains with the investor. So, while the investor gets their refund, they must also contractually agree to support the vendor's efforts to process the tax reclaim.

While this puts some people off—they lose interest in the claim process once they have their money, it can be a lucrative model for those who have the experience and knowledge. In terms of performance, it can benefit the investor to realise that performance earlier than normal.

Fiduciary Duty

For those of us who have been in the industry for some years, tax reclamation is a no-brainer. Why would you not do everything possible to optimise your investment efforts? This has led to some discussions about whether, in the institutional investment space, there is not a fiduciary duty on officers of a fund to require them to reclaim tax wherever they can.

I can recall meeting with a fund accountant to present the results of an analysis showing £1.4 m of claimable funds from their portfolio. The fund accountant decided not to do anything, to which my rather annoyed response was "that could be my pension fund you're dealing with". The reason given for this inaction was that the amount to be recovered was not "material" from an accounting point of view. My point about fund managers is that generally the money they are investing isn't their money, but it's your money. So, it's absolutely pertinent to ask questions about how a fund conducts itself in tax matters. If you're concerned about their "green credentials" you should be equally concerned about tax. In the US, there is a regulation called the Employee Retirement Income Security Act (ERISA[1]). ERISA is a federal law that sets minimum standards for most voluntarily established retirement and health plans in private industry to provide protection for individuals in these plans.

ERISA protects a plan's assets by requiring that those persons or entities who exercise discretionary control or authority over plan management or plan assets, anyone with discretionary authority or responsibility for the administration of a plan, or anyone who provides investment advice to a plan for compensation or has any authority or responsibility to do so are subject to fiduciary responsibilities. Plan fiduciaries include, for example, plan trustees, plan administrators, and members of a plan's investment committee.

The primary responsibility of fiduciaries is to run plans solely in the interest of participants and beneficiaries and for the exclusive purpose of providing benefits and paying plan expenses. Fiduciaries must act prudently and must diversify the plan's investments in order to minimise the risk of large losses. In addition, they must follow the terms of plan documents to the extent that the plan terms are consistent with ERISA. They also must avoid conflicts of interest. In other words, they may not engage in transactions on behalf of the plan that benefit parties related to the plan, such as other fiduciaries, services providers or the plan sponsor.

[1] https://www.dol.gov/general/topic/retirement/erisa.

Fiduciaries who do not follow these principles of conduct may be personally liable to restore any losses to the plan, or to restore any profits made through improper use of plan assets. Courts may take whatever action is appropriate against fiduciaries who breach their duties under ERISA including their removal.

In my book, literally speaking, I read this as inclusive of the types of activity we have discussed in this book, in terms of optimising withholding taxes that a plan is subject to when it invests cross-border. However, ERISA regulation does not specifically mention withholding tax, but if my plan administrator had just let $1.4 m go unclaimed, I know I'd have something to say to the regulator about it.

26

Tax Is a Product, Not a Task

This chapter describes the different approaches taken to withholding tax processing be financial institutions as opposed to third-party specialist vendors. The former tend to treat tax processing as a necessary evil, a task, while the latter treats the subject as a product. This leads to very different experiences for investors who may not understand the effect. This chapter should also act as a highlighter for financial institutions to show them how to improve their tax offerings.

The firms that process withholding tax generally fall into one of two categories. They are either financial institutions that have internal departments that process corporate actions as part of their safe keeping responsibilities to their customers or they are independent firms that have set up to provide tax processing services either directly to beneficial owners or to their financial institutions.

The independent firms' approach to this subject is usually driven by the source of their expertise. Their owners may have previously worked in financial institutions, as is the case with GlobeTax, so they will understand the difficulties they face. They may also have access to some technical expertise, as is the case with the GOAL Group, which developed a software solution. In both cases, these firms, apart from developing their respective solutions, must also sell those solutions to their prospective customers. It is therefore natural that these firms treat tax as a product. When you treat tax as a product, all the

R. K. McGill, *Cross-Border Investment Withholding Tax*, Finance and Capital Markets Series,
https://doi.org/10.1007/978-3-031-32785-8_26

corporate disciplines associated with product development, marketing, sales etc. are brought into clearer focus.

Financial institutions tend to take a different approach. To them, tax is an administrative burden and is most often seen as a cost of doing business. The people who work in these institutions are not usually proactively thinking of how they can improve the returns of their clients, it's not one of their key performance indicators ("KPIs"). For most staff in financial institutions, corporate actions are a reactive process, i.e., there is an event that triggers a series of actions, one of which might be a tax reclaim. It is only relatively recently that tax reclamation has been included in benchmarking of service levels and then, usually only at the binary level of "do you do tax reclamation or not?". It's usually left up to the client to make a fuss if they see a potential tax reclaim opportunity on their investment statement.

These two very different approaches lead to very different outcomes for investors. For financial institutions, tax reclamation is an administrative tax. So, the procedures are administrative, and no one really cares how long they take. The next procedural step takes place when the prior step is completed. For example, there is one Swiss bank that processes around 20,000 reclaims a year for their clients. However, they file these claims all at once and it takes them nearly a year to get all the relevant documentation in place. A third-party vendor treating this matter as a product recognises the inefficiency of this process. Typical outsourcing vendors will obtain a monthly data file from a financial institution that gives them the income data of clients that have signed up for the service either directly or via their financial institution. From this data, they can identify potential reclaims and begin the filing process much more quickly. Effectively this is real-time processing versus batch processing. The reason this is more efficient is simple. Once filed, a tax administration will typically pay out the refund within a certain time frame that is well-known in the industry. That clock only starts when the claim is received. So, the financial institution that batch processes once a year can be adding up to a full twelve months to the recovery time during which those funds are not available to the investor.

Exhibit 26.1 describes this efficiency differential. The financial institution processing in batch mode is storing up claims that could be but aren't filed until they have finished processing an entire year's worth of claims. The vendor files as soon as it can. The reason for this is in the pricing and business models of most vendors. The industry model for third-party vendors is usually based on two components (i) a percentage of the amount actually recovered and (ii) a contingent basis, i.e., the money must first be recovered before fees can be taken. It's this second component that drives the efficiency

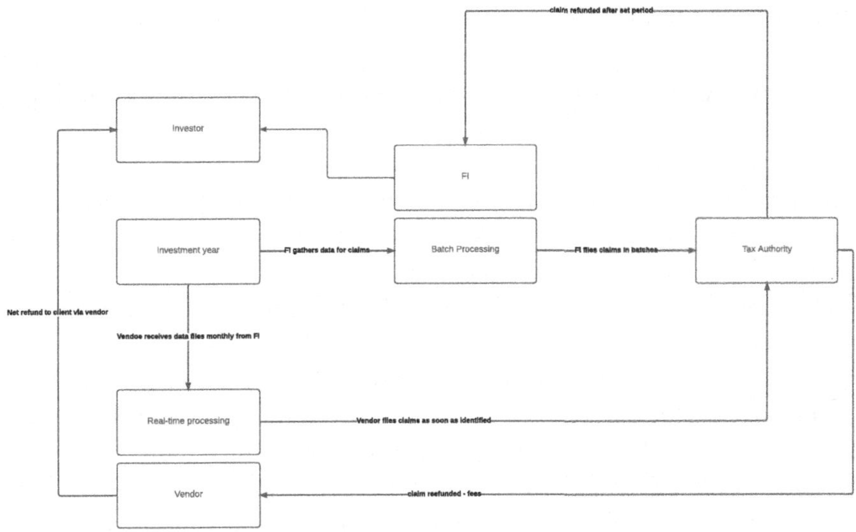

Exhibit 26.1 Batch processing v real-time (*Source* Author)

model. It's not in the interest of the vendor to wait and process in batch. They want to get the refund processed as fast as possible so they can get their fees. This is the difference between treating tax as a product (real-time processing) as opposed to a task (batch processing).

This contingent fee model has some interesting side effects. The first of these is a comparative effect. As far as tax reclamation goes, it does not matter what the size of a claim is, it's the same process once all the evidence is in place. So, for vendors, the major challenge is in justifying a larger absolute cash fee if the claims are large. If I have a $5 m claim, a 20% fee is $1 million. If I have a $1000 claim, the fee is $200—but the process, and by inference the processing costs are the same. So, why should I pay a different fee for the same process? The only counter to this objection is that some tax authorities do audit larger claims, notably the Swiss and German authorities, mainly because they are the ones most recently targeted in fraud cases. These audits are generally seeking to understand how the investor came to have the record date position that they did and whether the investment they held was for valid investment purposes. The Swiss tax administration, for instance, has two questionnaires that it sends to firms filing claims, the four-question questionnaire and the eight-question questionnaire. The eight-question questionnaire can get very detailed, even to the point of asking for copies of contracts of employment relating to anyone involved with the investor's financial affairs. How these questions are answered can be critical to the success of a claim.

Other tax authorities have taken this one step further by changing the claim procedure to require a claimant to provide evidence of the trading history leading up to their record date position on which they are claiming. Again, this is a response to recent fraud cases and, in the case of Germany, the "cum-ex" dividend scandal. Most financial institutions would not proactively provide such data because it's often difficult for them to get it from their systems while a vendor will know the risk and often proactively require that material before they process any claims.

The second side effect of a commercial approach to tax processing is the cash-offset effect. When a financial institution files claims on behalf of its clients, the cost is either absorbed as a cost of doing business or is allocated within their custody or brokerage fees. Either way, its rarely split out as a separate cost. The effect for commercial enterprise is much more direct. Since the vendor only gets paid when the claim gets paid, the time between being aware of. potential claim, filing it and getting a refund is critical. In effect, from a Cash perspective, the firm's cash flow is baked in for anything up to two years. In other words, if I file a claim today on a contingent basis, I must expend all the effort to gather the documentation, file the claim and chase it up, for two years before I get paid through my portion of the refund. So, third-party vendors need to pay close attention to cash flow effects because they are effectively financing a future cash flow from current activities.

There is another effect rarely discussed and that's the effect of macro-economic cycles on cash flow. In simple terms and remembering that cash flows are baked in for years forward, when times are good, corporations are healthy and many generate annual dividends. When times are bad, many companies go bust, while others tighten their belts and either do not distribute dividends or, if they do, the rate per share is substantially reduced. When the rate per share of dividends is squeezed, the number and value of reclaims drops. For a commercial enterprise treating tax as a product, they can, hopefully, predict these changes and adjust their own to offset lean years.

There are several financial institutions over the last few years that have started to strip out tax processing from their bundled fee custody model. It's clear that as soon as they do that, they have understood each part of the process and have priced it accordingly.

There is a big difference both in process and results, between treating tax as a product and treating it as a task.

Part VII

The Future

27

Digitisation of Tax

While transmission methods may advance, using DLT and other technologies and securities themselves become digital, some aspects of tax have heretofore been intractable to standardisation and automation. This chapter explores some of the ways in which those intractable issues may be solved. Not least of these will be digitisation of documentation for self-certifications of residency, the use of non-fungible tokens to represent tax reclaims, smart contracts to allow more efficient outsourcing and the use of high-technology vendor solutions by financial institutions to reduce cost and risk.

The word of the century, in financial circles at least, is digitisation. As I might paraphrase, "Digitisation. What is it good for? Absolutely nothing" and that would be correct. On its own, digitisation is useless. Its precursors are standards and automation. The world of withholding tax has been extraordinarily slow and inept at developing standards, preferring to sit within the International Standards ("ISO") community where tax matters tend to be addressed on a piecemeal basis as part of other corporate actions initiatives. It's been slower still at developing automation in this area. The main changes have been the development of the Electronic Submission Portal ("ESP") and the Managed Income Distributions at Source system "("MIDAS") by US firm GlobeTax. Similar systems have been developed by GOAL Group—the ADRoit system being an equivalent to ESP. TConsult's own platform, the Tax Compliance Toolkit ("TCT") is more oriented on the compliance obligations of financial institutions.

R. K. McGill, *Cross-Border Investment Withholding Tax*, Finance and Capital Markets Series,
https://doi.org/10.1007/978-3-031-32785-8_27

Tax administrations have also been active. The US is moving in 2023 to upgrade its traditional portals—The International Data Exchange System ("IDES") and its tax return portal—Filing Information Returns Electronically ("FIRE"). The latter is having a new interface installed between the users and the background functions, called the Modernised e-File system ("MeF"). MeF has decided to improve security by requiring all users to establish a unique identification account with ID.me. The UK tax authority, HMRC, now uses a portal for submissions of both FATCA and CRS reports.

However, all these systems merely lay the groundwork for potential digitisation. At one end, it's likely that, if you use a third-party, you'll be forced to use a proprietary format for data. At the other end, most tax administrations have settled on the use of the extended markup language, .xml, but otherwise, they use spreadsheets or paper. So, the direction of travel is good, but the degree of consistency is still not good enough, or fast enough. Withholding tax is a very data-heavy activity—number of shares, ISINs, CUSIPs, rate per share, trade history, record dates, pay dates and ex-dates, these are, or should be, relatively easy to consume. However, it's in documentation that the industry has failed most significantly.

The groundwork for digitisation is mostly focused on getting tax administrations and governments to accept and adopt digital versions of the paper forms they have historically mandated and to allow the use of digital electronic signatures in place of "wet" signatures. The US was the first to allow self-certifications of residency, one of the foundational components of their tax relief at source system. Even so, only a few firms have pursued this. Digitisation relies on automation and automation, in turn, relies on standards.

While there are a plethora of standards in financial services, the most common is ISO 20022, which is managed by the Society for Worldwide Interbank Telecommunications ("SWIFT"). I have the privilege of contributing as a member of three ISO standard committees—corporate actions, funds management and proxy voting. Withholding tax does not have its own committee, a notable thing in its own right. Withholding tax appears to be an adjunct to many other practices in financial services and its this, more than anything that I believe needs to change. In the Standards Release for 2021, there are only nine optional codes associated with withholding tax: TAXC, TAXR, TRAN, TRAX, TXDF, TXRC, UNFR, VATA, WITH and WITL. TXRC is an amount that was paid in excess of an actual tax obligation and was reclaimed. TAXR is an amount of withholding tax on a cash distribution. The reader may hopefully by now understand that the area of withholding tax is much more complex than this, in terms of how one financial institution may communicate with another.

When I first started working in this industry, I came across a description of SWIFT as the policeman of ISO standards in financial services. In one conversation, with an executive, I observed that the difficulties financial firms had could be solved simply by strictly enforcing the standard, i.e., if a message did not meet the standard, SWIFT should not allow the message to move across their network. It's worthwhile noting that SWIFT wears two hats. In addition to being the policeman of ISO standards, it also happens to run its own computer network over which ISO standard messages can be transmitted. While SWIFT is a not-for-profit organisation, it does charge its 8000 members for each message transmitted—which number in the billions each year. So, it's perhaps not entirely surprising that the response I received from the SWIFT executive was that a counterparty would prefer to receive a bad message than no message at all.

While my observation did not gain instant traction, it was interesting to see that sometime later, SWIFT implement an Event Interpretation Grid ("EIG") product. The EIG algorithm is applied to each message to determine the degree to which the content and format of the message was consistent with the Standard.

To me a Standard that allows for interpretation, is not a Standard, it's an opinion. Sea containers, on which ironically, the ISO system was founded, are all standard sizes. No one gets to change the height, width or depth on a whim.

Finally, I must mention artificial intelligence ("AI"). We are at the cusp of momentous changes driven by AI. The advent of ChapGPT has shown that AI can interact with us in astounding an very human-like ways. Some have likened our current state of development to that of the Wright brothers' first flight noting that only fifty summers later we were watching the take-off of 747 jumbo jets. How might we predict, or even imagine what AI could do in the world of tax? Certainly, I have been of the opinion in the past that while AI could replace some aspects of our society, it could never replace many of the aspects of withholding tax that has been stubbornly manual and paper-based for so many years. Now, I am not quite so sure.

There is a 2002 American movie, called Minority Report[1] whose premise is that crime will become obsolete in the future because we'll have access to enough data to predict crime before it happens. I can certainly see that AI should, in the not-too-distant future, be able to predict tax evasion, in real

[1] https://www.imdb.com/title/tt0181689/.

time. As systems become ever more complex and inter-connected, the data could be reviewed as soon as it's created. We already see the precursors to this with DAC 6, trying to describe the conditions that could lead to tax evasion. At present, we have to rely on reportability by intermediaries based on the characteristics of an arrangement. In the European Market Infrastructure Regulation ("EMIR"), we see the recording and analysis of broker conversations to identify key words and phrases that might be signs of activity that could de-stabilise markets. The technology is all there, we simply lack the ability, or perhaps the will, to engage an AI to review all the data and make inferences. I feel confident to say that AI could solve the problem of tax evasion by analysing behaviour, learning from how it's been done in the past and seeing merging trends in data.

I can also see how AI could be a better predictor of potential systemic weaknesses. If all the data on financial instruments and their trade data could be analysed by an AI, it should have the capacity to see those flaws. Of course, the monumental computing power required means that the tasks given to AI must be commensurately important to us, such as weather predictions to minimise global warming extreme events. Even so, today our weather prediction compute power is orders of magnitude better than it was just a few years ago.

On a more pragmatic level, the data volumes and complexity of withholding tax would seem to be childishly simple for an AI. It would be eminently possible for an AI to be given all the data on DTAs, investor types and trade data and have the AI automatically process tax relief at source on all cross-border transactions. All the investor would need would be a token in his wallet on his smart phone that could be used by his financial institutions.

So, now I must revise my prediction from the first edition of this book. Withholding tax can be fully automated and standardised and I believe, through AI, that becomes not only possible but inevitable. The drag on the timetable for this will be the penchant for humans to do things slowly and inefficiently.

Exhibit 27.1 provides an insight into what may be to come. Many firms will be disintermediated by AI because their function can be fully automated. An investor would have a wallet on their mobile device that includes a self-certification of tax residency in tokenised form. They can invest in securities through brokers or direct on exchanges. Connections with an AI allow the AI to monitor shareholders as these transactions take place. Transfer Agents will disappear. Assets transferred to custodians will also be monitored by AI so that trading activity and positions can be tracked for potentially dangerous

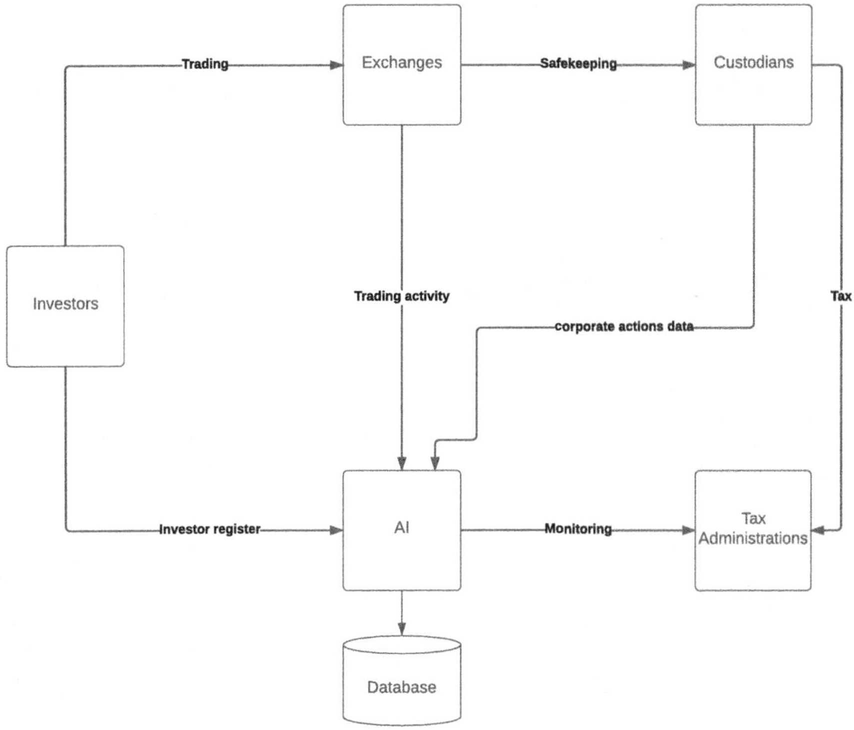

Exhibit 27.1 AI in tax

activity. Corporate actions themselves can be monitored and, most importantly, the tax implications of those corporate actions can be known almost immediately that a record date occurs.

The depth of knowledge of an AI in this space would eradicate the kind of cum-ex scandal that the Germans and others suffered. The AI would know the total position of every ADR so duplicate claiming could not occur[2] and the limit for every single investor would be known.

[2] At present, the ESO system would allow duplicate claims from a sophisticated investor. The only limit would be the omnibus position at the top of the payment chain. So, the total claims filed cannot exceed the limit, but that does not guarantee that there are no fraudulent claims within that limit.

28

Vendor Dynamics

In late 2022 I accepted an invitation to join the advisory board of RAQUEST GmbH, a subsidiary of Halvotech GmbH. I had been the managing director of GOAL so, I had relevant experience in withholding tax on which to call in order to support RAQUEST in their strategic planning. RAQUEST is a software vendor that licenses its software to financial institutions and institutional investors so that they have better tools to manage the tax relief and reclamation processes. In this chapter I have collaborated with RAQUEST's CEO, Alexander Lerch to explore why software solutions work in this sector, what they bring to their users and why a firm would use software rather than outsource.

A vendor is anyone that is not in the chain of payment but is or has been engaged to perform tasks related to withholding tax or is providing a product that facilitates that process. So, custodian banks and brokers are not strictly vendors, even though many charge clients for their tax services. GOAL Group, RAQUEST, GlobeTax, TAINA[1] etc. are all vendors.

The support of investors through the provision of appropriate services is often offered by custodian financial institutions to their investors as part of their securities services. However, the institutions face the same operational challenges, multiplied by the number of customers. For financial institutions, the performance of such services is further complicated by other aspects such as tax compliance, risk management, liability etc.

[1] https://www.taina.tech.

R. K. McGill, *Cross-Border Investment Withholding Tax*,
Finance and Capital Markets Series,
https://doi.org/10.1007/978-3-031-32785-8_28

This is the reason why many institutions often only offer the service to a limited target group, which either has a corresponding importance (such as high net worth individuals or institutional investors) or actively requests the service. As withholding taxes were not known by many investors for a long time, this led to a high amount of overpaid withholding taxes worldwide going un-reclaimed. However, a change in trend is emerging here: Investors are looking for more and more new ways to increase their after-tax returns, and the reduction of withholding taxes is moving into the focus of investors, which offers financial institutions in particular the opportunity to increase customer satisfaction and customer loyalty by providing appropriate services.

These services are usually offered in two ways: either the activities are performed in-house or outsourced to a specialised service provider (business process outsourcing or BPO).

Whether in-house or through a service provider, the goal is always to maximise the efficiency of the service and reduce the costs per case as much as possible in order to give as many investors as possible the opportunity to increase their after-tax returns. Since in most cases the service entails fees for the investor, a case-based profitability calculation per market and per investor is essential. Conclusion: The lower the case costs, the larger the recovery volumes that can be covered, with the result that many (especially smaller) investors can benefit from the service and obtain their rights.

One of the crucial questions is to what extent the execution of services can be automated and digitised through the use of software and IT systems in order to reduce unit transaction costs.

How Can Software Help and What Does It Need to Do?

Experience has shown that modern and highly specialised software solutions can reduce process costs and lead times by up to 90% through the targeted end-to-end automation of manual processes in financial institutions.

However, such a high degree of automation places numerous demands on the system used.

Modern software refers to systems which, from a technical point of view, are developed to the latest state of the art and can be used by numerous banks thanks to a high degree of standardisation. They should also offer a high degree of user-experience and have a user-friendly web-based interface.

Simple and seamless integration into the data and system landscape of the service providers is ensured through appropriate interfaces, such as application programming interfaces ("APIs") as well as the connection to foreign tax authorities. This latter aspect is becoming increasingly important, as the submission of paper-based documents is already no longer supported by tax authorities in some investment markets. By providing digital interfaces for the submission of applications, the degree of automation is further increased. End-to-end digitisation means that a system not only automates major parts of relief at source or reclaim processes but also monitors, allocates and posts the status of claims and resulting incoming payments.

The processing of withholding taxes is subject to numerous special regulations. Depending on numerous parameters such as the type of service (e.g., with or without power of attorney), the type of customer (private individual, legal entity, institutional investor), the tax domicile of the investor, the investment markets, the intermediaries involved and much more, a wide variety of regulations must be complied with, deadlines monitored, fees calculated, forms and additional documents provided and optimal application channels selected. Software must implement all these international specifics and be kept permanently up to date with legal changes in order to generate maximum benefit and ensure that, in principle, action is taken in the best interests of the investor.

In addition to creating forms, software-based solutions also generate cover letters required for communication with investors, custodian banks or tax authorities. Additional tax documents required for the tax reclaim process can be generated by the software, replacing tedious manual searches and extractions from banking systems. An example of such a document is a tax document issued by foreign banks in the Swiss investment market.

Overall, a professional solution is expected to analyse all potential recovery opportunities to maximise the investor experience and after-tax performance of the entire portfolio. Software solutions can also help banks identify open gaps in customer service, i.e., find and flag customers who have not yet enrolled in the withholding tax service. This would help account managers engage with their customers based on actual numbers and potential.

For financial institutions, ensuring tax compliance through software is an important aspect. Typical features such as the dual control principle, data historisation and separation, data security and auditability are examples of minimum standards. A preventative profitability calculation of applications regarding internal and external fees should also ensure that reclaims that do not make economic sense for the investor are avoided or are only made when, for example, the profitability limit is reached by further dividend payments.

This also highlights the fact that the use of such software should be accompanied by a change in approach from tax as a task, to tax as a product. The software should also validate all data, information that is missing or does not comply with the rules and regulations set by the respective tax authorities and/or custodian banks must be flagged.

Complementary reporting capabilities targeting different stakeholders and management levels provide a better overview and help organise workload and responsibilities. Real-time query and output functionalities support the handling of requests from investors or other stakeholders and enable operations staff to organise work as needed.

The more completely the process can be digitised, the greater the reduction in processing times and case-related processing costs, so that in the best-case scenario all investors can get their money more quickly and reinvest it through preventative relief at source or prompt recovery. This can create a win–win situation: the investor gets money back or increases their after-tax return in exchange for paying a service fee, and the service provider or financial institution increases customer loyalty, generates service revenue and can reinvest the withholding tax gained with the investor again. In order to operate the service economically, appropriate systems should allow for a high number of case volumes through bulk processing.

A complete mapping of the above-mentioned aspects frees the service provider from having to maintain specially trained personnel in large quantities and thus generates a positive aspect in terms of process and personnel costs as well as fail-safety with a simultaneous reduction in errors.

Outsourcing or In-House?

When looking for a solution that facilitates navigating the tax relief space, banks need to decide whether they want to handle the processing of tax relief at source, quick refund and tax reclaim themselves or outsource this part of their operational value chain. In the latter case, banks can opt for several outsourcing providers, e.g., one of the big four accounting firms or smaller specialised providers.

Once the strategic decision has been made to perform the processes in-house, banks need to look at options for standardising, automating and digitising the processing.

In principle, outsourcing only shifts the question of efficient processing to the service provider, who must then also ask himself how he can process and offer the service cost-effectively and efficiently.

From the perspective of the financial institution, the following high-level comparison of the two approaches can provide guidance for making a strategic decision for in-house processing or outsourcing (Exhibit 28.1).

	Business Process Outsourcing (BPO)	Software (in-house)
Data Delivery	There are expenses for the regular preparation and transmission of the data to the service provider in the required form	Costs are incurred for integration into the infrastructure (implementation and adaptation of the solution, connection of the interfaces to the core systems)
Data Security	Customer data is disclosed to external parties; it may be necessary to amend service contracts with customers and/or make a Transfer Risk Assessment ("TRA") under data protection laws, if the data transfer is cross border.	The sovereignty of the data remains with the financial institution, the service can be performed under power of attorney or without power of attorney, depending on the agreement with the customer
Data Exchange	A well-designed process organization for providing the required information to the service provider is necessary to avoid inefficient loops in case of missing accompanying documents, certificates, etc.	The provision of data and documents is carried out in-house in a direct way, if necessary by the software itself or via interfaces
Infrastructure	Typically, little or no additional IT infrastructure is required.	The setup and operation of a software solution is required, possibly in the cloud (if this is covered by the financial institution's IT policy)
Customer communication	Depending on the type of service, customer communication is handled by the service provider; the processing of customer queries must be clarified organisationally and approved by the financial institution.	Customer communication can be handled inhouse. In addition, comprehensive use of withholding tax data is possible, e.g., for sales purposes (reinvestment of reclaimed tax, proactive sale of withholding tax services, touchpoints with the customer).
Compliance/Risk	There is a shift of activities to the business process outsourcing provider, the operational responsibility of risk management as well as tax compliance has to be clarified	Responsibility for risk minimisation and tax compliance remain in-house and should be ensured by appropriate software functions
Reporting	Reporting is usually done by report outputs of the BPO provider according to the agreed service level agreements.	Due to the availability of data in-house, ad hoc analyses and insights are possible through corresponding reporting functions in the software or the connection to a data warehouse
Resources	Within the framework of outsourcing, depending on the characteristics, hardly any or no personnel operational resources are required.	Small personnel resources are required (depending on the degree of automation) to ensure that the services are carried out with the software; in some cases, external personnel trained in the software can be called in on a situational basis

Exhibit 28.1 Comparison of in-house to outsource processing (*Source* Alex Lerch, CEO RAQUEST GmbH)

Legal costs	Mostly service- or case-related costs are charged, but this is highly dependent on the BPO provider.	Depending on the software vendor and their licensing models, e.g., case-based costs or models with economies of scale may be possible
Know-How	Outsourcing means that tax expertise is shifted to the service provider and the institution does not have to maintain any know-how.	Tax expertise must be implemented in the software, but basic process know-how must be available in-house.
Service breadth	Outsourcing usually only makes sense for Reclaim services, due to the high demands on time critical process components and data integration into the core systems for Relief at Source processes	An infrastructural integration enables the handling of Reclaim, Quick Refund and Relief services for beneficial owners, provided that the software covers all areas. Customer queries can be answered directly in-house using the software
Process coverage regarding reclaim	In the context of outsourcing, process coverage usually ends with the application, as further steps require additional interfaces with the financial institution	The degree of automation can be extended with appropriate functional coverage and integration into the IT landscape, e.g., with regard to incoming payment matching and write-offs.
Quality of service	Usually, the quality of service is set in service level agreements. A direct short-term influence is not given and depends on the local workforce and management of the BPO provider.	The output from software based processing is standardized and therefore stable. Any additional manual work could increase/decrease the quality of service swiftly.
Place of processing & regulator frameworks	BPO providers need to abide by the respective laws on outsourcing activities in the country of the bank. The bank must monitor and document the compliance of the provider.	The software can be installed in any place and jurisdiction and the place of operations determines the set of regulations to be followed.
Overall cost of doing business	Banks would need to properly look at the cost components which will differ from internal costs, e.g. provider management costs, technical interfaces to BPO provider, BPO pricing per unit, internal costs for quality assurance, etc. BPO represents a shift to mostly variable costs.	Comparing internal to BPO costs banks need to look equitably on all cost components used when processing, e.g. work force, maintenance and release costs for software, overhead costs, etc. Internal costs are in most cases fixed costs (labour costs).
Corporate social responsibility ("CSR")	Banks might want to consider working conditions, ecological social and ethical aspects (ESG) when outsourcing to different jurisdictions.	When processing with internal staff using software CSR is under full control of the bank.

Exhibit 28.1 (continued)

Digital Processing and Interfaces

The growing trend towards digital application processes at the tax authorities is increasing the pressure on financial institutions and providers of withholding tax services to deploy specialised IT systems.

At the latest with this trend, individual in-house developments are coming under massive pressure. Tax administrations use a wide variety of technologies and procedures, and a standardised "one fits all" approach is currently not in evidence. These different approaches are driving up the cost of providing technical solutions, with the result that withholding tax service providers such as banks are increasingly having to rely on standard solutions because software technical mapping of the most diverse procedures is now only cost-efficient for specialised vendors with a broad customer base. This is particularly the case because internal IT departments of financial institutions are already massively challenged and in some cases overburdened with the numerous regulatory requirements, and digital processes often require faster response times for adjustments, innovations and bug fixes.

At present, two fundamentally different approaches are emerging among the authorities to digitising the application process:

1. Provision of digital interfaces
2. Provision of a web portal for uploading data

In principle, the first case is very well suited to the end-to-end digitisation of withholding tax processes, but country-specific details need to be considered more closely here, such as mass suitability, reliability, interface technology, data security, and so on. The existing or planned interfaces of different jurisdictions have so far varied greatly in their characteristics.

The second process is more difficult to digitise, but options exist here as well, such as the use of software bots to automatically enter the application data into the portals after it has been prepared in the withholding tax software, once the bots have been trained on the specifics of the portals in question. Both processes are subject to regular changes that must be continuously monitored and implemented in a timely manner, depending on the technology selected.

In some cases, manufacturers also offer their modules for digital submission separately (stand-alone), so that existing software solutions without their own digital connection to authorities can still be used for reclaiming.

Since the characteristics and architectures of the digital application procedures are defined by the tax authorities of the respective countries and no cross-national standardisation efforts are apparent, homogenisation is not foreseeable in the near future.

2. On the other hand, the automation of withholding tax service providers such as banks or BPO service providers as well as institutional investors, e.g., asset management companies. Here we speak of a business-to-business approach ("B2B").

The trend in recent years shows that withholding taxes have become more of a focus for investors, leading financial institutions to increasingly offer withholding tax services and use them as a means of customer retention and satisfaction. The use of specialised software has therefore received a real boost, not least because banks, for example, are excellently suited as providers of this service, since all the necessary information, data, documents and certificates are available in the custodian financial institutions in order to be able to process withholding tax services in a highly automated manner. The investor is relieved to the maximum for a corresponding service fee.

By using a B2C solution, the implementation is still the responsibility of the investor; by means of OpenBanking interfaces, parts of the necessary data can also be accessed and the application (e.g., also against payment of a fee or a percentage of the recoverable amount) can be supported. In cases where the custodian institution does not offer withholding tax services, this can be an alternative.

Differences Small/Large Bank When Using a Software Solution

When using software, the size of the bank also plays a decisive role. In the following explanations, "size" also refers to the number of investors with a securities account that are eligible for a withholding tax service due to the securities contained in their accounts.

Smaller Financial Institutions with a Smaller Relevant Customer Base

In smaller and partly specialised institutions, there is usually a smaller number of relevant investors, domiciles and investment markets; this generally leads to a lower potential for economies of scale and has to be addressed by appropriate licensing models of the software. Nevertheless, the provision of withholding tax services very often holds a high potential for reclaimable volume, depending on the composition of the clientele. Very often, primarily reclaim services are offered here, more rarely relief at source.

The decision to deploy software is often driven by little existing operational capacity or negligible tax expertise and, at the same time, high demand for competitive, high-quality tax services. Potentially, these companies have fewer resources available for IT implementation projects and interface connections, and decision-making processes are faster and easier. In particular, if the withholding tax service was not offered before the introduction of the software, or only to a very limited extent, an implementation close to the standard makes sense, on the one hand, to profitably use the best practices mapped in the systems, and on the other hand to spare the implementation costs and thus tied up internal specialist and IT resources. The service is then performed with the software either by existing employees or by using external resources, e.g., consulting services of the software manufacturer.

Larger (International) Financial Institutions with a Large Relevant Customer Base

Large institutions often have corresponding potential to scale. The software can be deployed across multiple branches or country organisations and can be used internationally and for all types of beneficial owners, served by the bank. In this context, so-called hub-and-spoke models are often set up, i.e., a central back-office organisation takes over the service for various international units, in some cases even for other financial institutions as part of an outsourced back-office service. In such cases, additional requirements such as client-related data separation play an important role. Due to its broad use, a large number of domiciles and investment markets are covered, the number of investors to be serviced requires a high mass suitability of the software.

These institutions also usually offer the full range of withholding tax services, from reclaim to quick refund to relief at source. This naturally holds great potential for economies of scale, which also places corresponding demands on the pricing models of the software manufacturers.

In turn, the introduction of software in large and complex organisations usually also means a high degree of organisational and technical dependencies that must be mastered in the software implementation projects. The software often has to be adapted to existing processes, special features and existing IT environments. A lot of experience and good project management on both sides are therefore indispensable to keep the effort for the implementation under control.

In operation, the software is usually operated by in-house staff and there is deep integration with upstream and downstream IT systems to ensure an optimal data flow and a high level of automation. Data security aspects hardly differ in large institutions from smaller ones, only the associated specifications are often more complex to implement.

On the surface, larger banks generally have more opportunities to make the most of a software solution. But mid-sized and smaller banks can also have a high level of motivation, a solid operating model and a suitable business model to work with a software solution.

29

Future of Tax Reclamation

As tax relief at source under TRACE, the Code of Conduct and the US Qualified Intermediary program all become the dominant cross-border tax processing models, the classical post pay date tax reclaim made to a tax authority will become increasingly boutique. This chapter explores the future of the post pay date tax reclaim and identifies whether and where this business will be viable for investors or for financial institutions.

The global trend in withholding tax is undoubtedly towards increased amounts of relief at source and quick refunds. While at the time of writing, only Finland has adopted and implemented trace, it is clear that other countries are paying very close attention to the degree of success that the finish is having with this system.

Challenges still exist. The fundamental flaw in OECD frameworks is that they are not legal frameworks they are merely frameworks that allow different jurisdictions to adopt the principles of those frameworks in different ways. Nowhere is this clearer than in the European Union withholding tax code of conduct. This code of conduct was built on the work of others commencing with Alberto Giovanni and his identification of the barriers to the free movement of capital within the European Union Member States. The fiscal compliance group FISCO continued that work and established a more detailed analysis of the withholding tax policies procedures and practises of the European Member States. In other words, FISCO identified more accurately what the actual problem was. Following on from the

R. K. McGill, *Cross-Border Investment Withholding Tax*,
Finance and Capital Markets Series,
https://doi.org/10.1007/978-3-031-32785-8_29

FISCO fiscal compliance group, another group will be set up to include both tax administrations and financial institutions and others with interests in this area to establish the parameters of a solution. This group, the Tax Barriers Business Advisory Group reported in 2013, 10 principles by means of which the barriers identified by Giovanini could be overcome. However while addressing its core remit, this group faced the existential issue of what the best method of implementation would be for this kind of solution will be.

Two options existed at that time. The first was to implement the recommendations of the Tax Barriers Business Advisory Group ("T-BAG") by means of a European Union Directive. The difficulty with the Directive is that it takes a long time, typically 5–10 years, to get the unanimous agreement of all of the Member States necessary for a Directive to take effect. The second solution was voluntary adoption. This has the benefit of being able to be implemented more quickly, but by definition, means a patchier implementation dependent on which countries feel themselves to me most closely aligned with the intended solution. In the end, voluntary adoption was the route that was taken and subsequent committees in the European Union effectively took the detailed analysis of the Tax Barriers Business Advisory Group and created from it a simplified framework which at best established several ideas that Member States could adopt at their discretion. It is my opinion the directive route would have been more successful and definitive given what we now know is occurring throughout the OECD with trace.

If the history of withholding tax has taught us anything, it is that in any different framework the more degrees of freedom you allow the subjects, the more holes you create in the relevant regulatory framework, the harder it is to achieve the intended objective.

So, as the introduction to this chapter noted the likelihood is that the standard refund process will, over time, become much more boutique in nature. The drivers for this are several.

The COVID-19 pandemic created financial turmoil and led to recession in some of the world's largest economies. At times like these, the natural cycle is that companies will likely reduce the value of dividends if they pay dividends at all. The net result being, especially if a large proportion of those dividends are taxed correctly at source, will be that the proportion of recoverable tax from a post pay date reclaim will drop. It is also true not such events tend to polarise investment strategies. While awareness of the withholding tax reclaim industry is relatively high with large institutional investors, they will probably be deploying their own resource to optimise their tax position because it's in their interest to do so. Smaller investors will usually have a lower level of awareness of this issue, be more prepared to simply accept tax as an inevitable consequence of securities ownership, and not have either the knowledge all the wherewithal to claim any of this money back.

In addition, tax administrations, whose role it is to implement procedures in line with double tax treaties, are increasingly likely to adopt a keep the cash strategy by implementing more and more invasive procedures for tax reclaims. We have already seen this in Germany and in Denmark which have both been subject to fraudulent claims after which larger claims are automatically audited, thus delaying the repayment of funds.

So, if we accept that the general trend is that most of withholding tax will be handled by financial institutions on behalf of tax administrations and that processing will increasingly be done in a digital universe, we must accept that the remaining proportion of entitlements will be left to financial institutions and a small number of third-party vendors. The costs associated with processing these post pay date refunds are likely to increase and the proportion of those claims that are viable to process will increase. It is logical therefore that a proportion of post pay date refund claims are never filed. This is not much different from the world that we have today in which the amount of over-withheld tax is approximately $200 billion a year with less than 7% of that tax ever being refunded back to the investors who put their money at risk in the first place.

I think it is likely that certain sectors of the withholding tax industry will transition into a fully digital world. We will see tax reclamation including tax relief at source being conducted predominantly on distributed ledgers using smart contracts and non-fungible tokens to replace documentation and some automated processing. I also think that the concept of tax certification of residency will be resolved in favour of a digital self-certification rather than an expansion of certifications issued by tax administrations.

Most tax administrations and legal frameworks ultimately hold the issuing corporation as being ultimately liable for withholding tax. It is a feature of the financial services industry but intermediation takes place at almost every level where corporations using financial instruments to finance themselves, use third-party financial intermediaries to conduct many of the activities for which they hold liability. Maintaining share registers, using paying and withholding agents who in turn use chains of other financial intermediaries whether they be brokers or custodians to manage the holdings of underlying investors through a series of omnibus accounts. Regulators have been hard at work too trying to protect the interests of investors in this extremely complex space. The European Union shareholder rights directive is a good example. However, the regulators are typically always behind the curve and not ahead of it. Their response to new regulation particularly in jurisdictions operating sophisticated relief at source systems such as the United States, is to require reporting of income and tax withheld in evermore complex ways.

Political issues should not be ignored either. The US has several initiatives which if implemented will cause enormous systemic problems. For example, President Biden has indicated that he would like to tax unrealised gains in the market. The IRS has had chapter one Section 871(m) on the books for over five years and has repeatedly delayed implementation because the industry has not been able to demonstrate that it is prepared to invest in systems necessary to be able to manage this tax. Ultimately, it is geopolitical influences that drive government and politicians to try to increase the tax take from the investment community without tipping that community into walking away. We've seen that most recently again in the US with Section 1446(f) regulations. These regulations require attacks on the game from the sale of an interest in a publicly traded partnership. This has changed the paradigm under which most custodian banks operate. Custodian banks are safe keeping securities whereas brokers are trading securities. Chapter three in Chapter 4 of the US Internal Revenue Code is generally focused on the taxation of US-sourced income when paid to non-us recipients. The implementation of 1446(f) means that as well as tracking income and applying the appropriate tax, the custodian now must have knowledge of the gain that was made when the security was sold. This is not a change of degree. This is a change of kind. In late 2022, most financial institutions that I spoke to we're effectively taking the policy approach to prevent their customers from investing in publicly traded partnerships and to dye vest existing owners prior to the implementation date of 1st January 2023. This one policy ensures that the financial institution is not subject to yet another set of US tax regulations. In addition to Chapter 1 for 31 and 61 for which they had to build and implement entire systems for client documentation data retention and reporting.

ADRs

There are some concerning outliers that may affect investors in the future. The first of these is the treatment of American depositary receipts. As I mentioned in a prior chapter the only person that can file a claim for a depositary receipt is the depositary bank that sponsored the ADR. However, when filing the claims the depositary will have used the ratio of the depositary receipt to the underlying security in order to construct a normal claim against the underlying security. In 2022 there were two binding rulings from the Danish tax council which addressed the Danish tax treatment of American depositary receipts. In one case, the American depositary receipt ratio was 14 to 1, and in the other case, the depositary receipt ratio was one to one. While these two cases were more particularly concerned with a proposed repurchase agreement, the general finding was that the shareholder is the depositary bank. Only if the depositary has completely waived actual influence and control over the underlying shares via the ADR program, the holder of an ADR certificate should be considered the shareholder for tax purposes.

The issue is therefore, whether the depositary is capable of filing claims on behalf of ADR holders Or whether, by virtue of the fact that the shareholder is deemed to be the ultimate beneficial owner of the underlying shares and the ADR, claims can only be filed by the ADR holder themselves. This would obviously place at serious risk an entire complex processing model that has been established over many years. Such considerations can, literally at the stroke of a pen, change the withholding tax landscape for an entire jurisdiction.

Fractional Shares

A more recent evolution in withholding tax is the holding of fractional shares. This situation has occurred simply because many of the corporations in which investors are interested have share prices which are extremely high. In these circumstances, the desire of the issuer to facilitate a wide base of share ownership can be damaged simply because of the cost of ownership. In the brokerage community, this has been relatively simple to implement because computer systems can be structured to allow for fractions of a single share. However, as far as the issuer is concerned generally speaking they do not deal in fractions of a share they deal in whole shares. So in the same way, for example, that an American depositary receipt is a security that may have a ratio of the receipt to the underlying securities, an analogous situation can exist with any security where a broker may choose to sell to its client a fraction of a share rather than a whole share. In processing terms, as I've said, this is not really a problem. What is a problem is that it's not clear that regulators have understood what is going on here. If one thing has been clear throughout this book, it is the concept of unintended consequences where the desire of the financial community and the investment community to create a smooth, streamlined and, preferably automated share owning democracy can easily be derailed if the tax consequences of such systems are not fully explored in advance rather than after the fact.

Taxation of Gains

It is rumoured that President Biden is considering taxation of unrealised gains. This would be a tax on a gain that has not resulted in income. I buy shares at $3 and hold them for a year, after which they are worth $10. Under this plan, I would owe tax on the gain, even though I have not realised that gain financially. This concept is fraught with problems, although that has never stopped the IRS in the past, and is likely to generate some substantial headwinds for the President, if he continues down that path. We already have Section 1446(f) as a tax on gross proceeds, although that is currently specific to PTPs which triggered a mass sell-off of PTPs by many non-US financial institutions.

What Does the Future Look Like?

Self-certifications of tax residency must be the way forward. They remove much liability and risk from financial institutions and place it where it belongs, with the investor themselves. If the first principle step is changing to the use of self-certifications, the next steps are surely the use of electronic signatures and then tokenisation of the forms as assets in their own right. Electronic signatures should be to a common published standard.

The industry widely uses omnibus accounts to save money and be more efficient. I concur with this and therefore, the resultant change should be the development of a standardised withholding statement that can be used in an ISO20022 format between financial institutions to allow the instruction of different tax rates on income received into those omnibus accounts.

Much of the rest of the withholding tax industry is composed of individual letters and forms created by tax administrations or vendors on an ad hoc basis. The EU is right when it says that a common easy-to-use communication system is required, probably web-based to provide so that financial institutions and institutional investors that make-up 90% of the industry, have a way to obtain consistent and accurate data at scale from multiple tax administrations. Having a French reclaim form in the French language is ridiculous when it's intended for non-French investors. All of the third-party tax reclaim vendors maintain databases of information on withholding tax processes and documentation requirements. What's needed is a collaborative effort similar to that of SWIFT in which this information is collated, validated and published for everyone.

30

Conclusions

We have come a long way in this second edition. The concepts have not changed, but the way in which they are implemented is changing more and more rapidly. I am happy to share my thoughts about the direction of the industry.

1. **Tax relief at source**. This will become the dominant operating model. Standard post pay date refunds will become an increasingly complex boutique activity attracting higher processing costs and prices. The relief at source model will, I think, evolve most quickly of all simply because the technology to facilitate it already exists and is relatively mature in other environments. The liability associated with relief at source will continue to be shifted towards the approved financial institutions acting as QIs or AIs and ultimately, investors. At some point control and oversight will need regulatory teeth to match the oversight. Anecdotally, 150 qualified intermediaries leave the QI program each year either because their contract has been terminated for non-compliance or because the cost of compliance was disproportionate to the perceived benefit.
2. **Self-Certifications of Residency**. I think that digitally signed self-certifications will become the norm in the near future. It is not in tax administrations' own interests to have their own manual processing of these certifications and the US and OECD seem convinced that a self-certification system will work. The US in fact has over twenty years of experience of this. The first step has already been taken, TConsult has

R. K. McGill, *Cross-Border Investment Withholding Tax*, Finance and Capital Markets Series,
https://doi.org/10.1007/978-3-031-32785-8_30

already launched an investor self-declaration system that complies with the US and OECD TRACE frameworks. UK-based TAINA also has a similar system. I suspect the next step will be the tokenisation of these documents and their use in a distributed ledger-based solution leveraging smart contracts.

3. **Fraud and Abuse.** I also think that the more obvious fraudulent activities, such as tax arbitrage, will be shut down faster in the future with the use of artificial intelligence by tax administrations who will use AI to identify patterns in trading and in claims processing. It is likely that more tax administrations will require evidence of trading history up to an including the record date to a basic requirement for tax reclaim.
4. **Batch processing.** This will disappear simply because it is inefficient and delays investor returns. Most tax processing issues have historically been dealt with within a manual batch processing model that reflected the fragmented approached taken by tax administrations. If either the financial institutions or the service providers can utilise the benefits of current technology, then batch processing should become a thing of the past and real-time reclaims will become a thing. Tax administrations will use algorithms to decide whether any specific flags can be set to determine whether a claim should be pulled from a queue for audit or whether it can be paid out immediately (either because the value is small or because the case itself is simple).
5. **Distributed Ledger.** This has already been tested in the laboratory by Ernst and Young.[1] I think we will see a live production environment within ten years. This may not use blockchain. It may instead use smart contracts to represent the total position of a company in a given corporate action. The smart part of the contract will allow investors, intermediaries on their behalf and vendors on behalf of investors to interact with the smart contract to establish an entitlement to tax relief. The smart contract allows for the full integration of the three possible relief models with financial institutions completing the smart contracts for relief at source and quick refunds and tax administrations completing the contracts for standard refunds.
6. **Standards.** SWIFT has already seen a great deal of competitive behaviour that seeks to disintermediate them from their core markets. Withholding tax is fundamentally a business process in three parts, each of which has its own characteristics that would be suitable for an ISO20022 implementation. I would expect an ISO20022 subcommittee to be set up to

---

[1] https://assets.ey.com/content/dam/ey-sites/ey-com/en_gl/topics/tax/tax-pdfs/ey-withholding-tax-distributed-ledger-report.pdf.

bring together these components as a way for SWIFT to stay relevant for its messaging platform. This will be the path that leads to step-change adoption by the financial services community.

7. **Adoption**. As the technology improves, the level of adoption within the payment chain for corporate actions will increase. Where today we might be at 5% adoption of tax relief for institutions that are more than three levels down in the payment chain, more automation and standards will increase this to above 20%. For the industry, this would be a truly huge improvement.
8. **Artificial Intelligence**. I think it is almost inevitable that AI will play some part in future of withholding tax and anti-tax evasion regulation. Many types of intermediaries may disappear through disintermediation disruption from new technologies.

The technology is out there. The desire from the investment community is there and financial institutions that treat tax as a product will be keen to leverage those technological advances to the extent that governments permit the technology to do its job, subject to the right control and oversight. I see an exciting time for withholding tax on the horizon. The rate of change will only increase.

Appendices

Appendix 1: Tax Barriers Business Advisory Group Report 2013

In 2013, I contributed to and co-edited the Tax Barriers Business Advisory Group final report to the European Commission. This report is one of the best available to give specific context to both the issues of withholding tax globally and the solutions that both business and tax administrations have agreed upon as the most effective.

Current Problems

Member States currently adopt a variety of different approaches to the issue of withholding tax, which has been described in previous reports and the work of Alberto Giovanini. These problems can be broadly categorised as follows:

1. Concerns over the legal basis under which cross-border tax simplification could be implemented
2. Lack of adequate or consistent interpretive guidance from Member States
3. Lack of a consistent tax relief model between Member States
4. A plethora of procedures, forms and information requirements from Member States
5. Lack of a mandate for the use of automation and standards.

R. K. McGill, *Cross-Border Investment Withholding Tax*, Finance and Capital Markets Series,
https://doi.org/10.1007/978-3-031-32785-8

The T-BAG Group has reviewed these issues in context to the different withholding tax systems currently operated by Member States in detail and its recommendations for specific issues to facilitate Member States adopting a simplified approach.

As part of its review, and in context to the FISCO recommendations, the T-BAG Group also reviewed the remedial tax reclaim processes of Member States and makes recommendations here for the provision of an EU-wide standardised tax reclaim which would lend itself to the transition by Member States from paper-based reclaim processing, to electronic and thus contribute to achieving the removal of some of the tax barriers laid out by Professor Alberto Giovanini.

International Context

A comparative analysis to the US system (US Revenue Code Chapters 3 and 4) allows the T-BAG Group to provide suggestions on those aspects of the US system which would work effectively in a European context, notwithstanding that at least one European Member State has already implemented a similar, albeit simplified system (i.e., Ireland). This applies particularly to the procedural aspects of contracts, documentation, withholding, information reporting and audits.

A comparative analysis of the work of the OECD allows the T-BAG Group to recommend several areas where there are common elements of an Authorised Intermediary system on which significant granular work has already been completed, e.g., self-certifications of residency, standardised messaging and from which, both business and Member States could benefit in terms of both reduced development and implementation costs in a European context.

Recent Changes

In normal circumstances Member States and the T-BAG Group itself would have had ample time to weigh considerations and recommendations on its mandate. However, in the last two years and more recently in the last six months, the rate of change in the international environment both inside the EU and outside it, has increased rapidly. Some of these changes are outside the direct mandate of the T-BAG Group. Others, albeit in principle within the mandate, have only recently become substantive and the Group has not had sufficient time to analyse them in detail nor make recommendations. Notwithstanding this, the T-BAG Group urges the Commission and Member States to take cognisance of this amplified rate of change which, we believe, increases the need for an integrated approach to short and long-term planning. Some of the issues which are not analysed in detail in this report but which should be included in further work are:

1. Effects of the widespread implementation of a Financial Transaction Tax (FTT).
2. Use of Legal Entity Identifiers (LEIs) as an additional beneficial owner identification tool;
3. Effects of the implementation of the Target 2 Securities (T2S) securities settlement platform.

For the avoidance of doubt, the Group recommends an explicit support for many of the elements of the TRACE Implementation Protocol (IP) for short-term solutions since many aspects of the IP (i) are congruous to the Group's recommendations and (ii) already have substantive implementation detail associated with them from which Member States can benefit.

Summary of the Proposed Solution Framework

The solution recommended has the following major characteristics. If the recommendations are approved by Member States, further work will produce the lower-level detail for a workable phased implementation.

1. Member States agree to a common standardised "Authorised Intermediary" Agreement ("AIA") which may be entered into between a financial intermediary and a Member State.
2. AI Agreements would provide rules for the conducts of (i) documentation of beneficial owners, (ii) application of relief at source on payments, (iii) withholding, (iv) information reporting and (v) control and oversight;
3. Member States agree a common form and distribution mechanism (e.g., website) for Guidance on the application of treaty benefits to different types of beneficial owners on which an AI may rely, subject to the understanding that such guidance does not over-rule a Member State's ability to question any specific case for a claim of treaty entitlement. It is envisaged that existing mechanisms for clarification of individual cases would still be available;
4. The identification of beneficial owners to be permitted by AIs through the mechanism of (i) Taxpayer Identification Numbers (TINs) issued by the beneficial owner's home State, (ii) application of the KYC rules of the AI's home State, to the extent that the source State accepts the degree to which, in its view, KYC rules establish beneficial ownership and (iii) agreement by Member States to the development and use of a common

and electronically transmissible self-certification of residency ("Investor Self-Declaration" or "ISD"). To the extent possible, the system should permit the use of Powers of Attorney ("PoA") to allow AIs and authorised third parties to facilitate any additionally required documentation;

5. Provided the documentation and identification rules are met, AIs would be permitted to make (or instruct) payments to eligible beneficial owners net of the appropriate treaty rate of withholding tax on the pay date.
6. Liability for underwithholding and/or incorrect documentation of beneficial owners should lie (i) with the beneficial owner (for incorrect or fraudulent representations), (ii) the AI for processing errors and (iii) the Source Member State for technical issues related to treaty eligibility, the latter being minimised through the clear Guidance proposal.
7. AIs servicing beneficial owners directly would provide annual information reports (i) to the source State at the beneficial owner level of disclosure and (ii) upstream at pooled level (by withholding rate applied) to other AIs in the payment chain. Such reports to be electronic and to a format standardised between Member States, e.g., XML;
8. Where a source country receives information reports from an AI and wishes to query the eligibility of any beneficial owner, Exchange of Information rules would be applied to permit the source country to apply directly to the home country using the TIN of the beneficial owner.
9. Under the terms of an AI agreement, AIs would be subject to a choice of internal review, certified by a responsible officer and subject to appropriate penalties, or external oversight by an approved independent third party by means of an "Agreed Upon Procedure" ("AUP") whose report would be available to the Source Member State. Governments would retain the right to undertake spot checks in both cases.
10. For those beneficial owners who were unable to meet the relevant documentation standards prior to the pay date, but where they can still prove eligibility under a treaty, Member States agree to develop a standardised, machine-readable tax reclaim form capable of being delivered electronically.

1. Introduction

Aim of the T-BAG Group

The aim of the Tax Barriers Business Advisory Group is to consider the follow-up of the Commission Recommendation on simplified Withholding Tax procedures from a business perspective and to identify any remaining fiscal barrier affecting the post-trading environment.

Structure of the Report

The Report is structured in four parts and assumes an understanding of the prior work and context of the Giovannini committee, subsequent Reports of FISCO and the Commission Recommendation on Simplified Withholding Tax Relief Procedures.

- Part 1 describes the current situation in Member States and the legal basis under which Member States may choose to adopt the committee's recommendations. This part also provides an example of harmonisation in the field of financial law.
- Part 2 describes parallel initiatives currently underway. A comparison is provided between the current EU work and related work at the OECD. This Part also describes the current situation in the US, including the US regulations (Chapter 3—QI and Chapter 4—FATCA).
- Part 3 provides a description of how, in practice, the current tax relief at source and reclaim procedures could be improved to work more efficiently. This Part also provides a guidance on how to improve the exchange of information, liabilities and the use of Tax Identification Numbers (TIN:s). The aim of the guidance is to reduce the current risks and compliance costs for investors, intermediaries, tax authorities and Member States.
- Part 4 provides a Summary and Conclusion to the Report.
- Appendices are provided where background or supporting material may be useful to understand the context of recommendations made in the body of the report.

A Glossary of terms is presented in order to explain commonly used and technical abbreviations and/or acronyms.

Mandate

According to its mandate, the T-BAG Group should:

1. Examine and update the current state of withholding tax relief and/or refund procedures in EU Member States with respect to double tax conventions and domestic law.
2. Suggest workable solutions to implement the principles outlined in the Commission Recommendation on Withholding Tax Relief Procedures (COM (2009) 7924 final), that might be acceptable to Member States' tax authorities.

This Introduction has been prepared by the Secretariat of the T-BAG Group.

This task should have regard to parallel OECD work in this area and would involve a two-step approach as follows:

1. short-term measures aimed at improving withholding tax relief procedures (e.g., widespread use of Taxpayer Identification Numbers; standardised claim forms; standardised residence certificate having a harmonised validity period; use of electronic systems; etc.); and
2. long-term, more ambitious and comprehensive solutions based on a simplified relief at source system.
3. Identify and suggest changes to address any possible other (remaining) tax barriers affecting the post-trading environment.

The present document has been produced by the T-BAG Group in line with its mandate. It is important to underline that the solutions proposed in this report relate to fiscal compliance procedures and are not aimed at any tax (rate) harmonisation. The aim of the proposed solutions is solely to remove fiscal compliance barriers related to EU clearing and settlement and to make local fiscal procedures work more efficiently. The aim is also to propose improved procedures adapted to the way financial markets operate today. Member States and the tax authorities will probably substantially gain by more efficient fiscal compliance procedures related to post-trading. And so will the industry, the investors, the taxpayers and the internal market as a whole.

The T-BAG Group has also considered some key documents and reports already provided in the fiscal compliance area related to post-trading, such as the Giovanini—, FISCO—and Monti Reports, the Commission Recommendation on Simplified Withholding Tax Procedures including its Economic Case and the relevant conclusions from the ECOFIN.

The T-BAG Group consists of a number of high-calibre experts from private bodies and the academic community. To facilitate the work of the Group, the Commission provided a Secretariat made up of a Chairperson and a Secretary from the Commission's Directorate General for the Internal Market and Services. Two officials from the Commission's Directorate General for Taxation and the Customs Union participated as Observers. The Organisation for Economic Co-operation and Development (OECD) is represented as Observer.

Prior Work

The Giovanini Reports

The Giovanini Group of financial market experts, which advised the European Commission on financial market issues, published two reports in 2001 and 2003. They asserted that "inefficiencies in clearing and settlement represent the most primitive and thus the most important barrier to integrated financial markets in Europe". Furthermore, the removal of these inefficiencies was "a necessary condition for the development of a large and efficient financial structure in Europe".

The first Giovanini Report identified 15 key barriers to an efficient pan-European clearing and settlement system for the EU. Two of these barriers (11 and 12) relate to fiscal compliance procedures. Barrier 11 relates to domestic withholding tax regulations, i.e., that foreign intermediaries cannot sufficiently offer withholding tax relief at source or only under the condition that they have a fiscal agent. Barrier 12 deals with national provisions requiring that taxes on securities transactions be collected via local systems.

The second Giovanini Report of April 2003 called for the following:

1. all financial intermediaries established within the EU should be allowed to offer withholding agent services in all of the Member States so as to ensure a level playing field between local and foreign intermediaries (Barrier 11); and
2. any provisions requiring that taxes on securities transactions are collected via local systems should be removed to ensure a level playing field between domestic and foreign investors (Barrier 12).

The Giovanini reports highlighted that national governments should cooperate closely with the private sector in removing these barriers.

Summary of the FISCO Reports

The EU Clearing and Settlement Fiscal Compliance Experts' Group ("FISCO") that was created in March 2005 following the Communication "Clearing and Settlement in the European Union—The way forward" had as one of its key objectives the resolution of Giovanini Barriers 11 and 12.

The FISCO Group published two reports—The FISCO Fact Finding Study and the FISCO Second Report on Solutions to fiscal compliance barriers related to post-trading within the EU. The two reports described as a serious problem the fact that withholding tax collection and relief procedures vary considerably between Member States and that different procedures often apply even to different classes of securities within the same Member

State. Many Member States restrict withholding responsibilities to entities established within their own jurisdiction. As a consequence, foreign intermediaries are often disadvantaged in their capacity to offer relief at source from withholding tax due to the significant extra cost of using a local agent or local representative in the discharge of their withholding obligations. The reports also pointed out that Member States' current relief procedures do not take sufficient account of the multi-tiered holding environment and often put tax collection responsibilities on an entity that is not connected to the beneficial owner/final investor. These procedures therefore assume that the market will organise itself to transfer information and (paper form) documentation on the beneficial owner up through the chain of intermediaries. In reality, however, this is costly and inefficient and may also create confidentiality and data-privacy issues. The FISCO Group concluded that the present fiscal compliance procedures hinder the functioning of capital markets and increase the cost of cross-border settlement. It said that the complexity and administrative costs resulting from the present procedures may lead investors to forego the relief to which they are entitled and may, for the same reason, discourage cross-border investment.

The FISCO Group proposed solutions aimed at improved, standardised, simplified and modernised withholding tax relief procedures that would be adapted to the way financial markets operate today. The present procedures are both costly and inefficient. The FISCO Group was of the opinion that:

- At-source relief procedures are the best method to improve the present situation because of the optimised cash flow they offer to investors;
- In order to make relief procedures simpler, paper-form certificate of residence should be replaced by alternative means to prove the investors' entitlement to tax relief, such as self-certification and know your customer (KYC) rules. Furthermore, intermediaries should be allowed to make use of modern technology to pass on investors' information to the withholding agents in electronic format.
- Many of the existing problems could be solved by shifting withholding responsibilities to intermediaries, i.e., by allowing all intermediaries in the custody chain either to assume full withholding responsibilities or to take responsibility for granting withholding tax relief by passing on pooled withholding tax rate information to the upstream intermediary. Avoiding the need for intermediaries to pass detailed information on beneficiaries up the chain would overcome data protection and client confidentiality concerns.

- Even though relief at source is the preferred relief method, there is a clear need also for efficient refund procedures. A supplementary standard and quick refund procedure should be implemented within the Member States by using similar formats for applications, by centralising refund procedures in each Member State to one tax authority or tax office only and by introducing a time-limit for making the refunds. The reclaim process should also be capable of electronic adaptation in order to optimise efficiency.

Commission Recommendation on Simplified Withholding Tax Relief Procedures.

On October 2009, the European Commission adopted the Recommendation on Withholding Tax Relief Procedures, COM (2009) 7924 final.

The aim of the Recommendation is to make it easier for an investor that is resident in one EU Member State to claim withholding tax relief on dividends received from another Member State. The Recommendation also encourages greater acceptance by Member States of electronic, rather than paper, information and suggests measures to eliminate the tax barriers that financial institutions face in their securities investment activities while at the same time protecting tax revenues against errors or fraud.

The Recommendation also suggests measures to eliminate tax barriers for the securities investment activities of financial institutions. This is important because a study carried out by the Commission services shows that, at present, the costs related to current reclaim procedures are estimated at a value of €1.09 billion annually, whereas the amount of foregone tax relief is estimated at €5.47 billion annually.

The Recommendation provides guidance on how to ensure that procedures to verify entitlement to tax relief do not hinder the functioning of the Single Market. In particular, the Recommendation encourages Member States to apply at source, rather than by refund, any withholding tax relief applicable to securities income under double taxation treaties or domestic law. Where tax relief at source is not feasible, the Recommendation suggests that quick and standardised refund procedures should be in place and lists possible elements of such refund procedures. It also encourages Member States to accept alternative proof of investors' entitlement to tax relief besides certificates of residence. The Recommendation further suggests how Member States can involve financial intermediaries in making claims on behalf of investors and, in particular, how the procedures could operate where there is a chain of financial intermediaries, in different Member States, between the issuer of the securities and a beneficiary. It also invites Member States to make greater use of existing channels for exchange of information between them and the exploration of new channels.

The Internal Market

The tax dimension was highlighted as a key issue of the Single Market in Professor Mario Monti's Report to President Barroso on "a new strategy for the single market" 2010. The Monti Report considered it important to cut the tax-related administrative burdens and compliance costs for businesses and citizens. Consequently, the Monti Report identified further work urgent on the elimination of tax barriers, including updating the rules on cross-border relief.

ECOFIN

The Economic and Finance Ministers of Member States Meeting in Council (ECOFIN) has many times stressed that post-trading of securities transactions is a key area for financial integration in the EU and that the removal of fiscal compliance barriers is urgently needed.

The Economic and Finance Ministers of Member States meeting in Council (ECOFIN):

- In November 2006, stressed that post-trading of securities transactions is a key area for financial integration in the EU and that the removal of fiscal compliance barriers is urgently needed;
- In October 2007, restated that concrete actions should be proposed promptly by the Commission on the basis of the work of the advisory groups; and
- In June 2008, noted the Commission's intention to adopt a Recommendation on withholding tax procedures by the first part of 2009 and to take into account the need to both simplify and improve tax efficiency.
- In June 2011, invited the Commission and the Finance Ministers of the participating Member States to report back on progress made on tax policy issues, notably to ensure the exchanges of best practices.

The actual financial crisis illustrates the importance of efficient, safe and sound post-trade within the EU. The current situation highlights the importance for the Member States to be competitive as issuers of different debt instruments, in order to obtain sufficient resources to manage the crisis. Considering the present lack of liquidity and financing needs, both for Member States and industry, the case for simplification in capital markets is stronger than ever.

Follow-up of the Commission Recommendation

When creating the Commission Recommendation on Simplified Withholding Tax Procedures, Member States were regularly updated, by presentations and discussions, at meetings of the Working Party No IV ("WP IV") on Direct Taxation—where all Member States are represented—of the European Commission's Taxation and Customs Union Directorate General and of the Commission's European Securities Committee (ESC).

After the adoption, Member States has actively discussed the follow-up of the Commission Recommendation at meetings of WP IV. It has during these meetings been highlighted among Member States that the Recommendation is an important step forward, but several issues need to be analysed further, such as the liability of foreign financial intermediaries and the need to improve exchange of information. Member States have reconfirmed that they are positive that the Commission goes ahead on this urgent dossier and explores these topics further.

The Commission has also performed successful missions to some Member States, including Finland and Germany, to study the practical transposition of the Recommendation.

Part 1—The Current State of Play

This part of the T-BAG Report is intended to establish the basis on which our recommendations are made. This Part in conjunction with prior reports, notably FISCO, has researched and documented both the legal and practical context in which any recommendations made would need to be workable.

Legal Barriers to simplification in Member States

Appendix 3 provides an analysis of the current legal barriers to simplification and expands on the comments below with reference to some of the ways in which Member States could approach and resolve these issues.

In a legal context, the EU has several mechanisms currently available which could be used as the basis for simplification. These include:

- Statutory harmonisation
- Enhanced Cooperation
- ECJ Case law
- EU Directive

Statutory harmonisation is both insufficient in itself and has practical difficulties associated with it which mean it is unlikely to be the sole method by which the recommendations of this report can be implemented. Not least of these are the disparities between the EC Mutual Assistance Directive and the EC Recovery Directive. These include levels of proof required to be able to apply the Directive, lack of obligations in the Directive and practical difficulties in identifying taxpayers in pooled investment vehicles.

There are alternatives to statutory harmonisation. Enhanced cooperation between Competent Authorities is referenced in the Markets in Financial Instruments Directive ("MiFID") in terms of strengthening duties of assistance. Level 4 legislation is also referenced as a possible legal approach. In addition, in many cases, national laws represent an impediment to simplification because they are not consistent across borders.

In recent years there has also been an observable increase in the number of cases brought to the European Court of Justice ("ECJ") which highlights another opportunity for simplification, at least in the case of providing greater clarity of interpretation of treaties. The practice of ECJ is based on several principles including those of (i) effectiveness, (ii) proportionality, (iii) equivalence and (iv) interpretation of national law with Community law. These are all discussed in detail in Appendix 3. The net effect of these issues is to formulate common practices supported by the case law in such a way as to effectively create a simplification through clarification. However, the use of ECJ as a strategy to achieve simplification is costly, long-winded and confrontational.

In its broadest sense, a bottom-up strategy of simplification whether through enforcement via case law or via statutory harmonisation or via existing alternatives, will face almost insurmountable obstacles of complexity. Adoption of a [Harmonisation] Directive also has advantages and disadvantages. In the current framework, Directives take extended periods of time to implement due to the need to not only define common simplification policies and procedures (which is common for all solutions) but also protracted negotiations between Member States which generally results in a "lowest common denominator" solution that may not be the most effective for the market or for investors.

Current State of Withholding Tax Relief Procedures in Member States

Tax relief procedures generally fall into one of three categories in Member States:

1. Tax relief at source, in which treaty entitlements or exemptions are applied on the pay date based on documentation available on the record date (in the case of equities) and an end-of-day holding (in the case of fixed income instruments);

2. Quick refund, in which an intermediary nets off an amount from tax withheld at statutory rate on pay date based on subsequent evidence of treaty entitlement prior to the date on which the intermediary is required to submit tax to its domestic tax authority; and
3. Long-form reclaims in which entitlements are claimed back using predominantly manual methods post pay date and within a statute of limitations period.

It is a common commentary in the investor community that it's one thing to have an entitlement and quite another and more difficult thing to receive an entitlement. This serves as an opposite commentary on the current state of play in the market today.

Some Member States allow permutations of the above methods. Relief at source is generally only offered by domestic financial institutions in each Member State which, in addition to applying domestic law, often have their own individual documentary requirements, deadlines and procedures. In addition, relief is often restricted to certain types of accounts and types of beneficial owners dependent on the individual advice received within the institution and their own business commercial restrictions. Long-Form Reclaims are generally filed directly with Member States' tax administrations using forms that differ in design, change periodically and have little or no standardisation or automation associated with them. Even so, in some, but not all Member States, long-form claims must be processed via a domestic financial institution. In all long-form reclaim cases, statutes of limitation vary by Member State as does the length of time that a Member State takes to pay reclaims out. These vary from a few weeks (e.g., Germany) to, anecdotally, over twenty years (e.g., Italy).

Irrespective of the relief methodology, all Member States require claimants to provide identification both that they are residents of a treaty State and that they are entitled to the benefit of the treaty. This is typically achieved today using certificates of residency issued by Member State's tax administrations either as explicit paper certificates or as stamps on treaty claim forms. Again, there is no standardisation and no automation within tax administrations even though businesses would be willing and eager to invest in and adopt such.

In all of the above, the legal framework in which investors and financial institutions have to work is based on the terms of the appropriate double tax treaty, assisted by a range of supporting frameworks, e.g., ECJ, Competent

Authority, whose purpose is most commonly to resolve disputes in specific cases, than to facilitate a simplification.

Relevant Existing EU Legislation and Case law

Arguments can be mobilised to develop a smooth legal basis for the national legal measures of Member States on procedural rights, and on the treatment of foreign resident taxpayers and their financial intermediaries in the particular areas of:

1. the standardisation of documentation;
2. coordination of the national public authorities in the exchange of information and in the facilitation of the provision of evidence;
3. the fair determination of the liability of financial intermediaries;
4. the application of a simplified relief at source system.

Taxation is within the competence of the Member States, although the power of the Member States to tax must be exercised consistently with primary and secondary Community law. It comes from such a division of power between the Member States and the European Union that tax matters cannot be harmonised unless the Member States reach a consensus in adopting explicit harmonisation measures. There are still alternatives to the traditional way of harmonisation. This can first be due to the development of forms of enhanced cooperation and the effective enforcement of rights between the authorities of the Member States. Furthermore, the ECJ has been scrutinising the legal practices of the Member States in light of the effective protection of taxpayer rights since decades. As a result of it, the Member States have been asked, from time to time, to remove restrictions on the fundamental freedoms, and streamline their legal systems.

The current situation is far from adequate, is inefficient and, in some cases, systems may even be in violation of EU law. More should be done in the area of withholding tax relief procedures to create a single and integrated EU financial market.

Although the progressive removal of tax barriers would be useful, the financial industry that benefits from the home licensing system of financial service providers must not dispense with all-encompassing, more systematic and categorical harmonisation. It has been still a problem that the single European passport that has been introduced in the financial law area cannot be extended to fiscal matters unless the Member States agree to adopt an appropriate legislative instrument of harmonisation. That would be necessary for entirely removing the barriers of non-harmonised national tax law to the freedoms of capital and services to be exercised in European capital markets.

The withholding tax procedures the market players experience are burdensome, and at times even discriminatory. In the following chapters, both the non-traditional ways of harmonisation and a proposal for the concept of a harmonisation Directive will be discussed.

Part 2—Comparative International Environment

This Part reviews other parallel situations and their respective solutions, in particular the US and OECD.

Comparison to US Tax Regulation

The withholding tax system in the United States has a number of common principles to those proposed by the T-BAG Group in this Report and also the OECD. The practical experience of the T-BAG Group in complying with those principles provides valuable information which can help Member States develop efficient policies and procedures that meet the needs of both governments and businesses, while at the same time enabling investors to benefit from improved relief procedures.

The US has two separate chapters of its Internal Revenue Code ("IRC") that are relevant to this report—Internal Revenue Code ("IRC") Chapter 3 and IRC Chapter 4. Chapter 3 encompasses the system known to most as the Qualified Intermediary ("QI") regime (that also deals with non-qualified intermediaries ["NQI"s]). Chapter 4 contains the so-called Foreign Account Tax Compliance Act provisions that were adopted on 18 March 2010, as a part of the Hiring Incentives to Restore Employment Act (colloquially known as "FATCA"). Both of these chapters of the IRC involve common principles—documentation of ultimate beneficial owners, information reporting to the US tax authorities, withholding on income distributions based on certain rules, information reporting and associated control and oversight procedures. They are however completely separate chapters of the IRC with different rules and very different objectives. It is important, however, to be aware that the US government is on record as having an objective to ultimately converge the procedural aspects of IRC Chapters 3 and 4 in an effort to streamline processing for financial institutions.

The QI regime has been in force since 1st January 2001, and has the objective of providing a relief at source tax environment based on foreign (i.e., non-US) financial institutions entering into a QI agreement with the IRS. The QI agreement lays down documentation and due diligence requirements that must be met to grant domestic or treaty relief from US withholding tax and to identify US individuals and trusts that are reportable on a recipient specific basis to the US tax authorities. The QI agreement also imposes certain information reporting requirements and allows but does not require QIs to assume withholding obligations. Control and oversight are organised under the QI agreement through a regular Agreed Upon Procedures ("AUPs") review by an external auditor. While institutions that do not sign an agreement with the US government are not subject to a QI contract, they are subject to the overarching terms of the regulations themselves. NQIs are subject to more restrictive and complex disclosure requirements than QIs.

In contrast, the provisions of FATCA came into force on 1st January 2013, although some obligations come into effect at later dates. The regulations have as their main objective the proper identification and reporting of the foreign accounts of US persons by foreign financial institutions (FFIs). The US is one of a few jurisdictions which claim a right to tax the global (as opposed to US-sourced) income of their Citizens. Chapter 4 is thus designed to address the failures of US Persons to disclose this global income required under domestic US law ("tax evasion"). To address this tax evasion issue, FATCA is designed to place an obligation on foreign financial institutions to identify and document all payees and subsequently to report certain income of those it finds to be US Persons. FATCA also provides for a 30% withholding tax on certain payments received by FFIs either because the financial institution failed to meet its obligations, did not agree to meet such obligations in contract and/or because account holders refuse to provide required documentation or information.

In that regard, these two Chapters of the US IRC, while apparently similar in many respects, are actually very different. Chapter 3 (QI) is a withholding tax relief regime designed to allow the correct level of tax to be withheld on US-sourced income payments based on exemptions and/or double tax treaties between the US and its partners. Chapter 3 also includes an information reporting regime with a limited scope (in view of both the limitation of the scope of QI agreements to US securities held on QI-designated accounts and the possibility to report most clients on a pooled basis). Chapter 4 (FATCA) on the other hand, is a tax evasion oversight system targeted at US persons with undisclosed (and therefore potentially untaxed) global income.

In the twelve years since implementation, the business has learned many lessons from implementing the QI regime. In their consideration of an Authorised Intermediary ("AI") system, Member States should capitalise on this experience.

FATCA, on the other hand, is seen by business as being, at best, disproportionate, (i) because of the lack of a true risk-based approach, to solve the issue of foreign account-based tax evasion and (ii) due to the considerable cost to implement changes to existing customer on boarding checks. In many cases, they also create significant legal conflicts either between domestic national law, EU law and US law for financial institutions and/or between financial institutions and their customers. In response to significant lobbying by the industry and many governments (including the EU) highlighting the legal obstacles that FATCA creates, the US, in the final regulations, created a two-tier approach by negotiating and agreeing bilateral intergovernmental agreements ("IGAs") designed to address these legal and privacy issues.

Financial institutions established in countries that have entered into an IGA with the US will not be subject to the FATCA provisions as contained in US domestic law but must instead comply with the provisions of the IGA entered into by their country of establishment. There are essentially two different IGA models. IGA Model 1 provides for reporting by local financial institutions to the local tax authorities that will transmit the information to the US tax authorities. A Model 1 IGA can be reciprocal or non-reciprocal. In its reciprocal form, the IGA requires information exchange from financial institutions established in both countries regarding holders of accounts maintained by those financial institutions that are resident in the other country. For this purpose, US citizens are required to be treated as US residents. In its non-reciprocal form, a Model 1 IGA provides for the exchange of information on US account holders only. A Model 2 IGA provides for direct reporting by local financial institutions to the US tax authorities when account holders consent to such reporting. Non-consenting account holders are initially reported on an aggregate basis but the US tax authorities are entitled to make a group request to the other country's tax authorities to obtain detailed information regarding the account holders included in the pool reported.

In both QI and FATCA, one of the business's biggest concerns is not just the way in which the rules are put into practice, but also the degree to which the tax authority concerned engages with the financial community to explain and help the development of workable solutions that meet both regulator's and business' needs.

Following the US trait, certain countries are starting to consider adopting regimes similar to FATCA. The UK has signed a tax information sharing agreement with the Isle of Man similar to IGAs—under which both governments will automatically exchange information on tax residents on an annual basis. The UK has further announced that it would pursue similar negotiations with other countries, and that the approach would closely follow the IGA.

While the T-BAG Group focuses in this chapter on granular implications of regulation, we also note in the conclusion of this chapter, that this is a very complex area and that there is a need for education and engagement, especially in the EU context which has the added complexity of different laws, languages and cultures.

Qualified Intermediaries

Control and Oversight

Any withholding system that permits foreign institutions to act as withholding agents, needs to have control and oversight processes. The US QI model uses three principles. The first establishes the obligations of foreign financial institutions, by contract, as the first element establishing the framework of control. The second ensures that the foreign institution is meeting its obligations, usually achieved through oversight by an authorised independent third party. The third ensures that the objectives of the system are not being abused either by incorrect identification of beneficiaries, entitlements or by inappropriate withholding or by means of formalised information reporting in cascade allowing for reconciliation with reports prepared by upper-tier custodians.

There are several aspects to the way that the US has implemented the enforcement and oversight regimes that the T-BAG Group wishes to comment upon.

Contracts

In order to be permitted to be a foreign Qualified Intermediary ("QI") and therefore withhold tax on behalf of the US Treasury, financial institutions must sign an agreement with the IRS ("QIA"). QIAs have a fixed term of six years. Failure to re-apply for QI status leads to a minimum two-year period without QI status.

For the industry, this requires contract management resources. If a contract is the preferred method, the T-BAG Group would suggest that a standardised EU Authorised Intermediary ("AI") Contract be developed and that renewal is automatic unless termination is triggered by one or other parties to the agreement. Tax authorities should commit to not impose obligations other than those specified in the relevant agreement (cf. in the case of the QI regime certain obligations followed from frequently asked questions published on the IRS website and from internal IRS instructions incorporated in Industry Memoranda) and to provide for realistic implementation deadlines when changes are made to the contract).

Audit v. AUP

Each QIA requires that the QI undergo an Agreed Upon Procedure ("AUP") twice during the six-year term of its QIA. Under the QI regime, unless the QI requests an IRS audit, the AUP applies and the QI is to be audited by a designated external auditor. The T-BAG Group considers AUP to be a more appropriate mechanism than audit conducted by the local tax authorities in cross-border situations given the legal issues that cross-border audits may create. In addition, the T-Bag Group prefers self-certifications over external audits. It is key that adequate audit guidance be provided and the specific procedures are defined by the tax authorities enabling the business to comply at a cost proportionate to the risk.

At the same time, it is worth noting that the EU Authorised Intermediary regime proposal looks to achieve the same overall outcome as the OECD's Tax Relief And Compliance Enhancement (TRACE) Implementation Package. Whist the OECD TRACE program currently suggests an approach of agreed-upon procedures, similar to QI we also considered IRS notice 2010–60.

In this notice, US Treasury notes that verification is crucial to achieving stated goals, but acknowledges cost should be reasonable. In this connection, it references the AML/KYC and similar regulatory rules as being similarly dependant on verification but as permitting audits that are either by external or internal auditors and that are not pursuant to agreed-upon procedures. This is in contrast to the QI requirements. Reliance on written certifications by senior management is also mentioned as a potential verification tool.

In particular, we recommend that the experience of QI's and external auditors or the IRS with respect to overall effectiveness cost and efficiency of external audits be considered in the development of the verification process. Further to the extent possible, verification processes of different regimes should perhaps be integrated. We also believe a simple verification process should be considered which is not one size fits all but rather includes several different approaches to verification (some more reliant on internal verification than others) which can be applied to AIs, as appropriate, depending on their overall record of tax risk management and compliance.

More importantly, the verification process should not rely on audits by external auditors. Based on the experience of QI's, such audits are costly and time-consuming. It is essential that the costs of implementing an AI regime (including the costs of verification) should be as reasonable as possible to assure participation and compliance. Therefore, the utilisation of external audits should be extremely limited. In light of the above, a verification process relying on internal verification by AI's (if supported by sufficiently robust procedures, processes and testing) should be viewed as a viable and preferable alternative.

Under the QI regime, alternatives to external audits relying on internal controls and testing have been permitted in certain situations. Under IRS

Procedure 2002–55 a QI may request a waiver of the external audit requirement if it has demonstrated substantial and robust internal controls with regard to its compliance with the QI agreement. Instead of an external audit, such a QI may perform an independent internal review. This internal review would include testing, checks, or other procedures deemed to be appropriate to determine whether the QI is compliant. The revenue procedure provides the QI may apply to the IRS for clearance to use this internal review process by submitting a formal description of the proposed testing program.

This does, however, in the European context, highlight the need for a standardised AUP acceptable across Member States.

Waivers

The US tax law recognises that some QIs may have relatively low amounts of US-sourced reportable income. This not only represents a low risk of tax evasion and underwithholding, but also a risk that the cost of complying with AUP requirements can be financially and administratively onerous and disproportionate to the tax and risk involved. Therefore, under the QI rules, a QI can apply for a waiver of the AUP requirement based on the threshold of reportable amounts in the audit year or based on the annual internal review program established by the QI. Three waivers are available, each with different information and procedural requirements: (1) if the reportable amount does not exceed $1 m, (2) if the reportable amounts exceed $1 m but does not exceed $4 m and (3) if the IRS approves QI's request to have its internal audit department perform the audit and report to the IRS.

To provide an incentive for maximum acceptance of a simplified system, the T-BAG Group would recommend some method whereby low-risk entities are either exempted from AUP or have a lower level of compliance burden.

Documentation

The US system permits financial institutions to apply for QI status when they are established in a jurisdiction the KYC rules of which have been approved by the IRS. To that extent, there is an implicit reliance by the IRS on the fact that a foreign institution (QI) is subject to its own domestic regulatory oversight.

The US also subscribes to the concept of self-certification using either a Form W-9 for its own (US) residents or a Form W-8 for non-US persons. There are several issues that cause business problems when using self-certifications:

1. There are different forms in the W-8 series (BEN, ECI, EXP and IMY). Having multiple forms causes account holders confusion as to which form they should be completing and incurs costs for business associated with checking that the form is correct according to any other information they hold about the account holder. Costs are also incurred by the business for training staff on how to analyse the forms and how to classify account holders based on the information provided by the account holder.
2. The US W-8 forms have a life span of three years from the end of the year in which signed, unless the recipient can obtain a US domestic tax identification number (TIN). This causes business challenges and cost associated with tracking the validity of documents on the one hand or the administrative task of obtaining a US tax ID for their account holder on the other. It also requires adjustments to reporting, withholding tax variances etc.
3. The forms can be used to assert entitlements under different income types. Part 1 of the W-8, for example, can be used to assert entitlement to an exemption for payments of portfolio interest even though Part 2 may be incomplete or incorrect. Equally Part 2, used to claim an entitlement under double tax treaty, requires certain account holders to know the exact clause in the relevant treaty under which they are claiming the entitlement. While business agrees that one form to serve multiple purposes is a good thing, the construction and instructions for such forms should be very clear to avoid large numbers of invalid forms due to a lack of understanding.
4. The forms must be delivered in paper form. Although there is an e-signature program under which, through a Memorandum of Understanding between a QI and the IRS, a "wet" signature is not required. The T-BAG Group would prefer, if originals are required, that they be required only of the institution acting as the custodian of the investor and that others in the chain with a need for such documentation be allowed to rely on suitably standardised electronic versions. Better is to allow for self-certifications that are compatible with all onboarding and communication channels (physical, internet, phone, …) and that allows for integration in account opening or other existing processes.
5. Each form is "owned" by the institution to which it is provided and would not, in the normal course of business, be available to any other institution. So, a single beneficial owner with multiple accounts may be providing several self-certifications to different institutions. The T-BAG Group notes that this is both a disincentive for beneficial owners and a risk that minor differences between forms create different tax results at different institutions such that the end investor suffers.

6. Substitute forms, including forms in foreign languages. That allows institutions with account holders who do not speak or read English to use substitute form W-8. Provided that at least the same data is present on the substitute as is present on the original IRS-approved form, and provided that the English version is also included.

The T-BAG Group is generally in favour of the self-certification principle. However, simplicity and standardisation will be key to a successful system. The T-BAG Group proposes an EU standardised self-certification, available in different EU languages and capable of being received, stored and transmitted electronically (including signature) as the preferred model. It ought to be possible to integrate self-certifications in existing account opening processes. Such a form should have an unlimited lifespan provided there are no material changes in circumstances that would affect the intent of the form.

Withholding

In the US system withheld tax is paid to the US Treasury (as opposed to information reports which are submitted to the IRS).

1. Withholding Agency

Foreign institutions who are QIs can withhold US tax on US-sourced income either directly as "Withholding QIs" ("WQIs") or indirectly via a US Withholding Agent or upper-tier QI if they are "Non-Withholding QIs" ("NWQIs"). Most QIs today are non-withholding preferring to use a US Withholding Agent ("USWA") to remit tax to the US Treasury on their behalf. However, this causes operational issues as there are two available systems enabling the USWA to know how much to withhold on any payment (given that it does not know who the beneficial owners are). These are (i) segregated pool accounts in which assets are segregated into "tax rate pools" prior to or on record date and (ii) withholding rate pool statements ("WRPS") made by the QI to the USWA on a payment by payment basis between the record date and pay date identifying the proportion of the income allocable to a particular tax rate. Please note that when a QI does not assume backup withholding (which is the withholding that must be applied when a US individual has not provided the required Form W-9) responsibilities it must provide a copy of the Form W-9 containing the personal details of its customer to its upper-tier custodian.

2. Source

The US regulations apply only to US source income, the definition of which presents challenges for business. While much income can be easily identified as to its source, there are occasions where the source is not clear. Heretofore, issuers have not generally categorised their distributions, leaving the matter to the industry to research and determine. This leads to the risk that different institutions, faced with the same income, define their source differently and thus withhold differently. This also impacts the consistency of information reporting.

3. Standards

The US has over 20 codes representing various income types as well as other codes representing exemptions, exceptions etc. While coding is a good thing to encourage automation, the T-BAG Group would support an ISO standard to apply to coding of income types.

4. Deposits

The US provides several mechanisms for the depositing of tax. The most used is a direct portal to US Treasury (EFTPS). With respect to the source of income and standards, the T-BAG Group would support a requirement on issuers of income to include a categorisation of their income, at least by country of source, using some standardised coding system.

Information Reporting

Information reporting is a fundamental concept in establishing a withholding system based on foreign financial institutions acting as withholding agents (QIs).

1. Cascade Nature

The US information reporting system, at least for non-US residents, is cascade in nature. This means that each entity in the chain must report to the IRS the US source payments made In principle, the IRS reconciles these reports (i) to the amount actually deposited at the US Treasury and (ii) upwards and downwards in the financial chain ending with the beneficial owner (in the case of a non-qualified intermediary ("NQI"). If payments were simple in nature, this system would work well. There are some problems however. For example, some issuers can re-classify their income after the end of the tax year. The regulations do provide a mechanism to address this (and any under or overwithholding) through "amended reporting". However, the IRS provides just one date (March 15th) on which all participants in the financial chain must file their reports. This single date is not workable in practice when a chain of intermediaries is involved. This has led to various commercial methods being used to solve the problem, all of which cause the cascade system to be inherently flawed.

The T-BAG Group has no issue with cascade reporting providing the rules and time frames given for allowing each participant in the chain to reconcile its books, receive and manage changes and make its final reports are adequate.

2. Paper v. Electronic

Currently, the US system supports both paper and electronic reporting at the same time, with electronic being mandatory for filings containing more than 250 forms.

This causes problems and costs both for business and for the IRS. The T-BAG Group would support a fully electronic system over the paper.

3. Domestic residents v. non-resident aliens

For income sourced in the US, the IRS requires separate reporting of US-sourced income to its own residents (Form 1099) on a recipient-specific basis and to non-residents (Form 1042-S) on a pooled basis (with certain exceptions). There are differences in the reporting requirements in terms of how income is pooled for non-resident reporting (1042), as well as different forms required (originals for 1099, downloadable for 1042).

All these different systems cause business an administrative burden and cost.

4. Pooled v. non-pooled Reporting

In some, but not all circumstances information reporting can be pooled in nature (aggregating all income paid to all beneficial owners of a particular type of income subject to the same income tax rate into one report) which benefits business by being simpler to administer. However, the system is not smooth and causes many institutions to be non-compliant. Errors caused by variations in the way reporting is constructed and/or understood mean that the principle of the cascade system in its ability to reconcile payments and tax withheld within a chain, can be damaged.

The T-BAG Group does not support pooling of reporting for authorised intermediaries but suggests that any proposed reporting system be at beneficial owner level and simple enough to administer so that most if not all intermediaries are likely to join the AI model.

Definition of "electronic"

The US has over time, changed both the format of data required as well as the delivery method. In Europe, it is likely that what constitutes "electronic" may vary by market. Currently "electronic" can mean a.pdf file, a spreadsheet or an ASCII file.

The T-BAG Group would support a single ISO-compliant standard, e.g., XML/XBRL for format and an "open" approach in which such standardised information (claims, reports etc.) could be delivered by any convenient, but secure carrier.

FATCA

The US has, for some time, had concerns that its taxpayers are evading taxes on their global income through the medium of foreign accounts, particularly in jurisdictions where secrecy laws acted to protect their identity. The use of collective investment vehicles, nominee accounts and other structural ways to hold investments can also act to create a barrier to transparency. The QI regime is perceived by the US authorities as only partially addressing such concerns and as lacking transparency with respect to non-US income of US persons. In addition, the relatively low number of foreign financial institutions that have entered into QI agreements with the IRS is further considered by the authorities as creating a barrier to transparency. The industry believes this view results, to some extent, from a misconception of NQI status and obligations.

FATCA was designed by the IRS to address these systemic problems. However, after the publication of the Proposed Regulations (RIN 1545-BK68) Relating to Information Reporting by Foreign Financial Institutions and Withholding on Certain Payments to Foreign Financial Institutions ("FFIs") and Other Foreign Entities issued on 8 February 2012 ("Prop.Regs."), it became clear that there are a number of operational issues prohibiting or making it unreasonably difficult to achieve compliance with

FATCA provisions. Recognising the need for cooperation in combating international tax evasion, but also the legal and practical restrictions, as well as costs of foreign financial institutions (FFIs) involved in achieving full compliance of FATCA, a number of countries expressed an intention to negotiate an IGA with the US, based on Model IGA agreements. Two Model IGA agreements have been developed so far.

The purpose of both Model IGAs is to reduce the compliance burden imposed on FATCA partner country FFIs and to overcome the obstacles created by local legislation regarding data privacy and withholding. Under Model 1 IGAs, the FFIs are required to report to their domestic tax authorities, whereas under Model 2 IGAs the FFIs will exchange information directly with the IRS. More importantly, under both Model IGAs the withholding is limited to a very narrow circumstances and applies only with regard to taxpayers and financial institutions that do not comply with the FATCA provisions. Specifically, an FFI is only required to withhold 30% of any US source withholdable payment made to a non-participating FFI, FFI that is not FATCA compliant or to an account holder that has not provided the required information or a waiver to the FFI.

The US Treasury Department has concluded several IGAs and announced that it is engaged in discussions with more than 50 jurisdictions that are interested to enter into IGAs.

Following the US trait, certain countries are starting to consider adopting regimes similar to FATCA. The UK has recently signed a tax information sharing agreement with the Isle of Man similar to IGAs—under which both the governments will automatically exchange information on tax residents on an annual basis. The UK has further announced that it would pursue similar negotiations with other countries and that the approach would closely follow the IGA. Russia has expressed similar intent to negotiate IGA-like agreements.

Many other countries have similar underlying principles under which they claim a right to tax the global income of their residents. This trend is likely to continue as global financial pressure on tax authorities results in a focus on ensuring disclosure so that tax revenues are optimised. It is natural to presume that EU Member States will feel a similar pressure.

The T-BAG Group understands the rationale of FATCA, however, the Group generally considers that the implications of FATCA are disproportionate with the intent and benefit for a number of the reasons given below. The comments apply to the FATCA regime under the Final Regulations and under the Model IGAs, unless indicated otherwise.

1. Multiple FATCA Regimes

As a result of the processes described above, currently, there are a number of FATCA models being advanced at the same time. As a result, multi-national financial institutions with subsidiaries and branches in various countries are faced with the implementation of the base FATCA model in the Final Regulations, IGAs negotiated based on Model 1, IGAs based on Model 2, and the IGA-like agreements entered into by other countries. Furthermore, even though the IGAs are negotiated on the basis of models, differences, however slight, exist among all negotiated IGAs. Some IGA's, the UK, for example, includes a "future-proofing" provision that the UK IGA will always benefit from any better terms offered by the US to any other FATCA Partner in an IGA. Notwithstanding that agreements may differ it is also possible that each country's implementing legislation will vary leading to different interpretations of key points. This means that IGAs and country-specific legislation will need to be constantly monitored.

The plethora of the FATCA models makes it extremely difficult, confusing and costly for financial institutions to comply with the law, making it practically unworkable. A standardised approach is recommended.

2. Definition of Financial Institution

In order to expand the number of entities over which the IRS can exert direct contractual control, FATCA and Model IGAs identify four different types of entities that can be defined as a foreign financial institution ("FFI"). Some of the definitions are rather broad and include entities that normally do not fall under the laws governing regulated financial entities. Because of the broad definition, FFIs that do not maintain financial accounts will also be captured even though they would not have anything to report on. The net effect of this expansion is that there are expected to be upwards of a million entities that fall into the definition of FFI and, consequently, be subject to the identification, reporting and withholding obligations. In addition, since the definitions of the FFI differ under Final Regs. Model 1 IGAs and Model 2 IGAs, the same Financial Institution could have a different FATCA status in different jurisdictions.

3. Contracts

FFIs will be required to sign an agreement "FFIA" which forces them to identify account holders, and, for certain legal entities, also the controlling persons of such account holders for the purpose of identifying any US persons, and imposes reporting and withholding obligations. Of particular interest is the development that the IRS has established a web-based method for FFIs to register and sign FFI Agreements, subject to experience, this concept has merit in an EU context. Under FATCA, the requirements will generally be incorporated into local law for FFIs in IGA countries while other FFIs must enter into an FFI agreement. No expiration dates have been set for FFI agreements.

There is concern that the IRS will be unable to cope with the number of FFIAs and equally, entities that were not previously defined as FFIs will have little or no capability to comply with the identification, reporting and withholding requirements. Furthermore, the same financial entity could be treated as an FFI in one country, but not in another. Therefore, as structured, the FFI concept is unworkable both for the IRS and business.

4. Waivers

FATCA provisions contain two contentious waiver issues which potentially put financial institutions in a position where compliance with US law may cause them to be in breach of local law.

FATCA recognises that there may be occasions where local law prohibits the reporting of the information required under FATCA that could identify US Persons (even if there are none in fact). To that extent, FATCA provisions require the FFI to obtain a waiver of such law from its account holders to permit such reporting.

This creates potential legal issues where it may be illegal for a resident account holder to provide a waiver of its own law, albeit failure to do so would place it in breach of US law.

In addition, the Final Regulations require FFIs to close accounts where such waiver is not provided or where the account is otherwise treated as recalcitrant.

There are concerns around these provisions including (i) potential contravention of SEPA regulation with respect to the right to have an account, (ii) changes to terms and conditions to accommodate a waiver principle may be open to legal challenge and (iii) the principle of a waiver may be deemed to be discriminatory.

5. Interpretation of US status

While opening the investment community to more transparency, FATCA also requires a more rigorous interpretation of legal status than FFIs have previously been familiar with. Financial Institutions currently apply KYC and AML rules but these are not deemed sufficient in all circumstances by the US to identify a US person. Additional tests might be applied by relationship managers for both entities and individuals, repeated regularly and to a substantially deeper level than currently will require significant training, additional systems builds and education of customers who may not see relevance to answering questions about a country they are not invested in. Furthermore, to the extent that other countries are also negotiating IGA-like agreements, the financial entities would need to identify the country of the tax residence of their account holders based on various other sets of rules and definitions.

If financial institutions are required to apply different rules by different EU countries for the same purpose, this will add to the cost and administrative burden, assuming that it is workable. A standardised approach is recommended.

6. Explicit Certification of Compliance

While the compliance with the QI rules is achieved through AUPs, FATCA compliance is likely to be more restrictive. Under Final Regulations, FFIs are required to explicitly certify that they have complied with FATCA obligations. Under the IGAs, the approach is different as the supervisory role will be mainly with the local tax authorities of the country of establishment of the FFI. The US tax authorities are however entitled to make inquiries directly to the FFI where it has reason to believe that minor errors have been made that resulted in incomplete information reporting or other infringements. In case the US tax authorities have determined that there has been significant non-compliance then it will notify the other contracting state and require it to apply the penalties as applicable under local law to address the non-compliance. In case the enforcement actions do not resolve the non-compliance within a period of 18 months, the FFI will be blacklisted as a non-participating FFI which will cause it to suffer a 30% US withholding tax on certain payments received.

7. Withholding tax as a penalty

FFIs are required to withhold 30% of any US source withholdable payment made to non-participating FFIs and recalcitrant account holders (account holders who have failed to provide required documentation or information). In addition, the Final Regulations and Model IGAs have reserved a right to expand the withholding to apply also to certain non-US source payments and sales proceeds. The IGAs have restricted instances whereby withholding is required by offering reporting alternatives.

Much has been said about the reporting model over the anonymous withholding model. Routinely, governments have expressed reporting as the desired outcome. Clearly today with investors foregoing tax relief due to the complex and costly processes tax authorities are not obtaining information on their residents cross-border investments. T-BAG envisages that the implementation of the AI regime will increase investor information reporting.

Documentation requirements and client identification procedures

The client identification and documentation procedures that apply under FATCA are extremely complex. The complexity is caused in part by the fact that the regime provides for a very high number of different statuses for legal entities and because of the complex combination of documentation requirements, due diligence requirements, documentation validity rules and presumption rules. The proliferation of statuses for legal entities is caused mainly by the very broad definition of financial institutions and the vagueness of concepts such as passive non-financial entities. The other issue with the documentation requirements under FATCA is the fact that these requirements are not sufficiently aligned with prevailing KYC procedures.

We should also point out that FATCA does require full paper file reviews in certain instances while financial institutions usually have well-developed client databases containing up to date identification data. Strict procedures and requirements generally exist for the maintenance and amending of these data. In spite thereof, FATCA only authorises electronic searches in limited circumstances thereby creating significant costs for financial institutions.

The T-Bag Group believes that the EU should advocate an approach whereby clear and realistic definitions are used and whereby documentation requirements be aligned with existing KYC requirements. In addition, financial institutions should be authorised to rely on their electronic data for due diligence purposes.

The T-BAG Group recognises Member State's legitimate wish to implement a relief at source and reclaim model for non-residents in an efficient way. Member States would also naturally wish to provide a disincentive to their own residents from evading taxes.

The T-BAG Group's overall view of FATCA is that, while the intent is understandable, it is not appropriate for the withholding tax system to be used for such a purpose and that other mechanisms exist, e.g., information sharing agreements, competent authority et al. which individually, in concert or adapted in some way would be more appropriate and effective for the intended purpose.

In comparing and contrasting the US QI system described here with the observations of business in the other chapters in this report, the Group notes that the US system, while conceptually simple is, in practice, still complex and costly at the operational level twelve years after its original implementation. The T-Bag Group does, however, support the principle that foreign intermediaries be allowed to act as withholding agents and offer withholding tax relief at source and that KYC documents can be relied upon for granting relief at source in many instances. To avoid the complexity of the QI and FATCA regimes, at the Member State and EU level, a strong focus on the principles of standardisation and use of electronic storage and transmission is recommended together with a well-thought through and continuous education and guidance program to provide for a high adoption rate by financial institutions.

Comparison to EU and OECD work

The OECD has in parallel with the EU, worked on improved withholding tax procedures. In January 2013 the OECD approved a standardised system of effective treaty and domestic relief (the TRACE Authorised Intermediary System) including a complete implementation package for countries to move forward ("the TRACE Implementation Package or IP). Section 4.1 provides some background on the work conducted within the OECD that has led to the approval of the TRACE Implementation Package. Section 4.2 and Appendix 5 compare the work with the EU recommendation in further detail.

Context

The OECD work on withholding tax relief procedures was initiated as a result of a growing awareness of governments and the financial industry of the need to improve existing withholding tax relief procedures. In 2006, the CFA established an Informal Consultative Group 6 (the ICG), composed of representatives from governments and the financial industry. The aim of the ICG was to analyse the compliance and administrative difficulties surrounding claims for tax treaty benefits on investment income derived through financial intermediaries and to consider whether there were administrative procedures that could be adopted to streamline those claims.

In January 2009, the ICG issued a report entitled "Possible Improvements to Procedures for Tax Relief for Cross-Border Investors" (the ICG Report). The ICG Report identified a number of inefficiencies in withholding tax relief procedures for cross-border portfolio investments and set out best practice recommendations for such procedures.

The ICG Report recommended that countries develop systems for claiming treaty benefits that allow "Authorised Intermediaries" to make claims from withholding agents for relief at source on a "pooled" basis on behalf of their customers that are portfolio investors. One of the major benefits of such an AI system (variations on which have been adopted by a few countries over the past decade) is that information regarding the beneficial owner of the income is maintained by the intermediary with the most direct account relationship with the investor, rather than being passed up the chain of intermediaries. The ICG also recommended that further work be undertaken to promote substantial uniformity across source countries with respect to the procedures to be followed by the AIs.

At the beginning of 2009, the CFA approved the establishment of a "pilot group", again composed of representatives from governments and the financial industry (the Pilot Group), to develop standardised documentation for the implementation of the "best practices" recommended by the ICG. In February 2010, the Pilot Group produced an "Implementation Package" containing model documents to be used by any country willing to implement the AI system recommended by the ICG (the Implementation Package or IP).

In February 2010, the CFA released the IP as a discussion draft for public comments. It also approved the creation of two working groups: (i) the TRACE Group, made up of government representatives from OECD countries, to take forward the work on the IP and develop a plan for multi-country adoption of the AI system (working in close consultation with a dedicated Business Advisory Group) and (ii) a joint government/business group of IT experts to ensure that the proposed information reporting and automatic exchange of information processes that are part of the recommended AI system can function effectively.

In December 2012, the TRACE Group approved a revised version of the Implementation Package which takes into account the comments received on the Pilot Group's draft.

The TRACE IT Expert Group has:

- developed an electronic format for the information to be reported by financial institutions to tax administrations and for the exchange of information between tax administrations. This format, using eXtensible Markup Language ("XML"), is called the TRACE XML Schema. XML is the modern industry-standard markup format, as used in the OECD Standard Transmission Format (STF), and the EU format developed from STF for the Savings Directive, FISC 153.
- designed and conducted a Proof of concept test to confirm that the TRACE XML Schema fulfilled the objectives of the TRACE project from the perspective of the financial intermediaries and the tax authorities of the source and residence countries involved recommended the use of secure file transfer protocol ("sFTP") as the transmission method for reporting by financial institutions to tax administrations and for the exchange of information between tax administrations, or alternatively, the existing EU CCN system for exchange between tax administrations, where available.

In January 2013, the CFA endorsed the Implementation Package and approved further work in two areas: a) exploiting synergies between TRACE and other reporting regimes (including FATCA, the Common Model for Residence Country Reporting) and any EU follow-up work on the FISCO Feasibility Study and b) developing a plan for a multi-country adoption of the Authorised Intermediary system and assisting countries progress towards adoption.

Comparison of the EU Recommendation with the TRACE IP

The EU Recommendation and the IP support a withholding tax relief system that has many similar features. However, there are also some differences. The main differences are that:

1. the Recommendation only provides the general framework of such withholding tax relief system and does not always specify how each of the features of the system should be put into practice, while the Implementation Package is very detailed and consists of a self-contained set of all the agreements and forms that would pass between a source country, the AI and the investors participating in the system; and
2. the scope of the Recommendation is limited to EU resident investors, investing in securities from another EU Member State through a financial institution established in an EU Member State or EFTA Member Country, while the IP is designed to apply in a global context.

The IP is fully consistent with the EU Recommendation and could serve as a basis for any country wishing to implement the Recommendation. In the long term, the EU-specific context might possibly justify different approaches for putting the EU Recommendation into practice, from those followed in the IP. In particular, one could consider:

1. EU financial institutions to be authorised by the EU Member States in which they are established, similar to MiFID (instead of EU source countries);
2. Submitting Authorised Intermediaries to an audit by the tax authorities of the EU Member State in which they are established only, audits which would be recognised by the source EU Member States (instead of submitting them to a review by an independent reviewer and/or audit by the source country tax authorities)
3. Requiring EU based AIs to report investor-specific information via the tax authorities of the Member States in which they are established, who would exchange the information with the relevant source and residence countries (instead of reporting to the source country as envisaged by the IP).

Appendix 5 provides a detailed comparative analysis.

From a business perspective and in a strictly EU context, some of these options may present benefits. However, unlike the approach followed in the IP, each of the above options would require the adoption of a Directive. As a result, they would not offer any solution in the short to medium term. As a practical matter, this potential approach would need to be tempered by adopting enhanced tax relief arrangements that can be implemented in the most expeditious manner. In addition, these options would only function in an EU context: other solutions would need to be adopted for the cases in which the investor, issuer or intermediary is located outside the EU Consideration should therefore be given to the risk that operating two separate systems in parallel may increase costs for tax authorities, financial intermediaries and investors.

Guidance

Part 3—Proposed Solutions

Financial intermediaries may provide some form of a withholding tax service to their clients that hold portfolio debt and equity investments. This is especially relevant for custodian banks. The custodian's tax services in this context focus on the collecting and filing of tax documentation to enable investors to make a relevant claim under either a treaty or domestic law. In order to claim the benefit of a relevant treaty, it is common for there to be some form of documentation to evidence entitlement. As set out in this report, this ranges from the provision of a certificate of tax residence to a treaty claim form or income payment information, among others. Such a tax service can take on a number of forms but may include the following tasks:

1. the collection of tax documentation from clients;
2. the submission of relevant tax documentation to local withholding agents;
3. the submission of reclaims to a source country tax authority; and
4. the renewal of such tax documentation under power of attorney.

Custodian banks may service a diverse client base—e.g., clients from multiple residence countries; of different legal forms and business purposes.

While ultimate responsibility for any tax relief claim will normally reside with the beneficial owner, an FI will wish to check such entitlement. As noted within this report, the question of treaty eligibility or otherwise can be a difficult area in certain circumstances. The areas of difficulty typically arise on questions of interpretation around whether the claimant is:

- a person for the purposes of the relevant treaty;
- a resident within the meaning of the relevant treaty; and
- and the beneficial owner of the income received.

Typically the qualification of entities such as partnerships, corporations, Collective Investment Vehicles, pension funds, Trusts, Charities, International organisations and others causes the greatest concern. Specifically, the complexity of the qualification of CIVs has been recently recognised and addressed in the OECD Report on 31st May 2010, titled The Granting of Treaty Benefits with respect to the Income of Collective Investment Vehicles. We also note the on-going work of the OECD in clarifying the meaning of the term "beneficial owner" in articles 10, 11 and 12 of the OECD Model Tax Convention.

The authors of this report believe that any question of liability in the context of the application of an incorrect withholding tax rate on a portfolio investment income payment has to be placed within the context of the need for appropriate clear guidance from the Authorities. Increased effective guidance will enable all participants—i.e., both FIs and claimants of lower rates of withholding tax—to appropriately commercially allocate risk to the appropriate party.

Clear guidance issued by the respective competent authorities enables investors to determine any tax relief to which they may be entitled and enables FIs to determine the parameters of any tax relief service and the respective rates to apply.

In turn, this will reduce risks and compliance costs for investors, FIs and Governments. Finally, it will enable tax authorities to concentrate their investigations on risk rather than the more standard portfolio investor entitlements. Of course, it will still be necessary for Tax Authorities to have the ability to provide investor-specific rulings or opinions but certainty in the first instance will increase confidence for all participants.

The owner of the guidance is by nature the competent authority of the source country. However, a standardised format and a central information platform hosted by the EU will increase the effectiveness of the Single Market significantly. We suggest that a streamlined ruling process be devised where generic entity-level rulings can be requested to confirm whether such an entity is entitled to either a lower rate of withholding tax either under a treaty or domestic law. Such rulings should be limited to portfolio investors and subject to certain conditions and appropriate limitations. Such conditions could include a general tax avoidance limitation.

In order to request such a ruling, the ruling applicant should be required to provide the following: an overview of the entity—this should include references to source country tax law and commercial law where applicable and include confirmation as to whether the entity is opaque/transparent under source country tax law; and whether the entity is subject/liable to tax in the source country on income received.

To provide for a level playing field and to avoid different stances being taken by FI's, we recommend that rulings of this nature are made publicly available on the internet. This should assist tax authorities in that it will avoid duplicative requests for clarification.

Relief at Source

The aim of this chapter is to provide an overview of proposals for Relief at Source, introducing the notion of contracts signed between the different parties that could lead to a short/mid-term solution.

Authorised Intermediary Agreement

Bilateral agreements, i.e., voluntary adoption, can be seen as a practical route to establish financial intermediaries as AIs. While EU regulation through Directive is an alternative, this would be limited to EU participants. In any case, contracts would be needed for non-EU participants and the financial industry recognises that an EU regulation may be difficult in the short term.

The different types of bilateral AI agreements could be described as follows:

1. Local to Local
2. Residency to Source Country

Local to Local

Under this option, the country of residence of the intermediary would grant its resident financial institutions the ability to act as an authorised intermediary (AI) for the purpose of information reporting and as a withholding agent. In this case, the home country would act as an agent for the source country. In the short term, this would initially be possible for EU or EFTA resident intermediaries.

In the mid/long term, non-EU intermediaries meeting criteria to be defined/agreed by EU Member States would be treated the same as an EU or EFTA resident intermediary. Business suggests that criteria could be by reference to EOI provisions. The prerequisites of such a system would include:

1. Source country must have agency agreements with all countries in which AIs are established.
2. All Member States to agree on the content of the agreement. There are benefits to a local–local AI system:
3. Each resident intermediary would have to sign only one contract. This solution would lead to the kind of simplifications encouraged by the EU Commission Recommendation of 19th October 2009;
4. Familiarity with governing law.

However, this solution may actually require changes in local law to account for procedures in case of underwithholding.

Country of Residency to Source Country

In this model, an intermediary would sign a contract with each source country. The benefits of this methodology include:

1. This solution can be quickly implemented by the source countries who wish to do so (no dependency on countries of AIs);
2. Non-EU or EFTA resident intermediaries would be treated the same as residents. This would avoid discrimination of third countries.

However, EU or EFTA resident financial institutions would have to sign up to 27 contracts. In order to ease the process, one solution would be a package including all agreements and forms to be filled in, duly signed and forwarded to the competent authorities.

AI Contract Model

The main elements which would need to be taken into account for such agreements are:

1. Governing law;
2. Procedural requirements;
3. Nature of income covered;
4. Withholding agent status;
5. Terms of reporting obligations;
6. Authority to disclose;
7. Liability;
8. Penalties;
9. Rates of withholding (which could be delegated to guidance);
10. Documentation requirements (including retention period and validity);
11. Statute of limitations covering both claim and review period;
12. Control and oversight (to include detail of reviewer);
13. Dispute procedures;
14. Term of contract and termination provision.

This list is not intended to be definitive.

Documentation

Given (i) an AI Agreement to codify the obligations of AIs, together with (ii) adoption of the principles and guidelines issued by the various Member States, (iii) appropriate documentation of beneficial owners and (iv) the use of TIN's to facilitate the exchange of information, withholding agents would be able to withhold at the correct relief rate at the time that the distribution is made to the investor.

With reference to (iii), documentation to evidence status and legal form of those investors claiming relief either "at source" or in a tax reclaim, in the main are the same. These are discussed at some length in Chapter 9 and include:

1. KYC documents;
2. Powers of Attorney;
3. Certificates of Tax Residence.

Information Reporting

In order to meet the tax authorities' requirements, AIs will be asked to provide detailed information about reportable payments and beneficial owners. The frequency of the reporting could be on a monthly basis with a year-end summary report.

Having reviewed the US withholding tax system, certain conceptual elements do seem to provide both access to reconciliation of payment chains between AIs as well as disclosure. However, other elements were deemed by the T-BAG Group to be disproportionate to an efficient system.

The T-BAG Group proposes that the AI closest to the beneficial owner be responsible for reporting at the beneficial owner level directly to the source Member State. The AI would, in the envisioned model, report upwards to other AIs in the payment chain at a pooled level.

Reporting Models

Information reporting could be implemented in a number of ways as exemplified below.

Reporting via source state of income

In this model, the AI issues a report directly to the source state of income payment. It is up to the source state of income payment to issue the information reporting to the residence state of the final beneficial owner, whether automatically or via specific request. This option brings a harmonised solution among EU Member States.

Reporting via home state of AI

In this model, the AI issues reports to its home state Tax Authorities. It is up to the home state to report/forward the information reporting to the source state of income payment and to the residence state of the final beneficial owner.

Reporting via source state of income and residence state of beneficiary

The intermediary issues a report to the source state of income payment and to the residence state of the final beneficial owner. Of the described reporting models the Group prefers the source state of income model as it is most compatible with current practices in global context.

Standards and Automation

Transmission of report data is currently neither coordinated nor standardised between tax authorities. The T-BAG Group strongly recommends that attention is given to these subjects in any planned implementation. However, the

T-BAG Group recognises that each Member State has different levels of standard and automation in place ranging from standard paper delivered forms (which vary by Member State) to electronic data files (which vary in format and delivery mechanism). Therefore, the work involved in moving towards a more harmonised, standardised and automated system will be different for each Member State and maybe a significant driver for the speed with which a phased voluntary adoption can occur.

Standards

Current standards employed by the industry include both ISO (currently ISO15022 and planned ISO20022) and XML among others. Equally, there are several options open to Member States for the transmission of such standardised information. In cases where reporting is comprised solely of data an ISO standard is feasible, although financial intermediaries are not expected to have fully implemented ISO20022 for several years and there are no ISO15022 standards that currently address the reporting requirements. XML and it's subsidiary XBRL offers more opportunities for rapid implementation. XBRL is a subset of XML and is designed for financial reporting and is congruent with ISO20022. The US and UK already mandate in regulation that financial reporting must be in XBRL format. IRS in FATCA Final Regulations preamble also notes that it intends to mandate XBRL as a standard for information reporting under IGAs commencing in 2015. As there are over 50 countries with which the US is currently negotiating IGAs, it is likely that, by the end of 2013, most of the key investment markets will be familiar with the concepts of XML/XBRL. This technology may therefore be useful as a bridging technology, quick and low cost to implement and congruent to the longer term solution of an ISO20022 standard.

Automation

Most, but not all, banks are members of the Society for Worldwide Interbank Financial Messaging ("SWIFT") which operates a secure messaging computer network over which data can be moved between participating users. However, to date, no tax authorities have a presence on the SWIFT network for the receipt of reports. In addition, while standardised in principle, the reality of ISO standardised messages sent over the SWIFT network suffer from consistency problems in that counterparties on the network can independently agree on the location of data in messages passed between them. The theory is that a message of any given type, if it meets the ISO standard should be readable by any other institution on the network. However, this is not the case. Were this model to be replicated in the information reporting between AIs and Member States, it is possible that each Member State could specify its own format for the location of data within messages. Thus each AI sending reports to up to 27 tax authorities could find it costly and challenging to send a report containing the same data elements, but differently ordered, thus removing almost all of the benefits of standardisation and automation which the financial services industry would want.

The internet also offers opportunities to develop secure data transmission methods and many emerging types of institutions, notably central securities depositories, are or have developed proprietary systems with underpinning ISO standards. In this respect, XML and XBRL also offer flexible and rapid implementation approaches. XML establishes a taxonomy (or dictionary) by means of which any party can transmit to any other party, a document containing "tags" to identify where specific data elements appear in the document. This means that an XML/XBRL Information Report can be formatted visually in any way a tax authority wishes and the required data within the document is machine readable irrespective of where the data element appears in the document. The T-BAG Group recommends that, in any information reporting requirement, Member States mandate XML/XBRL formatting, to allow both tax authorities and AIs flexibility to adopt standardisation and automation in an efficient way and at their own pace.

The T-BAG Group recommends that the information to be provided by the financial intermediaries should be standardised in line with the OECD and limited with respect to content.

Report Content

In order to fulfil the requirements of Member States, give comfort about the proper execution of the AI agreement and prepare the field for a quick and efficient audit, we propose that the following information would have to be included in information reports. As mentioned before some information can be provided on a monthly basis and others on an annual basis:

1. AI Identification number
2. Payee—intermediary
    (1) Payee—details
    (2) Name
    (3) Intermediary approval number
    (4) Address
3. Payee—beneficial owner details
    (1) Name
    (2) Home State TIN
    (3) Country of Residence

   (4) Address
   (5) Beneficial Owner Type

4. Income Payment Details

   (1) Issuer tax residence (country of taxation)
   (2) Nature of Income (standardised income type code)
   (3) Unique security identifier
   (4) Gross amount
   (5) Net amount
   (6) Tax rate

Intermediary reporting to upstream agent/intermediary (pool reporting).

1. AI Identification number
2. Pool reporting rate
3. Income payment details a. b. c. d. e. f.
4. Issuer tax residency (country of taxation)
5. Nature of Income (standardised income type code) ISIN
6. Gross amount
7. Net amount
8. Tax rate

All granted and tax withheld and deposited with the respective tax authorities. This information should allow any future reconciliation between exemption.

The possibility for an AI to shift part of its responsibilities (information reporting responsibility and/or withholding responsibility) to another upstream AI, or third party, should also be anticipated in order to allow small AIs to contract and be compliant at low cost. The contract, reporting and audit scope should take this possibility into account.

Withholding

The T-BAG Group considers that tax should be paid to the source country directly in order to avoid having Member States transferring money between them and obliging them to maintain multilateral reconciliation processes.

Control and Oversight

All Member States can be expected to require a control and oversight methodology to ensure proper and efficient operating of an AI system. In essence, there are three different possibilities:

1. Audit of AIs by the home country tax authority
2. Agreed Upon Procedure ("AUP") conducted by independent

3. Self-verification

It should be noted that there is a legal difference between an "audit" and an "Agreed Upon Procedure". An audit requires an auditor to give a legal opinion upon which the recipient can rely. There are associated liabilities with an audit process that do not exist within an AUP model. Equally, a greater range of independent, suitably qualified firms would naturally be available to AIs within an AUP model than would be available within an audit model. An AUP is simply a procedure agreed upon by a tax authority. While an independent firm, who may well offer traditional audit services, can conduct an AUP, they would not be acting in the legal capacity of auditors.

In respect of the audit by the local authorities, this is unlikely to be an acceptable solution in the current financial climate. For example, we understand that some tax authorities may be reluctant due to staff and budget constraints—we are currently seeing this in the development of enabling legislation for Intra Governmental Agreements in the UK. Another approach could be to appoint an external auditor but this would result in transferring the audit cost to the AIs.

In light of the above, we recommend an AI verification process which similarly relies primarily on internal controls and self-audits for those AI's that have previously demonstrated a record of compliant behaviour, strong internal controls and verification processes. The extent to which the AI verification requirements rely on internal processes could depend on an AI's overall risk profile based on, among other factors, its approach to tax (and overall) risk management and its history of compliance under domestic regulation. Specifically, the following factors, among others, could be considered in determining whether a particular AI's verification process should be reliant on internal controls and processes:

Compliance record;

1. A record of internal KYC/AML reports supported by robust internal controls and including annual reporting to local bank regulators;
2. An established verification process relying on internal health checks or similar testing programs which is part of the AI's existing tax risk management framework and which is performed by an independent department of the AI;
3. The inclusion in internal audits of testing (in addition to the above health checks) to verify compliance with existing operational tax requirements
4. A process involving annual internal compliance certifications by the affected departments to an independent department with oversight

responsibilities and/or by the AI to its parent company. An internal AI compliance verification process would include the following features:-

(1) Detailed written AI internal policies and procedures;
(2) Identification of responsible parties within each affected business and operational unit and other key controls;
(3) Required regular testing (by an objective independent business unit and/or internal audit) meeting specified requirements and documented in written test reports;
(4) Regular certifications (perhaps every second or third year) to the home country competent authority by senior management of the participating AI (supported by sub-certifications from affected businesses) regarding compliance with internal procedures; and
(5) In the event, the certification reports an un-remediated material deficiency and if, in the discretion of the competent authority an audit is necessary to assure remediation of that deficiency, an external audit firm would be engaged by the AI to do an independent audit. The scope of the audit would be pre-agreed by the AI and the competent authority and would be limited to the identified problem area (e.g., business line or legal entity) and issues. The audit would focus, as appropriate, on assuring that the remediation is implemented, the deficiency corrected, and the procedures are otherwise compliant.

Tax Reclaims

Overview

As this report notes, the preference is for Member States to adopt a unified simplified withholding tax relief at source system, i.e., one solution for all European Union source Member States that provides for a withholding tax relief at point of payment process for non-resident portfolio investors.10 We have not addressed claims made by domestic investors—i.e., investors resident in the same country as the source payment. We recognise that this solution may involve significant change for certain countries in that new process and procedures would need to be adopted. As a point of record, this report is supportive of the Commission's Recommendation of 19 October 2009 on withholding tax procedures.

The following section makes certain suggestions as to how existing documentation requirements, in order to benefit from a reduced withholding tax rate either under a double tax treaty or domestic law, could be simplified and so lead to processing efficiencies for both claimants and intermediaries.11 Such simplification would also have benefits for tax authorities in that it should reduce processing costs and, to some degree, improve the general compliance environment.12 The proposals outlined below should be seen as evolutionary in that they represent a progressive step towards the final goal of a unified simplified tax relief system. In assessing whether or not this progressive step should be adopted, tax authorities should consider whether it would make better sense to go directly to the end solution as set out.

As a general matter, reduced rates of withholding tax on portfolio securities income are claimed through one of two means—tax relief at source (i.e., at point of income payment) or through a retrospective tax reclaim.13 Tax relief at source may, in certain markets, be obtained without detailed tax documentation but more commonly documentation will be required. Such documentation may encompass treaty claim forms and certificates of tax residence etc. Tax reclaims will generally require a tax treaty claim form to be completed and such a form may also require further documentation such as a certificate of residence, tax voucher etc. Portfolio investors in this context is taken to mean those investors qualifying under a relevant double tax treaty for the general rate of withholding tax on dividends. i.e., investors holding a shareholding meeting a minimum threshold as envisaged under Article 10 2(a) of the OECD Model Tax Convention on Income and on Capital will not be said to be a portfolio investor.

It is worth noting that relief at source is the preferred withholding tax claim method for both investors and intermediaries as tax reclaims, by their very nature, possess a number of specific issues.14 The key issues being:

1. Reclaims have a time value of money cost;15
2. Reclaim timeframes can vary from market of investment to market of investment, but a recent study by the British Bankers' Association noted that indicative timeframes for receiving a reclaim can range from 2 weeks to a minimum of ten years;17
3. As reclaims typically require a form to be produced and income-specific information recorded, this means that such reclaims have a higher processing cost compared with tax relief at source that allows for one-time documentation (or documentation requiring only periodic renewal).

The OECD in a recent report made further comments with regards to the problems associated with tax reclaims and this report endorses those comments.

Treaty forms, whether relief at source or reclaim, have certain core similarities in terms of the information requested from the claimant. As such, this report argues that it should be possible to standardise documentation, for both purposes, to support a common tax claim process and deal with source country concerns around receiving sufficient evidence of entitlement to a lower withholding tax rate. The benefit of having one form to access multiple markets of investment would reduce complexity within the European Union and should remove a barrier to cross-border investment.20 We would further argue that standardised documentation should significantly reduce the costs of processing different paper forms and documents. These costs incurred in processing forms have been estimated as ranging between €50 and €140 per refund claim. As such, any simplification should result in lower costs for all participants in the process—i.e., government, intermediaries and investors.

A significant benefit of simplification should be an increase in claims by eligible investors. This increase may result from the investor better understanding the claim process or the reduction in the cost to claim leading to a low-value claim being economically worthwhile.

This report recommends, in line with the recommendation made by the 2007 FISCO Report, that a simplified form for all Member States (i.e., one form covering all Member States) should be developed. Such a simplified form should not be restricted to EU investors. That is any investor investing into an EU country should be able to use this standardised form. The simplified form should be issued with associated detailed guidance from each member state so that any points of detail or definition have appropriate guidance allowing both investors and intermediaries to understand and operate the claim process.

Any such form should be capable of dealing with domestic exemptions (e.g., pension, charity etc. result of ECJ cases; infringement procedures etc.) and not be limited to claims pursuant to a double tax convention. Furthermore, we believe that international organisations or sovereign entities should be able to use any standardised form. We accept there may be some difficulties in designing such a form but guidance may represent a potential solution. For example, there may be policy issues around whether sovereign entities may benefit from any domestic law provisions providing for sovereign immunity. A recent OECD paper described those issues and such concerns could be dealt with through guidance—e.g., it could be clearly stated that the doctrine of sovereign immunity will not apply to income paid to a trading entity regardless of the fact that it is ultimately owned by a sovereign body.

The benefits of providing a standardised form can be seen to be multi-dimensional in that it will have an impact on all participants in the claim process:

1. the investor—simplification should lead to a greater degree of clarity around eligibility and reduce costs of compliance. At present, where

investors are presented with an unclear claim process this may lead to investors having to take tax advice (and so a cost) or forgoing tax relief that they would otherwise be entitled to;

2. financial intermediaries—a standardised form with clear guidance should reduce costs of compliance, reduction in processing costs and make it easier to offer a service; and
3. government—a simplification of the claim process may lead to increased capital inflow where investors, previously unable to obtain tax relief on portfolio income, may make investment decisions based on an increased post tax yield.

Increased clarity around the claim process should help improve the general compliance process and reduce the potential for erroneous claims arising from a lack of familiarity with the claim process.

Common Reclaim Form

In designing a standardised claim form, capable of use in both a relief at source and reclaim situation, for use within all European Union countries, consideration should be paid to existing tax claim forms. Following a review of existing tax forms from Member States it is clear that existing tax forms have a common core set of questions used to determine eligibility for lower withholding tax rates. Appendix 7 details the output of this review and the findings have been summarised below. In essence, a withholding tax claim will require both the provision of core data and a number of key representations to be made by the claimant.

The recurring data/representations can be said to cover the following common elements:

1. Claimant details (e.g. name and address);
2. Claimant type (i.e., individual, company, pension fund etc.);
3. Home country identification;
4. Resident country tax identification number (TIN);
5. Treaty Article under which claim is made;
6. Whether the investor meets the provisions on any limitation of benefits provision ("LOB");
7. A beneficial ownership representation;
8. A "no treaty abuse" representation;
9. A "subject to"/"liable to" tax representation; 24
10. Whether (in the context of a company) the claimant operates through a branch in the source country and whether the income received is attributable to that branch;

11. Whether the beneficiary holds above a certain threshold of the share capital of the distributing company; and
12. Details regarding the income-paying event (i.e., security details, distribution dates etc.);
13. Amount of the claim
14. Details of the refund mechanism (account number for credit of refund).

It is worth noting that the recurring data and representation can be seen to be broadly consistent with the data/representations envisaged under the OECD's draft Implementation Package.

For completeness, it should be noted that documentation simplification is a significant process enhancement issue but thought does need to be given to the wider process. As the Commission's recommendation stated in respect of refund procedures: "Such procedures should comprise the following:

1. permission for information agents or withholding agents to submit refund applications to the tax authorities of the source Member State on behalf of the investors;
2. use of a single contact point for the introduction and handling of all the refund applications and publication of the relevant information on refund procedures on a website, in at least one language customary in the sphere of international finance;
3. use of common formats for refund applications which would be able to be filed electronically;
4. refunding in a reasonable period of time and normally, at least, within 6 months of receipt of the refund application by the relevant tax authority, provided that all necessary information is available".

This report endorses these recommendations.

Know Your Customer ("KYC") information

Financial institutions are generally obliged to perform certain KYC due diligence at the account opening stage and on certain specified transactions on an ongoing basis. However, it should be noted that KYC as a general matter is not geared towards establishing either tax entitlements or tax residency. As such KYC has an inherent limitation in this regard.

While the FISCO Report proposed that for individuals it may be sufficient to rely on such KYC in order to determine access to tax relief, the financial institutional preference is for a tax-specific form. Such a form eliminates potential ambiguity or incorrect determinations based on partial information. Source countries would need to be in a position to satisfy themselves that such KYC would be sufficient to determine access to reduced rates of withholding tax. While it should be noted that several countries—such as Austria and Germany—have for a number of years applied a KYC-rule for interest payments made to non-resident investors, in practice however this can be difficult. The US Qualified Intermediary regime currently allows for KYC information to be used in place of tax-specific forms.

Where such KYC is deemed to be sufficient, it is likely that the financial institution will need to inform the claimant that will make certain tax-based determinations—including residency and beneficial ownership—based, in part, on the country of birth and identity documentation provided. There are some issues with this approach, not least that individuals are potentially highly mobile and financial institutions may in practice default to asking for additional evidence to support a claim for a reduced withholding tax rate. Therefore, this would mean in practice that KYC may be insufficient and may require additional information and evidence to support a claim. This report therefore suggests that if Governments believe that KYC can be used to determine treaty access, the inherent limitations should be accepted and should any incorrect treaty determinations be made based on such KYC this should not give rise to any financial penalties or similar for the financial institution.

Powers of Attorney

Tax authorities should accept the use of a power of attorney ("PoA") by a financial intermediary or third-party service provider acting on behalf of the beneficial owner. In order to operate a modern outsource solution for clients, this is a key requirement and need for the industry. In practice currently today the PoA is used, unless the source country does not accept their use, by an intermediary to complete documentation on their client's behalf. In order to do so an intermediary will ask their client to provide certain standing representations. We recommend that the standardised reclaim form be capable of completion under such a PoA.

Certification

A number of forms require home state tax authorities to validate the form, i.e., by means of either stamping a form, to evidence treaty residence, or by providing a certificate of tax residence to append to the form. This process is in itself a time-consuming process for all participants in the process. We further note that ever-increasing cross-border investment is likely to mean that burdens on tax authorities to provide such certification will increase. This point was raised at first by the FISCO Group in its "Second Report on Solutions" in 2007.i27 FISCO requested to abolish the currently customary certificates of residence that need to be issued annually by the responsible tax office of the beneficial owner. This idea was raised in a recent OECD report that noted:

> "the U.S. Internal Revenue Service processed 2.4 million certificates of residence for the fiscal year ending 30 September 2007, over a 60 percent increase from just a few years earlier. This procedure has been centralised into one service centre, and a user fee has been instituted to help defray the costs. As a result, the costs of granting and claiming treaty benefits have been shifted from the source country (the one asking for the forms) to the residence country (the one providing the forms) and then charged to the investors, who benefit from the treaty. There has been some debate over whether this is an appropriate allocation of costs".28

It is also worth noting that the use of certificates of tax residence is in itself of questionable value. Again a recent OECD report commented on the limitations of this certification process as a checking tool for the source country.

This report concurs with both the Second FISCO Report and the OECD report and proposes that any requirement for a certificate of residence be eliminated to be replaced by a common standardised form of self-certification.

Collective Investment Vehicles

It is important to note that certain Member States have placed processes around claims made by collective investment vehicles ("CIVs"). In this context, collective investment vehicles mean funds that are widely-held, invest in a diversified portfolio of securities and are subject to investor-protection regulation in the country in which they are established. As a general comment, it is felt that these processes are somewhat unclear both as a legal matter (i.e., whether the collective investment vehicle is treaty entitled in its own right or whether any treaty determination should be made at the level of the holder of the units or shares in the collective investment vehicle) and as an operational matter (i.e., how should the process work). Any uncertainty regarding treaty eligibility is especially problematic for a CIV, which must take into account amounts expected to be received, including any withholding tax benefits provided by treaties, when it calculates its net asset value ("NAV"). The NAV, which typically is calculated daily, is the basis for the prices used for subscriptions and redemptions. If the withholding tax benefits ultimately obtained by the CIV do not correspond to its original assumptions about the amount and timing of such withholding tax benefits, there will be a discrepancy between the real asset value and the NAV used by investors who have purchased, sold or redeemed their interest in the CIV in the interim.

In May 2010 the OECD released its report on "The granting of treaty benefits with respect to the income of Collective Investment Vehicles". Based on this report the Commentary on the OECD Model Tax Convention includes for the first time statements regarding the application of the Convention on CIV.

According to the OECD commentary a CIV should be treated as a person and as a resident for treaty purposes if the tax law of the country where such a CIV is established would treat it as a taxpayer.30 As it is a consistent objective of CIV regimes to ensure that there is only one level of tax at either the CIV or the investor level, there are a number of countries where the CIV is in principle subject to tax but its income may be exempt from tax. Even in these cases the requirements to be treated as a resident may be met if the requirements to qualify for such an exemption are sufficiently stringent.31 Moreover, a CIV, defined as a vehicle that is widely held, holds a diversified portfolio of securities and is subject to investor-protection regulation in the country in which it is established, will also be treated as the beneficial owner of the dividends and interests that it receives, so long as the managers of the CIV have discretionary powers to manage the assets generating such income.

In order to provide more certainty regarding treaty eligibility of CIVs the OECD-Commentary concludes that tax authorities may want to reach a mutual agreement clarifying the treatment of some types of CIV in their respective States. With respect to some types of CIVs, such mutual agreement might simply confirm that the CIV satisfies the technical requirements (person, resident, beneficial owner) and therefore is entitled to benefits in its own right. In other cases, the mutual agreement could provide a CIV a administratively feasible way to make claims with respect to treaty-eligible investors.

In light of the importance of certainty regarding the treaty eligibility of CIV this report recommends that EU countries consider the recent amendments made to the OECD Model Convention.

Such considerations should take account of the fact that a high percentage (approx. 75–80%) of CIV established within the territories of the EU Member States are compliant with the Directive 2009/65/EC of 13 July 2009 on the coordination of laws, regulations and administrative provisions relating to undertakings for collective investment in transferable securities (UCITS).

The Directive contains rules for the authorisation, supervision, structure and activities of UCITS established in the Member States.

For the purpose of the Directive UCITS means undertakings with the sole object of collective investment in transferable securities or in other liquid financial assets of capital raised from the public and which operates on the principle of risk-spreading.33 The Directive contains obligations regarding the investment policies of UCITS.

UCITS may be constituted in accordance with contract law (contractual funds) trust law (unit trusts) or statute (corporate funds). Not subject to the directive are:

1. Collective investment undertakings of the closed-ended type
2. Collective investment undertakings which raise capital without promoting the sale of their units to the public within the Community or any part of it
3. investment undertakings the units of which, under the fund rules of the instruments of incorporation of the investment company, may be sold only to the public in third countries.

To pursue activities UCITS have to be authorised in accordance with the Directive by the competent authorities of its home member state.36 Further they are under the supervision of the competent authorities of the home member state.

Given the regulatory framework of UCITS, it is unlikely that they will be used for treaty shopping as UCITS are subject to investor protection regulation, havė to hold a diversified portfolio and will be widely held. Considering the intention of the UCITS Directive to approximating the conditions on Competition between UCITS at Community level, while at the same time ensuring more effective and more uniform protection for unit-holders we recommend that UCITS funds should be deemed to be treaty entitled in their own right. The treaty entitlement should be determined by reference to the fund's place of incorporation/establishment. As proposed by the OECD such entitlement could be clarified by a mutual agreement between Member States.

Automation

We believe that the recurring data and representations noted above could be used to develop a common form for use by all Member States. However, we note that this reference to a form should not be read as a preference for a physical form (i.e., a paper-based solution) and indeed these data fields could be developed as the data set necessary for any e-filing reclaim solution. In line with the comments made above any such form should be produced in an international language used in financial transactions.

This report as a general matter supports electronic filing of tax documentation in order to secure withholding tax relief. Electronic filing in this context is taken to mean the use of the transmission of defined data (the schema) by secure electronic means (the transmission format). A number of Member States, such as the Netherlands and Germany, already provide for a degree of such e-filing, although such e-filing is currently limited to tax reclaims.

There are a number of benefits of moving towards an e-filing solution and such a system should provide for:

- A reduction in processing costs for both intermediaries and government;
- A better compliance regime in that governments will be better able to run database queries and so check data received on a real-time basis; and
- The elimination of a paper-intensive process.

The success of moving to an e-solution will largely depend on the solution chosen.

We are also mindful of the OECD Treaty Relief and Compliance Enhancement Implementation Package. The transmission format and exchange method should be standardised in order to keep costs proportionate to the end goal.

As noted above, a standardised form with a standardised data set would allow for the basic building blocks of a e-filing/e-reporting solution to be developed.

Exchange of Information

Exchange of information between governments is an essential part of withholding tax systems described in the EU Recommendation as well as the Implementation package developed at the OECD. This section contains a number of considerations in this regard.

Use of Tax Identification Numbers

Tax Identification Numbers ("TINs") are used to identify taxpayers and are an excellent feature for effective control through any tax exchange of information process. This was highlighted in the (Second FISCO Report 2.5). TINs can be useful for processing information received from a treaty partner. The provision of TINs is also important when either making or answering a request or providing information to a treaty partner country by means of spontaneous information exchange since it will facilitate the quick identification of the taxpayer.

In more recent years some governments have sought to introduce TIN requirements for non-resident investors seeking tax treaty or domestic law tax relief in a source country. It has been widely documented that this approach raises discrimination concerns highlighting barriers to the principle of free movement of capital.39.

The T-BAG Group considers that there are two elements relevant to the use of TINs in the context of this report:

1. TINs provide Member States with an excellent method to optimise exchange of information and to match and reconcile information reporting.
2. TINs should be issued by the residence country not the source country

Legal basis for exchange of information

It is understood that the EU is studying an approach in which financial institutions would report information to their own tax authorities, which would in turn exchange relevant parts of the information with source and residence countries. This contrasts with the OECD AI system where financial institutions would report information to the source countries which would exchange it with the residence countries. Such alternative approaches would work only to the extent the country of establishment of the intermediary has treaties with both source and residence countries of the investors allowing such exchange of information.

The T-BAG group considers that efficient relief procedures should be available to all eligible investors, independent of the treaty network of the country of establishment of their financial institution. Therefore, the alternative approach under analysis by the Commission, if adopted, could mean remote access to the system would disadvantage foreign intermediaries and their customers. Nevertheless, the cost for tax administrations and financial institutions to administer both approaches in parallel must be taken into consideration before pursuing such an approach.

Liability

Within the Second FISCO Report (2.2.3), the importance of the liability on Financial Intermediaries in their role as facilitators of withholding tax relief mechanisms has been discussed. Consideration however needs to be given to various factors that may result in a deemed tax underwithholding and the need to limit the liability on Financial Intermediaries as a result.

Business did not take into account the legal position with regard to liability for under-withholding across the various EU Member States. The need for harmonisation and the options available to Member States have been documented in (Chapter 3). However, business believes liability arises in the following three areas:

- The party (or parties) with withholding responsibility
- The party (or parties) that are held liable for any underwithholding
- Any factors that may be relevant in determining which party (or parties) are held liable for underwithholding in different situations.

The following assumes that tax relief has been provided "at source" in accordance with the EU recommendations. Different conclusions may be reached where tax relief has been provided by means of alternative "at source" or tax reclaim arrangements.

Business believes that the determination of liability for underwithholding (i.e., identifying the party that must pay) should be distinguished from the collection of that liability. It does not necessarily follow that the party that collects the liability should be the party that is liable for underwithholding.

Determination of liability

Liability may rest with different parties depending on the generic cause of the under-withholding. Based on practical experience the most common generic causes for underwithholding are:

1. Technical issues surrounding the eligibility or otherwise of a particular investor type, where there is no clear guidance from the source country
2. Processing errors by a Financial Intermediary (FI)
3. Incorrect or fraudulent representations by a client of an FI.

Although in all three cases, the FI might seek to recover the underwithholding and might generally be able to pursue this under its standard indemnity arrangements with its customers, an ultimate liability of the FI for an underwithholding only exists with respect to cause 2.

Business submits that for underwithholding attributable to cause 1, ultimate liability should rest with the source country. For underwithholding attributable to cause 3, we consider that ultimate liability should rest with the client, i.e., the claimant. It is proposed that a FI will be required to operate under the best practice recommendations regarding the "reason to know" standard. By adopting the best practice recommendations liability of the FI under cause 3 should only be created when the FI is acting in collusion with the client.

This position is distinct from the OECD Implementation Package approach which provides for strict liability for underwithholding for authorised intermediaries (see Appendix 5).

Collection of liability

It is recognised that Governments will seek to ensure that they have the ability to recover any tax underwithholding in an effective and efficient manner. It is further recognised that the most efficient approach may involve the Tax Authorities in a source country seeking repayment of taxes from the FI. However, it is submitted that the cause of the liability should be carefully balanced with the obligation imposed on the FI. We believe that there are three recovery scenarios for a source country:

1. FI unable to recover tax under-withheld
   a. In the event the FI cannot recover the tax which was under-withheld, business considers that the tax authority should address the request to the claimant directly. Within an EU context, the tax authorities have the tools to recover taxes directly from the claimant/taxpayer. This is facilitated under mutual assistance directives within the EU the most recent of which is Council Directive 2010/24/EU.
2. Incorrect or fraudulent claims paid directly to the end investor
   a. Given that the end investor is the party that has received the benefit of the underwithholding, the underwithholding is solely resulting from its fraudulent/negligent behaviour and the end investor is ultimately responsible for returning the relevant tax to the source country. It follows that the source country should go directly to the end investor as also proposed under option 1 (outlined above). Where appropriate, relevant recovery assistance agreements could be invoked by the source country in cooperation with the residence country to recover the tax.
3. Other cases
   a. the source country would go directly to the withholding agent/first FI in the chain who would reimburse the source country. Thereafter it would be necessary for the indemnification arrangements in place between the various parties to be exercised in order to attempt to ultimately recover the funds from the investor. This option is likely to be the preferred option for many source countries. However, we

consider this would be the most cumbersome option to operate as it potentially requires multiple indemnification agreements to be exercised in the investment chain. In certain cases such as the inability to recover underwithholding (under recovery scenario 1) from the end investor, business believes that ultimate liability should rest with the source country.

b. the source country would go directly to the last FI in the chain who would exercise the relevant indemnification agreement to recover the under-withholding from the investor/CI. The FI would reimburse the source country in all cases except where it is unable to recover underwithholding under recovery scenario 1 from the end investor.

Having reviewed the various recovery scenarios business believes that option b represents the optimal approach for recovery of tax not withheld. It is submitted that option b minimises the overall administrative burden by directly targeting the relevant link in the chain. This should ensure the efficient recovery of tax. In addition, business believes that to the extent that FIs have a role in the recovery of taxes, the following matters should also be considered:

1. the need for clear guidance regarding the entitlement to tax treaty benefits or otherwise;
2. equality of treatment in relation to the liability of an FI and a local withholding agent operating in the source country;
3. penalties and fines should be proportionate to the error/fraud committed and any interest penalties should be aligned with the source country central bank rate.

In conclusion, the party liable for the recovery of tax depends on the reason for the underwithholding occurring. Where information has been supplied incorrectly or fraudulently by the investor, the source country should pursue the investor/beneficial owner for the recovery of tax. Where the FI has failed to operate under best practice "reason to know" recommendations or commits processing errors which result in underwithholding, the FI should be liable for the recovery of tax.

Recommendations of the T-BAG Group 10. Final Conclusions

Overarching Principles

The overarching principles that has driven business in researching, discussing and making these proposals to Member States is the need for both governments and business to reduce costs and make the withholding tax system more efficient, reliable and accessible for all those involved in it. The core principles needed to achieve this, wherever possible are: (i) agreement to common simplified approaches, (ii) standards and (iii) automation. So, while the conclusions of this report go into some granular detail about the different elements of an efficient withholding tax system, e.g., documentation, liability, exchange of information, reporting and tax reclaims etc., a common thread in many proposals is the development and use of voluntarily agreed standards between Member States and wherever possible for information to be transmitted securely in electronic form.

The T-BAG Group reviewed both FISCO reports, together with an analysis of the US withholding tax system and projects in hand by the OECD to establish, from experience, some of the best practices that could be incorporated into an EU withholding tax system.

The prior FISCO reports concluded that the most effective system for the E.U would be an "Authorised Intermediary" type system in which relief at source would be the base model with optional post pay date tax reclaims available in all Member States. The framework solution proposed takes this principle and addresses some of the challenges that this concept produces at an intermediate level of granularity. If Member States approve this proposal, at this level of granularity, further work will need to be conducted to produce the finalised framework.

Legal Basis

In Chapter 2 and Appendix 5, the Report outlines several arguments which essentially reach the conclusion that there is no substantive legal obstacle to the implementation of the FISCO Report recommendation nor to the subsequent implementation proposals outlined in this report.

Implementation

The T-BAG Group believes that voluntary adoption by Member States would be the most effective way to implement the report's recommendations and that there are self-evident economic benefits to government, investors and business. The alternative method of a Directive would probably take seven to ten years to accomplish (cf. European Savings Directive) and would result in more complexity and cost for governments and the industry in the interim. Some Member States (e.g., Slovenia, Ireland) are already adopting their own variations on an AI model.

A Directive need only be envisioned if it transpires that certain Member States have not taken any voluntary action to adopt the recommendations in a phased approach.

The measure of Member State adoption should be proportionate to the economic benefits/costs. However, the T-BAG Group believes that the degree of cost-saving and efficiencies gained by early adopters will be a compelling driver for other Member States. However, a Directive would also be helpful to address binary points.

Summary Conclusions

As a result, this report makes a series of pragmatic recommendations which the T-BAG Group urges be considered for implementation either by voluntary adoption by Member States (preferred) or by Directive.

The principle recommendations flow from the FISCO Report (2010) in which Member States were urged to and have in principle agreed, to a common policy in which Member States move towards a consistent and simplified withholding tax model based on the availability of both tax relief at source and post pay date refunds.

In this report, the group has provided more detailed recommendations. Tax relief at source will be applied by financial intermediaries, authorised in contract by Member States, and supported by a simplified requirement for documentation of beneficial ownership, integrated with existing international regulatory principles such as KYC and AML. The group also makes specific recommendations with respect to post pay date refunds. These recommendations focus on improvements to efficiency and use of technology that will lead to a more consistent reclaim process for Member States, intermediaries and investors alike.

Structural changes intended to support this policy include recommendations on improved quality and distribution of guidance from Member States on the interpretation of both double tax treaties and domestic law reliefs, use of common and standardised forms and procedures, adoption of technology allowing for electronic transmission and processing of documentation, clarification of the liability of financial intermediaries and the implementation of control and oversight mechanisms, including annual information reporting and exchange as well as independent oversight. In particular, the report provides (i) specific suggestions for determining the liability of intermediaries in context to the proposed system, (ii) a proposed more formalised and standardised guidance and exchange of information from and between Member States, (iii) suggested content for AI agreements, (iv) proposals for documentation of beneficial owners including self-certification of residency, (v) proposals for tax information reporting content and audits as a control and oversight system based on a recommendation for Home State oversight and reporting with exchange of information rules permitting the transfer of such information to the source State.

The T-BAG Group believes that there is ample legal precedent, to allow Member States to harmonise and simplify their withholding tax procedures, as envisioned in the FISCO Report, either on a voluntary basis or via a Directive or both. Due to the difficulties and time frame likely under a Directive based approach, the T-BAG Group favours a voluntary solution adopted by Member States to be implemented in a phased way.

In total, the implementation of these recommendations will achieve the objectives of the Commission and Member States, to improve the efficiency of the markets by removing the barriers to the free flow of capital resulting from the current inconsistent, fragmented and inefficient relief mechanisms.

Appendix 2: European Union Withholding Tax Code of Conduct

Introduction

Nature and Scope of the Code

This code provides a set of pragmatic approaches to improve the efficiency of current WHT procedures in particular for refunds but also including procedures for relief at source.

- Entitlement to submit refund claims or apply for relief
- Efficient and user-friendly digital WHT procedures
- Efficient Internal IT Systems
- Effective reliefs and provision of refunds in a short period
- User-friendly forms
- User-friendly documentation requirements
- Set up a single point of contact
- Relief at source

It should be noted that whereas some of the suggestions may be carried out relatively quickly and cheaply, others may take longer and involve substantial investments, in particular when it comes to IT systems.

The code is envisaged to apply to WHT procedures on cross-border passive income (mainly dividends, interests and royalties), that is sourced in an EU Member State, and that is paid to EU residents and to non-residents.

Securities income covered within the scope of Union legislation does not fall within the scope of this code.

It should be noted as well that some of the suggestions requiring the assumption of important responsibilities and obligations by financial intermediaries may lead to liability for failures to comply with such obligations.

Background and Context

WHT are a source of income for Member States and raise revenues used to fund public expenditures. However, burdensome procedures for WHT reliefs and refunds have long been identified as a barrier to a well-functioning capital market.

They hinder cross-border investment, disrupt financial processes such as clearing and settlement, increase the cost of cross-border trading and are a barrier to achieve a single European securities market. They are particularly burdensome for individual and small investors. The resulting misallocation of financial resources undermines investment within the EU.

This code comes as a response to the September 2015 Commission's initiative to build a Capital Markets Union (CMU), which proposed to draft a Code of Conduct on WHT as one of its main deliverables and the work of the EU Commission Expert Group on barriers to free movement of capital (composed mostly of non-tax experts).

Based on the work of the group, in March 2017 the Commission adopted a report on national barriers to capital flows (2017 Report), where inefficiency in cross-border WHT reclaims and refunds procedures has been identified, among others, as one of the biggest barriers to an effective capital market.

In particular, the 2017 Report identified a series of best practices on WHT recovery proceedings (in addition to relief at source) and reiterated, as way forward, the need to work together with national tax experts on a Code of Conduct.

The Report stresses that existing WHT procedures can be generally demanding, resource-intensive and costly for investors. The end result is that many individuals simply forego their right to claim back WHT.

Member States have already taken important steps and made significant investments in upgrading their WHT systems. The report by the Expert Group on barriers to free movement of capital is one in a long series of initiatives undertaken at the EU level to make WHT procedures more efficient. The report published in 2017 by this expert group still considers Council

Directive 90/435/EEC of 23 July 1990 on the common system of taxation applicable in the case of parent companies and subsidiaries of different Member States and Council Directive 2003/49/EC of 3 June 2003 on a common system of taxation applicable to interest and royalty payments made between associated companies of different Member States.

WHT procedures as a current barrier in post-trading environment and recommends making WHT procedures more efficient.

Recently, as committed in the CMU Action Plan, the Commission set up the European Post Trade Forum (EPTF), an expert group tasked "to undertake a broader review on progress in removing Giovannini barriers, including WHT, after the recent legislation and market infrastructure developments".

Entitlement to Submit Refund Claims or Apply for Relief

Description

Possibility of beneficial owners, non-resident financial institutions and other representatives submitting refund claims or applying for relief.

For instance, beneficial owners, including those with a low-value portfolio, are able to claim a refund or apply for relief on their own behalf, without any intermediary; non-resident intermediaries are allowed to claim a refund and apply for relief on behalf of their clients in a non-discriminatory manner.

Problems It Can Address

- Economic impossibility for beneficial owners with a low-value portfolio to obtain the refund or apply for the relief to which they are legally entitled.
- Limits to competition between financial intermediaries.
- Lack of level playing field between resident and non-resident intermediaries due to barriers, such as the mandatory requirement for a resident representative.
- Additional costs for non-resident intermediaries to provide WHT services.

Possible Ways to Get There

- Tax administrations allow non-resident beneficial owners to submit claims or apply for relief on their own behalf.
- Tax administrations allow non-resident financial institutions or other representatives of the beneficial owners, within the limits of what is currently allowed by law, to claim relief on behalf of their customers.
- Tax administrations do not require non-resident beneficial owners, institutions or other representatives to maintain a resident fiscal agent and/or representative or to use resident tax advisory firms to claim relief, within the limits of what is currently allowed by law.

Efficient and User-Friendly Digital WHT Procedures

Description

Digitalisation of the reclaim process; digitalisation can be defined as the adoption or increase in the use of digital or computer technology by an organisation. It takes time, demands resources and can be carried out with various degrees of maturity (in the case of WHT processes, it can range from using emails and/or publishing forms online to full online processes).

Efficient Internal IT Systems

Problems It Can Address

- High compliance costs for taxpayers and administrative costs. Unnecessary in-person/by-phone contacts.
- Delays in processing of claims for refund or applications for relief.

Possible Ways to Get There

Tax administrations identify which forms need to be filled in and publish them online.

The whole reclaim process can be completed online through a user-friendly portal. To ease the submission of supporting documents, tax administrations allow file upload easily.

Permits global custodians and other financial institutions to submit claim in respect of multiple beneficial owners at once.

To receive data quickly and efficiently, tax administrations implement a system to system option for qualified intermediaries.

Tax administrations ensure that the external IT systems (i.e., the approach described in this section) are connected to their internal IT systems (described in the following section).

Tax administrations use IT systems for efficiently processing reclaims and refunds, as well as, when applicable, a relief at source system.

Problems It Can Address

- Administrative burden of paper-based procedures;
- Delays in processing claims for refund or applications for relief due to time-consuming and lengthy administrative procedures;
- Inefficient work process when information from different sources has to be gathered manually.
- Risk of fraudulent behaviour, such as, double refund applications and unjustified reclaims or application for relief.

Possible Ways to Get There

The IT systems would be:

- effective and make the best possible use of data, allowing tax administrations to easily retrieve, cross-check and match data gathered from various sources and those already available to the tax administrations;
- connected to the online e-filing system used by beneficial owners and/or financial intermediaries to reclaim WHT;
- smart in the sense that automatically alerts tax administrations of possible risks in the refund claims, to minimise the likelihood of fake or fraudulent claims being processed;

- able to keep its data secure;
- able to allow tax administrations to simply and rapidly create statistical reports on claims processing;
- cost-effective.

Effective Reliefs and Provision of Refunds in a Short Period

Description

Provide relief and refunds in an appropriate period of time and normally within 6 months of receipt of a fully documented and valid claim for refund or application for relief by the relevant tax authority. The assumption is that taxpayers truthfully submit refund claims and supporting documentations to tax administrations, respecting deadlines, and in accordance with the law.

User-Friendly Forms

Problems It Can Address

- Monetary disadvantages for the beneficial owner or payor, i.e., high opportunity costs.
- Difficulties in finding the facts due to the amount of time passed.
- Legal uncertainty, also in respect of further similar transactions.

Possible Ways to Get There

- Tax administrations publish on their websites documentation requirements, description of the law and deadlines, if any, that taxpayers need to respect for submitting their claims.
- Effective IT systems (described in the previous section) available to taxpayers and tax administrations.
- Tailored forms, easy to fill in online.
- The tax administrations make the forms for the submission of refund claims or applications for relief as user-friendly as possible.

Problems It Can Address

- Difficulties in completing forms, particularly for non-resident beneficial owners or financial intermediaries that may not be familiar with local language or tax administration.
- Administration costs and barriers that prevent claiming refunds or applying for relief.

Possible Ways to Get There

To ease the submission of documentation, yet within the limits of what is currently allowed by law and in particular tax treaties, tax administrations:

- strive to provide electronic forms, which are tailor-made, interactive, comprehensive and self-explanatory;
- provide proactive, transparent and comprehensive guidance to different types of taxpayers (small retail investors, pension funds, insurance groups, transparent funds and their investors etc.) on different incomes (dividends, interests etc.) or key definitions (beneficial owner etc.) and communicate in a tailored-made way (considering, for instance, the applicable tax treaties) to meet the needs of these target groups, so that taxpayers can quickly find the forms they need to fill in and reduce mistakes in doing so;
- make forms and guidance available in addition to the national language in at least one foreign language customary in the sphere of international finance;
- ensure guidance is kept up to date as treaties and domestic law changes and
- the European Commission provides and keeps up to date a single webpage listing all links to national websites where forms and guidance can be found.

User-Friendly Documentation Requirements

Description

Tax administrations provide clear requirements in relation to which supporting documents taxpayers have to provide in order to substantiate their claims for refund or applications for relief vis à vis tax administrations; document requirements are published online in at least one language customary to the sphere of international finance; documents requested are relevant and necessary.

Problems It Can Address

- Time and cost for taxpayers in fulfilling their reporting responsibilities.
- Lack of clarity regarding the requirements that beneficial owners and financial institutions have to fulfil in order to effectively prepare claims for refund and applications for relief.
- Financial institutions have to ask their clients multiple times for supporting documents.

Possible Ways to Get There

To simplify documentation requirements, yet within the limits of what is currently allowed by law and in particular tax treaties, tax administrations:

- publish online clear and comprehensive documentation requirements for different entity and income types, when applicable;
- when appropriate, simplify documentation requirements for cases of minor risk; Example: https://ec.europa.eu/taxation_customs/national-tax-websites_en
- allow supporting documents in electronic formats, as far as legally possible;
- avoid requesting excessive information from taxpayers;
- avoid requesting documents that it is not possible for the taxpayer to obtain with reasonable effort;
- avoid excessive, ad hoc, non-standardised requests to taxpayers for information, unless necessary for compliance, relying on risk assessment;
- avoid recurrent documentation requirements, if information is already available to tax administration;
- accept certain valid documentation to support a series of different claims, when appropriate;
- accept tax residence certificates in the format provided by the residence country of the beneficial owners as proof of their tax residence;

- allow proofs of the beneficial owners' entitlement to treaty benefits other than tax residence certificates in relation to the amount(s) in question issued by the residence country, for example, such as:
  - allowing claimants to use self-certification of tax residence, where enough information is available possibly in combination with
  - allowing claimants to rely on financial institutions' "know your customer" (KYC) procedures to certify tax residence;
- set up a central information platform (example: the European TIN Portal) which provides information about WHT reclaim and refund procedures and on the different formats used for tax residence certificates in the EU.

Set Up a Single Point of Contact

Description

Tax administrations have a single point of contact for all aspects concerning the WHT procedures. The single point of contact can be easily found, i.e., on the website of the tax administration.

Problems It Can Address

- Taxpayers' compliance burdens.
- Dispersion of expertise on WHT procedures within tax administrations.

Possible Ways to Get There

- Identify a single point of contact for refund claims and applications for relief. A single point of contact is the point of reference for providing easy to understand and accessible guidance to taxpayers, also in one additional foreign language customary in the sphere of international finance.
- Single points of contact are easy to find on the websites of the tax administrations. The European Commission provides and maintains a single webpage listing all links to Member States' single points of contact.

Relief at Source

Description

Relief at source is a category of WHT procedures in which treaty entitlements or exemptions are already applied when the underlying payment is made, provided all necessary information is available. No WHT—or less WHT—has to be paid to the tax administration by the withholding agent or distributing paying agents. Relief at source is not necessarily always the best practice and, in some cases, a relief at source simply is not possible. In some cases improving withholding tax procedures by making WHT relief by refund quicker and more efficient can be more appropriate. Carrying out relief at source requires the assumption of important responsibilities and obligations by financial intermediaries which can be held liable for failures to comply with their obligations.

Problems It Can Address

- Some risks of errors and fraud, including multiple refunds for the same underlying claim.
- Opportunity costs and delays in receiving the refund.
- Costs beneficial owners and financial intermediaries face in processing refund claims.
- Administrative costs involved in processing refund applications.

Possible Ways to Get There

- Tax administrations try to carry out tax relief at source systems in the least burdensome manner for investors and financial intermediaries, balancing however the need for simplification with the necessity of ensuring compliance.
- For example, tax administrations may grant WHT relief at source relying on a system of authorised information agents and withholding agents, in which the information agent closest to the beneficial owner:
  - verifies whether the beneficial owner is entitled to tax relief;
  - passes to the next information agent in the custody chain pooled WHT rate information;

- reports investor-specific information to the source Member State when needed;
- and the withholding agent applies WHT relief at source on the basis of
- pooled WHT rate information.

- Another way to grant relief at source is a system where the tax authorities verify whether the beneficial owner is entitled to tax relief:
  - The beneficial owner applies for full or partial exemption from WHT before the underlying payments are made;
  - If the conditions are met, the tax authorities issue a certificate of exemption; o The beneficial owner hands this certificate to the payor and the latter applies WHT relief at source accordingly.
- Tax administrations cooperate to ensure that information agents and withholding agents comply with their obligations.

Follow-Up

- Member States are encouraged to commit to the code and to follow it to improve the status quo by 2019.
- With a view to arriving at a comprehensive EU wide review of developments in line with the code, Member States are encouraged to collect information about progress achieved and to share this information and best practices with the Commission and with each other.
- To keep each other informed of progress achieved and of possible obstacles encountered, Member States' tax experts will meet at least twice in 2018.
- After 2019, the code of conduct could be reviewed to take into account any significant change. The need for such a review will be considered regularly.

Appendix 4: List of AIs for Finland TRACE Framework

Name of the Authorised Intermediary	Business ID in Finland	Tax identification number (TIN) in the country of domicile	Country of domicile	Date of registration
A/S Arbejdernes Landsbank	3176870-9	DK31467012	DENMARK	01.01.2021
Ålandsbanken Abp	0145019-3		FINLAND	01.01.2021
Ålandsbanken Abp (Finland), svensk filial	2743004-3	SE516406-0781	SWEDEN	01.01.2021
AS SEB Pank	2382421-3	EE10004252	ESTONIA	01.01.2021
BAWAG P.S.K. Bank für Arbeit und Wirtschaft und Österreichische Postsparkasse AG	3238229-3	AT09015/0111	AUSTRIA	01.10.2021
BNP Paribas—United States Of America Branch	3243618-3	US94-1677765	USA	01.01.2022
BNP Paribas Australia Branch	3315507-6		AUSTRALIA	01.10.2022
BNP Paribas London Branch	3315522-8		UNITED KINGDOM	01.10.2022
BNP Paribas S.A. Niederlassung Deutschland	3188677-2	DE04722015370	GERMANY	01.01.2021
BNP Paribas S.A., Belgium Branch	3315508-4		BELGIUM	01.10.2022
BNP Paribas S.A., Jersey Branch	3315510-5		JERSEY	01.10.2022
BNP Paribas S.A., Succursale Italia	3315509-2		ITALY	01.10.2022
BNP Paribas S.A., Sucursal en España	3315517-2		SPAIN	01.10.2022
BNP Paribas SA	3243619-1	FR662 042 449	FRANCE	01.10.2022
BNP Paribas Singapore Branch	3315516-4		SINGAPORE	01.10.2022
BNP Paribas, Paris, Zurich Branch	3315520-1		SWITZERLAND	01.10.2022
BNP Paribas, Succursale de Luxembourg	3315515-6		LUXEMBOURG	01.10.2022
Carnegie Investment Bank, filial af Carnegie Investment Bank AB (PUBL) SE	3176039-5	DKR29WNF.99999.BR.208	DENMARK	01.01.2021
Ceskoslovenska Obchodni Banka, A.S.	1091403-3		CZECH REPUBLIC	18.03.2021
Citibank Europe plc	3145255-2	IE132781	IRELAND	01.01.2021
Citibank, N.A.	2382869-5	US13-5266470	USA	14.04.2022
Clearstream Banking Ag	1926619-1	DE04022013205	GERMANY	01.01.2021
Clearstream Banking S.A.	2383001-5	LU19702200132	LUXEMBOURG	01.01.2021
DANSKE ANDELSKASSERS BANK A/S	3192018-4	DK31843219	DENMARK	18.02.2021
Danske Bank A/S	2383204-5	DK61126228	DENMARK	18.01.2021

(continued)

(continued)

Name of the Authorised Intermediary	Business ID in Finland	Tax identification number (TIN) in the country of domicile	Country of domicile	Date of registration
DELEN PRIVATE BANK	2597268-2	BE0453076211	BELGIUM	30.03.2021
DELEN PRIVATE BANK LUXEMBOURG	2760967-6	LU19872202776	LUXEMBOURG	30.03.2021
Deutsche WertpapierService Bank AG	2382403-7	DE4722012006	GERMANY	01.01.2021
Djurslands Bank A/S	3190382-7		DENMARK	12.02.2021
Dragsholm Sparekasse	3272901-5	DK63370215	DENMARK	07.03.2022
Erik Penser Bank AB	2382478-2		SWEDEN	01.01.2021
Evli Oyj	3239286-2		FINLAND	02.04.2022
Forvaltningsinstituttet for Lokale Pengeinstitutter	3191329-1	DK52033810	DENMARK	05.03.2021
Frørup Andelskasse	3194086-3	DK0038136216	DENMARK	08.03.2021
FYNSKE BANK A/S	3195120-4	DK25802888	DENMARK	16.03.2021
Handelsbanken, filial af Svenska Handelsbanken AB (publ), Sverige—Denmark Branch	3223807-2	DK24246361	DENMARK	14.07.2021
Handelsbanken, filial av Svenska Handelsbanken AB (publ.) Sverige—Norway Branch	2383062-1	NO971 171 324	NORWAY	01.01.2022
Hsbc Bank Plc	1773534-5		UNITED KINGDOM	01.01.2021
HSBC Trinkaus & Burkhardt GmbH	1561395-0	DE103/5702/0455	GERMANY	01.01.2021
Hvidbjerg Bank A/S	3188503-2	DK64855417	DENMARK	03.02.2021
Hypo Vorarlberg Bank AG	3211072-2	AT98/930/2369	AUSTRIA	14.05.2021
ITI Capital Limited	3184807-1	GB8057363326	UNITED KINGDOM	08.01.2021
J.P. Morgan SE	3255668-7	DE047 220 3354 9	GERMANY	20.12.2021
J.P. Morgan SE—Dublin Branch	3310271-6		IRELAND	22.01.2022
J.P. Morgan SE—Luxembourg Branch	3315466-3	LU20228400026	LUXEMBOURG	22.01.2022
J.P. Morgan Suisse SA	2680868-1	CH060.292.380	SWITZERLAND	16.02.2021
JP Morgan Chase Bank, National Association	2382445-9	US13-4994650	USA	18.02.2021
Jyske Bank A/S	1732335-9	DK17616617	DENMARK	01.01.2021

(continued)

(continued)

Name of the Authorised Intermediary	Business ID in Finland	Tax identification number (TIN) in the country of domicile	Country of domicile	Date of registration
Komercni banka a.s.	2485037-6		CZECH REPUBLIC	01.01.2021
Leleux Associated Brokers	2987794-9		BELGIUM	01.01.2021
Maj Bank A/S	3194087-1	DK36085916	DENMARK	08.03.2021
Merkur Andelskasse	3194085-5	DK24255689	DENMARK	08.03.2021
Mizuho Trust & Banking (Luxembourg) S.A.	2383191-5		LUXEMBOURG	21.01.2021
Nordea Bank Abp	2858394-9		FINLAND	01.01.2021
Nordea Bank Abp, filial i Norge	3177830-9	NO920058817	NORWAY	01.01.2021
Nordea Bank Abp, filial i Sverige	3177272-4	SE663000019501	SWEDEN	01.01.2021
Nordea Danmark, Filial af Nordea Bank Abp, Finland	3175963-4	DK25992180	DENMARK	01.01.2021
Nordnet Bank AB Suomen sivuliike	2329589-2		SWEDEN	01.01.2021
Nykredit Bank A/S	2382890-0	DK10.51.96.08	DENMARK	12.01.2021
OP Säilytys Oy	2771050-4		FINLAND	29.04.2021
RBC INVESTOR SERVICES BANK S.A.	2382486-2		LUXEMBOURG	01.01.2021
RBC Investor Services Trust, UK Branch	2382178-4		UNITED KINGDOM	13.01.2021
Ringkjøbing Landbobank A/S	3319723-3		DENMARK	20.10.2022
SIP Nordic Fondkommission AB	2530153-9	SE556708664901	SWEDEN	01.01.2021
Skandinaviska Enskilda Banken AB (publ)	2382849-2		SWEDEN	01.01.2021
Skandinaviska Enskilda Banken AB (publ) Helsingforsfilialen	0985469-4		SWEDEN	01.01.2021
Société Générale	2382464-3	FR552120222	FRANCE	01.07.2021
Söderberg & Partners Wealth Management AB	3211747-3	SE556674-7456	SWEDEN	18.05.2021
S-Pankki Oyj	2557308-3		FINLAND	22.01.2021
Spar Nord Bank A/S	2070811-0	DK13737584	DENMARK	01.01.2021
Sparekassen Danmark af 1871	3197783-4	DK64806815	DENMARK	16.03.2021
Sparekassen Kronjylland	3240314-6	DK17912828	DENMARK	06.10.2021
Sparekassen Sjælland-Fyn A/S	3315250-2		DENMARK	01.01.2023
SÜDWESTBANK—BAWAG AG Niederlassung Deutschland	3194089-8	DE99157/01884	GERMANY	08.03.2021

(continued)

(continued)

Name of the Authorised Intermediary	Business ID in Finland	Tax identification number (TIN) in the country of domicile	Country of domicile	Date of registration
Sumitomo Mitsui Trust Bank (USA) Limited	2039904-7		USA	09.02.2021
Svenska Handelsbanken AB (Publ)	2383300-5	SE502007-7862	SWEDEN	01.01.2021
Swedbank AB	3185963-5		SWEDEN	26.01.2021
Swedbank AS	2383049-6	EE10060701	ESTONIA	01.01.2021
Sydbank A/S	2382393-1		DENMARK	01.01.2021
The Hongkong and Shanghai Banking Corporation Limited	3126666-1		HONG KONG	01.01.2021
Totalbanken A/S	3191638-8	DK10349818	DENMARK	17.02.2021
UB Securities Oy	0772898-5		FINLAND	01.01.2021
UNION BANCAIRE PRIVEE, UBP SA	3265973-1	CHE-105.923.869	SWITZERLAND	03.02.2022
Vestjysk Bank A/S	3181346-9	DK0034631328	DENMARK	05.01.2021

Index

R. K. McGill, *Cross-Border Investment Withholding Tax*, Finance and Capital Markets Series,
https://doi.org/10.1007/978-3-031-32785-8